THE POLITICS OF CANDU EXPORTS

IPAC
The Institute of
Public Administration of Canada

IAPC
L'Institut d'administration
publique du Canada

The Institute of Public Administration of Canada Series in Public Management and Governance

Editor: Donald Savoie

This series is sponsored by the Institute of Public Administration of Canada as part of its commitment to encourage research on issues in Canadian public administration, public sector management, and public policy. It also seeks to foster wider knowledge and understanding among practitioners, academics, and the general public.

For a list of books published in the series, see page 320.

DUANE BRATT

The Politics of
CANDU Exports

IPAC
The Institute of
Public Administration of Canada

IAPC
L'Institut d'administration
publique du Canada

UNIVERSITY OF TORONTO PRESS
Toronto Buffalo London

© University of Toronto Press Incorporated 2006
Toronto Buffalo London
Printed in Canada

ISBN-13: 978-0-8020-9091-1
ISBN-10: 0-8020-9091-5

Printed on acid-free paper

Library and Archives Canada Cataloguing in Publication

Bratt, Duane, 1967–
    The politics of CANDU exports / Duane Bratt.

    (Institute of Public Administration of Canada series in public management
and governance)
    Includes bibliographical references and index.
    ISBN-10: 0-8020-9091-5   ISBN-13: 978-0-8020-9091-1

    1. CANDU reactors.   2. Nuclear industry – Political aspects – Canada.
    3. Canada – Foreign economic relations.   Canada – Foreign relations – 1945–.
    I. Title.   II. Series.

    HD9698.C22B73 2006   382'.45621483'0971   C2005-907883-9

University of Toronto Press acknowledges the financial assistance to
its publishing program of the Canada Council for the Arts and the
Ontario Arts Council.

University of Toronto Press acknowledges the financial support for
its publishing activities of the Government of Canada through the
Book Publishing Industry Development Program (BPIDP).

Contents

Tables and Figures

Tables

Figures

Acknowledgments

This book is the culmination of over a decade of thinking and writing about the export of CANDU nuclear reactors. My interest in nuclear issues began as a senior undergraduate and was the topic of my master's thesis at the University of Windsor in 1992. Since that time, I have worked on many educational, teaching, and research projects, but have continued to possess a keen interest in Canadian nuclear policy. Over the years, my writing was kept current and theoretically probing through the publication of a series of scholarly articles on different facets of this important aspect of Canadian foreign policy.

I need to acknowledge the assistance and support of a number of individuals and institutions. For a project with such a long gestation, it is likely that I may have missed someone. To those that I have left out, I offer a contrite apology. There are two individuals who are most responsible for assisting me through the completion of this project. Going in chronological order, the first is Terry Keenleyside who was my thesis supervisor at the University of Windsor. It was while writing my MA thesis that my fascination with nuclear exports was developed. It was also during this time that my extensive CANDU research files started to be compiled. These tasks could not have been completed without the mentoring of Professor Keenleyside.

Following the completion of my PhD at the University of Alberta (a time when my intellectual interests took me in different areas), I took a position as a sessional instructor in the Department of Political Science at the University of Calgary. There I met Jim Keeley. Professor Keeley has an encyclopedic brain for international relations, especially international nuclear regimes. Not only that, but the man has a wide collection of Canadian, American, and United Nations documents on the creation of the international nuclear non-proliferation regime from the 1950s and 1960s. Professor Keeley was kind enough to allow me to browse through his documents as well as his collection of nuclear books. *The Politics of CANDU Exports* benefited enormously from the research that I conducted in his office. He also provided many useful comments on earlier drafts of the manuscript.

Obtaining Canadian government documents on the subjects of nuclear weapons and CANDU exports is no easy task. Access to information does exist, but it can be a cumbersome and expensive process. Therefore, it is crucial that the academic community share what documents that do come into the public eye. I would like to thank Erika Simpson of the University of Western Ontario for passing on many important documents. Despite the frequent blackened out sections, the documents that you provided reinforced some of my speculations with proof and, in some cases, opened up new areas for examination.

There are three institutions that I would like to thank for their support. The formative stages of this book occurred during the period when I received my BA and MA from the University of Windsor. As an MA student, I received some financial support that allowed me time to write my thesis. The book took its real shape while I was working at the University of Calgary and Mount Royal College. Although neither institution supplied direct funding for this book, each place provided necessary office space and administrative support. In addition, I would like to thank the following colleagues for allowing me to share my ideas with them: Don Barry, Rob Huebert, Keith Brownsey, Bruce Foster, Mike Fellows, David Sabiston, and Marco Navarro. I would especially like to acknowledge Rosemary Gardner for her administrative support.

I would like to recognize the work of the wonderfully patient Emily Andrew at UBC Press. Even though we could not consummate this book with UBC Press, the assistance and encouragement that Emily provided over what seemed like a long road was invaluable. In the same vein, I would like to thank the anonymous peer reviewers, some who read the manuscript several times, for providing me with a list of helpful suggestions. I did not always agree with your thoughts, but they always led to a tighter and more substantive argument.

The Politics of CANDU Exports would never have been printed without the assistance of two key institutions. The University of Toronto Press, and especially Virgil Duff, accepted the manuscript and carefully guided this first-time author through the maze that is academic publishing. The Institute of Public Administration of Canada (IPAC) provided essential subvention funding, which allowed the manuscript to be published. Many people at IPAC need to be thanked: Joseph Galimberti, the Institute's executive director; Patrice Dutil, the director of Research; Keith Brownsey, chair of the Research Committee; and Donald Savoie.

An author's first book is not only a time-consuming assignment, it is also an emotionally exhausting one. Therefore, I would like to thank all of the past and present members of the Calgary Field Lacrosse Club. Having to think about offensive strategies, slides, and clears was a necessary diversion from the topics of fissile materials, nuclear waste, and IAEA safeguards. The time spent on the field whether it was at Willowridge, or more exotic locales like Vail, Colorado, or Santa Fe, New Mexico, was, in its own way, helpful to the writing of this book.

Finally, I would like to acknowledge the patience of Teresa, Chris, and Dorothy. Too many nights and weekends were spent cooped up in my upstairs office struggling for the right words. I may have been at home, but only in body, not in spirit. While others may have assisted this book in material or expertise ways, Teresa, Chris, and Dorothy supported me the most by giving up the most valuable commodity – space and time – that allowed me to finish this project. *The Politics of CANDU Exports* is dedicated to them.

List of Acronyms

AECB	Atomic Energy Control Board
AECL	Atomic Energy of Canada Limited
BJP	Bharatiya Janata Party
BNFL	British Nuclear Fuels Limited
BOT	Build, Own and Operate, Transfer
BWR	Boiling Water Reactor
CANDU	Canada Deuterium Uranium
CAPD	Civilian Atomic Power Division
CCNR	Canadian Coalition for Nuclear Responsibility
CDM	Clean Development Mechanism
CEAA	Canadian Environmental Assessment Agency
CGE	Canadian General Electric
CIDA	Canadian International Development Agency
CIRUS	Canada-India-United States Research Reactor
CNA	Canadian Nuclear Association
CNEA	Argentine Nuclear Energy Commission
CNNC	China's National Nuclear Corporation
CNP	Campaign for Nuclear Phaseout
CNS	Canadian Nuclear Society
CNSC	Canadian Nuclear Safety Commission
COG	CANDU Owners Group
CTBT	Comprehensive Test Ban Treaty
DEA	Department of External Affairs
DFAIT	Department of Foreign Affairs and International Trade
EC	European Community
ECC	European Economic Community
ECIC	Export Credits and Insurance Corporation

EDC	Export Development Corporation
EMR	Department of Energy, Mines, and Resources
EPR	European Power Reactor
EU	European Union
EURATOM	European Atomic Energy Agency
FBR	Fast Breeder Reactor
G7	Group of Seven
GATT	General Agreement on Tariffs and Trade
GCR	Gas-Cooled Reactor
GDP	Gross Domestic Product
GE	General Electric
HWR	Heavy-Water Reactor
IAEA	International Atomic Energy Agency
IIPA	Independent Integrated Performance Assessment
INES	International Nuclear Event Scale
INFCIRC	Information Circular (IAEA)
ING	Intense Neutron Generator
IPAC	Institute of Public Administration of Canada
ITC	Department of Industry, Trade, and Commerce
JAEC	Japanese Atomic Energy Commission
KANUPP	Karachi Nuclear Power Plant
KEPCO	Korean Electric Power Corporation
KWU	Kraftwerk Union
LWR	Light-Water Reactor
MITI	Japanese Ministry of International Trade and Industry
NATO	North Atlantic Treaty Organization
NEI	Nuclear Energy Institute
NGO	Non-Governmental Organization
NNWS	Non-Nuclear Weapons States
NORAD	North American Aerospace Defence Command
NPD	Nuclear Power Demonstration
NPT	Nuclear Non-Proliferation Treaty
NRCan	Natural Resources Canada
NRU	Nuclear Research Universal
NRX	Nuclear Research X-perimental
NSG	Nuclear Suppliers Group
NWS	Nuclear-Weapons States
OCI	Organization of CANDU Industries
OECD	Organization of Economic Cooperation and Development

OPG	Ontario Power Generation
PAEC	Pakistan Atomic Energy Commission
PKK	Kurdish Workers' Party
PNE	Peaceful Nuclear Explosion
PRC	People's Republic of China
PWR	Pressurized-Water Reactor
R&D	Research and Development
RAPP	Rajasthan Atomic Power Plant
RBMK	Light-Water Graphite Reactor
RCMP	Royal Canadian Mounted Police
ROC	Republic of China
ROK	Republic of Korea
SALT	Strategic Arms Limitation Treaty
SCFAIT	House of Commons Standing Committee on Foreign Affairs and International Trade
SGN	Saint-Gobain Techniques Nourvelles
SIPRI	Stockholm International Peace Research Institute
SNN	Societatea Nationala Nuclearelectrica (Romania)
TAEK	Turkish Atomic Energy Authority
TEK	Turkish Electrical Authority
TRR	Taiwan Research Reactor
UN	United Nations
UNAEC	United Nations Atomic Energy Commission
UNDP	United Nations Development Program
UNSCEAR	United Nations Scientific Committee on the Effects of Atomic Radiation
US	United States
USSR	Union of Soviet Socialist Republics
WNA	World Nuclear Association
WTO	World Trade Organization
ZEEP	Zero Energy Experimental Pile

THE POLITICS OF CANDU EXPORTS

1 Introduction

In 2002, Atomic Energy of Canada Limited (AECL) celebrated its fiftieth anniversary. AECL is the Crown corporation in charge of the design, development, supervision of construction, and sale of the Canada Deuterium Uranium (CANDU) nuclear power reactor. While AECL celebrated its anniversary with a number of commemorative events, questions about the future of the CANDU and the Canadian nuclear industry abounded. In recent years, a number of major incidents have dramatically increased public attention on the Canadian nuclear industry. In 1996, Canada announced the sale of two CANDU nuclear reactors valued at $4 billion to China. In 1997, Ontario Hydro was forced to suspend operations of seven of its nuclear power plants because of poor performance. In 1998, India and Pakistan, which had received large amounts of Canadian nuclear assistance in the 1950s, 1960s, and early 1970s, including the purchase of CANDU reactors, exploded a series of nuclear bombs. In many respects, it was a return to the mid-1970s, when the international dimensions of Canada's nuclear policy first attracted the attention of Canadians through such events as the 1974 Indian nuclear test that involved Canadian nuclear technology – in particular, the CIRUS rewsearch reactor – and a scandal that involved AECL's sales agents paying nuclear officials in South Korea and Argentina to purchase CANDUs.

The questions that people started raising in the late 1990s were very similar to the ones that were asked in the mid-1970s. How safe are nuclear reactors? Do they pose a threat to the physical environment, or, because of the climate change debate, might they be embraced as a clean energy source? What are the financial benefits, or costs, of nuclear power? What are the links between nuclear power and nuclear bombs?

Why was Canada selling nuclear reactors to China, India, and Pakistan? The purpose of this book is to tackle these questions.

In doing so, this book provides the most comprehensive account of the history of CANDU exports to date. Every CANDU sale, and even some important unsuccessful attempts, from 1956 to the present will be examined in detail. In the process, much will be revealed about Canada's bilateral relationships with India, Pakistan, Taiwan, Argentina, South Korea, Romania, China, and Turkey. The book also traces the changes that have occurred in the international environment throughout the history of CANDU exports. For example, it will chart the development of the international nuclear non-proliferation regime through the creation, and strengthening, of institutions and treaties including the International Atomic Energy Agency (IAEA), the Nuclear Non-Proliferation Treaty (NPT), and the Nuclear Suppliers Group (NSG). I will also assess how CANDU exports are being affected by the increasing importance of human rights and environmental protection in world politics. It should be noted that much of the work on this book was carried out in the late 1990s. Some topics have been brought up to date to reflect important recent developments, but others, where it is believed that the points have not been changed by subsequent developments, have been left unchanged.

There is a substantial international political dimension to the export of nuclear reactors. Since the end of the Second World War, CANDU exports have been an important component of Canada's foreign policy.[1] This can be illustrated in a variety of ways. The building and maintenance of nuclear reactors constitute a large-scale industrial project between, at a minimum, two countries. It costs billions of dollars and employs tens of thousands of people over a multi-year timeline. Nuclear reactor exports, then, involve both a high-profile and a long-term relationship between those countries. This naturally results in a great deal of attention being focused on the type of political regime that receives a CANDU from Canada. This attention is magnified when the recipient state is not one of Canada's traditional trading partners like the United States, Western Europe, or Japan.

There is also substantial governmental involvement in the international nuclear trade at both the supplier and the recipient end. With the exception of the U.S. firms of Westinghouse and General Electric (GE), most nuclear suppliers, like AECL, are government owned. In addition, and even when the firms are privately owned, politicians and bureaucrats try to help secure nuclear reactor exports. In the Canadian case, prime ministers from Louis St Laurent to Jean Chrétien, with ample support from bureaucrats in the Department of Foreign Affairs and International Trade (DFAIT) and Natural Resources Canada (NRCan), have tried, with varying degrees of success, to flog CANDUs. To cite one example, Jean Chrétien, both as prime minister and earlier as energy minister, has been called 'a great booster of nuclear enterprise both at home and abroad.'[2]

In addition to the above characteristics, which the international nuclear trade shares with all multinational industrial megaprojects (like dams or airports), the export of nuclear technology and materials presents a series of unique challenges. First, successive governments have considered the CANDU to be 'Canada's last and/or best chance for developing and maintaining a high-technology-based and internationally competitive and respected industry.'[3] The prestige of nuclear power has meant that the CANDU has assumed an important place, one that extends beyond simple monetary value, in Canada's international trade.

Second, there is the existence of an international nuclear regime. The main components of the nuclear regime are the IAEA; the NPT; regional nuclear free-zones, as set out in the Treaty of Tlatelolco and the Bangkok Treaty; the NSG and its 1993 guidelines; the European Atomic Energy Agency (EURATOM); the nuclear export policies of individual supplying countries like Australia, Canada, and the United States; and the security pledges of the nuclear weapons states (NWS) as upheld in some United Nations resolutions. The existence of an international nuclear regime illustrates how important reactor sales are to international relations and, consequently, to Canadian foreign policy.

There is also the fact that the process of nuclear fusion, like the invention of fire, can be extremely beneficial to humankind or it can be very destructive. The central dilemma of nuclear power has been how to harness it for peaceful uses without allowing its destructive capability to jeopardize human survival. A complicating factor in this respect is that nuclear power, while possessing both the peaceful and violent characteristics of fire, increases them exponentially. This has meant that there is considerable overlap between, on the one hand, Canada's efforts at creating and maintaining an international nuclear non-proliferation regime and, on the other, its concurrent efforts at exporting the CANDU. This is why Ottawa has placed severe restrictions on which countries can be sold AECL reactors. For example, Canadian

Table 1.1. Countries that have signed a Nuclear Cooperation Treaty with Canada (as of January 2002)

Argentina	Indonesia
Australia	Japan
Brazil	Republic of Korea
China	Lithuania
Colombia	Mexico
Czech Republic	Philippines
Egypt	Romania
EURATOM (Austria, Belgium,	Russia
Denmark, Finland, France,	Slovakia
Germany, Greece, Ireland, Italy,	Switzerland
Luxembourg, Netherlands,	Turkey
Portugal, Spain, Sweden,	Ukraine
United Kingdom)	Uruguay
Hungary	United States

laws prohibit AECL from selling to countries that have not signed a Nuclear Cooperation Treaty with Canada.[4] Table 1.1 provides a list of all countries that have signed a nuclear cooperation agreement with Canada.

Finally, if the threat of nuclear weapons was not dangerous enough, nuclear reactors carry the possibility of an environmental catastrophe. There have been a number of serious accidents since the invention of nuclear reactors. This feature of CANDU exports will be dealt with in more detail in chapter 3, but for now, three examples should suffice. In 1952, Canada's first research reactor, the NRX, was seriously damaged when a power runaway caused a number of steam explosions. Although there were no deaths, the reactor was greatly damaged, and only an intensive and expensive salvage effort could restore it. In 1979, the Three Mile Island reactor in Pennsylvania suffered a loss of coolant. As was the case with the NRX, there were no deaths and no injuries, but the accident generated an enormous amount of publicity that greatly inflated its seriousness. The media attention was largely due to some unfortunate timing – *The China Syndrome*, a big-budget Hollywood thriller about a nuclear meltdown starring Michael Douglas, Jane Fonda, and Jack Lemmon, had been released less than two weeks prior to the Three Mile Island accident. If Three Mile Island was largely a media-created nuclear incident, the 1986 accident at Chernobyl, Ukraine, was most definitely not. Chernobyl, which led to the immediate death of thirty-one people and whose meltdown had serious ramifications throughout Europe, was the worst nuclear accident in the world and has come to symbolize the environmental risks of nuclear power.

Since CANDU exports represent an important facet in the making, of Canadian foreign policy, a number of questions spring forward: Who is involved in the decision-making process? Which individuals, offices, and interest groups influence the government's decision-making process? How are these decisions made? The political dynamic involved in CANDU exports can best be analysed by identifying and sketching out the positions of the various governmental and non-governmental actors who play a role in the decision-making process. This type of political approach is fundamental to explaining and understanding CANDU exports. This is because, at its most basic level, Canadian foreign policy decision-making is conducted through a prioritization of competing interests and objectives. Why should Canada export, or not export, nuclear reactors? Where should Canada export nuclear reactors? What conditions, if any, should Canada attach to its nuclear exports? These are explicitly political questions and must, therefore, be ultimately decided by the Canadian government.

The decision to export CANDUs is embedded in a number of political, security, and economic factors. Before briefly identifying these factors, which will be sketched out in greater detail in chapters 2 and 3, it is important to state two caveats. First, the debate over CANDU exports cannot be reduced to a simple case of economic interests versus security concerns. This is because, for example, there are economic arguments that favour CANDU exports and there are economic arguments that oppose CANDU exports. Second, the arguments, both for and against, have changed over time. For example, the use of nuclear exports to combat the spread of communism has become irrelevant since the end of the Cold War. The factors that facilitate CANDU exports centre on the economic benefits that would accrue to Canada through the export of nuclear reactors, as well as the economic consequences of insufficient exports. Political rationales have included the goals of containing communism and assisting the developing world through economic development and technology transfer. The most important constraining factor has been preventing the spread of nuclear weapons. Other constraining arguments include the role of government subsidies in the nuclear industry, the protection/promotion of human rights, and the preservation of the environment.

Origins of Canada's Nuclear Program

Whoever found it first,
Would be sure to do their worst.

From the song 'Manhattan Project' by Rush

The War Years

There can be no doubt that the foundation of peaceful nuclear power had its origins in the search for ways to harness the military applications of the atom. C.J. Mackenzie, who was president of the National Research Council during the Second World War, affirmed in 1961 that Canada's participation in the atomic weapons program with the United States and Great Britain allowed it to get in 'on the ground floor of a great technological process for the first time in Canadian history.'[5] Code-named the Manhattan Project, this weapons program was created in 1942 to construct atomic bombs for use against the enemy states of Germany and Japan. The results of this multinational team of scientists were seen in the bombings of Hiroshima and Nagasaki. Canada's role in the Manhattan Project, which was decidedly as a junior partner to the British and especially the Americans, was a result of two major factors. First, Canada could supply uranium. At the time, there were only two known supplies of uranium outside of Nazi-controlled continental Europe – one in Belgian Congo, the other on the shores of Great Bear Lake in the Northwest Territories. In addition, the only North American uranium refinery was in Port Hope, Ontario. The second factor was location – Canada was far from the fighting in Europe and Asia, which allowed the scientists to work in peace a safe distance away from Nazi or Japanese bombing raids.

A research laboratory was established in August 1942 at the Université de Montréal, where Canadian scientists were joined by a team of British scientists who had been working on the secrets of the atom at the Cavendish Laboratory at Cambridge University. The Americans had three labs at universities across the country: the University of California at Berkeley, the University of Chicago, and Columbia University in New York. A core of European scientists who had fled the Nazis also assisted the Americans. The Montreal lab conducted research into the measurements and theoretical analyses of the nuclear properties of heavy water,[6] uranium, and graphite. In addition, there were frequent scientific exchanges between all of the allied scientists. Despite the differing objectives of the three countries – let alone the various laboratory teams – it was hoped that the project would continue in this spirit of cooperation. Unfortunately, this was not to be.

In 1943 the Americans decided to take almost all control of the atomic weapons program away from their Canadian and British allies. The Canadians were informed of this decision via a January 1943 letter from James B. Conant, who headed the American scientific administration on defence matters, to C.J. Mackenzie, who was in charge of the Montreal laboratory. There were a number of reasons for this shift in U.S. policy. An obvious one was that the Canadians and British were more reliant on American cooperation than the other way around. 'The United States,' as Wilfrid Eggleston has noted, 'was already doing ten times as much as the United Kingdom; and Canada was hardly as yet in the picture at all. The United Kingdom had confessed that the production of an atomic weapon was beyond its heavily engaged resources.'[7] On 2 December 1942, Enrico Fermi succeeded in creating the first self-sustaining atomic chain reaction at the University of Chicago lab. This led the Americans to believe that they could develop the bomb on their own. The increased role of the U.S. Army in the bomb program – personified in General Leslie Groves – also led to a consolidation of American control. With Groves at the helm, there was an increased demand for secrecy and security. The American military was also concerned about an agreement that the British had reached with the Soviets calling for the exchange of information on new weapons. Finally, there was a growing awareness of the profit potential from civilian uses of atomic energy. The Americans were concerned that companies like Britain's Imperial Chemical Industries and Canada's Defence Industries Limited could emerge as potential post-war rivals. The Americans 'were determined not to see the commercial benefits of scientific advances that had cost the U.S. taxpayer hundreds of millions of dollars to achieve siphoned off by others who had contributed little or nothing to the effort.'[8]

In retrospect, the decision by the Americans to decrease their cooperation in the Manhattan Project was actually a blessing for Canada. The Americans assumed more control over the weapons program, leaving the Canadians to follow an almost independent path towards the creation of controlled nuclear power. Buckley has argued that 'the semi-idleness' of the Canadian scientists in Montreal gave them 'an unexpected opportunity to pursue a number of interesting theoretical and speculative lines of inquiry. The long and successful line of Canadian heavy water-natural uranium reactors, from the first small research units to the huge CANDU power reactors, owes much to the pioneering work carried out as the team waited for its "war work" to begin.'[9]

The Americans' initial decision to restrict atomic cooperation was, after much negotiating, eventually reversed at the highest political level. In August 1943, Canadian Prime Minister Mackenzie King hosted British Prime Minister Winston Churchill and U.S. President Franklin Roosevelt at the Quebec Conference, which formalized nuclear cooperation among the three powers. The leaders ended the rivalry between the nuclear teams when they pledged to pool all available staff and brainpower in pursuit of the atomic bomb. A key clause of the document called for the British government to 'recognize that any postwar advantage of an industrial or commercial character shall be dealt with as between the United States and Great Britain on terms specified by the President of the United States to the Prime Minister of Great Britain.'[10] The conference also established a Combined Policy Committee made up of three Americans, two Britons, and Canada's 'Minister of Everything,' C.D. Howe, to supervise nuclear cooperation. Some of the areas where the committee believed that cooperation could take place included the fundamental properties of reactor materials, research uses of radioisotopes, and the design of natural-uranium power reactors.

On 13 April 1944 the committee decided that a heavy-water reactor, which could produce plutonium for the atomic bombs, should be built in Canada. A pilot-scale research reactor, the Zero Energy Experimental Pile (ZEEP), was designed in 1944–5. ZEEP was built at Chalk River Laboratories, about 200 kilometres northwest of Ottawa on the Ottawa River, on the Ontario–Quebec border. When ZEEP went critical on 5 September 1945, it was the first reactor outside of the United States to do so. A full-scale heavy-water research reactor, the Nuclear Research X-perimental (NRX), became operational in 1947. At the time, it was widely considered to be the most powerful research reactor in the world, and it would continue to serve the needs of nuclear scientists and engineers for the next four decades.

In short, Canada's development of nuclear technology came out of wartime imperatives. The Manhattan Project should be viewed in the context of the larger war effort against the Axis powers. However, just as other wartime inventions had civilian applications – radar and synthetic rubber for example – so too did nuclear technology. Hiroshima and Nagasaki demonstrated the military applications of the atom, but there was also widespread agreement, especially in Canada, that nuclear power could be of tremendous civilian use, primarily as an almost inexhaustible energy source. This can be seen in the statement that C.D. Howe made to provincial premiers in October 1945: 'the real significance does not lie in the fact that this new bomb has accomplished an almost incredible feat of destruction, important as that fact may be; its significance is that this bomb is a sign which all can appreciate that the basic problems of the release of energy by atomic fission have been solved, and that the unbelievably large amounts of energy which scientists have long believed to be associated with matter can now be made available for practical use.'[11] Therefore, at the end of the war, Ottawa, unlike its allies in Washington and London, made a conscious decision to concentrate its efforts exclusively on developing the peaceful aspects of nuclear power.

Post-War Development

When the Second World War ended in 1945, there was no question that Canada would continue to exploit the atom. Its political leaders, most notably C.D. Howe, were determined not to lose the unique technological advantage that it had acquired during the war. So, attention quickly turned to electricity production, and Canada decided to pursue a nuclear power reactor based on a heavy-water, natural-uranium design. There were a number of key factors for this decision. First, as noted earlier, Canada possessed a rich reservoir of uranium deposits in the Northwest Territories (Great Bear Lake, later known as Port Radium) and Ontario (Port Hope and Elliot Lake). Second, the use of natural uranium would avoid the costly construction of a uranium enrichment facility. Third, Canada, through the Manhattan Project, had developed a cadre of nuclear scientists and engineers who possesed a significant body of technical knowledge about heavy-water reactors. Finally, and, not unimportantly, there was a strong desire to develop a nuclear system independent from the Americans and the British.

In 1947, following the completion of the ZEEP and NRX projects, the scientists at Chalk River proposed that Canada design and build an even more powerful research reactor: the Nuclear Research Universal (NRU). The decision to spend over $26 million (a significant sum of money at the time) was to ensure that Canada would always have one operational reactor. What would happen if NRX were to suffer an accident (as it did in 1947 and in 1952)? Moreover, nobody knew at the time what the lifespan of a research reactor was. Was it ten years, or only five? If Canada was left for a long period without a working reactor, the team of scientists and engineers, which had painstakingly been put together, would be left idle. In this situation, there was a good chance that this critical mass of nuclear knowledge would be broken up, and Canada's independent nuclear research program would be disbanded. A second reactor was necessary if Canada was to remain at the forefront of atomic energy development. After much negotiation within the government, approval for the NRU was finally given in January 1951. It would suffer start-up and construction delays, fore-shadowing future problems with the CANDU design, before it finally went critical in 1957. The NRU, although similar to the NRX in size and basic operating design, had a number of important new features: 'it would have a closed cooling system, operate at a higher temperature, and, most importantly, have an on-power refueling mechanism, which meant that fuel rods could be replaced without interrupting operation of the reactor.'[12]

The decision to build the NRU was a momentous one in Canada's nuclear history because it was the first major development that was not part of its wartime commitment. By setting aside the necessary funds to build the NRU, Ottawa provided a visible sign of support that Canada would develop an indigenous nuclear technology. In fact, the NRU was the first purely Canadian-designed reactor; the NRX had entailed a joint Canadian-British collaboration. Robert Bothwell, who was com-missioned to write a history of AECL, has argued that the NRU 'kept Canada in the nuclear game, a fully paid-up participant in the small international club of atomic powers. It allowed independence and reci-procity with the Americans and the British; if Canada were not in the "big leagues" that some dreamed of, then surely it occupied a very solid middle position without the expense and complications that a weapons program entailed.'[13]

By the early 1950s, it was evident that the next stage in Canada's nuclear development was designing a reactor for generating power. This led to the creation of the new Crown corporation, AECL, in 1952, with the mandate to develop the peaceful uses of nuclear power. AECL was now responsible for the Chalk River laboratories. According to Howe, AECL was established to 'relieve the National Research Council of responsibilities that have become more industrial than research and ... concentrate the management in one agency charged solely with respon-sibility for expediting development in this expanding field.'[14]

AECL formed a partnership with Ontario Hydro and Canadian Gen-eral Electric (CGE) to develop a made-in-Canada power reactor. AECL had recognized that a power reactor was crucial if 'Canada [was] to hold her position in this new field.'[15] The federal cabinet approved the building of a demonstration power reactor in 1955. Seven years later, Canada's first power reactor, and the prototype for the CANDU, the 20-megawatt Nuclear Power Demonstration (NPD) plant, went into commercial operation. The NPD was built on a site near Chalk River and produced power for twenty-five years before being decommissioned in 1987. The NPD was a crucial stage in the development of the CANDU. As Fawcett has noted, 'all the elements defining the distinctive CANDU reactor type – natural-uranium fuel, heavy-water moderator and coolant, horizontal zircalloy pressure tubes, and a bidirectional fuelling method – were first brought together in NPD.'[16]

This NPD project was followed a few years later by a larger prototype, the 200-megawatt Douglas Point station on Lake Huron (site of the current Bruce Nuclear Power Development site), which went into service in 1968. Douglas Point was also a cooperative effort between AECL and Ontario Hydro. Robert Bothwell has argued that the AECL–Ontario Hydro relationship was 'central to the development of Canada's nuclear industry.'[17] AECL was responsible for the reactor design and construction of the plant's nuclear section. Ontario Hydro was in charge of the construction of the conventional parts of the plant and would operate the plant. An important point to stress with regards to the Douglas Point station was the fact that it was the Diefenbaker government that gave it its approval. Since the Liberals had made every previous nuclear decision, the fact that the Progressive Conservatives were now supporting the Canadian nuclear industry demonstrated the non-partisan nature of the development of the atom in Canada. In fact, the decision of the Conservatives to maintain Eldorado Nuclear and AECL as Crown corporations – the Liberals had been planning to privatize them – indicates that they viewed nuclear power as a crucial aspect of Canada's industrial policy.[18] The Douglas Point station was the first reactor to be called a CANDU, and along with the success of NPD, it showed that the heavy-water model was a viable technology in large-scale power reactors. The future CANDU design was now set and Canada began a building boom that would see reactors built in New Brunswick, Quebec, and, especially, Ontario. (See table 1.2 for the evolution of nuclear reactors in Canada; table 1.3 for the current status of reactors; and figure 1.1 for a map of nuclear activity in Canada.)

Canada's unique historical development of the CANDU was quite

Table 1.2. Evolution of nuclear reactors in Canada

Reactor	Type	Units	Online	Current status
ZEEP	Research	1	1945	Decommissioned
NRX	Research	1	1947	Decommissioned
NRU	Research	1	1957	Operational
NPD	CANDU Prototype	1	1962	Decommissioned
Douglas Point	CANDU	1	1965	Decommissioned
Pickering A	CANDU	1–3	1971–3	Suspended
Pickering A	CANDU	4	1971–3	Operational
Gentilly 1	CANDU	1	1972	Decommissioned
Bruce A	CANDU	1–2	1977–8	Suspended
Bruce A	CANDU	3–4	1977–8	Operational
Pickering B	CANDU	4	1982–6	Operational
Pt. Lepreau	CANDU	1	1983	Operational
Gentilly 2	CANDU	1	1983	Operational
Bruce B	CANDU	4	1984–7	Operational
Darlington	CANDU	4	1990–3	Operational

Table 1.3. Current status of nuclear reactors in Canada

			Decommissioned	
Research	Operating	Suspended	Research	Power
8*	17	5	3	3

*There are two research reactors at Chalk River and six at Canadian universities (Alberta, Saskatchewan, RMC, Dalhousie, L'Ecole Polytechnique, and McMaster).

distinct from the American experience, which developed its civilian light-water reactor based on research spun from its highly successful nuclear naval reactor program. The CANDU reactor, in contrast, was developed as a commercial power reactor from the start. Once the war was over, Canada's research was largely focused on exploring the civilian potential of nuclear energy, and there were three factors that were critical to the development of its nuclear industry. First, Canada concentrated its efforts on a single reactor design. The federal government, which financed the research and development that led to the CANDU, did not have the resources to invest in several different types of reactors. In both Britain and France, for instance, civilian nuclear development suffered because of infighting between competing reactor designs. Canada, as a much smaller country, could not afford that type of internal technological competition. Second, Canada had to ensure that it

Figure 1.1. Map of nuclear activity in Canada

Canada's Nuclear Reactors and Uranium Mines

▲ CANDU reactors [# of reactors x net MW(e)]

1. Bruce A: 4 x 770 (2 mothballed for refurbishment)
   Bruce B: 3 x 795 + 1 x 849
   Douglas Point: 1 x 208 (decom) - large prototype CANDU
2. Pickering A: 4 x 515 (2 mothballed)
   Pickering B: 4 x 516
3. Darlington: 4 x 881
4. Gentilly-1: 1 x 250 (decom) - Boiling water CANDU
   Gentilly-2: 1 x 635 CANDU 6
5. Point Lepreau: 1 x 633 CANDU 6
6. Nuclear Power Demonstration: 1 x 22 (decom) - first CANDU

● Research reactors (thermal power)

A. U of Alberta, Edmonton: SLOWPOKE II, 20 kW
B. Saskatchewan Research Council, Saskatoon: SLOWPOKE, II 20 kW
C. AECL Whiteshell Laboratories, Pinawa
   a) WR-1 organic-cooled, 60 MW (decom)
   b) SLOWPOKE Demonstration, 2 MW (decom)
D. McMaster U, Hamilton: MNR, 5 MW pool
E. U of Toronto: SLOWPOKE II, 20 kW (decom)
F. Royal Military College, Kingston: SLOWPOKE II, 20 kW
G. AECL Chalk River Laboratories
   a) NRU, 135 MW
   b) NRX, 42 MW (decom)
   c) PTR, 100 W (decom)
   d) ZED-2, 250 W
   e) ZEEP, 250 W (decom) - first reactor outside USA
   f) MMIR 1 and 2: 10 MW each, medical isotope production
H. MDS Nordion, Ottawa: SLOWPOKE II, 20 kW (decom)
I. Ecole Polytechnique, Montreal: SLOWPOKE II, 20 kW
J. Dalhousie U, Halifax: SLOWPOKE II, 20 kW

■ Uranium Mines/Mining Areas

1. Cluff Lake (closed)	7. Rabbit Lake
2. McClean Lake	8. Beaverlodge (closed)
3. Midwest	9. Port Radium (closed)
4. Cigar Lake	10. Eliot Lake (closed)
5. McArthur River	11. Bancroft (closed)
6. Key Lake	

Copyright September 2005
Canadian Nuclear Society
www.cns-snc.ca

Source: Canadian Nuclear Society, www.cns-snc.ca/nuclear_info/canadareactormap.gif

produced an independent reactor design. If Canada were simply providing a carbon of a Westinghouse design or a Kraftwerk Union design, then it inevitably would become a branchplant nuclear producer. Third, it had to make sure that the science worked. Canada put all its eggs in the CANDU basket, and a failed system could have meant hundreds of millions of dollars wasted and, more importantly, an opportunity wasted.

Instead, as over thirty-five power reactors at home and abroad testify, the science did indeed work.

The Decision to Export

When U.S. President Dwight Eisenhower delivered his 'Atoms for Peace' speech to the United Nations in 1953 (an event that will be explained in more detail in chapter 3), the major nuclear countries began a race to establish their share in the international nuclear reactor marketplace. The Americans, the British, the French, and the Canadians were soon competing to see who would be the first to establish a successful power-reactor design. Once a design had been established and tested as a power source domestically, it would open the door to the export market. Britain was first off the block with exports of its magnox reactors to Japan and Italy in the 1950s. However, being first, did not necessarily mean being best. Britain's reactor design was heavily flawed, and it has been shut out of the export market ever since.

Canada developed its nuclear industry gradually through the building of research reactors, power prototypes, and eventually, full-scale power reactors. Throughout this process, it was always assumed that when ready, Canada, like the other major nuclear powers, would be pursuing the export market. For example, in a 1955 briefing to the federal cabinet, AECL outlined one of its major objectives: 'To carry out the power reactor development programme in such a manner as to ensure that the Canadian manufacturer will be in a position to design, fabricate and construct power reactors and their components for the domestic and *the foreign market.*'[19]

Given Canada's small domestic market, it was realized early that Canada's nuclear industry must have an international dimension. 'The only way,' as AECL President Lorne Gray asserted in 1968, 'that a full workload could be provided over the five-year period and beyond would be if Canada were to gain orders for nuclear power stations abroad at reasonably regular intervals.'[20] The 1981 *Nuclear Policy Review* later explained that 'Canada's exports of nuclear equipment and technology represent both a natural extension of, and a support for, the domestic nuclear power programme.'[21]

Canada was also motivated for finding markets for its substantial reservoir of uranium. For most of its known existence, uranium was viewed as an unwanted by-product of radium. Its major use had been simply to add colour to glass and ceramics, and it took the discovery of nuclear fission for uranium's true potential to emerge. To ensure that

Table 1.4. Canada's nuclear reactor exports

Country	Ordered	Online
India (CIRUS – research reactor)	1956	1960
India (RAPP I – CANDU power reactor)	1963	1973
Pakistan (KANUPP – CANDU power reactor)	1965	1972
India (RAPP II – CANDU power reactor)	1966	1981
Taiwan (TRR – research reactor)	1969	1971
Argentina (Embalse – CANDU power reactor)	1973	1984
South Korea (Wolsung I – CANDU power reactor)	1973	1983
Romania (Cernavoda I – CANDU power reactor)	1978	1996
Romania (Cernavoda II – CANDU power reactor)	1982	Under construction
South Korea (Wolsung II – CANDU power reactor)	1990	1997
South Korea (Wolsung III – CANDU power reactor)	1992	1998
South Korea (Wolsung IV – CANDU power reactor)	1992	1999
China (Qinshan I – CANDU power reactor)	1996	2002
China (Qinshan II – CANDU power reactor)	1996	2003

uranium, which has some of its largest deposits in Canada, remained valuable required the worldwide expansion of nuclear power. Greater reliance on nuclear power, preferably from Canadian-designed reactors, would mean that uranium mines in Elliot Lake and elsewhere could maintain production. This would ensure a steady stream of revenue that could finance full-employment at the mines. Gordon Churchill, the minister of trade and commerce in the Diefenbaker government, explicitly made this point to the House of Commons in 1958 when he stated that one of the major objectives of the nuclear program was 'to expand the civil market, both domestic and foreign for Canadian uranium.'[22]

Beginning in 1956, AECL launched a sales effort aimed at a select number of developed countries: Britain, the United States, France, Japan, Australia, Denmark, the Netherlands, and Italy. AECL also targeted a number of the larger and/or more industrially advanced developing countries: Greece, Indonesia, Turkey, Chile, Mexico, Egypt, Hungary, Venezuela, Yugoslavia, Russia, the Philippines, and Thailand. In the end, AECL succeeded in selling research and CANDU power reactors to India, Pakistan, Taiwan, Argentina, South Korea, Romania, and China (see table 1.4 for a list of all nuclear reactor exports).

Organization of This Book

In the first two chapters following this introduction, I explain the arguments that facilitate and constrain CANDU exports. Chapter 2 examines the economic and political justifications that have made the sales of CANDUs an important objective of successive Canadian governments. Chapter 3 sets out a series of constraining influences that have been prominent in the debate over CANDU exports. These factors, which involve a mix of security, economic, and political arguments, include the fear of nuclear proliferation, the issue of human rights abuses in recipient states, the environmental concerns associated with nuclear power, and the extent of government subsidies in the Canadian nuclear industry.

The next four chapters are devoted to analysing how the clash of foreign policy objectives has been played out in each CANDU sale. Chapter 4 looks at the initial period of 1945 to 1974, beginning with Canada's first nuclear transaction – a research reactor to India in 1956 – and ending with India's explosion of a nuclear device in 1974. Chapter 5 examines the period of 1974 to 1976, when Canada's nuclear export policy responded to India's nuclear explosion by terminating its nuclear cooperation with India and Pakistan and renegotiating its nuclear safeguards agreements with Argentina, South Korea, Japan, and the European Community. Chapter 6 assesses the period 1977 to 1989, when Canada suffered the consequences of its unilateral actions in the area of nuclear proliferation during the preceding period. Chapter 7 looks at the period of 1990 to 1996, when Canada experienced a nuclear renaissance with new CANDU sales to South Korea and China.

This book concludes with chapters 8 and 9. Chapter 8 looks at four recent, but separate, events to determine the future interplay of Canada's competing foreign policy objectives in the area of CANDU exports: (1) Ontario Hydro's 1997 decision to shut down seven of its CANDUs; (2) the 1998 nuclear tests by India and Pakistan; (3) the attempted sale of a CANDU to Turkey; and (4) the decision to assist Romania with the construction of its Cernavoda II reactor. Chapter 9 systemically identifies which foreign policy objective was most dominant in each time period. It also identifies which foreign policy objectives have consistently explained Canada's decision-making when it comes to CANDU exports.

2 Justifying CANDU Exports

CANDU exports are not normal business transactions. They require a long-term, intensive, and expensive bid process and are frequently accompanied by high-level government involvement. For example, the Turkish Electrical Authority (TEK) asked for preliminary proposals in October 1992 and, for eight years, kept changing the bid process before finally announcing its decision to cancel the project in July 2000. In its pursuit of the nuclear contract, AECL spent several million dollars redrafting and refining its bid, and even enlisted Prime Minister Jean Chrétien's lobbying in Ankara on its behalf. A further political complication is the significant anti-nuclear movement that has emerged in Canada and other countries that publicly challenges all attempts at exporting the CANDU. Given the volatile and controversial nature of the international nuclear trade, why, then, does Canada try to export CANDU reactors? What benefits, if any, does Canada amass, or hope to amass, through these exports? There are numerous economic and political arguments that provide the basis for the intensive efforts by AECL and the Canadian government in finding buyers for the CANDU.

The purpose of this chapter is to identify these arguments. The first part looks at the economic justifications for CANDU exports. In assessing these economic arguments, five dimensions must be explored: (1) the benefits that accrue to Canada from the export of nuclear reactors; (2) the competition that exists among the world's reactor suppliers; (3) the markets that exist for reactor exports; (4) the consequences for the Canadian nuclear industry of insufficient exports; and (5) the pro-nuclear lobby in Canada. The second part looks at the political arguments that help to justify CANDU exports. In particular, Canada has historically used CANDU exports to pursue two political foreign policy objectives: assisting the developing world and the containment of communism.

Economics

Benefits

Canada achieves enormous economic benefits from its nuclear industry.[1] The most obvious benefit is the amount of revenue the industry generates. The Canadian Nuclear Association (CNA) estimates that the industry contributes over $6 billion annually to Canada's gross domestic product. This puts $700 million a year of tax revenue into the coffers of the federal and provincial governments.[2] Exports make up an important component of these revenues. For AECL, exports constitute 70 per cent of its total commercial income. For example, in the period 1979–92, its revenues were over $2.4 billion.[3] CANDU exports, in particular, bring in hundreds of millions of dollars to the Canadian economy. In 1996, the sale of two CANDUs to China represented a $4-billion contract that contained $1 billion in Canadian content.[4]

When hundreds of millions of dollars of foreign exchange enter Canada, its balance of payments is advanced. In 1994, nuclear exports exceeded $800 million, while uranium exports totalled over $1 billion.[5] Canada's balance of payments is also enhanced because 'imports constitute a very small portion of the nuclear industry's inputs.' As a result, the nuclear industry generates a positive trade balance of over $1.5 billion.[6] Specific sectors of Canada's balance of payments are also enhanced by CANDU exports. For example, former international trade minister Michael Wilson maintained that CANDU exports were a positive influence on Canada's trade balance in 'high value-added goods and services' – an area in which Canada continually possesses a trade deficit.[7] In a related point, CANDU exports also demonstrate to sceptical onlookers that Canada is an 'industrial country capable of supplying large-scale, high-technology systems and is not just a purveyor of natural resources.[8] In a major cost-benefit analysis of the Canadian nuclear industry commissioned by AECL in the early 1990s, Ernst and Young emphasized this point by showing that the nuclear and aerospace industries were the only two Canadian high-tech industries with a surplus trade balance.[9]

Another economic benefit of CANDU exports is that they can be used to break into new markets. Since nuclear reactor exports involve a substantial commitment between two countries, it can be surmised that a sale in this area will lead to increased trade in many additional sectors. As Michael Wilson pointed out, 'one of the keys to opening the door to Canadian business' in South Korea was 'the CANDU reactor. It has been our "flying wedge" into the market of a trading partner whose importance will grow in the coming years.'[10]

Employment in Canada is also positively influenced by exports. AECL, alone, employs more than 3,500 full-time people.[11] It is true that most of these jobs are dependent on domestic projects, but there would definitely be job losses in the absence of foreign sales. To get a better indication of the employment in the Canadian nuclear industry, we need to examine the component suppliers as well. There are over 150 industrial companies that participate either as major component suppliers or as subcontractors. Some of these suppliers are

- Babcock & Wilcox: the primary manufacturer of nuclear steam generators
- Sulzer Bingham Pumps: supplies the primary heat transport pumps
- Velan Valves: manufactures industrial steel valves
- Canatom: one of the largest domestic engineering and construction firms that specializes in nuclear reactors
- Zircatec Precision Industries: supplies fuel bundles
- Cameco (the successor to Eldorado Nuclear): is one of the world's major uranium producers
- Theratronics International: produces medical equipment and is a market leader in radiation treatment[12]

The Ernst and Young study estimated that in 1993 the industry directly employed around 30,000 people.[13] In addition, indirect employment – 'defined as the number of person years required to produce the commodities for all but the first stage of production' – was estimated to be a further 10,000.[14] Exports are necessary to provide a steady workload for the nuclear design teams and components industry. In fact, Ernst and Young calculated that 'indirect employment in Canada will rise by 2,500 when each new CANDU export project is being built abroad.'[15]

CANDU exports also help Canada deal with the problem of economies of scale. It is necessary to export nuclear equipment and technology because Canada's domestic market is simply not large enough on its own to sustain a nuclear industry. In this regard, Canada is at a disadvantage with other nuclear supplier states, in particular the United States, which have much larger domestic markets. Exports, then, are crucial to Canada's nuclear equipment suppliers because these sales allow them to maintain the necessary infrastructure needed to produce components. The domestic market alone would not provide enough orders to make it economically feasible for companies to maintain the necessary manufacturing capability. To ensure that Canadian supplying firms remain in the nuclear industry, Canada must produce a satisfactory level of reactor exports; without these supplying firms, there would be no domestic nuclear industry.

Related to the problem of scale is the question of research and development (R&D). Typically, AECL spends between $175 and $250 million each year on R&D, part of which is appropriated by the federal government. In 2001–2 this appropriation was $136.6 million.[16] Since its formation in 1952, AECL has received over $4.9 billion in nuclear R&D funds from the Canadian government.[17] AECL has one of the highest levels of investment in R&D among Canadian companies.[18] CANDU exports help to justify this investment and exports help to spread out these substantial costs over a larger market.

Canada has greatly benefited from this investment in R&D. In particular, the level of spending has allowed the Canadian nuclear program to make a significant contribution to pure research. Pure, sometimes called basic, research can be defined as research 'done solely to increase knowledge without any practical application in view.'[19] Although the amount of basic R&D conducted by AECL has been greatly reduced since the 1995 program review, during previous decades the fields of physics and chemistry, to name just two, saw an increase in its scientific knowledge as a result of the research conducted by Canadian nuclear scientists. Chemistry benefited from research into radiation chemistry, nuclear fission and fusion, high-temperature-solution chemistry, isotope separation, radiation-induced creep and growth, and channelling (the ability of energetic positively charged particles to penetrate further into crystalline material by following preferred directions between the regularly spaced atoms in the crystal), hydrogen uptake by zirconium, and zirconium corrosion.[20] Physics benefited from research into the structure, composition, and behaviour of the nuclei; neutron-scattering; positron annihilation; and theoretical physics.[21] 'Canadian scientists,' as Brian Buckley has concluded, have 'made major contributions to the development of reactor physics, notably in accurately predicting changes in reactivity associated with fuel use as well as alternative methods of producing high-energy neutrons as a possible foundation for power production.'[22]

Canadian scientists have also conducted applied research that has led to numerous technological spin-offs. Investment in R&D in the utilization of atomic energy in Canada has not only given rise to the CANDU reactor but also has led to the development of medical and industrial applications of radioisotopes.[23] One of the prides of the Canadian nuclear industry was the invention of the cobalt-60 beam for cancer therapy. The cobalt-60 had the capability of destroying selected cancer cells while, at the same time, leaving healthy cells untouched. This represented a major scientific breakthrough and quickly became the standard medical treatment for cancer around the world. By 1951, the cobalt-60 was being successfully tested in Saskatoon and in London, Ontario. Within a few years AECL was exporting the devices to hospitals and cancer treatment centres worldwide. Cobalt-60 has, to a lesser extent, also been used for non-medical purposes. Just as cobalt-60 destroys cancer cells, it was discovered that small dosages of radiation could also kill the micro-organisms that caused food spoilage. The accuracy of the radiation treatment for cancer left healthy tissue untouched; similarly, irradiation does not affect the taste, texture, colour, or nutritional value of the food. Soon, food irradiation plants, complete with large quantities of cobalt-60, were being built. Cobalt-60 units, primarily used for cancer treatment, became one of AECL's most important products.[24] About 85 per cent of the cobalt-60 used for medical or industrial purposes and about half of the cancer therapy machines come from Canada.[25]

There have been other technological spin-offs that have resulted from nuclear R&D. Given the initial high cost of uranium in the early days of the nuclear age and the fact that only a small fraction of neutrons was available to generate power, a major concern of nuclear scientists – and those in government who paid the bills – was neutron economy. In fact, W.B. Lewis, one of the senior architects and administrators of the CANDU program until his retirement in 1973, declared that neutron economy would be a fundamental aspect of all nuclear research.[26] One way to increase neutron economy is through 'accelerator breeders,' which can create artificially fast neutrons by bombarding uranium with an intense beam of protons accelerated to an energy of several hundred MeV.[27] This research has led to the industrial use of particle accelerators. In addition, there have been a number of other spin-offs: cooling systems for fighting forest fires, flight simulators for pilots, sensing and measuring instruments that measure the condition of equipment, and vibration technology for hard-rock mining.[28]

The Nuclear Competition

To understand properly the competition that exists in the international nuclear reactor trade, one must distinguish between the different reactor types (also see the appendix). The dominant design in the world is the light-water reactor (LWR). There are approximately 330 LWR plants currently operating throughout the world, representing over 75 per cent of all nuclear power plants in operation. This type of reactor has been operating for more than thirty-five years. The largest nuclear supplier state in the world – the United States – uses LWRs, but it is also used by other suppliers like France and Germany. The second major type of nuclear reactor is the heavy-water reactor (HWR). The Canadian-designed CANDU is the principal HWR. Since Canada is the only supplier that specializes in the HWR, it possesses certain advantages and disadvantages in the export market. Germany can also produce an HWR, and has sold two reactors already (both to Argentina), but the HWR is not its specialty, and this has allowed Canada to price the CANDU at a much lower level than the German HWR. Traditionally, Canada's toughest competition has come from the United States (Westinghouse and General Electric), France (Framatome), and Germany (Siemens AG).[29] Tables 2.1 and 2.2 indicate the market share of each of these supplier countries.[30]

The golden age of the nuclear industry was the 1960s and 1970s with over 80 per cent of all nuclear power plants being ordered in those years. During this critical time period, Canada, despite having clear technical advantages over competing reactor designs, found it difficult to obtain sales. Mark MacGuigan, minister of external affairs from 1981 to 1982, complained that 'marketing the CANDU ... was a difficult sell. Canada lacked the political and economic clout to make other nations want to oblige us.'[31] In 1981–2, the Department of Energy, Mines, and Resources (EMR) conducted a comprehensive review of Canada's nuclear policy and it also found that competing supplier states maintained 'broad institutional and political aspects' that Canada has found difficult to overcome.[32] In its review, which looked at long-range prospects, EMR identified a number of advantages that LWR suppliers had:

• Most are large multinational companies with established reputations in the energy systems supply field, both nuclear and conven-

Table 2.1. Share of nuclear reactor export market, 2001

Country	Operable	Under construction	Shutdown
United States	52	1	1
Soviet Union/Russia	17	0	3
Canada	10	2	0
France	8	0	0
Germany	4	2	1
Britain	0	0	2
Sweden	2	0	0
China	1	0	0

Source: International Nuclear Safety Center, *Data for Nuclear Power Plants*, www.insc.anl.gov/plants/

Table 2.2. Historical export markets for nuclear power reactors, 2000

Country	Customers
United States	Belgium, Brazil, India, Japan, South Korea, Mexico, Netherlands, Slovenia, Spain, Sweden, Switzerland, Taiwan
Soviet Union/Russia	Armenia, Bulgaria, Cuba, Finland, Hungary, Lithuania, Slovakia
Canada	Argentina, China, India, South Korea, Pakistan, Romania
France	Belgium, China, South Korea, South Africa
Germany	Argentina, Brazil, Netherlands, Spain, Switzerland
Britain	Japan, Italy
Sweden	Finland
China	Pakistan

Source: International Nuclear Safety Center, *Data for Nuclear Power Plants*, www.insc.anl.gov/plants/

tional, with a number of reactor units operating in a variety of different countries. They have credibility as suppliers.

- Several of the competitors are high-technology based manufacturers with an abundance of skills and resources. The propriety rights for LWR technology generally emphasize standardization and cost reduction to boost competitiveness, and uses R&D and engineering primarily to the extent that these contribute to the attainment of competitive goals.
- Competitors tend to have broad and diversified product lines; most also provide non-nuclear generating capacity which allows economies of scale and spreading of commercial risks.
- They tend to have worldwide networks of resident overseas offices

permitting maintenance of a constant presence in prospective markets.

- Some competitors have the advantage of a continuing strong domestic supply experience upon which to base overseas marketing efforts.
- Some suppliers conduct existing utility business with prospective customers and have local manufacturing outlets which support localization objectives of prospective clients.
- Most suppliers are capable of mounting broadly based industrial financing and trade packages commensurate with the size and scope of the reactor systems proposals.
- Major suppliers have excess production capacity and, therefore, foreign sales are eagerly sought.
- LWRs are marketed by several firms, providing customers with the advantage of choosing from a number of suppliers.[33]

Since the early 1980s, after most of the nuclear power plants had been built, all nuclear suppliers have faced the same problem: overcapacity. In each supplying country, the individual nuclear industries were created when energy demands were high and when the future growth of nuclear power appeared endless. However, the demand for nuclear power has decreased in both the domestic markets of the major suppliers and in the export markets. This trend is expected to continue. A 1999 Organization of Economic Cooperation and Development (OECD) report suggested that while the worldwide demand for energy continues to grow, nuclear energy remains static.[34] It is estimated that in OECD countries, because there are few new plants being built and many older plants are being decommissioned, the share of electricity from nuclear plants will decrease from about one-quarter to one-eighth by 2020. Thus, suppliers are faced with preserving their industries until demand for nuclear power again increases.

In a situation where many capable suppliers are searching for available markets, there is going to be intense competition. The stakes are very high: the survivors will gain potential billions, while the losers will disappear from the industry.[35] As a result of this stiff competition, suppliers have utilized many 'sweeteners' to increase sales. Historically, these 'sweeteners' have included generous financial arrangements between suppliers and recipients, and in some cases the bribery of officials; assurances of a reliable uranium fuel supply, both natural in the case of Canada and enriched in the case of everybody else; the

supplying of additional fuel-cycle facilities; increased technology transfers; and a willingness to relax safeguards designed to limit nuclear
proliferation. Many of these 'sweeteners' are now officially banned due
to export control agreements by the Nuclear Suppliers Group and the
OECD's Consensus Agreement. However, today's suppliers may discover new 'sweeteners' such as ignoring a potential customer's weak
environmental and/or human rights standards.

Many experts believe that nuclear power can recover its share of the
electricity market. Projecting energy trends is never an easy task and
achieving a consensus can be very difficult. Nuclear energy has been no
exception. Every time the price of oil or natural gas skyrockets, nuclear
power suddenly looks much more attractive. Similarly, the debate over
climate change has led the nuclear sector to emphasize the fact that,
unlike coal-fired plants, nuclear power does not emit sulphur dioxide,
nitrogen oxides, or particulates. In both cases, proponents of nuclear
energy quickly emerge to predict a building expansion. A prototypical
statement comes from Gary Kugler, a senior vice-president of AECL,
who has suggested that 'most people would agree that oil and gas are
going to be volatile in terms of price. When you are talking about
energy security for modern economies, you have to think of 20, 30 and
50 years. And when you do that, there is no solution, except nuclear on
a large scale, unless the environment is going to be seriously damaged.'[36] In addition, the first generation of nuclear power plants built in
the 1960s and early 1970s are starting to show their age. If countries
decide to replace their aging nuclear plants with new nuclear plants, as
opposed to switching to other energy sources, the downward trend
could reverse. For example, in the fall of 2001, the British Energy PLC
submitted a proposal to the British government to build up to ten new
nuclear plants. Nevertheless, the optimists who believe that nuclear
energy can hold its market share, or even expand, remain, at best, a
significant minority of energy experts.

The Nuclear Market

A further complication that the Canadian nuclear industry faces in its
pursuit of exports is the current size of the export market for nuclear
reactors. There are three factors affecting this. First, what is the overall
demand for electricity? Electricity demand is highest in the developed
world, but the largest increase in electricity demand has been among
the Asian tigers. Second, what are the energy alternatives that exist

Table 2.3. The ten largest consumers of nuclear power, 2003

	No. of reactors	Total MW(e)	Nuclear percentage of electricity capacity
United States	104	98,530	20
France	59	63,293	78
Japan	53	44,153	39
Germany	19	21,141	30
Russia	30	20,793	16
South Korea	18	14,870	39
United Kingdom	27	12,082	22
Ukraine	13	11,195	46
Canada	14*	9,998	12
Sweden	11	9,460	46
Top ten total	348	305,515	N/A
World total	439	360,046	N/A

*Canada has twenty-two reactors, but between 1997 and 2003, eight were suspended.
Source: World Nuclear Association, 'World Nuclear Reactors 2002–2003 and Uranium Requirements,' www.world-nuclear.org/info/reactors.htm

within a particular country? If a country has extensive oil reserves, like Saudi Arabia, its need for nuclear power is obviously quite weak. Third, what is the technological capability of the state? Part of the technology capability is the ability of a state's infrastructure to support nuclear power. This can range from the existence of nuclear research facilities to a satisfactory electrical grid system.[37] The combination of these three factors has meant that the nuclear market is quite small, as only thirty-one countries in the world possess an operational power reactor.[38]

The nations of the Western industrialized world are best suited for nuclear power and, in fact, nuclear energy plays a very significant role in their electricity market. In 1998, for example, 345 nuclear reactors supplied 23.8 per cent of OECD countries' electricity.[39] Unfortunately, the Canadian nuclear industry has been largely shut out in exporting to all OECD states (see table 2.3). For example, Japan may not compete in the export market, but it has a flourishing domestic nuclear industry. This greatly restricts the size of the potential nuclear market because any country with an indigenous nuclear industry is likely to have some form of market protection that constrains the importation of reactors. Thus, early on, AECL presumed, probably rightly so, that the Western industrialized countries would exclude foreign competition to protect their domestic nuclear industries. After all, it is likely that Canada would take similar steps to ensure that the extent of foreign penetration of its nuclear market remained very low.

Trade protectionism is not unique to the nuclear reactor market. Although trade barriers have been greatly reduced over the years thanks to the work of the General Agreement on Tariffs and Trade (GATT) and the World Trade Organization (WTO), there remain a number of sectors where protectionist policies remain entrenched. Agriculture and textiles are two obvious examples of persistent trade irritants, but a better comparison to the nuclear sector is the aerospace sector. As in the nuclear sector, the aerospace sector has only a few companies competing in a multibillion dollar high-tech market with very tight margins. Many of the purchasers are government-owned airlines, and each supplier also has a high degree of economic importance and political symbolism, including very close ties to the home government. The leading suppliers in today's market are Boeing (U.S.), Airbus (Europe), Bombardier (Canada), and Embraer (Brazil). Bombardier's business model closely resembles AECL's as it is 'structured around government incentives, government subsidies, government contracts, government-led export promotion, and government "tied aid" to developing countries.'[40] This has led to a high-profile and intransigent trade dispute between Bombardier and Embraer. The WTO has been forced to arbitrate, largely unsuccessfully, the dispute over the fifty-to-seventy-seat regional aircraft market between Canada and Brazil, each country accusing the other of unfair trade practices that include export credits and loan guarantees.[41]

The principal export market for Canada and the other nuclear suppliers has been, and remains, the developing world. Given the protectionist nature of the industrialized countries towards nuclear reactors, the developing world has become a 'dumping ground' where nuclear suppliers deposit their wares.[42] This is likely to continue, as the OECD estimates that the developing world, including China and the transitional economies of Eastern Europe, will be the only parts of the world with an increase in the use of nuclear power.[43] However, most developing countries do not possess the necessary technological infrastructure to justify their acquisition of nuclear power. Therefore, the major market for reactors lies with a small group of newly industrialized countries. In addition, once these countries develop a domestic industry, they will eventually be forced to export for the very same reasons that the current suppliers export. That this is already starting to happen is evident in Argentina's export of research reactors to Peru, Algeria, and

Albania, China's nuclear cooperation with Pakistan, and India's offer to build nuclear research reactors in Egypt and Syria.

Consequences of Insufficient Exports

Despite the limited opportunities presented by a small market and tough competition, Canada has been under pressure to maintain a sufficient level of CANDU exports to sustain the domestic industry. This was a powerful rationale throughout the 1970s and 1980s. Since the early 1990s, the economic rationale has accentuated the commercial opportunities and downplayed the link by maintaining the domestic nuclear industry to one based on commercial opportunities. Nevertheless, given that this was a historic justification for exports, and continues to be cited by AECL and the Canadian Nuclear Association, it needs to be explained in greater detail.

Stark consequences were predicted in the 1970s and 1980s for the nuclear industry if Canada failed to obtain sufficient exports. One important consequence would be that Canada would move back down the nuclear learning curve. In particular, Canada could go from a 'manu- facturing *capability*' to a 'manufacturing *potential.*' The difference be- tween capability and potential 'is essentially between possession of an active and a latent industrial function, and between being competitive and being uncompetitive at a given time in world reactor markets.'[44] The Canadian nuclear industry warned that insufficient exports would lead to Canadian firms leaving the nuclear industry. Ottawa had been quite receptive of these concerns. The Department of Energy, Mines, and Resources (EMR), in its 1982 nuclear review, surveyed the nuclear component companies and found that 'almost all' of the suppliers would abandon the industry if sufficient exports were not secured.[45] EMR concluded that 'if a sizable number of main components suppliers were to leave the nuclear market, the vigour with which the CANDU reactor could be promoted in exports, as well as domestic markets, would seriously degenerate.'[46] The Canadian nuclear industry has been more resilient than the EMR review predicted. In the twenty years since the review, only seven foreign reactors, and no new domestic reactors, have been built. A few firms have left, but the nuclear industry has been able to retain its capability to build CANDUs. Nuclear component suppliers have seemingly mastered the ability of leaving the nuclear sector when there is no work and quickly reconstructing their nuclear capability when necessary orders arrive. Nevertheless, this argument should not be totally dismissed as a reason for promoting CANDU exports. This is because Canada still needs to maintain a 'critical mass' of suppliers, otherwise it will need to rely on foreign firms. Thus, Canadian political leaders continue to remain sensitive to the needs of domestic nuclear component suppliers.

The Canadian nuclear industry has also threatened that, eventually, if enough exports are not arranged, the ultimate collapse of the industry could occur. The loss of an industry that has contributed approximately $23 billion to Canada's gross domestic product between 1962 and 1992 would be devastating.[47] In addition to these GDP losses, there would be other, more far-reaching consequences should be domestic nuclear industry disintegrate: it could adversely affect Canada's energy supply, security, and balance. The result would be higher energy costs, a less self-sufficient energy supply, and a less-reliable energy supply.[48] Currently, between 15 and 17 per cent of Canada's electricity is supplied by nuclear power.[49] Without it, Canada would be forced to spend over a billion dollars a year 'importing fuel for electricity generation.'[50] Ernst and Young have determined that 'from 1965 to 1989, nuclear energy saved the Canadian economy approximately $17 billion in foreign exchange.'[51]

In this scenario, Canada would also suffer a massive 'brain drain' of high-tech personnel skilled in the nuclear field. It is not just the number of employees that is important, it is also the type of employees. This industry utilizes a very high proportion of scientists and engineers, more so than many other industry, and these workers constitute a scarce resource in Canada. Ernst and Young estimated that over 3,200 scientists and engineers are employed in the nuclear industry.[52] As a result, these jobs take on considerable importance.

Finally, the creation of an indigenous nuclear technology has provided Canada with an important element of national prestige. An important reason for the continuation of the Canadian nuclear project following the end of the Second World War was a belief by the key decision-makers, most notably C.J. Mackenzie and C.D. Howe, that Canada, for the first time in its history, had the unique opportunity of being at the forefront of a revolutionary advance in science and technology. The sentiment that Canada was becoming a scientific power through its work on atomic energy was also recognized internationally. Margaret Gowing, the official historian of the British nuclear program, wrote:

Atomic energy had helped to carve a new status for Canada in the post-war world. It had brought her to the top diplomatic tables and it had demonstrated and enhanced her underlying scientific, technological, and industrial strength. The NRX reactor – planned by a wartime hotchpotch of Canadians, British, New Zealanders, and French and other European refugees – was the most successful experimental pile in the world. In these circumstances Canada was relaxed and generous, ready to help the British and the Americans without bothering too much whether she got back as much as she gave. An odd twist of wartime fate had made her into an important country, atomically speaking.[53]

For example, in the first twelve years after the war, there were a series of United Nations commissions with a mandate to eliminate or control nuclear weapons. Sitting at the negotiating table were the two super-powers (the United States and the USSR), two other permanent members of the Security Council (Britain and France), and Canada. The only reason that a middle power like Canada was treated as an equal of the superpowers was because of its role in the development of the atom.[54]

National prestige has been frequently identified as a key incentive for a country to develop nuclear weapons. In Canada's case, national prestige was a key incentive in the maintenance of nuclear science and technology, including the CANDU. The CANDU and its scientists have received a number of national and international technological achievement awards. In 1987, the reactor was named as one of Canada's top ten engineering accomplishments, and in 1984 AECL scientist Bertram Brockhouse won the Nobel Prize in Physics. As a result, the CANDU has benefited from a degree of national myth-making. This image of the CANDU as a matter of prestige cannot be overstated. As George Lermer has pointed out, 'massive "sunk costs" in the CANDU program combined with high technological achievements make CANDU a package of prestige that politicians would disassociate from only at their peril.'[55] Since the early 1960s, the example of the Avro Arrow has been brought up as a warning to the government to protect the nuclear industry. As the *Toronto Star* editorialized in 1979, the failure to support the Canadian nuclear industry 'would be the Avro Arrow mistake again, on a vastly greater scale.'[56] The explicit warning against Canada's giving up on another high-tech industry is a powerful force for the continued maintenance of the nuclear industry.

The Pro-Nuclear Lobby

It is not just the economic benefits or even the consequences of insufficient CANDU exports that makes the economic argument central to the decision-making process, it is also *who* is making these arguments. There are a variety of different domestic actors with competing and complementary interests involved in the export of CANDUs. By identifying who they are and sketching out their positions, we can start to see the political dynamic of CANDU exports at work. Obviously, the primary actor involved is AECL. AECL is the designer, engineer, distributor, patent holder, and marketer of the CANDU. AECL's mission is 'as a leading supplier of full-scope nuclear power capabilities. This gives it the capacity, in collaboration with Canadian and international partners, to capture a substantial share of the emerging global nuclear power market with a competitive and superior product.' AECL has asserted that its research, development, and engineering role has 'enhanced national science and energy objectives and contributed to the evolution of Canada's nuclear policies.'[57] Its headquarters and its engineering design centre are in Mississauga, Ontario, but its major research and development laboratories remain in Chalk River.[58] In addition, AECL maintains offices in the major cities of the countries to which it has either sold a CANDU or hopes to sell one; these include Seoul, Beijing, Bucharest, Buenos Aires, Ankara, Jakarta, and Bangkok.[59]

The provincial utilities – Ontario Power Generation (previously called Ontario Hydro), Hydro-Québec, and New Brunswick Power – are also charter members of the pro-nuclear lobby. They are the owners and operators of all of the CANDUs in Canada. Ontario Power Generation (OPG) is the largest owner of CANDUs with fifteen operational reactors (four remain suspended, although their restarting is currently under study). These reactors generate between 40 and 60 per cent of Ontario's electricity (depending on how many reactors are operational). In fact, as was shown in chapter 1, the partnership between Ontario Hydro and AECL was instrumental in the development of the CANDU. New Brunswick Power only owns one reactor, but the Point Lepreau reactor, which began power production in 1983, has been one of the most efficient reactors in the world and accounts for over 21 per cent of the province's electricity needs. Hydro-Québec, because of its large reserves of hydro-electric power from James Bay and Churchill Falls, has the smallest interest in nuclear affairs of the three provincial utilities. The Gentilly-2 is Hydro-Québec's only reactor and it generates less than 3 per cent of Quebec's electricity needs. The provincial utilities have an ongoing vested interest in the maintenance of the Canadian nuclear industry through continued CANDU exports even if they have, so far, refused to provide financial support for AECL's export program.

Federal (AECL) and provincial (Ontario Power Generation, Hydro-Québec, and New Brunswick Power) Crown corporations dominate much of the Canadian nuclear industry. However, the private sector is also heavily involved in the nuclear industry as component suppliers (see fig. 2.1). As stated earlier, there are over 150 private sector companies in Canada that provide components for the CANDU. They can be divided into six sectors: (1) manufacturing (Babcock and Wilcox, Sulzer Bingham Pumps, Velan Valves); (2) engineering (Canatom); (3) operation and maintenance (subcontractors to the provincial utilities); (4) uranium mining (Cameco); (5) construction; and (6) others (hospitals and universities that rely on nuclear medicine and radiology, and companies like Nordion which is a world leader in medical radioisotope technology).[60]

The Canadian Nuclear Association (CNA) is the industry's collective voice. Formed in 1960 to promote nuclear power, its membership includes AECL, the major component suppliers, the uranium producers, and the electrical utilities. In addition, a key government department – the Department of Foreign Affairs and International Trade (DFAIT) – is a member. The CNA's mandate is to 'create and foster an environment favourable to the healthy growth of sound applications for nuclear energy.' On the issue of exports, the CNA is committed 'to sponsoring activities relating to the successful marketing of nuclear-related products and services in Canada and around the world.'[61]

The Canadian Nuclear Society (CNS) could also be listed as another pro-nuclear interest group. However, unlike the CNA's explicit lobbying, the CNS is a professional society, like the Canadian Association of Physicists or the biological and chemical societies. The CNS, which was formed in 1979, is 'dedicated to the exchange of information in the field of applied nuclear science and technology. This encompasses all aspects of nuclear energy, uranium, fission and other nuclear technologies such as occupational and environmental protection, medical diagnosis and treatment, the use of radioisotopes, and food preservation.'[62] Given this mandate, the bulk of CNS members are individual professionals from educational institutions.

There are also umbrella organizations like the CANDU Owners Group (COG) and the Organization of CANDU Industries (OCI). COG was formed in 1984 by the provincial utilities that owned CANDUs (Ontario Hydro, Hydro-Québec, and New Brunswick Power) and AECL. The purpose of COG is to provide a framework that will promote closer cooperation among the owners and operators of CANDU stations in

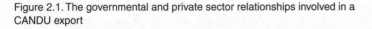

Figure 2.1. The governmental and private sector relationships involved in a CANDU export

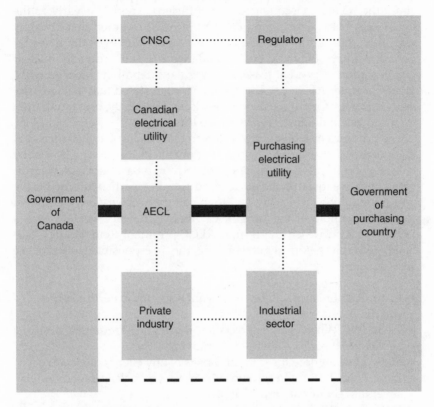

matters relating to plant operations and maintenance, and to foster cooperative development programs leading to improved plan performance. OCI was founded in 1979 to represent Canadian private sector companies engaged in CANDU exports. 'Its purpose is to represent companies in the Canadian private sector engaged in the supply of goods and services for CANDU power plants in export markets. In doing so, it provides a focal point for industrial collaboration between the private sector of Canada's nuclear industry and foreign purchasers of a CANDU plant.'[63]

The above groups can be viewed, in general, as the pro-nuclear export lobby. These groups, as Morrison and Wonder have noted, 'all have a strong interest in seeing that nuclear exports continue at the highest possible level.'[64] In particular, the nuclear industry has frequently emphasized the benefits of CANDU exports while warning about the severe consequences of insufficient exports. As early as the mid-1960s, Lorne Gray, then president of AECL, warned that 'the only way, then, that a full workload could be provided over the five-year period and beyond would be if Canada were to gain orders for nuclear power stations abroad at reasonably regular intervals.'[65] More recently, in 1997, former AECL president Reid Morden stated that 'a successful export strategy for our industry today is, in the end, the best foundation for a successful domestic future down the road.'[66]

The pro-nuclear lobby is also quick to react to any public criticism of the industry. For example, many components of the pro-nuclear lobby will respond in print, via letters to the editor, on any story they see as being negative towards the nuclear industry.[67] A particular target is the anti-nuclear lobby (see chapter 3 for a comprehensive description). An excellent example of the pro-nuclear lobby's defence strategy was a 1997 speech, in which the former AECL president Reid Morden outlined, with full rhetorical guns blazing, the 'irresponsible tactics' of the anti-nuclear lobby:

- Tactic One. Pretend you have relevant scientific expertise, when you don't.
- Tactic Two. When challenged on one misleading argument, simply move onto the next – always be a moving target.
- Tactic Three. Ignore the costs and risks of any energy alternative.
- Tactic Four. Talk about the consequences of a nuclear tragedy – never talk about risk or probability.
- Tactic Five. When in doubt, always evoke the most scary images. Nothing beats drama to raise funds.
- Tactic Six. Always, always repeat. There's nothing like repetition of a lie to make people think it's the truth.
- Tactic Seven. Pretend you are interested in energy or the environment, when your real agenda is simply anti-nuclear, full stop.[68]

Politics

Assisting Developing Countries

Furthering Canadian economic interests has always been an important objective of Canada's foreign policy. Beyond economics, however, Canada has additional foreign policy objectives in the political and security realms. In the political realm, one of its foreign policy goals has been to assist in the economic and political growth in developing countries. There are many rationales for pursuing this foreign policy objective, including reducing global poverty, enhancing Canadian prosperity and security, and advancing global human security.[69] Furthermore, some critics have viewed development assistance and international peacekeeping as the 'twin pillars' on which Canadian post-war international activity has rested.[70] Canada's participation in multilateral forums like the World Bank, the United Nations Development Program (UNDP), the Development Assistance Committee of the OECD, as well as its creation, in 1968, of a domestic aid agency – the Canadian International Development Agency (CIDA) – can all be viewed as efforts to formalize its development strategies.

One way that Canada's development policy was pursued, particularly in the early years of its post-war liberal internationalism, was through its membership in the Commonwealth.[71] In 1955, Lester Pearson, then external affairs minister, asserted that he viewed the Commonwealth as 'a bridge of understanding between the West and Asia and Africa [whose value] is very great in this age of suspicion and strain where there are few such bridges.'[72] The Commonwealth was seen as a forum in which economic cooperation between its old, rich, and white members (Australia, Canada, New Zealand, and the United Kingdom) and its new, poor, and multiracial members (Ceylon/Sri Lanka, India, Malaysia, Pakistan, Singapore) could take place. A prominent example of foreign assistance inside the Commonwealth was the introduction in 1950 of the Colombo Plan, which was initiated by the Commonwealth but later included the United States and most of Southeast Asia. The plan was an attempt at alleviating the problems of poverty, illiteracy, and overpopulation in Asia through technical aid, training, and a series of megaprojects, including, as we will see in chapter 3, a nuclear research reactor.

An important rationale for CANDU exports for most of the post-war period, up until the late 1970s, was the objective of development assistance. Nuclear technology transfers were viewed as a specific mechanism through which Canada could assist the developing world. Canada believed that the peaceful benefits of nuclear power should be at the disposal of all states, and many of its early nuclear pioneers accepted that nuclear energy could bring enormous benefits to underdeveloped countries. W.B. Lewis was consistent in his belief that since Canada had nuclear technology, it had a responsibility to share it with the developing world. As early as 1947, Lewis had drafted a paper entitled 'World

Possibilities for the Development and Use of Atomic Power,' which advocated the sharing of nuclear knowledge between the developed and underdeveloped world.[73]

Decades later, Prime Minister Pierre Trudeau would reiterate the obligations that Canada had in trying to assist developing countries. In a 1975 speech to the Canadian Nuclear Association entitled 'Canada's Obligations as a Nuclear Power,' Trudeau asserted that 'it would be unconscionable under any circumstances to deny to the developing countries ... the advantages of the nuclear age ... Technological transfer is one of the few, and one of the most effective, means available to us of helping others to contribute to their own development ... Nuclear technology is one of the most certain means of doing so ... The decision taken by Prime Minister St. Laurent to enter a nuclear-assistance program with India was a far-sighted and generous act of statesmanship.'[74] Therefore, Canada sought to use the transfer of nuclear technology as a way of aiding underdeveloped states.

Since the locus of Canada's foreign assistance was the Commonwealth,[75] India and Pakistan were viewed as logical recipients of Canadian nuclear assistance. J.G. Hadwen, a former ambassador to Pakistan and high commissioner to India, noted that the common belief in external affairs during the 1950s and 1960s was that 'Canada, during the war period, had developed considerable expertise in the generation of electricity by nuclear processes. We believed that Canadian technology was the most efficient of the nuclear technologies available. We thought of it as the safest of alternatives and as the one best suited to peaceful generation of electricity.'[76]

Containing Communism

Canada's second major foreign policy goal, especially in the early years of the post-war, was anti-communism. Throughout the Cold War, a central pillar of Canadian foreign policy was preventing the spread of communism. Events in the late 1940s, such as the Berlin blockade and the communist coup in Czechoslovakia, resulted in Canada's opinion of the Soviet Union changing from valued ally against Nazi Germany to the leader of a hegemonic communist bloc bent on world domination. Canada shared this fundamental shift in opinion with its key allies in Washington and London. When the United States adopted a policy of containment in response to the Soviet threat, Canada immediately followed suit.

Canada implemented its policy of communist containment in many well-known ways. It joined Western defence alliances like the North Atlantic Treaty Organization (NATO) in 1949 and the North American Aerospace Defence Command (NORAD) in 1958. It sent troops, under UN authorization, but U.S. command and control, to fight in the Korean War in 1950. Finally, the containment of communism meant that during most of the Cold War, Canada maintained limited diplomatic, economic, political, and social relations with the Soviet bloc and communist China.

One of the sparks that started the Cold War was the defection of Igor Gouzenko in 1945. Gouzenko was a low-level cipher clerk in the Soviet Embassy in Ottawa who brought with him hundreds of documents detailing the extent of an elaborate Soviet spy ring in Canada, the United States, and the United Kingdom. One of the key targets of Soviet espionage was to acquire details of the Manhattan Project. 'The Soviet spy network,' as Prime Minister King wrote in his diaries, 'lead right into the Research Buildings here in Ottawa, the Laboratories in Montreal, to British scientists working there who have even more knowledge of the atomic bomb developments than almost anyone; to persons in our own External Affairs Department and in the Registry Office in Earnscliffe [official residence of the British High Commissioner].'[77]

The Gouzenko revelations affected Canada's nuclear development in a number of significant ways. First, the United States – viewing its Canadian and British allies as security sieves[78] – greatly restricted the extent of its nuclear cooperation with its former partners. In August 1946, six months after Gouzenko's defection, the United States passed the McMahon Act, which made it illegal for Americans to transfer nuclear technology to foreigners. This U.S. action reinforced Canada's desire to pursue an independent nuclear course which would ultimately lead to the invention of the CANDU. Second, Canada became deeply concerned about the theft of nuclear technology by the Soviets. In fact, the protection of nuclear secrets became a significant aspect of Canada's counter-espionage efforts. Third, given the lack of trust that existed during the Cold War, it was unthinkable that Canada would consider selling nuclear technology, especially its prized CANDU, to a communist state. It was not until the mid-1970s, during the era of détente, that Canada finally negotiated a nuclear cooperation agreement with a communist country. Finally, in addition to protecting it own nuclear research, Canada wanted to prevent countries from working with the Soviet Union on nuclear projects. A reactor sale meant a long-term partnership between supplier and recipient, and Canada did not want to see stronger economic or political relations emerge between the Soviet Union and other states, especially vulnerable developing countries. During the Cold War, as the Indian case would show, Canada would rather weaken its nuclear safeguard demands than allow the Soviets to use a nuclear reactor to establish closer ties with a developing country.

Canada also linked communist containment with its efforts in foreign development assistance. Indian Prime Minister Jawaharlal Nehru advised the West that 'the best defence against communism was to raise living standards' in the poorest regions of the world.[79] Ottawa took heed of Nehru's advice, and the Colombo Plan should be viewed in this way. In fact, Pearson justified the Colombo Plan on the basis that 'if southeast Asia and south Asia are not to be conquered by communism, we of the free democratic world ... must demonstrate that it is we ... who stand for national liberation and economic and social progress.'[80] Canadian officials made the argument that its relatively small military and financial contribution to NATO was offset by its role in fighting communism through providing development assistance. Escott Reid, a senior external affairs official, wrote in 1970 that 'Canada can do relatively little to assist in preventing war by maintaining armed forces ... if Canada were to double its present defence expenditures of 1.8 billion Canadian dollars a year, this would increase the total expenditures of the NATO countries by ½ percent. But if Canada were to increase its net expenditures on foreign aid to poor countries by 1.8 billion Canadian dollars a year, this would increase the total expenditures of the wealthy white countries on foreign aid to poor countries by 33 percent.'[81]

The commercial imperatives for exporting nuclear reactors constitute a major influence on the Canadian government. Despite the intense competition from other nuclear suppliers and the relatively small market that exists, Canada needs to produce foreign sales of the CANDU. The benefits of exports combined with the potential adverse consequences of limited exports have meant that commercial influences play a significant role in Canada's CANDU export policy. In addition, Canada has other foreign policy objectives that it has tried to meet through the export of CANDUs. Whether it is helping to assist developing countries or containing the spread of communism, Canada's political interests have also been used to justify CANDU exports. The combination of these economic and political arguments constitutes a powerful force for facilitating Ottawa's pursuit of as many CANDU sales as possible.

3 Constraints on CANDU Exports

Canada's economic and political interests in exporting CANDUs are balanced by other security, political, and economic interests that have been prominent in the debate. These objectives, taken individually or as a group, have usually been seen as constraints. However, it is important to note that there have been times when these considerations have, in fact, facilitated exports. For example, it has been argued that international trade, including nuclear exports, can actually be used to change the human rights record of other countries. Similarly, maintaining nuclear cooperation with developing countries can help to prevent environmental disasters. Thus, while this chapter may be titled 'Constraints on CANDU Exports,' the real story is much more nuanced.

The first constraining argument is that Canada must help prevent the proliferation of nuclear weapons. A second is that Canada should refrain from selling nuclear materials to regimes that violate human rights. A third concerns the effect of CANDU exports on the environment. Finally, in the fourth argument, critics raise issues about the extent of Canadian government subsidies that accompany exports. These four arguments, with various degrees of support, have been recognized in governmental policy statements, critiques from the anti-nuclear movement, and academic literature.

Nuclear Proliferation

A major constraint against CANDU exports is Canada's commitment to nuclear non-proliferation, of which there are two types: horizontal and vertical. Horizontal proliferation is defined as increasing the number of actors that possess nuclear weapons. An example of horizontal nuclear proliferation was when China successfully tested a nuclear weapon in 1964. Traditionally, horizontal proliferation was viewed as restricting the number of states that have nuclear weapons, but today it also includes preventing non-state actors, like terrorist organizations, from acquiring the bomb. The Nuclear Non-Proliferation Treaty (NPT) recognizes five nuclear weapons states: the United States, the Soviet Union/Russia, the United Kingdom, France, and China. There are three non-NPT states that possess nuclear weapons: India, Pakistan, and Israel. North Korea is widely believed either to have nuclear weapons already or to be on the verge of developing them. Vertical proliferation is concerned with the quantitative and qualitative expansion of the nuclear weapons systems of those states that already have the bomb. The development of the hydrogen bomb was an example of vertical proliferation. While Canada has promoted the prevention of vertical proliferation through arms control agreements like the Comprehensive Test Ban Treaty (CTBT), it has been more concerned with horizontal proliferation. This is because horizontal proliferation creates more decision-makers capable of launching a nuclear war, which in turn increases regional and global instability.

If a country wants to obtain nuclear weapons, there are three options that it can choose from: it can purchase, steal, or develop them. The first two options involve acquiring major parts or even a complete weapon (by purchase or theft) from a country possessing such weapons. The third, and the most expensive and time-consuming one, is building nuclear weapons through the development of nuclear technology and capabilities. In this option, there are two elements necessary for the construction of a nuclear weapon: the knowledge or the technology and the actual fissile material, consisting of highly enriched uranium or plutonium. These can be attained directly by building a facility solely for the purpose of creating weapons-grade fissile materials, or indirectly by using fissile materials created from peaceful nuclear energy facilities.

Building power reactors or a civilian research reactor for the purpose of diverting plutonium for weapons production is extremely inefficient. The plutonium that is diverted from commercial nuclear reactors is inferior to plutonium produced specifically for weapons production. In addition, power reactors are more expensive to build and operate than facilities designed to produce weapons. Yet the use of a civilian nuclear program to pursue, and in some cases, develop a nuclear weapons arsenal is precisely the path followed by India, Pakistan, North Korea,

South Africa, Israel, Iraq, Argentina, Brazil, Taiwan, South Korea, and Iran.

How does a civilian nuclear program assist the production of nuclear weapons? The most obvious way is the clandestine diversion of pluto-nium from a civil program to a military program. This is why the prevention of fissile material diversion is the principal aim of the Inter-national Atomic Energy Agency (IAEA) inspectors. A second way is the training of nuclear scientists and engineers – 'dual-use people.' In the 1950s and 1960s, Canada and the United States assisted India's civilian nuclear program by training thousands of Indian nuclear scien-tists and engineers. Unfortunately, some of these people later partici-pated in the development of India's nuclear weapons arsenal. Munir Ahmed Kahn, the former head of Pakistan's nuclear program, stated clearly the indispensable role of technical training in the civil-military linkage:

The Pakistani higher education system is so poor, I have no place from which to draw talented scientists and engineers to work in our nuclear establishment. We don't have a training system for the kind of cadres we need. But, if we can get France or somebody else to come and create a broad nuclear infrastructure, and build these plants and these laborato-ries, I will train hundreds of my people in ways that otherwise they would never be able to be trained. And with that training, and with the blue-prints and the other things that we'd get along the way, then we could set up separate plants that would not be under safeguards, that would not be built with direct foreign assistance, but I would now have the people who could do that. If I don't get the cooperation, I can't train the people to run a weapons program.[1]

In a third way, a legitimate civilian power program provides camou-flage for a parallel weapons program. This can create a situation in which the IAEA devotes its scarce resources to conducting inspections on acknowledged safeguarded nuclear facilities, while a clandestine weapons facility goes undetected and uninspected. Clearly, the larger and more widespread the legitimate sector, the easier it is to hide the illegitimate sector. A final link is that a large civilian program creates a powerful nuclear lobby within a state. In many developing countries, nuclear scientists, like Homi Bhabha in India and A.Q. Khan in Paki-stan, have become national heroes because they were able to master highly sophisticated and modern technology. The temples that they built – reactor sites – were proof of their wizardry and mystique. 'Nuclear establishments,' as George Perkovich has noted, 'can be seen as avatars of modernity, national prowess, and power, and the leaders of these establishments are well-positioned to persuade leaders and publics to give them rein to bring greatness to their nations.'[2] The nuclear establishment thus becomes a powerful bureaucratic actor that, if it desires, could move its country down the path of weapons production.

To help ensure that civilian nuclear programs do not lead to weapons production, an elaborate system of international nuclear safeguards has been developed. William Epstein has defined safeguards as 'the regulations and restraints that a nuclear supplier country imposes on its exports of nuclear materials and equipment.'[3] Safeguards have both technical, as well as political, objectives. Technical safeguards centre on controls over the use of nuclear technology, especially fissile material, and aim to structure international nuclear cooperation so that it directly restricts the development or military application of sensitive nuclear capabilities. A second type of safeguard is political, focusing on a state's motivation for producing nuclear weapons. Mitchell Reiss has remarked that 'the capability without the motivation is innocuous. The motivation without the capability is futile.'[4] Accordingly, the IAEA has developed safeguards to guard against both functions. In its *NPT Model Safeguards Agreement*, the IAEA states that the technical objective of safeguards is 'the timely detection of diversion of significant quantities of nuclear material from peaceful nuclear activities to the manufacture of nuclear weapons or other nuclear explosive devices or for purposes unknown, and deterrence of such diversions by the risk of early detection.'[5] The IAEA states that the political objectives of nuclear safeguards are

1 to assure the international community that States are complying with their non-proliferation and other 'peaceful use' undertakings, and
2 to deter (a) the diversion of safeguarded nuclear materials to the production of nuclear explosives or for other military purposes and (b) the misuse of safeguarded facilities with the aim of producing unsafeguarded nuclear material[6]

Political safeguards, then, emphasize the ramifications of any military application of nuclear weapons by the near-nuclear-weapons states, such as bilateral or multilateral diplomatic pressure.[7] Political pressure can also take the form of imposing economic sanctions, such as when the United States, Japan, Canada, and other nations cut off their foreign aid to India and Pakistan following their nuclear tests in May 1998.

Nuclear safeguards are not a foolproof method for preventing proliferation. This point was made right at the dawn of the nuclear age. The Acheson-Lilienthal Commission, appointed by U.S. President Truman to examine the international aspects of atomic activities, reported in 1946 that

> there is no prospect of security against atomic warfare in a system of international agreements to outlaw such weapons controlled only by a system which relies on inspections and similar police-like methods. The reasons supporting this conclusion are not merely technical, but primarily the inseparable political, social, and organizational problems involved in enforcing agreements between nations each free to develop atomic energy but only pledged not to use bombs ...
>
> So long as intrinsically dangerous activities [that is, production and use of weapon-usable materials such as plutonium and highly enriched uranium] may be carried out by nations, rivalries are inevitable and fears are engendered that place so great a pressure upon a system of international enforcement by police methods that no degree of ingenuity or technical competence could possibly hope to cope with them.[8]

Joseph Stanford, former director of the Legal Advisory Division of the Department of External Affairs, similarly acknowledged that 'safeguards by themselves cannot prevent the proliferation of nuclear weapons. All they can do is detect breaches of the safeguards.'[9]

It may be true that nuclear safeguards are not perfect, but they do matter. They provide a 'legal barrier' against the spread of nuclear weapons. They 'embody the norm of non-proliferation' that raises the political stakes for any state deciding to proliferate. Safeguards also serve as an important 'confidence-building measure' that allows civilian nuclear activity to progress.[10] As Richard Kokoski has emphasized, safeguards 'have the potential to slow the progress of a country determined to develop a nuclear weapon capability, and this delay may provide sufficient time for security issues to be adequately addressed, for a change of leadership to occur, for a negotiated end to the programme to be reached or for the decision to be reversed for some other reason.'[11] While IAEA on-site inspections failed to discover the extent of Iraq's nuclear weapons program in the period prior to the Gulf War in 1991, it did discover North Korea's covert efforts to build nuclear weapons. In the words of Tariq Rauf, a noted nuclear proliferation expert, Iraq represented a failure of the IAEA 'not to detect' their weapons program earlier, but North Korea was not a failure. 'It was the IAEA that found the plutonium problem in time.'[12]

Regardless of the presence of safeguards on its reactors, opponents of Canada's nuclear export policy charge that the CANDU's unique heavy-water design is desirable to those states that would like a weapons option. Critics suggest that there are three features of the CANDU that make it a proliferation-prone reactor. First is the fact that the CANDU is a very efficient producer of plutonium, one of the key ingredients of a nuclear weapon. Second, while most reactors need to be shut down to refuel, the CANDU's online refuelling capability (which makes it an efficient reactor) also allows for the clandestine diversion of spent fuel. As David Martin notes, 'this makes monitoring and verification of CANDU fuel much more difficult.'[13] Finally, the CANDU's fuel is natural (rather than enriched) uranium. Since enrichment technology is complicated and expensive, the use of natural uranium has been an important selling feature of the CANDU. Unfortunately, it also allows a potential proliferator to have a 'safeguard-resistant independent fuel cycle.'[14] This concern with the CANDU's technology was explicitly noted in a 1977 U.S. report, the Ford-Mitre nuclear policy review, which concluded that the CANDU 'is more suitable for reliable weapons' than conventional light-water reactors (LWRs).[15]

However, there is no consensus that the CANDU is a greater threat to non-proliferation than the LWR. AECL scientists argue that there is a difference between reactor-grade plutonium (produced by a CANDU) and weapons-grade plutonium. Weapons-grade plutonium contains at least 93 per cent Pu-239, while reactor-grade plutonium is only 60 to 70 per cent Pu-239. It is technically possible for a potential proliferator to increase the Pu-239 ratio to 93 per cent, but this is a very difficult, risky, and expensive procedure.[16] Other experts have defended the CANDU's online refuelling capability, stating that 'safeguarding this type of fuel management, although more expensive, is probably easier than in the case of bulk refuelling, due to the small number of fuel elements involved in each transfer operation.'[17] In addition, the diversion of plutonium from a CANDU would 'produce local hot spots within the reactor core, resulting in less than optimal reactor performance.' This would 'likely be detected by the safeguards systems employed in CANDU reactors.'[18] In the final analysis, and despite the protestations of the

Canadian anti-nuclear movement, one cannot state definitively that one specific type of reactor poses a greater risk for proliferation than any other reactor.

Regardless of the type of nuclear reactor, there are problems with the application of nuclear safeguards. As the historical record of the international nuclear trade shows, the intense competition among nuclear suppliers has led to the development of 'sweeteners' offered to potential purchasers. The most insidious form of sweetener has been the relaxation of safeguards on reactor exports. Purchasing states, which wish to develop a nuclear program without foreign interference, place incredible pressure on the suppliers to reduce safeguards. Although the near-nuclear-states argue that they have the best of intentions, and that safeguards are an infringement on sovereignty, the truth is that some of the clients desire nuclear reactors to produce nuclear weapons in addition to their stated purposes of using them as a peaceful energy source. When the goal of purchasing countries to avoid safeguards collides with the fierce competition among suppliers, the result is, all-too-often, a reduction of safeguards. The major nuclear suppliers eventually reached a consensus on 'full-scope safeguards' by the early 1980s, but with new suppliers like China and Pakistan that are outside many parts of the non-proliferation regime, the problem of different safeguards standards still exists.

One way to prevent competition on safeguards among nuclear suppliers is through agreement by the suppliers on common export controls, which perform a number of very useful functions. They

1 help to channel trade to legitimate, peaceful activities and away from illegitimate ones
2 impose delays and additional costs on detected weapon programs
3 create a level playing field for industry, by establishing an agreed upon set of rules applied under transparent national decisions
4 render patterns of trade transparent, thereby making it easier to monitor trade and identify malefactors
5 insulate industry from the political and economic risks of trade in highly sensitive areas
6 give industry the incentives and tools to police itself
7 symbolize and give meaning to the anti-NBC [nuclear, biological, and chemical weapons] norm
8 are a necessary part of implementing treaty commitments to prevent trading sensitive materials and technologies with non-parties[19]

Canadian Policy Statements on Nuclear Non-Proliferation

As chapter 1 showed, Canada's initiation into the world of the atom was its role in the Manhattan Project. In the late 1940s and early 1950s, even as Canada was developing what would become the CANDU power reactor, there continued to be a military component. NRX and NRU were used to produce plutonium for American bombs, and uranium was exported to the United States and United Kingdom for their weapons program. Nevertheless, over the years there was a steady evolution in Canadian foreign policy that nuclear power should be developed for peaceful purposes only. Part and parcel of this philosophy was that all the benefits of nuclear power, except, of course, nuclear weapons, should, in principle, be at the disposal of all states, albeit subject to international inspection and control. Ottawa's official policy had two fundamental aspects: (1) promote the evolution of a more effective and comprehensive international non-proliferation regime; and (2) ensure that Canada's nuclear exports did not contribute to nuclear weapons proliferation.[20] This section will trace the development of Canada's non-proliferation policy from Mackenzie King to Jean Chrétien. It will show how Canada's policy emerged out of unilateral decisions and bilateral relations, and through multilateral forums and organizations.

Canada came out of the Second World War with the industrial and technical basis to develop a new energy source and with vast unexploited uranium reserves. It also had the world's only working reactor outside the United States. This led to the development of a nuclear industry almost by accident. Despite its experience and expertise with nuclear technology, however, there was a tacit consensus – with almost no public discussion or opposition – that Canada would not build or acquire its own nuclear weapons. The earliest, and most famous, public renunciation of nuclear weapons was delivered by C.D. Howe during question period in the House of Commons on 5 December 1945: 'We have not manufactured atomic bombs, we have no intention of manufacturing atomic bombs.'[21]

Why did Canada – despite having the technical capacity and resources – not develop atomic weapons in the years immediately following the war? After all, the United Kingdom, with considerably fewer advantages, diverted significant amounts of money from its post-war rebuilding efforts to develop an independent nuclear arsenal. Brian Buckley, a former DFAIT officer, recently completed a study to figure out this historical puzzle. Buckley concluded, after a wide examination of primary and secondary material, including archival material pertaining to then defence minister D.C. Abbott, the cabinet's defence committee, and the full cabinet that there was 'no direct or indirect evidence that the military case for the acquisition of an independent atomic arsenal was ever seriously debated, publicly or privately, in any of the major policy-making mechanisms of government.'[22] In short, not only did Canada not 'go nuclear,' but it also never considered the option.

What explains this decision to ignore the military aspects of the atom? The conventional opinion, as expressed by Canadian-born UN official and disarmament advocate William Epstein, is that Canada's policy 'reflected nation-wide abhorrence of these weapons, the desire to prevent their proliferation, and to see them entirely eliminated, and the hope to benefit from the promising peaceful uses of nuclear energy.'[23] This may be the commonly held view after decades of building an anti-nuclear myth, says Buckley, but it does not answer the question of why Canada ignored the bomb at the start.[24]

The more important question is why Canada ignored the bomb in the crucial formative decade of 1945–55? Countries pursue nuclear weapons to address a perceived security threat or as a matter of national prestige.[25] Neither of these two prerequisites applied to Canada. Canada felt relatively secure. Its planners knew that any threat to the country, and the most likely seemed to be a world war involving the Soviet Union, would automatically affect the United States. And since the Americans had nuclear weapons, there was little need for Canada to possess an independent capability. As to perceptions of prestige, Canada had only shaken off its self-image as a small, quasi-colony with a population of 13 million in 1945. It did not see a need to try to assert itself as a great power.

A comparison of Canada with Britain illustrates the point. 'It was taken for granted,' renowned Canadian foreign policy commentator John Holmes has written, 'that a country of Britain's assumed stature in the world would have [the bomb]. The Canadian situation was the reverse. At no time was serious consideration given to producing Canada's own bomb ... There is no evidence of Canadian anxiety to have a finger on the control of such a weapon. Canadians were beginning to refer to themselves as a middle power, but few had ambitions for the responsibilities of great-power status.'[26] With no pressing need to acquire nuclear weapons, there was little desire to pay the substantial financial costs of building nuclear weapons.

On 15 November 1945, the Tripartite Declaration on Atomic Energy was announced by the United States, the United Kingdom, and Canada.[27] Its purpose was to discourage the development of nuclear weapons and encourage exploration into the possible peaceful uses of atomic energy. In particular, it asked for international action 'to prevent the use of atomic energy for destructive purposes; and to promote the use of recent and future advances in scientific knowledge, particularly in the utilization of atomic energy, for peaceful and humanitarian ends.' The three leaders also announced that the United Nations would establish an atomic energy commission with a mandate to enhance exchanges of scientific information for peaceful purposes; control atomic energy to the extent necessary to assure its peaceful us; eliminate from national armaments atomic weapons and all others adaptable to mass destruction; and establish safeguards by way of inspection and other means to ensure compliance.' Six months later, Canada enshrined the goals of the Tripartite Declaration in its own domestic legislation. In June 1946, Canada announced the incorporation of the Atomic Energy Control Act. The purpose of this Act, according to the minister of reconstruction and supply, C.D. Howe, was 'to encourage further research and development towards a peaceful and constructive application of atomic energy, under proper safeguards.'[28]

In December 1953, United States President Dwight Eisenhower made his famous 'Atoms for Peace' speech to the United Nations General Assembly.[29] Eisenhower used his speech to outline the extent of nuclear proliferation, weapons tests and stockpiles, and raised the deadly spectre of nuclear warfare. The solution to the nuclear arms race, according to Eisenhower, was 'Atoms for Peace' which called for the formation of an international agency that would regulate nuclear trade. In addition, this international nuclear agency would facilitate the transfer of nuclear technology from states possessing this capability to those wishing to acquire it for peaceful purposes. As Eisenhower stated, 'experts would be mobilized to apply atomic energy to the needs of agriculture, medicine and other peaceful activities. A special purpose would be to provide abundant electrical energy in the power-starved areas of the world.'

Eisenhower's proposed new international nuclear agency was designed to replace the United Nations Atomic Energy Commission (UNAEC), which was created with the very first resolution of the UN General Assembly in 1946 and lasted until 1952. The UNAEC was one of the first casualties of the Cold War and was essentially irrelevant months after its creation. With the failure of international cooperation on atomic matters, the United States brought in its infamous McMahon Act which outlawed all U.S. nuclear cooperation. The 'Atoms for Peace' proposal was an explicit reversal of the McMahon Act and represented a new belief that the best way to halt nuclear proliferation was not through isolation and secrecy, but through the dissemination of scientific knowledge in a spirit of openness and cooperation.

Canada fully endorsed 'Atoms for Peace.' It meshed with Canada's belief that the atom held great peaceful benefits for humankind. 'Atoms for Peace' also provided an opportunity to re-emphasize that 'Canada is the only country in the world with sizeable atomic energy establishments where no bombs are being made, and where all the thinking and planning is focused on peacetime aspects.'[30] Health and Welfare Minister Paul Martin Sr., who, in 1957, would become the Secretary of State for External Affairs, told the United Nations that Ottawa was 'prepared to broaden its existing programme of exchanging research institutes and is now in a position to furnish considerable additional information on the structure and operation of research reactors.'[31] Canada responded favourably to 'Atoms for Peace' because it represented its belief in the peaceful possibilities that the atom possessed. Canada also had less altruistic reasons for supporting Eisenhower's proposal. Opening the floodgates to the worldwide development of civilian nuclear power would mean Canada would benefit from increased uranium development, giving a boost to both its then-fledgling nuclear industry and its manufacturing and construction companies.

The agency that Eisenhower asked for came into being in 1957 with the formation of the International Atomic Energy Agency.[32] The IAEA had the twin objective of promoting 'the contribution of atomic energy to peace, health and prosperity throughout the world,' while, at the same time, ensuring 'that assistance provided by it or at its request or under its supervision or control is not used in such a way as to further any military purpose.' The first objective would be achieved by fostering 'the exchange of scientific and technical information on peaceful uses of atomic energy.' The second would be achieved through the establishment of a nuclear safeguards system that would ensure that nuclear materials were not diverted from peaceful uses to build nuclear weapons. This safeguard system would include nuclear material accounting reports, containment and surveillance measures, and on-site inspections of individual nuclear facilities.[33]

Canada played a major role in the negotiations that led to the formation of the IAEA.[34] In fact, Canada would have a seat on the IAEA's board of governors and W.B. Lewis would sit on its scientific advisory committee. 'Canada has achieved this position,' as Bill Bennett, the head of AECL, explained, 'largely because of the emphasis which has been placed on fundamental research since the inception of the Chalk River project.'[35] As then external affairs minister Sidney Smith stated, 'Canada wholeheartedly supports the newly established international atomic energy agency.'[36]

The second pillar of the international nuclear non-proliferation regime was the Nuclear Non-Proliferation Treaty (NPT). If the IAEA's purpose was to promote the peaceful uses of nuclear energy, the purpose of the NPT, opened for signature in 1968 and ratified in 1970, was to prevent the proliferation of nuclear weapons states.[37] As the NPT made clear in its preamble, 'the proliferation of nuclear weapons would seriously enhance the danger of nuclear war.' The NPT established two classes of countries: nuclear-weapons states (Britain, China, France, Soviet Union, and the United States: the only countries which had already tested nuclear weapons)[38] and non-nuclear-weapons states (everybody else). The essential bargain contained in the NPT was the inalienable right of the world's non-nuclear-weapons states (NNWS) to develop nuclear energy for peaceful purposes and to have access to the full range of peaceful nuclear technologies developed by the richer countries, including the five nuclear-weapons states (NWS). The NPT's preamble stated that 'the benefits of peaceful applications of nuclear technology ... should be available for peaceful purposes to all Parties to the Treaty.' Article IV enunciated this commitment in more detail. All parties to the Treaty would 'have the right to participate in, the fullest possible exchange of equipment, materials and scientific and technological information for the peaceful uses of nuclear energy.' NNWS, especially in the 'developing areas of the world,' would benefit from nuclear supplier states pledged to 'cooperate ... to the further development of the application of nuclear energy for peaceful purposes.'

Contained in the NPT were many safeguards designed to end the proliferation of nuclear weapons by NNWS. The NNWS, in Article II, pledged 'not to receive' any 'nuclear weapons or other nuclear explosive devices' and 'not to manufacture ... acquire ... seek or receive any assistance in the manufacture of nuclear weapons or other nuclear explosive devices.' Article III specified that the NNWS would also agree to 'accept safeguards' from the IAEA 'for the exclusive purpose of verification of the fulfilment of its obligations assumed under the Treaty with a view to preventing diversion of nuclear energy from peaceful uses to nuclear weapons or other nuclear explosive devices.' These safeguards, unlike those in the original IAEA statute which were facility-based, would apply to all the fissionable material within the territory of a NNWS. NPT safeguards were developed in conjunction with the IAEA in 1970.[39] The IAEA was also charged with administering the NPT safeguards regime. NPT safeguards are commonly referred to as full-scope safeguards because they comprehensively covered the entire fuel cycle and all of a country's known nuclear facilities.

As an incentive for NNWS to sign the NPT, the NWS pledged to make strides to end their nuclear arms race. The preamble of the NPT declares the intention of the NWS 'to achieve at the earliest possible date the cessation of the nuclear arms and to undertake effective measures in the direction of nuclear disarmament.' Under Article VI, the NWS agreed 'to pursue negotiations in good faith on effective measures relating to cessation of the nuclear arms race at an early date and to nuclear disarmament.'

Canada, befitting its role in the international nuclear community, played a significant role in negotiating the NPT and was an original signatory of the treaty. Ottawa believed that the NPT was an important step in preventing nuclear war. 'The treaty' would 'be an important factor in maintaining stability in areas of tension, in creating an atmosphere conducive to nuclear-arms control and generally enhancing international stability.'[40] External Affairs Minister Mitchell Sharp, in announcing Canada's proposed ratification of the NPT, stated that 'as a leading proponent of the treaty and one of the major "near-nuclear" signatories, Canada has an opportunity to provide leadership by demonstrating our faith in the non-proliferation treaty.'[41] The basis for Canada's support of the NPT was more than just a desire to stop the spread of nuclear weapons. Canada also believed that its commercial interests were being met by the NPT. The treaty would also enhance the 'development of the nuclear programmes of signatories for legitimate peaceful purposes' and the 'international trade in nuclear material and equipment.'[42]

Many near-nuclear-weapons states found the NPT discriminatory because it made a distinction between nuclear-weapons states and non-nuclear-weapons states, and because it held the membership in the 'nuclear club' at five. The NPT set up a permanent hierarchy of two classes of countries: five countries that could legally possess nuclear weapons with everybody else prohibited. The states that initially refused to sign the NPT included India, Pakistan, Argentina, South Africa, and Israel, the so-called near-nuclear-weapons states, as well as both China and France, which were nuclear-weapons states. Canada acknowledged the discriminatory nature of the NPT, but also felt that it was a necessary agreement. Commenting on the NPT, General E.L.M. Burns, Canada's representative on the UN Disarmament Committee, stated that, 'while this is an inherently discriminatory approach to the problem, it is the only rational one.'[43]

The international nuclear non-proliferation regime suffered a major setback in 1974 when India exploded a nuclear device. Canada felt partially responsible for India's action because the plutonium used in the device came from a Canadian-built research reactor. In response, as will be detailed more extensively in chapter 5, Canada suspended, and then terminated, all nuclear assistance with India. In announcing the suspension of Canada's nuclear cooperation, External Affairs Minister Mitchell Sharp stated that India's explosion was a direct violation of Canada's policy of nuclear power for peaceful uses only. Sharp maintained that Canada could not be expected to 'assist and subsidize, directly or indirectly, a nuclear program which, in a key respect, undermines the position which Canada has for a long time been firmly convinced is best for world peace and security.'[44]

In December 1976, Canada announced a new nuclear non-proliferation policy. In the House of Commons, External Affairs Minister Don Jaimeson stated that 'shipments to non-nuclear weapon states under future contracts will be restricted to those which ratify the Non-Proliferation Treaty or otherwise accept international safeguards on their entire nuclear program. It follows from this policy that Canada will terminate nuclear shipments to any non-nuclear weapon state(s) which explode a nuclear device.'[45] This new policy strengthened its 1974 position that had been Canada's immediate response to the Indian nuclear explosion. This 1976 statement was the most stringent of any of the nuclear suppliers until the United States matched Canada in 1978. It was not until 1995, at the NPT extension conference, that all the treaty parties finally agreed that nuclear exports 'should require, as a necessary precondition, acceptance of full-scope Agency safeguards.'[46]

Canada's 1976 non-proliferation statement did contain one small loophole, but it was closed by Prime Minister Brian Mulroney in 1992. At a commencement address at Johns Hopkins University in Baltimore, Mulroney eliminated the possibility of nuclear cooperation in the absence of the NPT. The 1976 policy statement had referred to 'otherwise accept' full-scope safeguards. This meant that nuclear cooperation was possible as long as a country submitted to IAEA inspections of their entire nuclear program, it was not necessary for them to sign and ratify the NPT. This possibility was now ended. Later in the speech, Mulroney went further by suggesting that 'as part of an effective international effort, Canada would be prepared to terminate all of its economic cooperation programs, including aid and tariff preferences, with any country' that did not sign the NPT.[47] Although other prominent non-signatories included Israel and Pakistan, it was clear that Mulroney's comments were aimed squarely at India, with whom Canada retained an extensive aid program. In addition to these public statements, quiet diplomacy had been used to try to pressure India and the other nuclear-threshold states to ratify the NPT.

Canada's commitment to the NPT has always transcended party politics. Regardless of whether the Liberals or the Progressive Conservatives were in power, Canada remained committed to the objectives contained in the NPT. Policies on the NPT articulated by Pierre Trudeau were carried forward by both Brian Mulroney and Jean Chrétien. Indeed, the foreign policy review initiated by Chrétien after the October 1993 election asserted that 'our highest priority is to secure international agreement to indefinitely and unconditionally extend the NPT' and strengthen 'the capacity of the IAEA to effectively safeguard civilian nuclear systems.'[48] The Liberal government had an opportunity to demonstrate its commitment to nuclear non-proliferation at the 1995 NPT review and extension conference.

The NPT conference was a success: the signatory states decided to make the treaty permanent. The Canadian delegation played an important role in the conference decision for indefinite extension.[49] It was Canada that presented and worked to obtain over 100 co-sponsors for the resolution that formed the basis for the decision. Although extension was an important step in strengthening the international non-proliferation regime, the nuclear threshold states of India, Israel, and Pakistan still show no signs of adhering to it, and North Korea has since renounced the treaty. Nevertheless, the final result was that the NPT was extended indefinitely and Canada played a key role in that process.

Canada's most recent comprehensive policy statement on nuclear non-proliferation was given in 1999. It was drafted in response to a December 1998 House of Commons Standing Committee on Foreign Affairs and International Trade report entitled *Canada and the Nuclear Challenge: Reducing the Political Value of Nuclear Weapons in the Twenty-first Century* in December 1998.[50] In the policy statement, Ottawa reiterated its view that the 'preservation and enhancement of the NPT and the nuclear disarmament and non-proliferation regime is integral to Canada's national security and to the human security of future generations of Canadians.' In addition to reinforcing specific aspects of its non-proliferation policy, Ottawa also used this occasion to place specific demands on the troublesome states of India and Pakistan: 'freeze their nuclear weapons programs; adhere to the CTBT; participate in the negotiation of a Fissile Materials Cut-off Treaty and agree to a moratorium on the production of fissile material; refrain from missile tests; institute and enforce sound export controls with respect to sensitive technology and materials; and sign and ratify the NPT as non-nuclear-weapon States.'

Canadian Nuclear Schizophrenia[51]

These government statements on nuclear policy show that since the Second World War, Canada has gradually toughened its stance against nuclear proliferation. It has aspired to exploit the peaceful benefits of nuclear power while refraining from developing its own nuclear weapons. Moreover, Canada has maintained the same policy with regards to its CANDU exports. Nevertheless, some aspects of Canadian policy have been, and remain, at odds with this policy. Canadian uranium exports were initially used to fuel the nuclear weapons programs of both Britain and the United States. Chalk River, which contained the NRX and the NRU reactors, was designed both to advance Canada's civilian nuclear program and assist the United States military nuclear program by producing plutonium for American bombs. This strategy reflected the contradictory nature of Canada's nuclear policy. Ottawa would keep its own nuclear heart pure by investing only in civilian applications of the atom, but it would also play its role in the Western alliance by assisting and supporting the strategy of nuclear deterrence against the Soviet Union.

There may be some controversy over whether any Canadian uranium fuelled the bombs that landed on Hiroshima and Nagasaki, but there is no dispute that Canadian uranium was an integral part of the Manhattan Project.[52] In fact, the major architects of Canada's civilian nuclear program, Wilfrid Bennett Lewis and C.J. Mackenzie, believed that Canada's development of nuclear power could be financed, in part, by the sale of plutonium (which was about $5,000 an ounce) to the United States.[53] By 1959, Canada's annual uranium exports had reached more than 15,000 tonnes and were worth over $300 million. Historian Ron Finch, in his 1986 book *Exporting Danger*, estimated that Canada provided the Americans and British with enough uranium for 15,000 nuclear bombs.[54] It was not until 1965 that Ottawa decided that, henceforth, 'export permits will be granted, or commitments to issue permits will be given, with respect to sales of uranium covered be contracts entered into from now on, only if the uranium is to be used for peaceful purposes.'[55]

The Chalk River facility, beyond supplying plutonium, contributed in other ways to the American and British nuclear weapons programs. Throughout the 1940s and early 1950s, the Canadian program did not totally abandon its military origins. C.D. Howe made many references in the House of Commons to the military role of Canada's *civilian* nuclear program. In 1953, Howe remarked that 'we in Canada are not engaged in military development, but the work that we are doing at Chalk River is of importance to military developments.'[56] A year later, Howe explained that 'while the reactor was primarily a research tool, much of the information obtained in its design and operation has been of great value to the military program.'[57] As O.M. Solandt, a senior civilian analyst in the Department of National Defence, said during the Korean War, 'There is no question that other friendly countries have always regarded the Chalk River Project as a major Canadian contribution to defence.'[58] It is impossible to separate pure research into the properties and potential of the atom into peaceful and defence purposes, and civilian and military uses of that research cannot be divorced. For example, in the early 1950s, the U.S. Navy used Canadian technology to design a small reactor for powering its nuclear submarines. A final bit of evidence of Chalk River's military role was the stationing of a United States military liaison officer.

While it is true that Canada never designed, nor even desired, an indigenous nuclear weapons capability, Canada did debate, and then acquire, U.S. nuclear weapons. John Clearwater, a former civilian analyst with the Department of National Defence, is the author of two books on the presence of American nuclear weapons in Canada. In *Canadian Nuclear Weapons*, he details the period from 1963 to 1984, when Canadian weapon systems were equipped with U.S. nuclear warheads. During this period, Canadian bases at home and in West Germany possessed a nuclear capability. Canada deployed four nuclear weapons systems: the BOMARC surface-to-air anti-bomber missile; nuclear bombs carried by the CF-104 Starfighter; the Honest John short-range battlefield rocket; and the Genie air-to-air unguided rocket. Clearwater estimates that 'at the height of the Canadian nuclear deployments, the greatest number of weapons which could have been available to Canada would have been between 250 (low estimate) and 450 (high estimate).'[59]

Clearwater's second book, *U.S. Nuclear Weapons in Canada*, describes the nuclear weapons that the United States stored at its bases in Newfoundland and the Canadian arctic from 1950 until 1971: 'The first known presence of nuclear weapons in Canada came in September 1950, when the [U.S. Air Force] stationed eleven Mk4 "Fat Man"-style atomic bombs at Goose Bay, Newfoundland.'[60] U.S. bombers equipped with nuclear weapons also made overflights of Canadian territory, a practice authorized as early as 1948. A major focus of *U.S. Nuclear Weapons in Canada* is command and control. Washington was not committed to consulting with Ottawa let alone obtaining its consent to use nuclear weapons; its only obligation was to inform.

Canada's decision to acquire American nuclear weapons was consistent with the decisions of its NATO allies.[61] In fact, as Tom Keating has persuasively argued, although 'Canada's struggle with American nuclear strategy and nuclear weapons has been viewed in bilateral terms, the country's multilateral security connections have been most influential in shaping the direction of Canadian policy.'[62] In 1957, NATO decided to adopt tactical nuclear weapons as part of its effort to deter Soviet aggression. The cover story in the November/December 1999 *Bulletin of the Atomic Scientists* provides significant evidence of 'where, when, and under what circumstances the United States deployed nuclear bombs overseas.'[63] During the 1950s and 1960s, it reports, West Germany, Italy, Turkey, Netherlands, Greece, Belgium, Denmark (in Greenland), and Iceland all hosted U.S. nuclear weapons. Even Britain and France, which had independent nuclear capabilities, stored U.S. nuclear warheads. At the peak of U.S. overseas nuclear deployments, there were more than 7,000 nuclear weapons in Europe.

Canadian policymakers were under pressure to acquire nuclear weapons for the military. The Canadian military had a strong desire that it should be trained in the use of atomic weapons. Solandt made the case for the Canadian use of American nuclear weapons in the early 1950s, arguing that 'it becomes increasingly obvious that should there be another total war it will be predominantly atomic. It will not be so many years before no first-class armed force, no matter how small, will be able to engage in battle unless it has atomic weapons. ... We must begin now to lay a foundation of knowledge that will ultimately enable the Canadian Forces to use atomic weapons.'[64] Ten years later, the Pearson government implemented Solandt's recommendations. But the result was that American nuclear weapons, under American command and control, could be launched from Canada. In fact, 'Canadian deployments were little more than extensions of U.S. military deployments and strategy.'[65]

Eventually, Canada did reverse course and began, in 1968, to remove all nuclear weapons systems from its bases. The process of nuclear weapons removal allowed Pierre Trudeau to give his famous nuclear suffocation speech to the United Nations General Assembly in 1978. During this speech, Trudeau bragged that Canada was 'not only the first country with the capability to produce nuclear weapons that chose not to do so, we are also the first nuclear-armed country to have chosen to divest itself of nuclear weapons.'[66] What Trudeau did not mention in his speech was that there were still nuclear weapons in Canada. In fact, it would not be until 1984 that Canada was completely free of nuclear weapons.

Despite having removed U.S. nuclear weapons from its forces and territory, Canada remains firmly under the protection of the American nuclear umbrella. It participates in the nuclear defence of North America not only through its membership in NATO but also through NORAD. And even if Canada were not a member of these alliances, it is likely that Washington would continue to view an attack against its northern neighbour as an attack against the United States. Thus, it can be argued that American nuclear deterrence would extend to include Canadian territory irregardless of Ottawa's nuclear policy.

Canadians generally believe in nuclear non-proliferation, and Canada was the first country capable of building nuclear weapons that decided not to. It has continued to refrain from developing nuclear weapons and, in a precedent-setting move that Ukraine and Kazakhstan later followed, removed all nuclear weapons from its soil. Canada also implemented a policy of not assisting in any country's production of nuclear weapons through either CANDU or uranium exports. However, Canada continues to accept the protection of the American nuclear umbrella. There is a certain logic to the Canadian position, but one can also understand why countries like India and Pakistan, which may not live in such a secure environment, view the Canadians as hypocrites for preaching against the development of nuclear weapons while at the same time accepting their protection.

Regional Conflicts

Canada's principal defence against the spread of nuclear weapons has been its reliance upon the international non-proliferation regime. In particular, the chief form of prevention has been the use of nuclear safeguards. Safeguards may 'legally secure' the CANDU, but they do not, in and of themselves, ensure that the reactor will not be used for military purposes. This point was conceded by former Secretary of State for External Affairs Mark MacGuigan in the specific context of whether Argentina would have violated its legal guarantee not to use Canadian nuclear technology for military purposes in the early 1980s: 'The only genuine question anyone could raise was whether the then government in Argentina could be trusted to respect them.'[67]

Since a reliance on treaties exclusively cannot ensure the absence of weapons proliferation, Ottawa also needs to take into account the implications of nuclear sales within the context of regional conflicts. Nuclear proliferation requires both technological capability and political motivation. Since it is virtually impossible to divorce the military and civilian aspects of the atom, it is necessary for suppliers to identify those countries that may have a political motivation for acquiring nuclear weapons. One obvious incentive for the acquisition of nuclear weapons is the existence of a regional conflict. The potential military use of nuclear power means that states that have either been involved in a regional conflict or might be expected to in the near future will consider a nuclear reactor possessed by their adversary to be a threat to their security. For this same reason, some states will want their own reactors for defensive or even offensive purposes. Thus, Ottawa must be cognizant of the implications for regional stability in concluding any of its CANDU exports.

The Canadian government's 1982 *Nuclear Policy Review* acknowledged the importance of this factor: 'Apart from specific safeguards requirements, Canada makes political and economic assessments of potential reactor customers and discourages sales to countries which may be subject to domestic or external instabilities or security threats.'[68] Unfortunately, a cursory glance at the list of CANDU purchasers shows that most have been involved in a regional conflict so grave that it led to war: India versus Pakistan, Taiwan versus the People's Republic of China (PRC), and South Korea versus North Korea.

Human Rights

Since the end of the Second World War, the promotion of human rights has been a broad foreign policy goal of successive Canadian governments.[69] It is true that this commitment to human rights has been 'neither sustained nor widespread. But there has been a historical empathy with those whose human rights have been violated and a desire to give expression to these symbolic interests.'[70] Ottawa has officially promoted human rights in many ways. It was an original signatory to the Universal Declaration of Human Rights and many of the subsequent UN-sponsored protocols. Although, as a major study on human rights and Canadian foreign policy concluded, 'it was not until the mid-1970s that Canada was prepared to assign staff and resources to the task of promoting international respect for human rights. Until then the government had not spoken out with any force on human rights.'[71]

Since the mid-1970s, Ottawa's rhetoric, both at home and abroad, was increasingly used to promote human rights. In 1977, External Affairs Minister Don Jamieson stated that 'Canada will continue to uphold internationally the course of human rights, in the legitimate hope that we can eventually ameliorate the conditions of our fellow man [sic].'[72] Parliament's Special Joint Committee on Canada's International Relations declared in 1986 that 'the international promotion of human rights is a fundamental and integral part of Canadian foreign policy.'[73] The 1995 foreign policy review proclaimed that human rights were a 'fundamental value' and 'a crucial element in the development of stable, democratic and prosperous societies at peace with each other.' It added that Canada would 'make effective use of all of the influence that our economic, trading and development assistance relationships give us to promote respect for human rights.'[74] During his tenure as Canada's foreign affairs minister (1996–2000), Lloyd Axworthy made human rights a central plank in his human security agenda. Axworthy's work on human rights was reflected in, among other things, his initiatives on the protection of children in armed conflict and in his support for the establishment of an International Criminal Court.

In the last two decades, Ottawa has tried to go beyond statements and speeches and has taken steps to institutionalize its promotion of human rights. It created a human rights office in both DFAIT and CIDA, set up human rights training programs for Canadian officials, and asked Canadian embassies to submit reports on their states' human rights records. Human rights also became one of CIDA's six program priorities in making decisions to grant development assistance.

Despite these efforts, a 'rhetoric-reality' gap has emerged in Canadian human rights policy. Canada's efforts to implement the promotion of human rights into its foreign policy have been largely inconsistent and episodic.[75] In some cases, like the work of Prime Ministers Diefenbaker in 1960–1 and Mulroney in 1985–7 on the issue of South African apartheid, Canada was a human rights leader. However, in other cases, like ignoring atrocities in East Timor in the 1970s and quickly normalizing relations with China in the aftermath of the 1989 Tiananmen Square massacre, Canada was prepared to deliberately neglect human rights considerations. In general when the promotion of human rights has come into conflict with other important foreign policy goals – that is, security or commercial interests – it is the human rights goals which have tended to suffer.[76]

CANDU exports, when you come right down to basics, are essentially trade issues. In other words, why should the issue of human rights play a larger role on Canada's trade policy in some sectors (nuclear materials) as opposed to others (agriculture or automobiles)? The answer is that CANDU exports do not easily fit into the traditional framework of human rights versus security or commercial interests. Instead, as the earlier section on nuclear non-proliferation demonstrated, the fault line for CANDU exports lies between human rights *and* security concerns versus commercial interests.[77] This means that the goal of human rights is not isolated but rather is working in tandem with other Canadian foreign policy goals. Thus, an initial assumption could be made, based on how Canada's competing foreign policy goals line up, that human rights may have a different impact on CANDU exports than they would on other trade products.

There are other reasons why human rights are an important lens through which to evaluate CANDU exports. First, most of the countries to which Canada has sold nuclear reactors have been dictatorships with very poor human rights records: Pakistan and Taiwan in the 1960s; Argentina, South Korea, and Romania in the 1970s; and China in the 1990s. The issue of exporting nuclear reactors to human rights violators raises several unique questions. A reactor transaction requires a long-term relationship. In several cases described in later chapters, Canada was willing to attempt to forge close economic and political ties with states that abuse their own people. In fact, Canada's representatives in international forums have pointed out the human rights abuse of the very countries (i.e, Argentina and Romania) with which it was eagerly pursuing reactor export deals. The most notable example occurred in September 1979, when External Affairs Minister Flora MacDonald made a speech at the United Nations condemning Argentina's human rights record, while at the same time other members of the government were in Buenos Aires trying to sell them a CANDU (this episode will be dealt with in more detail in chapter 6).

Concluding a foreign sale of any large-scale industrial project, like a nuclear reactor, requires a great deal of sales ability. This frequently involves the senior levels of the political leadership. What happens when Canada conducts these high-level bilateral negotiations with a noted human rights violator? There is a certain amount of public distaste when Canadian politicians woo foreign dictators to buy a reactor. The most recent and high-profile example of this was the Team Canada Trade Summit to China in 1994. During this visit, Prime Minister Chrétien, nine provincial premiers, and numerous other ministers, bureaucrats, and Canadian business executives tried to convince Chinese officials like Li Peng (the architect of the 1989 Tiananmen Square massacre) to buy Canadian goods and services, including, of course, CANDUs.

Moreover, regimes that have very poor human rights records can also be quite unstable. There may be some exceptions, like the Soviet Union or Castro's Cuba, but, in general, countries that rely on state repression tend to be at risk. Politically at-risk nations often seek quick, and radical, change in the components and character of their regimes. This change can range from more moderate forms like a coup d'état (Argentina and Pakistan) to more extreme forms like revolutions (Iran and Nicaragua). Since 'repression often leads to civil unrest and revolution,' as T.A. Keenleyside has noted, this 'may be damaging to global security and, hence, to Canadian strategic interests.'[78] Political instability also means that, in a long-term relationship such as that entailed by a nuclear reactor transaction, it is almost impossible to maintain a continuity of political responsibility and accountability. Governments that take power by force do not always adhere to the international agreements that their predecessors have made. More specifically, will a military regime honour a previous regime's pledge to only use nuclear technology for peaceful purposes? Canada's principal tool for preventing nuclear proliferation has been through its safeguards agreements, which require a certain level of trustworthiness between the parties to any transaction. Can a regime that violates its own domestic social contract by subjecting its citizens to human rights atrocities be trusted to adhere to its international responsibilities?

Finally, Canada's export of nuclear reactors is a highly visible sign that Canada is supporting, rather than condemning, the actions of a human rights violator. This is because CANDU exports help to establish, or strengthen, bilateral ties. Thus, Canada can be seen as giving legitimacy to a repressive state. Given Canada's reputation in the world as a human rights leader, this type of legitimacy is a useful commodity for repressive states wishing to justify their actions. It is even possible that Canada is doing more than just supplying moral support and political legitimacy. Canada may be propping up a repressive regime by providing it with greater energy resources produced by nuclear reactors. This point is especially relevant if the transaction is also being subsidized by Canadian taxpayers (see the section below on government subsidies of CANDU exports). A more secure energy source results in a stronger economy, thus providing a state with greater resources with which to crack down on opposition movements. If the Argentina junta circa 1974 or the current Turkish government had had additional resources, it is probable that they would have been used to further crackdown on labour movements or the Kurdish separatists. In other words, Canada may actually be increasing the scale and scope of human rights abuses by exporting CANDUs to the offending state.

The above section shows the arguments for restricting CANDU exports based on a state's poor human rights record. However, it would be a mistake to assume that the protection or promotion of human rights has only been used in an attempt to constrain CANDU exports. In fact, some Canadian politicians and officials have explicitly argued that the sale of CANDUs can advance the human rights record in recipient countries. This counter-argument has its roots in the general debate about the best strategy of promoting human rights in other countries. What is the better approach to improving human rights: the sticks of economic sanctions, political isolation, or humanitarian intervention? or the carrots of trade, investment, diplomatic ties, and cultural exchanges? The purpose of nuclear power is to generate electricity to create economic growth and prosperity. Since there is a strong correlation between economic prosperity and democracy and human rights, it could be argued, notwithstanding the arguments raised earlier, that CANDU exports can be used to advance human rights. This debate will be discussed in more detail in chapter 6 when the sale of two CANDUs to China is explored.

Nuclear Safety and Environmental Values

Since the 1960s, there has been a steady increase in interest about environmental issues in Canada. Marcia Valiante, an environmental lawyer at the University of Windsor, has written that environmental protection has come to be accepted as one of the fundamental values of Canadian society, at least on paper. International instruments, domestic policy documents, legislation, and court decisions abound with eloquent statements of commitment to biodiversity, sustainable development, and the health of future generations. Yet, efforts to implement those commitments reveal great uncertainty and disagreement over the pace and direction of environmental action.[79]

The Atomic Energy Control Board (AECB) was created in 1946 to control, promote, and regulate nuclear technology. In its early years, the AECB's 'existence revolved around developing and actively promoting nuclear technology; this included setting up Crown corporations such as Eldorado Nuclear and Atomic Energy of Canada Limited.'[80] Today, the AECB is exclusively a regulatory body with a mandate 'to ensure that the use of nuclear energy in Canada does not pose undue risk to health, safety, security and the environment.'[81] It regulates the nuclear industry through a licensing system. There are about 4,000 different licenses that regulate nuclear facilities and materials. The AECB also administers import-export licenses that are used to enforce Canada's nuclear non-proliferation policy. In 2001, the AECB was converted into the Canadian Nuclear Safety Commission (CNSC).[82]

Canadian officials have frequently voiced concern regarding the possible environmental dangers of nuclear power. Since the 1950s Canada has been a charter member of the United Nations Scientific Committee on the Effects of Atomic Radiation (UNSCEAR).[83] The earliest high-profile statement on the environmental implications of nuclear power came from Prime Minister Pierre Trudeau. In a 1975 speech to the Canadian Nuclear Association, Trudeau reminded the industry that it had an obligation to provide 'safe sources of energy' and to 'preserv[e] the environment.' This must be done through all of the stages of nuclear power 'exploration, mining, processing, fabrication, design, and sales.'[84]

The purpose of this section is to explain how people's fears over the environmental risks of nuclear power have been used to try to constrain

CANDU exports, the safety of nuclear reactors being the biggest environmental threat. The most common potential reactor accident involves the loss of coolant. During nuclear fission, an incredible amount of heat is generated which, therefore, requires an effective cooling system. The major source of coolant is basic water, which is why reactors are situated near lakes or major rivers. A loss-of-coolant accident was what occurred at the Three Mile Island nuclear power station in Pennsylvania in 1979. If a loss-of-coolant accident lasts long enough, a second and much more severe type of nuclear reactor accident could occur: a core meltdown. A core meltdown means that the excessive heat has melted through the thick steel of the reactor's pressure vessel, through its concrete floor, and down into the earth, possibly releasing very large quantities of radioactive gases into the atmosphere. This phenomenon is called the China Syndrome. Other types of reactor accidents can include power surges, steam explosions, and radiation leaks.

The most infamous nuclear accident occurred at Chernobyl, Ukraine. On 26 April 1986, technicians at the number four reactor at the Chernobyl nuclear plant performed an unorthodox safety test of the reactor's systems. During the test there were a number of errors, including shutting off the reactor's safety systems, which led to a massive power surge. This resulted in successive steam explosions that completely destroyed the reactor plant. The graphite moderator also caught fire. The explosions released large amounts of radiation into the atmosphere. This was the world's most serious nuclear accident, which was caused by an unfortunate combination of factors, including human error, inadequate reactor design, and poor regulatory oversight. According to Valery Legasov, deputy director of the Soviet's Kurchatov Institute of Atomic Energy and the head of the accident investigation team, 'if at least one violation of the six committed had not been done the accident would not have happened.'[85]

The Chernobyl accident had an immediate impact. The explosion killed two workers at the reactor, and an additional twenty-nine firefighters and emergency clean-up workers later died as a result of fatal exposure to radiation. Of the approximately 600 workers and emergency personnel on site, 134 of them were treated for acute radiation sickness. Due to the fear of radiation exposure, the town of Pripyat, located only three kilometres from the plant, was evacuated within thirty-six hours of the accident. In total, Soviet authorities evacuated approximately 250,000 people from the republics of Ukraine, Russia, and Belarus. The radiation also spread throughout the rest of the northern hemisphere, most notably into the bordering countries of Finland and Sweden. For several weeks, the level of radiation in the atmosphere was above normal.

There have been some lingering long-term health and environmental effects from the accident. The UNSCEAR, which has been monitoring the accident since 1986, reported in 2000 that there have already been 1,800 reported cases of thyroid cancer in Ukraine, Belarus, and Russia among individuals exposed to radiation during childhood. It concluded that 'there can be no doubt about the relationship between the radioactive materials released from the Chernobyl accident and the unusually high number of thyroid cancers observed in the contaminated areas during the past 14 years.' UNSCEAR also identified 'anxiety and emotional stress' among parents and children which has led to other health and social problems in the most heavily infected areas. Nevertheless, more serious health problems, like leukaemia or birth defects, have not arisen.[86]

Following the Chernobyl accident, it was understandable for Canadians to wonder whether a similar accident could happen to a CANDU. Three weeks after Chernobyl, Pat Carney, minister of energy, mines, and resources, asked AECB to undertake a scientific review. After comparing the different reactor designs and safety systems, the AECB found that there were great technical differences between Chernobyl's RBMK-type reactor and a CANDU. For example, the RMBK used an inflammable graphite moderator, lacked a thick concrete containment, and its safety system was linked to its control system. The AECB concluded that the Chernobyl accident was so unique, not just technologically but also because of some very lax bureaucratic operating policies, that it was impossible for a similar accident to occur to either a domestically or foreign operated CANDU.[87] In addition to the AECB report, the province of Ontario commissioned an independent study, led by University of Toronto professor F. Kenneth Hare, to examine the safety of Ontario's nuclear reactors. It also concluded that 'Ontario Hydro reactors are being operated safely and at high standards of technical performance. No significant adverse impact has been detected in either the work-force or the public. The risk of accidents serious enough to affect the public adversely can never be zero, but is very remote.'[88] The two external reviews of the CANDU system did produce a number of recommendations to further improve reactor safety, but they both emphasized that the technology was sound and that CANDUs were being operated at a very high safety standard.

Notwithstanding the significant technological differences between RBMK and CANDU reactors and the differences in bureaucratic culture between the Soviet Union and Canada, the Chernobyl accident had, and continues to have, a major influence on the perception of nuclear power in Canada. Nuclear scientists may maintain that nuclear projects should be based on a scientific basis, not the whims of public opinion. However, all aspects of nuclear energy, including export policy, are fundamentally political acts, and in politics, perceptions matter. It matters if Canadians believe that Chernobyl was more disastrous than it really was, or if they believe that a similar accident could happen in Pickering. Elected officials make decisions not just on scientific facts but also on public opinion, even erroneous public opinion.

How common are serious reactor accidents? Table 3.1 lists a summary description of the IAEA's International Nuclear Event Scale (INES). Reactor accidents, those with an INES rating between 4 and 7, are very rare. For example, in the period from June 1995 to June 1996, the IAEA recorded seventy-three events: thirty-five of them were either 0 or below scale; twenty-seven were at Level 1; eight at Level 2; and only three at Level 3.[89] In short, in that one typical year, there were no nuclear reactor accidents. Moreover, in the history of nuclear power, there have been only eight accidents worldwide, with only one (Chernobyl) at Level 7.[90] This is a very good safety record.

Despite the hysteria over nuclear accidents, nuclear energy has a much better safety record than any other energy source. Chernobyl was the worst incident in the history of nuclear power, but as tragic as it was, the death toll was only 31. In comparison, 84 people died when the oil rig Ocean Ranger sank off the coast of Newfoundland in 1982; 200 people died in a gas explosion in Guadalajara, Mexico, in 1992; 2,500 people died in a hydro-dam failure in Macchu, India, in 1979; and 53 people died in a coal-mine disaster in Shanxi, China, in 2003. Table 3.2 compares the fatalities caused by the production of different energy sources. Clearly, nuclear power is the safest energy source.

Despite the empirical evidence about the safety of nuclear reactors, the Canadian nuclear industry needs to address the 'social implications.' The 1998 House of Commons Committee Report, *Canada and the Nuclear Challenge*, pointed out that there is a 'deeply entrenched fear and mistrust of nuclear technology ... within some segments of our society. This "dread factor" is real and palpable. It is an important element in decision-making processes concerning nuclear matters, as it will undoubtedly affect the public confidence resulting from such

Table 3.1. Summary description of the international nuclear event scale

Level	Descriptor	Criteria	Example
7	Major accident	Major release of radioactivity, widespread health and environmental effects	Chernobyl, Ukraine, 1986
6	Serious accident	Significant release of radioactivity, likely to result in full implementation of local emergency plans to limit serious health effects	Kyshtym reprocessing plant, Russia, 1957
5	Accident with off-site risk	Severe damage to reactor core and/or radiological barriers; limited release of radioactivity, likely to require partial implementation of planned countermeasures	Three Mile Island, U.S., 1979
4	Accident without off-site risk	Minor external release of radioactivity; significant damage to reactor core and/or radiological barriers, or fatal exposure of a worker	Saint Laurent A1, France, 1980
3	Serious incident	Only very small release of radioactivity to environment; severe spread of contamination within facility and/or acute health effects to a worker	Vandellos 1, Spain, 1989
2	Incident	Significant spread of contamination inside the facility and/or overexposure of a worker	
1	Anomaly	Anomaly beyond the authorized operating regime	
0	Deviation	No safety significance	

Source: IAEA, 'The International Nuclear Event Scale,' Fact Sheet, www.iaea.or.at/worldatom/inforesource/factsheets/ines.html

Table 3.2. Immediate fatalities by energy source, 1969–86

Energy option	Number of events	Fatalities	Percentage of all energy fatalities
Hydro-electric	8	3,839	35
Coal	62	3,600	33
Oil	63	2,070	19
Natural gas	24	1,440	13
Nuclear	1	31	0.3

Source: Hans Tammemagi and David Jackson, Unlocking the Atom: The Canadian Book on Nuclear Technology (Hamilton: McMaster University Press, 2002), 67.

processes.'[91] A Senate committee report on nuclear safety stated authoritatively that 'no serious injury or death to workers or the public has been recorded in more than 20 years of operation of CANDU reactors in Canada.'[92] Nevertheless, this means that even if the possibility of a serious CANDU accident in Canada or elsewhere is extremely rare, the *perception* of reactor safety can play an important role in constraining CANDU exports.

In addition to the safety of the nuclear reactors, there are other potentially dangerous environmental concerns. One concern is the extent to which the public is exposed to the radiation that is emitted from nuclear power. Radiation from the nuclear fuel cycle is regularly produced in the following ways:

- *Mining and milling:* release of radon gas; spread of dust; groundwater contamination.
- *Conversion, enrichment and fuel fabrication:* release of uranium in gaseous and liquid effluents.
- *Power generation:* release of gaseous fission products and contaminated water; low-level waste, decommissioning wastes.
- *Reprocessing:* release of gaseous fission products; liquid effluents; low-level waste.
- *Transportation:* radiation from the transport package.
- *Waste disposal:* migration of radioactive elements from the disposal area into the environment, particularly over the course of decades or centuries.[93]

According to the UNSCEAR, nuclear power's contribution to radiation (excluding accidents) is virtually insignificant as it accounts for less than 0.05 per cent of the world's release of radioactivity. This compares very favourably with coal since 'a 1,000 MWe coal-fired power plant releases about 100 times as much radioactivity into the environment as a comparable nuclear plant.'[94] The vast majority of radiation comes from natural elements and medical sources.

A second concern is the safe disposal of vast amounts of radioactive nuclear waste. A nuclear reactor, like most other large-scale industrial projects, produces hazardous wastes. Nuclear waste is commonly divided into low-level and high-level. Low-level consists of all radioactive waste that is not spent fuel. This includes mops, clothes, and equipment involved in cleaning up slightly radioactive spills. The more critical environmental concern is the disposal of high-level waste, which

Table 3.3. Half-lives of some radionuclides

Substance	Half-life in years
Thorium – 232	14×10^9
Uranium – 238	4.5×10^9
Uranium – 235	0.71×10^9
Plutonium – 239	24,000
Carbon – 14	5,730 years
Cesium – 137	30 years
Strontium – 90	28 years
Hydrogen – 3 (tritium)	12 years

Source: Hans Tammemagi and David Jackson, Unlocking the Atom: The Canadian Book on Nuclear Technology (Hamilton: McMaster University Press, 2002), 264.

is made up of over 200 radioactive elements, including uranium, pluto-nium, cesium, and strontium. High-level nuclear waste is a by-product of the energy process and is contained in the spent fuel rods from nuclear reactors. Spent fuel nuclear waste has two important character-istics. 'First, it is very small in volume compared to wastes created by many other industries or by burning coal for energy.'[95] On discharge from a CANDU, only about 1.1 per cent of the fuel material can be viewed as waste. 'This is,' as Hans Tammemagi and David Jackson point out, 'dramatically different from coal, oil and other fossil fuels that undergo a complete physical transformation during their combus-tion process.'[96] On average, a CANDU will generate about 30 tonnes of high-level nuclear waste per year. In total, Canada's reactors have accumulated 1.3 million bundles of nuclear waste, enough to fill up three hockey rinks.[97] The second characteristic is that 'the waste is contained; it is not emitted into the environment.'[98] High-level waste is intensely radioactive and requires heavy shielding to protect those who handle it against its penetrating radiation and intense heat. Moreover, the elements of nuclear waste frequently have half-lives that can range from several hundred years to tens of thousands of years (see table 3.3 for a list of nuclear half-lives). However, it is also true that the most highly radioactive substances die out very quickly, while those with the least amount of radioactivity have the longest half-lives. So cesium-137 decays within thirty years, while plutonium-239 has a half life of 24,000 years.

How do you dispose of high-level nuclear waste? In the short term, high-level waste is stored in either water-filled pools or dry-storage cement canisters onsite at Canada's nuclear reactors in Ontario, Quebec, and New Brunswick. The CNSC estimates that this amount of nuclear waste can be safely stored onsite for several more decades.[99] The long-term disposal of high-level waste is a tremendous technological and managerial undertaking, and no country has yet to come up with an acceptable procedure.[100] In the case of Canada, the nuclear industry has proposed burying all nuclear waste in titanium or copper corrosion-resistant containers 457 to 914 metres below the surface of the granite rock of the Canadian Shield. This is a very controversial plan and has been opposed on technological, social, ethical, economic, and environmental grounds. For instance, the Campaign for Nuclear Phaseout (CNP) has criticized the Canadian Shield plan arguing that waste containers could leak and contaminate underground rivers and lakes; there could be accidents with the transportation of nuclear waste from the reactors to the disposal site in the Canadian Shield; earthquakes on the site could lead to the release of radioactivity; storing so much nuclear waste in one place could lead to accidental explosions; and a lack of public consultation.[101]

In March 1998, a government commission appointed by the federal minister of the environment completed a comprehensive review of plans for high-level waste disposal. The commission report concluded that 'from a technical perspective, safety of the [deep geological] concept has been on balance adequately demonstrated for a conceptual stage of development, but from a social perspective, it has not. As it stands, the AECL concept for deep geological disposal has not been demonstrated to have broad public support. The concept in its current form does not have the required level of acceptability to be adopted as Canada's approach to managing for nuclear fuel waste.'[102] Following this review, on 25 April 2001, Ottawa introduced Bill C-27, legislation that creates a Waste Management Organization and gives approval for pursuing the Canadian Shield proposal.[103]

The issue of nuclear safety and environmental protection has traditionally been viewed as a constraining factor against CANDU exports. However, it is now being argued that nuclear power, and therefore CANDU exports, do indeed possess some environmental benefits. In particular, the issue of climate change, principally through global warming, has suddenly made nuclear power appear more environmentally friendly. This is because nuclear power, unlike other conventional energy sources, does not contribute to the emission of greenhouse gases, the major cause of climate change.

The nuclear advantage looks very impressive when it is compared with coal and natural gas, the other two major electricity sources. Nuclear power has zero emissions of carbon dioxide, sulphur dioxide, or nitrous oxide, but a coal plant emits six million tonnes of carbon dioxide and sixteen thousand tonnes of nitrous oxide and a natural gas plant emits 140 million tonnes of carbon dioxide.[104] According to the World Nuclear Association, 'if all the world's nuclear power were replaced by coal-fired power, electricity's carbon dioxide emissions would rise by a third.'[105] Without a doubt, coal, which contributes about 20 per cent of Canada's energy supply, is the worst environmental offender.

These facts have naturally led the nuclear industry to proclaim that nuclear power is the solution to the problem of climate change. The Nuclear Energy Institute (NEI) has stated that, 'around the world, nuclear energy is, and will continue to be, the primary large-scale source of electricity produced without emitting greenhouse gases.'[106] The World Nuclear Association maintains that 'one-third of human-induced greenhouse gases come from the burning of fossil fuel to generate electricity. Nuclear power plants do not emit these gases and are the single most significant means of limiting the increased greenhouse gas concentrations while enabling access to abundant electricity.'[107] A joint International Atomic Energy Agency–World Nuclear Association study showed that 'the planet avoided approximately 600 million tonnes of carbon emissions in 2000 thanks to the 438 nuclear reactors operating that year.'[108] Finland and the United States, among others, have realized that they cannot reduce greenhouse gas emissions without the use of nuclear power.[109] The Canadian nuclear industry has echoed these sentiments. Robert Van Adel, the president of AECL, writes that 'in terms of emissions – the key for clean air and climate change – it is worth noting that a typical CANDU plant in a single year avoids the discharge of about five million tonnes of carbon dioxide (greenhouse gas), sulphur dioxide (acid rain) and other key by-products such as particulates, that lead to the creation of smog ... Without present-day nuclear capacity, Canada's greenhouse gas levels would be some 15–20% higher.'[110]

Governments in Canada are also starting to recognize the nuclear advantage. Former natural resources minister Ralph Goodale asserted that 'without nuclear power in Canada, our greenhouse gas emissions would be between 10 to 15 percent higher than they are now. A typical CANDU saves the equivalent of 5 megatonnes of CO_2 per year.' He added that 'nuclear power is a crucial component of global climate change strategy.'[111] This was reiterated in 2003 by Goodale's successor, Herb Dhaliwal. 'The Government of Canada is committed to ensuring that the nuclear industry continues to be an important part of our energy mix. And I am convinced that it can play an important role in meeting the global demand for cleaner energy. It is a viable option to help Canada meet its objectives, especially for climate change and sustainable development.'[112] In July 2003, the Ontario government announced that nuclear power would now be eligible for the same tax breaks as other renewable resources like wind and solar power.[113]

The Kyoto Protocol is a 1997 international agreement on climate change where countries made pledges to reduce carbon emissions. Canada, which ratified the Kyoto Protocol on 17 December 2002, has committed to reducing its overall level of greenhouse gases by 6 per cent below its 1990 level and to achieve that reduction between 2008 and 2012. The protocol came into force when fifty-five signatories representing 55 per cent of the world's emissions ratified the protocol. As of April 2005, 150 countries representing 61.6 per cent of emissions have ratified the Kyoto Protocol. The only major emitters who have not ratified the Kyoto Protocol are the United States and Australia.

The Canadian government and the nuclear industry have argued that maintaining and enhancing the use of nuclear energy is the best way of achieving the emission targets contained in the Kyoto Protocol. For example, Ralph Goodale asked rhetorically, 'Without those zero-emission CANDUs, how would we hope to meet the climate change commitments Canada made in Kyoto?'[114] This is because 'a typical nuclear plant of 1,000 Megawatts capacity operating at 80 per cent capacity factor will offset the emission of over 5 million tonnes of CO_2 annually.'[115] The International Nuclear Forum, an informal group of the world's nuclear industry associations, has suggested that

- recognition of the contribution from operating nuclear energy facilities as an integral part of current and future greenhouse gas abatement strategy
- accreditation of current and future emission avoidance from non-emitting and low-emitting technologies, including nuclear energy facilities, in the design and implementation of all the Kyoto Mechanisms
- distribution of emission allowances in global electricity sectors based on electricity generated to ensure an emissions trading system that is non discriminatory of non-and low-emitting technologies

- equal application of full life-cycle analysis, to all energy generation technologies, in order to account for greenhouse gas emissions from every stage of energy generation[116]

At the Climate Change Conference in Berlin in fall 1999, Canada campaigned to have nuclear energy included as part of Kyoto's Clean Development Mechanism (CDM). The CDM allows firms in developed countries to receive emission credits for investing in projects in developing countries that reduce or avoid greenhouse gases. Since countries that plant forests can use this to offset their other emissions, it was believed that building more nuclear plants could be utilized for the same purpose. This led Canada to argue, along with France and Japan, that selling reactors to developing countries should result in emission credits. Canada could point to the sale of two CANDUs to China in citing the benefits of nuclear power to reducing global warming. According to the Canadian Nuclear Association, 'the use of nuclear power at Qinshan will reduce the quantity of carbon dioxide produced in China by 9 million tonnes per year compared with coal, which would have been used if nuclear power was not available. From the project commissioning in 2003 to the end of 2012, this project will avoid, in total, over 85 million tonnes of carbon dioxide.'[117] Nevertheless, this initiative was opposed by a number of European states like Britain, Norway, and Germany, who claimed that it would simply replace the environmental hazard of greenhouse gases with that of nuclear waste. The British environment minister argued that 'nuclear is not a creator of carbon dioxide but it's not a renewable source of energy in quite the same category as wind or water power.'[118]

The environmental movement is, not surprisingly, outraged at the suggestion that nuclear power could be used to combat climate change. 'Nuclear power is not the solution for climate change,' criticized Irene Kroch of the Nuclear Awareness Project, 'it is a cynical gambit on the part of the global nuclear power industry to save itself from being phased out.'[119] Nuclear critics accept that reactors do not directly emit greenhouse gases. Nevertheless, they maintain that if all the stages of the nuclear process – uranium mining, enrichment, transport, constructing power reactors, decommissioning – are taken into account, then nuclear power does indirectly emit greenhouse gases. However, a recent study that examined the entire CANDU fuel cycle still determined that 'over one hundred times as much CO_2 is avoided by deployment of the CANDU fuel cycle in place of coal plants in Canada than is released by CANDU construction, the fuel production process, and decommissioning. The electrical output per unit of CO_2 released overwhelms that from the direct use of fossil fuel for electrical energy.'[120]

Comparing life-cycle emissions of carbon dioxide also shows nuclear in a very favourable light, not just with 'dirty' energy but also in comparison with renewable energy sources like solar and wind power. Over the course of its life-cycle, coal produces about 1,000 CO_2 emissions (grams/kilowatt-hour), solar between 60 and 150, wind between 3 and 22, and nuclear only 6 CO_2 emissions.[121] Anti-nuclear critics maintain that even if nuclear reactors provide some environmental benefits through the reduction of greenhouse gases, these are heavily outweighed by the environmental damage caused through the production of radiation, nuclear waste, and the possibility of a severe-reactor accident. They argue that the solution to climate change is not through the maintenance or expansion of nuclear power, but through energy efficiency and the greater utilization of renewable energy sources like wind or solar power.[122]

Ever since the oil shocks of the early 1970s, energy efficiency has been seen as the answer. Nevertheless, the demand for energy, especially electricity, has been persistent in its upward climb. In the case of wind and solar power production, it is true that they are providing more and more electricity to the grid, but they are currently unable to even come close to providing the vast amounts of electricity that the world requires. Not only that, there are also environmental costs with wind and solar power.[123] For example, 'a 1,000 MWe solar electric plant would generate 6,850 tonnes of hazardous waste from metals-processing alone over a 30-year lifetime.' Meanwhile wind farms require millions of kilograms of concrete and steel, thousands of kilometres of land, and are a major killer of birds.

Renewable energy is not a panacea. There is no energy source that is 100 per cent green. There are just different degrees and types of environmental damage. However, while the nuclear industry has already internalized its environmental costs, other energy sectors, in contrast, have failed to take 'on such long-term commitments, along with the difficult burden of trying to prove their safety over thousands of years. Many industries have always discharged their wastes directly into the environment and haven't been held to account for them.' With a heightened attention to climate change, it is very possible that 'the public may come to view nuclear power more realistically now that there are other technological risks to compare it with.'[124]

Not every environmental group challenges the positive link between nuclear power and climate change. When Ontario Hydro temporarily shut down some of its nuclear reactors in 1997, it had to make up the loss of electricity production by increasing its use of coal power. 'Ontario then became one of the leading sources of air pollution in North America due to the chemicals and smog from these plants. Health authorities in Toronto have estimated that several hundred additional deaths annually can be attributed to this degradation of air quality.'[125] The air quality in Ontario did not go unnoticed by environmental groups. In June 2002, the Ontario Clean Air Alliance released a report that acknowledged some of the environmental benefits, like cleaner air, of nuclear power. The report argued that Ontario's air will become cleaner when its suspended nuclear reactors come back onstream because it will reduce the province's dependency on dirty coal plants. 'A return to service of the Pickering A and Bruce A nuclear reactors would permit a dramatic reduction in Ontario's coal-fired electricity generation.'[126]

Despite the benefits that nuclear power has on the problem of climate change, the issue of nuclear power is still clouded with other environmental issues like nuclear waste and reactor safety. This is why Robert Morrison concludes that 'climate change will be an important issue for nuclear energy, but it is not likely to be its saviour.'[127] As Steven Mark Cohn has written,

> ultimately the debate over the long run implications of greenhouse constraints for nuclear power is similar to the general debate over the future of nuclear power. Once time horizons approach fifty to one hundred years, basic intuitions about technological trajectories, ecological risk taking, and societal dynamics govern forecasting outcomes. The underlying disagreement between those who perceive fission power as the logical next step for energy sector development (due to its large fuel supply and potential for continued technical change) and those who see it as a dead-end (due to its inherent hazards) is likely to continue.[128]

Government Subsidies

Ottawa has heavily subsidized the nuclear industry, and there are several ways that CANDU exports have specifically benefited from these subsidies. In the post-war era, atomic energy was one of the leading sectors for government scientific research and development. This can be seen by the extent to which the federal government supported the

Table 3.4. Federal government research and development subsidies to AECL, 1952–2002 (in 2001 dollars)

Dates	$millions
1952–9	193.8
1960–9	453.3
1970–9	869.3
1980–9	1559.0
1990–9	1628.2
2000–2	348.8
Total	5052.4

Source: Compiled from data in Atomic Energy of Canada Limited, Annual Reports, 1951– 1952 to 2001–2002.

Table 3.5. Comparing government research and development subsidies on nuclear technology, 1980–2000 (in 2000 US dollars)

	1980 ($millions)	1990 ($millions)	2000 ($millions)
Canada	74.6	91.98	68.7
France	n/a	385	497*
United Kingdom	549	188	n/a
Japan	2,226	2,501	2,603
United States	2,179	663	35
All IEA countries	6,794	4,199	2,709

*France's data are from 1999.
Source: World Nuclear Association, 'Expenditure by IAE Countries on Fission R&D,' www.world-nuclear.org/info/inf68.htm. Data for Canada from Atomic Energy of Canada Limited, Annual Reports, 1980–1981 to 2000–2001.

research and development efforts of AECL: from 1952 to 2002, AECL was given over $5 billion in nuclear R&D subsidies (see table 3.4). While Canada is not unique in its support of nuclear R&D it trails all of its G7 competitors by significant margins. Table 3.5 lists the amount of R&D spending on non-military nuclear technology.

Ottawa has also provided grants and loans that have been used to help finance specific CANDU exports (see table 3.6). Canada's initial nuclear exports to India and Pakistan were both in conjunction with foreign-aid projects. For example, Canada's first export, the CIRUS research reactor to India in 1956, was part of the Colombo Plan foreign-

Table 3.6. Federal financing of nuclear reactor exports

Country	Aid	EDC loans ($millions)
India (CIRUS)	9.5	0
India (RAPP I)	0	37
India (RAPP II)	0	38.5
Pakistan (KANUPP)	25.5	25.5
Taiwan (TRR)	0	0
Argentina (Embalse)	0	124 and (US$60)
South Korea (Wolsung I)	0	300 and (US$112.5)
Romania (Cernavoda I–II)	0	2897.3 and (US$1139.4)
South Korea (Wolsung II–IV)	0	0
China (Qinshan I–II)	0	1500 and (US$350)

Source: The figures for India and Pakistan were compiled from data in Department of Energy, Mines, and Resources, Nuclear Policy Review, Background Papers (Ottawa: EMR 1981): 314..For Argentina, South Korea, and Romania, the data are from Export Development Corporation, Annual Reports, 1974–79. Additional information on Romania was acquired from Canada, News Release No. 199 (17 September 1991), Uranium Institute News Briefing NB00.38–8, and 'Government Approves Export Financing for Romanian Reactor,' Nuclear Canada (8 January 2003). For China, the data are from Natural Resources Canada, Speeches 96/116 (26 November 1996).

aid package to south Asia. This meant that Ottawa paid $9.5 million out of a total cost of $17 million for the reactor. Likewise, Pakistan's KANUPP power reactor was partially financed by a grant from CIDA.

All developed countries have a specialized and well-funded governmental agency to assist companies in trade promotion – the U.S. Export-Import Bank. In Canada's case, the Export Development Corporation (EDC) has provided loans to further CANDU exports. In 1969 the Export Development Act converted the Export Credits and Insurance Corporation (ECIC) into the EDC. The EDC was created to promote international trade by assisting Canadian companies in foreign markets. The EDC provides a number of financial services: short-term export credit insurance; bonding and surety services; political risk insurance; short-term credit guarantees; and medium and long-term loans to foreign borrowers and buyers.[129] The international nuclear market is a multibillion dollar industry where competition is intense and sales are few. In this environment, it is only natural that AECL would rely heavily on EDC for assistance. In fact, EDC loans have frequently represented the lion's share of the total cost of the reactor. For example, the Wolsong I sale to South Korea in 1973 was $576.5 million with EDC providing a $430-million loan. As Robert Morrison has commented, 'because CANDU sales are large, lumpy and difficult to predict in terms of their funding needs – either AECL needs hundreds of millions or none at all – they tend to exhaust the funds available for a given country, or to drive out competing projects.'[130]

EDC has two types of accounts. The Corporate Account is for regular transactions and is accountable to international agreements on trade promotion like the WTO's Subsidy and Countervail Measures Agreement and the OECD's consensus rules. Although EDC is a Crown corporation, the corporate account is intended to be self-sustaining. This means that EDC operates it on commercial, as opposed to concessional, terms. The second type of account is the Canada Account,[131] which is used in situations where EDC may view a financial transaction as being too risky because of the size of the transaction, market risks, or financing conditions, or a combination of these. The Canada Account is used if the minister of international trade, in consultation with the finance minister, believes that the transaction is in Canada's national interest. Any loan over US$50 million also requires full cabinet approval. In addition, Canada Accounts are negotiated, structured, and administered like the corporate account, the difference is that all of the money, and the accompanying financial risk, is with the Government of Canada. These types of loans are fully repayable, but they may involve concessionary terms. The criteria for using the Canada Account include

- EDC's usual lending or insurance criteria (Canadian content, financial and technical capability of the exporter, technical and commercial viability of the project, etc.)
- the government's general willingness to consider the country risk in question and the creditworthiness of non-sovereign borrowers
- national interest considerations such as
  - economic benefits and costs to Canada, including the employment generated or sustained by the transaction
  - importance of the transaction to the exporter
  - importance of the export market to Canada, and
  - foreign policy implications, including Canada's bilateral relationship with the country in question

The use of the Canada Account is critical to CANDU exports. Larry Shewchuck, an AECL spokesperson, claims that Canada Account financing is 'hugely important because international reactor exports are a very competitive industry. We have to compete with reactor sales from foreign countries and they too get a lot of government support.'[132] In fact, many CANDU exports have benefited from the use of EDC's Canada Account, including Wolsung I ($250 million), Embalse ($124 million), Cernavoda I (US$300 million), and Qinshan I and II ($1,500 million, US$350 million). Since nuclear transactions are so large, they take up a very high percentage of the Canada Account. As of 1999, CANDU exports represent over half of the $5.2 billion that EDC has committed from the Canada Account.[133]

Since EDC loans, by OECD consensus, are commercial transactions, the government should actually be making money from loans that support CANDU exports. Robert Morrison, a former director general of Uranium and Nuclear Energy Policy at Natural Resources Canada, has claimed that 'the record for repayment of loans for CANDU sales has been good.'[134] In fact, the record is a lot more mixed than what Morrison describes. There were indeed no problems with the majority of EDC's loans (India, Pakistan, South Korea, and China), but the loans to Argentina and Romania in the 1970s required a significant amount of financial restructuring that included debt forgiveness. In 1991, EDC loaned Romania $330 million from its Canada Account to finish construction of the Cernavoda I reactor. Cernavoda I was completed in 1996, but within two years Romania was already delinquent in its repayment schedule. EDC reported in 1998 that the loan to Romania had $9 million in payments past due, and still had $293 million outstanding.[135] By 2003, all EDC loans for Cernavoda I had been repaid, paving the way for new financing for Cernavoda II.[136]

Ottawa has also supported the Canadian nuclear industry in other, more indirect, ways. Peter Berg has noted that 'Canadian taxpayers have also supported prototype and commercial reactors, heavy water plants, the high costs of regulating the industry, and the exemption of provincial utilities from federal income taxation.'[137] The Campaign for Nuclear Phaseout has determined that the total amount from all nuclear subsidies (CANDU and non-CANDU projects) for the period 1953–2000 has been over $16 billion (in 2000 dollars).[138] Provincial governments have also helped to subsidize the nuclear industry. For example, Ontario Hydro has benefited from reduced-debt servicing costs through the provision of loans guaranteed by the province.[139] In other cases, provincially owned utilities have also unwittingly subsidized the development of the CANDU. During the construction of the Gentilly-2 reactor in the late 1970s, Hydro-Québec was responsible for a $1-billion cost overrun.[140]

Ottawa will be on the hook for future costs from the nuclear industry. In particular, there is the looming cost of decommissioning reactors. Decommissioning is defined as the measures taken at the end of the nuclear facility's operating lifetime to assure the continued protection of the public from the residual radioactivity and other potential hazards in the retired reactor. In 1999, Canada's Auditor General reported that 'there are significant costs associated with decommissioning [AECL's] facilities and remediating its sites, including costs of residual waste storage and disposal. Generally accepted accounting principles require that these costs be recognized in a rational and systematic manner over the estimated lives of the corresponding facilities. However, [AECL] expenses these costs as the activities take place and has not recorded a liability for them. Government funding of these costs is similarly recorded. Failure to record a liability for these costs is not in accordance with generally accepted accounting principles.'[141] AECL estimates that decommissioning will be $377 million,[142] but David Martin has suggested that the final cost of decommissioning could be as high as $1 billion.[143] If the higher amount is correct, who will pay this additional $600 million? Even AECL has acknowledged that it does not have the money. AECL chair Bob Nixon said in 1997 that 'if AECL were to do this [deal properly with decommissioning], with present levels of funding, there would be little left for its prime task, the development of nuclear power.'[144] This means that, ultimately, Canadian taxpayers would be on the financial hook for cleaning up old nuclear reactors.

Developing countries, for reasons of political and economic nationalism, seeking to acquire nuclear energy, tend to be very eager to develop as much of an indigenous nuclear industry as possible. As a result, they often demand that transfers of nuclear technology accompany any nuclear reactor transaction. Consequently, almost every nuclear transaction, regardless of whether the supplier is the United States, Germany, or Canada, involves a degree of technology transfer to the recipient country. In fact, nuclear suppliers frequently use technology transfers as sweeteners in order to secure reactor sales. Critics have argued that the use of nuclear technology transfers to acquire CANDU exports can be seen as another form of government subsidy. After all, Ottawa has invested billions in nuclear R&D, and now, for the sake of selling a CANDU, is willing to give away the technology. Technology transfers have also had an adverse effect on the amount of actual Canadian content in several of the reactors. This is because there is a corresponding scale between the amount of reactors a country has purchased and the amount of technology that is transferred. For example, Wolsung III and IV only contained 25 per cent Canadian content.[145]

In the case of India, so much Canadian technology was transferred with CIRUS and RAPP that the Indians were eventually able to build their own reactors, RAPP III and IV, which were based upon RAPP I and II purchased from Canada. In fact, many of India's indigenous reactors, like Madras I and II and Narora I and II, are referred to as 'CANDU clones' because they are essentially modified versions of the heavy-water Canadian reactors. India has fourteen power reactors built with another two under construction. Four of these were purchased from abroad (two from Canada and two from the United States), but the rest are Indian-made 'CANDU clones.'[146] In short, a consequence of Canada using nuclear technology transfers to acquire initial CANDU sales is that it may inhibit CANDU sales in the long term.

The Canadian nuclear industry might prefer that all CANDU exports have 100 per cent Canadian content, but it understands that the needs of purchasing states to develop their own independent nuclear capability through technology transfers makes that unrealistic. AECL realizes that a reactor sale with 25 per cent Canadian content is better than no reactor sale with 100 per cent Canadian content. Moreover, notwithstanding the arguments of the preceding paragraphs, there are some benefits to including technology transfers as part of a CANDU export.[147] Technology transfers can be used to lock in customers to the CANDU purchase. In this way, sharing some of the design features may facilitate additional sales and/or upgrades. This is especially important in countries like South Korea, which have different types of reactor models operating. When Seoul has to decide on its next reactor purchase, the extent to which it already has access to the nuclear technology would be a factor in its decision-making. Sharing CANDU technology also creates a larger pool of scientists, engineers, and technicians in multiple countries. This has a number of advantages. It provides potential customers with a choice of suppliers for the CANDU, which alleviates the unease they may have in dealing with a monopoly. It allows for other countries and companies to provide a wide variety of support services to AECL. The possibility that the CANDU will benefit from additional refinements and efficiencies is increased when you add to the number of scientists working with the technology.

In fact, this was one of the purposes for the creation of the CANDU

Owners Group. The wider the base of CANDU knowledge, the greater the opportunity to penetrate new markets. For example, the Korea Electric Power Corporation (KEPCO) is a one of AECL's subcontractors in the sale of two CANDUs to China. Providing access to some nuclear technology does not necessarily mean that a country automatically becomes totally self-sufficient. India was able to 'clone' the CANDU and build its own reactors, but its version quickly became obsolete because it lacked access to AECL's further scientific enhancement of the CANDU system. As chapter 5 will show, the Indian nuclear program suffered greatly when Canada applied sanctions in 1974 because its knowledge of the CANDU had not sufficiently evolved.

Technology transfers of any product, including nuclear reactors, are complex economic issues. In the case of the CANDU, the key questions are, What types of knowledge are being transferred, and how much technology is being transferred? If AECL transfers too much of the CANDU's secrets it may preclude future exports, but if it transfers too little it may also preclude future exports. A thorough cost-benefit analysis needs to be assessed when determining the extent of technology transfers that can be part of a CANDU export.

The extent of Canadian government subsidies have created political and policy concerns within Canada. For example, can society accept cuts in health care, education, and other forms of social spending when the nuclear industry is receiving hundreds of millions of dollars annually? Canadians have begun to question the types of priorities their government has been promoting. Moreover, as David Martin and David Argue have asserted, 'the context of current decisions about the ongoing taxpayer subsidization of the nuclear industry is the fiscal restraint now being exercised by governments in many other areas of expenditure.'[148]

The Anti-Nuclear Lobby

Canadian foreign policy decisions are not always decided on the strength of the competing arguments. In many cases, it is the political/economic strength of the groups that are making those arguments. The decision to export CANDUs is no exception. The previous chapter sketched out the pro-nuclear lobby that is comprised of AECL and its nuclear component suppliers, the large provincial utilities, and the nuclear scientific community. This section will highlight the anti-nuclear lobby; these are groups that are philosophically and fundamentally opposed to CANDU exports.

The foremost anti-nuclear group is the Canadian Coalition for Nuclear Responsibility (CCNR), which was established in 1975 and acts as an umbrella organization for the entire anti-nuclear movement. CCNR's board of directors contains many prominent academic scientists such as Gordon Edwards (the president of CCNR) and Fred Knelman. Its main issues include many of the constraining variables that were discussed earlier in this chapter: the link between the peaceful and military application of nuclear power, government subsidies to the Canadian nuclear industry, and the negative environmental consequences of nuclear power. CCNR has been able to penetrate the public consciousness on nuclear issues through its submissions to government bodies and agencies, its press releases, and acting as a frequent interview source by the media. This gives CCNR a platform to participate and influence the public debate over CANDU exports. Despite having a budget that is comparatively minuscule, CCNR is considered a threat by AECL and the rest of the Canadian nuclear industry. In fact, in 1985, AECL compiled a secret dossier on the Canadian anti-nuclear movement, including CCNR, to determine its strength. It determined that CCNR had the following strengths:

• Many of the current members of the group are well-respected throughout the environmental movement.
• The group has good volunteer researchers and well-placed sources of information.
• It is a national group with national linkages.
• The group normally hears about any nuclear issue that surfaces.
• It is good at accurately explaining technical issues to the general public in an entertaining way.
• It has a strong capability to critically examine complex scientific data.[149]

A second major anti-nuclear group is the Campaign for Nuclear Phaseout (CNP). The CNP was formed in 1989 and is supported by over 300 non-governmental organizations like CCNR, Concerned Citizens of Manitoba, Council of Canadians, Down to Earth, Energy Probe, Greenpeace, Inter-Church Uranium Committee, Mouvement Vert Mauricie, Sierra Club, and Women's Health and Environments Network. The CNP is mandated to carry out education programs by

• educating the Canadian public and decision-makers about issues relating to nuclear power and uranium mining

- conducting research into issues relating to nuclear power and energy alternatives
- producing and disseminating educational materials to supporting groups, and
- acting as a liaison between public interest groups across Canada

In that vein, it publishes a number of regular and special publications. CNP has been focusing its efforts on: '1) issues related to Canada's planned import of plutonium and the export of CANDU reactors; 2) research and education on renewable energy alternatives for Canada; 3) the production of a catalogued inventory of nuclear contamination and waste sites across Canada.'[150]

Finally, the Canadian environmental lobby has been a strong force in the anti-nuclear movement. The Sierra Club, Greenpeace, Energy Probe, and Friends of the Earth have all been active in the past two decades in the domestic nuclear debate. For example, Norm Rubin, the president of Energy Probe, has been and continues to be recognized as a high-profile critic of Canada's nuclear policies. These groups have also attempted to play a role in nuclear exports. This can be seen when the Sierra Club launched a 1996 court action against the Chrétien government's decision to sell two CANDUs to China without conducting an environmental assessment of the project.

There are a number of security, political, and economic considerations facing the Canadian government that constrain its instinctive economic and political interests in exporting CANDUs. The overriding preoccupation is to maintain and strengthen the international nuclear non-proliferation regime. However, there are, as indicated, three additional considerations which might (some would say should) act as constraints on CANDU exports: not selling nuclear materials to regimes that violate human rights; the effect of CANDU exports on the environment; and the extent of Canadian government subsidies that accompany CANDU exports. The actual influence of these constraining factors will be tested in subsequent chapters.

4 The Need to Establish Markets, 1945–1974

The initial period of Canada's nuclear reactor export policy was between 1945 and 1974. The central theme of this period was Canada's need to establish foreign markets for its unique technology of a heavy-water nuclear reactor. Although a number of sales were concluded, particularly to India, the early years of Canada's efforts to export nuclear reactors were not especially successful economically. It discovered that the market for nuclear reactors was small and competition, especially from the Americans, was keen. In addition, there was a nagging feeling that grew throughout the years that Canada might be unwittingly supporting the nuclear weapons aspirations of its customers. In the end, this period began with great optimism as Canada set out to wander the world with the intention of fully exploiting the peaceful benefits of nuclear energy, but it ended with a bang – India's 1974 nuclear weapons test.

India: CIRUS, 1956

Canada's first nuclear reactor export was concluded in 1956, with the gift of a $9.5-million research reactor to India. The 40 megawatt Canada–India–United States research reactor (CIRUS) was part of the Colombo Plan, a developmental aid program for the impoverished countries of south Asia that was modelled upon the successful Marshall Plan for Western Europe. India was an obvious target for Canadian nuclear exporters because India, despite its underdeveloped status, had, in fact, been working on a nuclear program. As a U.S. State Department official commenting in the late 1940s panted out, '[T]he aspirations of Indian officials in atomic energy development appears illimitable.'[1] By 1948,

India had already established an Atomic Energy Commission, and, in 1954, both the Department of Atomic Energy and an atomic energy research establishment were created.[2] This led to the construction of India's first research reactor, Apsara, which went critical in August 1956. Notably, the construction of this reactor was built entirely by Indian scientists and engineers, with the only foreign assistance being the British supply of fuel.

Prime Minister Jawaharlal Nehru and Dr Homi Bhabha were the two indispensable driving forces behind India's atomic project. During Britain's colonial rule, Nehru was, along with Mahatma Gandhi, one of the leaders of the Indian independence movement. Later, as modern India's first prime minister, Nehru remained a staunch nationalist who was determined to chart India's own way in the world. As such, he possessed great support among the Indian people. If he wanted India to acquire nuclear technology, then the Indian people would go along, not just because of the institutional power of the office but also because of Nehru's moral authority. In addition, while Nehru may have been the politician, he did have scientific training from Cambridge, and would always maintain an ardent interest in scientific developments. Bhabha – the father of India's nuclear program – was a Cambridge-trained physicist, but he was also a natural political animal.

Making this partnership even tighter was the fact that, on a personal level, the two men were very close. Bhabha 'had ties with Nehru through family and science, having tea or dinner with Nehru almost every two weeks. These men shared the same patrician background with proximity to wealth and political influence; both had been to Cambridge, both lived like bachelors and considered themselves connoisseurs of art, music, and food. Their mutual attraction enabled them to speak the same language.'[3] Both men were firmly convinced that harnessing the power of the atom was crucial to India's economic development. In a major speech at the United Nations in the early 1950s, Bhabha had stated that 'the industrialization of the underdeveloped areas, for the continuation of our civilisation and its further development, atomic energy is nor merely an aid; it is an absolute necessity.' For his part, Nehru believed that India's only way out of its 'vicious circle of poverty' was 'by utilising the new sources of power which science [had] placed at [its] disposal.'[4]

The Indians did realize that they would eventually need foreign help with their nuclear program. As David Hart has noted, 'it was felt necessary to obtain foreign assistance for the building of power reactors, partly because other countries had more experience, and partly because many of the large scale, sophisticated pieces of equipment were just not obtainable in India.'[5] In addition, as Canadian officials were quick to recognize, India would be more receptive to Canadian nuclear assistance because it would be 'less embarrassing to receive direct assistance from [Canada] in this rather delicate field than from either of the larger atomic powers whose motives might be questioned by groups in India as well as by other Asian countries.'[6] This opened the door for nuclear exports.

It was Canada who first proposed engaging in a nuclear transaction with India. In March 1955, Nik Cavell, the administrator of Canada's aid to the Colombo Plan, inquired whether AECL president Bill Bennett thought 'it would be possible for AECL to build a nuclear power plant in India.'[7] Unfortunately, Canada's first nuclear power plant – the NPD – was still in the final design and political approval stage, and, in fact, would not become operational until 1962. Thus, Bennett suggested that, instead, India be supplied with a replica of the NRX research reactor. Officials at the Department of External Affairs also thought that it was an excellent idea to give India a nuclear research reactor as part of the Colombo Plan. External Affairs Minister Lester Pearson thought it was 'a most important gesture, the effects of which might be very great indeed.'[8] Negotiations between Canada and India soon followed and a contract was signed in April 1956.

It is important to stress that CIRUS was a research reactor, not a power reactor. The purpose of a research reactor is to allow a country's scientific community to examine nuclear technology. A country needs to start with research reactors before moving on to power production. There were several reasons why the first nuclear transaction was a research reactor as opposed to a power reactor. First, Canadian nuclear experts believed that the Indians lacked the personnel and facilities to operate and maintain a power reactor.[9] Second, a research reactor would be a teaching tool to allow the Indians – as it had with the Australians, Belgians, Danes, and Swiss – to build up their atomic knowledge.[10] Third, as stated above, Canada itself did not yet have an operational power reactor. Finally, it would have been politically difficult for Ottawa to authorize a heavily subsidized power reactor for India when it had rejected a similar request from Nova Scotia.[11]

In analysing Canada's research reactor export to India, it can be said that there were many economic factors that influenced Canada's decision to proceed with the export of CIRUS. The most important was that

CIRUS would be Canada's first export, and Canada wanted desperately to break into the international nuclear export market. Concluding this first transaction would make Canada's nuclear industry look credible to the international community. Exporting the NRX design would make Canada the first country to have built an experimental nuclear reactor in the developing world. Canada had previously been seen as a junior partner in the development of nuclear energy; and, therefore, to be seen as an independent producer, it needed another country to show faith in its system. This was especially true because of the unique nature of Canadian nuclear technology that was based on heavy water. Since the United States relied on a light-water reactor, and the British on a graphite system, Canada had not only to sell 'itself' as a reliable and competent high-tech supplier to a sceptical international community, but also had to sell its radically different technology.

In addition, the consensus in the 1950s was that nuclear energy would be a substantial growth area. Since, at this stage of the international nuclear trade, buyers were 'first-time buyers, and the first sale could lead to a significant amount of repeat business,' that first sale was crucial.[12] As Canada's reactor technology was still relatively unproven and developing, India, it was hoped, would become Canada's testing ground leading to eventual worldwide CANDU sales. In realizing this, Canadian officials were quick to comment that

> the United Kingdom and the United States are showing great interest in the development of atomic energy in Asia and you may be sure that Canadian companies would welcome an opportunity to gain a foothold in this part of the world. The commercial interest which the United States is taking in the development of atomic energy in Japan makes it perhaps all the more imperative why Canada should assist in making comparable advances in this field.[13]

The economic importance of that first export was enhanced when India started negotiating with other countries for the reactor, in particular, the Americans, the British, and the Soviets. The American Embassy in New Delhi was advising Washington 'that serious consideration should be given to the immediate provision to India by the United States of an atomic reactor unit.'[14] Meanwhile, the British had reached a nuclear agreement with India in December 1955 that called for the export of a '"swimming pool reactor," enriched fuel, and technical assistance.'[15] Like Canada, these countries were also motivated by the need to establish the credibility of their domestic nuclear programs. However, all three countries had a greater reputation for high-tech industrial production than did Canada. This was a substantial handicap and therefore the necessity of making the sale was greater for Canada than for the other suppliers.

The policy of aiding Canadian market expansion in Asia was an additional economic consideration. One of the purposes of the Colombo Plan was to allow Canada to make commercial inroads into south Asia. Therefore, it was hoped that Canada could penetrate this market, not only through nuclear sales but also through trade in many different sectors. As C.D. Howe put it in a letter to Pearson, CIRUS would allow Canada to gain a good trading position in the area, and this was obviously more preferable than allowing 'the United States or the United Kingdom to do so.'[16] A final economic consideration was that India could be used as a testing site for Canadian nuclear technology. It was felt that Canada's 'scientific community' would gain experience from having 'the N.R.X. function under different climatic and topographic conditions.'[17]

In addition to these economic factors, Ottawa had political interests that facilitated the CIRUS transaction. First among them was the nature of the Canada–India relationship at the time. The two British Commonwealth countries were collaborating actively in the United Nations in the pursuit of global peace and security. Canada also recognized India as the world's most populous democracy and as a leader of the nonaligned countries. Canada and India enjoyed warm, cordial relations reinforced by personal friendship at the highest level. For example, AECL's W.B. Lewis had studied with Dr Bhabha at Cambridge in the 1930s, and the two had continued their friendship even when Lewis moved to Canada and Bhabha moved to India.[18] Some writers have even referred to this era as characterized by an Ottawa–New Delhi entente.[19] This entente was solidified through Canadian-Indian cooperation during a number of crises in the early 1950s, including the Korean War, the International Commission for Supervision and Control in Indochina, and the Suez Crisis. This cooperation led Canadian diplomats to hold their Indian counterparts in a great deal of respect. John Holmes wrote that 'the eminence of Mr. Nehru, the ghost of Mahatma Gandhi, and the cantankerous brilliance of Mr. Krishna Menon combined to make India in the 1950s a middle power of such influence that in all things except military and economic strength and a permanent seat in the Security Council it was a great power.'[20] Both Prime Minister

Louis St Laurent and External Affairs Minister Lester Pearson 'attached the highest importance to Canadian–Indian relations, viewing India as a necessary bridge between what would now be called the First World of Western industrial democracies and the Third World of developing and impoverished states.'[21] CIRUS was a perfect tool to accomplish this goal because nuclear energy constituted a high-technology transfer of a product whose objective was to support economic development.

A second political consideration was that India was a strategically important country in the context of the Cold War. Canada had to ensure that India did not fall into the communist bloc. Indeed, another purpose of the Colombo Plan, under which this export was arranged, was to prevent the expansion of communism. Nehru himself had argued that India's nascent democracy was facing a dual threat: '[F]irst by a direct onslaught by communism; and secondly by an internal weakening, largely due to unfavourable economic conditions ... policy should be directed against this second danger, for it was this which would create the conditions in which communism would flourish.'[22] Canadian officials accepted Nehru's analysis, particularly after the victory of the communists in the Chinese civil war in 1949 and communist North Korea's invasion of South Korea in 1950. External Affairs Minister Lester Pearson commented that 'there is no more important question in the world today ... that communist expansionism may now spill over into southeast Asia.'[23] This sentiment was virtually without opposition in Canada. The Canadian news media wholeheartedly endorsed the Colombo Plan rather than rearmament as being a better way to spend money 'in the fight against communism.'[24] The leader of the opposition, John Diefenbaker, also asserted in the House of Commons that '$50 million a year ... would be cheap insurance for Canada ... to halt communism in Asia.'[25]

Canadian officials clearly believed that CIRUS represented a significant bulwark to communist expansion in India. Moreover, if Canada did not help with India's nuclear development, the Soviets would gladly take Canada's place. The Soviets were in a zero-sum game with the Americans in attracting allies around the world, especially in developing countries. China had already been 'lost' to the communists and if India were to follow, the West would feel even more threatened with the two most populous countries in the world as members of the communist bloc. There were a number of incidents that suggested that the Indians were establishing closer relations with the Soviet Union: the Indians had been purchasing arms from the Soviets; in 1953, India and the Soviets completed a trade agreement; the Soviets, in competition with the Colombo Plan, had developed their own aid package, which eventually led to India acquiring Soviet steel mills. Nehru had told the Canadian High Commissioner how impressed he had been by Soviet hydroelectric technology. Bhabha, in a rare bending of Soviet security and intelligence policies, had even been allowed to inspect Soviet nuclear facilities in 1955. From the Canadian side, it appeared that the potential of Soviet–Indian nuclear cooperation was becoming a distinct possibility. This allowed Canadian officials to rationalize that it was better if India acquired 'nuclear expertise and facilities through cooperation with countries like Canada than as a result of assistance from the Soviet Union.'[26]

Canada's economic and political arguments heavily outweighed any qualms that it might have had about nuclear proliferation. In fact, during the initial stages of the negotiations between Canada and India the issue of nuclear proliferation was largely ignored. A major eight-page memorandum from Jules Léger, the Under-Secretary of State for external affairs, to Pearson on 21 March 1955 had only one paragraph dealing with CIRUS safeguards, and it concluded that 'there would apparently be no significant security problem.'[27] Later on, Canada began to slowly realize the potential military uses of the plutonium that CIRUS would produce. When Bhabha visited Canada in October 1955, he was presented with a Canadian proposal that the irradiated fuel rods (which contained the plutonium) would be returned to Canada. However, Bhabha refused, making it very clear that it would be an infringement on Indian sovereignty if it did not have clear and absolute ownership of the fuel. Canadian negotiators tried several different tactics – including a visit by Pearson to India to sway Nehru himself – and drafted many proposals designed to prevent India from possessing full control of the spent fuel, but the Indians held firm. The CIRUS agreement fell silent on the issue.

Fearing the possible loss of the deal, the Department of External Affairs dropped its demands on the repatriation of the irradiated fuel rods. Léger allowed that 'there might also be some problems regarding control over the plutonium produced by any reactor which we might supply.' Nevertheless, he felt that 'this could presumably be surmounted, especially if we assume that a country like India will acquire a reactor from some source (friendly or otherwise) and will be producing this material.'[28] In other words, India was going to acquire nuclear technology without safeguards, so Canada might as well be the supplier.

Léger also identified another problem for the Canadians: there had not been an international agreement on the export of nuclear technology in place at the time of the CIRUS transaction. According to Léger, '[I]t was too bad that no international agreement existed for the export of nuclear technology, and it was unlikely that an international atomic energy agency would be constituted for some time. In the meantime, it was every country for itself.'[29] Eisenhower's famous 'Atoms for Peace' speech had been made in December 1953, and it was widely known, throughout the CIRUS negotiations, that the creation of a new international agency – the IAEA – responsible for the regulation of atomic power was imminent. In fact, 'members of the Canadian Delegation, and no doubt the chief Indian negotiators also, were very conscious' during the negotiations over the statute of the IAEA 'of their implications for the Canada-India Reactor Project where the arrangements to be made for the provision of the fuel elements would be directly affected by the safeguard provisions eventually adopted by the Agency.'[30] Nevertheless, the fact remains that the IAEA did not become functional until 1957, so, in reality, it did not exist when the contract for CIRUS was finalized.

How could Canada convince India to accept unilateral safeguards prior to any negotiations that the IAEA would hold on creating an international standard on nuclear safeguards? In addition, the CIRUS agreement, as Canada's representative later explained to the United Nations General Assembly First Committee in 1965, 'came into existence ... at a time when the concept of safeguards was much less highly developed than it is today.'[31] Since nuclear safeguards were in such an embryonic stage, it is no wonder that external affairs was unprepared for dealing with issues like spent fuel rods, export controls, and onsite inspections. Finally, the Canadian negotiators were hamstrung by the fact that they could not refer to any precedents, after all this was one of the very first times that a bilateral nuclear reactor transaction had taken place.

Another crucial determinant that explains Canada's ambivalence towards the non-proliferation issue was that Canada trusted the Indian government. Inside Canada, there was, as Robert Bothwell has asserted, 'considerable trust in the political reliability of the Indian government.' In addition, it could be argued that 'the domestic constraints of the Indian political system' were the best protection against any military applications of CIRUS.[32] If Canadian diplomats did exhibit some apprehension about India's intentions, they were shamed into

recanting. This is because Bhabha had argued that within the Commonwealth 'India's word' should be 'a sufficient safeguard' and Canadian
reservations 'only served to call into question Indian credibility.'[33]

Canada's negotiating position was also hindered by a distinct lack of
coordination between AECL and the Department of External Affairs.
DEA memorandums emphasized that it would handle all of the political negotiations, while AECL would be limited to providing technical
information. Unfortunately, as Iris Lonergan pointed out, 'AECL gave
out technical information rather selectively and appeared to place more
trust in Indian fellow scientists than in Canadian diplomats. The lack of
technical knowledge in External Affairs about nuclear technology and
safeguards severely hampered the Canadian and was one of the determining factors for the mishandling of the spent fuel ownership and
disposal question.'[34]

There were additional arguments with which Ottawa tried to convince itself that there was only a minimal threat of nuclear proliferation
by India. Canada felt that once the IAEA became operational, it could
safely handoff to them the issue of CIRUS's safeguards. In other words,
CIRUS could be safeguarded retroactively. In addition, there were
fears that the other potential suppliers (the United States, United
Kingdom, and Soviet Union were now joined by France and Belgium)
might supply the reactor to India, and they would not place any
safeguards on it.[35] Finally, Canada felt that India did not have the
capability to build a nuclear military device either immediately or in
the foreseeable future.[36]

As a result of Canada's economic and political interests, combined
with the minimizing of its proliferation concerns, the CIRUS transaction was completed with minimal safeguards. The only safeguard contained in the agreement was Article III: 'The Government of India will
ensure that the reactor and any products resulting from its use will be
employed for peaceful purposes only.'[37] This meant that there were
serious loopholes. For example, peaceful purposes were never defined,
and this would come back to haunt the Canadians when New Delhi
claimed that its 1974 nuclear explosion was for peaceful purposes. A
second loophole was the fact that the fuel question was not settled
satisfactorily at the time of the agreement's ratification. Instead, two
alternatives were suggested: (1) 'arrangements for the provision of the
fuel elements' would be 'agreed upon by the two Governments before
the reactor' was 'ready to operate'; or (2) 'if an international agency
acceptable to both Governments' came into being, the terms of the

agreement would 'be in keeping with the principles of that agency.'[38] In the end, Canada suggested letting the IAEA resolve the fuel question despite 'the fact that there was no guarantee, and perhaps no real hope, that India would be more cooperative with the agency than it had been with Canada.'[39]

It was completely unrealistic of Canada to believe that the Indians would cooperate with the IAEA. This assertion is not based on the benefits of twenty-twenty hindsight, but rather it is based on the events of the period. During the negotiations over the formation of the IAEA – which were occurring simultaneously with the CIRUS negotiations – India worked strenuously against nuclear safeguards. India opposed, on general principles, the idea that nuclear safeguards would 'vest the Agency with far-reaching powers to interfere in the disposition of the atomic fuel of the future power-industries of countries receiving aid, and thus, in the economic life of the countries concerned.'[40] In a more specific case, Arthur Lall, a senior member of the Indian delegation to the UN, told Ambassador Arnold Heeney, the head of Canada's delegation to the IAEA negotiations, that Agency safeguards should be restricted to fissionable materials which the Agency supplied. India would oppose any inspections of source materials or fissionable materials acquired under a bilateral agreement.[41] Canada rejected this interpretation. Heeney argued that 'if fissionable material' did require to be safeguarded, 'surely safeguards [were] required irrespective of whether it was acquired from the Agency or whether it [was] acquired under a bilateral agreement under Agency auspices.'[42] The Indians also put forward an amendment during the IAEA negotiations that would allow parties to 'contract' out of safeguard controls.[43] Although Canada and the other delegations easily defeated this amendment (only the USSR and Czechoslovakia supported the Indians), it illustrated not only India's views on nuclear safeguards but also Canada's intimate knowledge of those views.

There was one area where Canada was in agreement with India about restricting the scope of international safeguards. Both India and Canada believed that there should be no international controls on natural uranium. Canada may have been striving for safeguards on nuclear reactors, but it did not want to see the development of controls on natural uranium. In a memo to his ambassadors in Washington and New York, Pearson explained that it 'undoubtedly would damage' Canada's 'position as a potential major supplier of uranium and adversely affect her relations with other countries.'[44] The contrast between its position on reactor safeguards and uranium safeguards is a good example of the tension in Canadian foreign policy between international security and national commercial interests that has been inherent in Canada's nuclear policy.

India eventually became an original signatory to the IAEA, but it continued its criticism of the Agency's safeguards framework. India agreed to the statute at the Conference on the Statute of the IEA on 23 October 1956, but in July 1957, just before the IAEA came into force, the Indians reiterated that

> if safeguards are applied by the Agency only to those States which cannot further their atomic development without the receipt of aid from the Agency or other Member States, the operations of the Agency will have the effect of dividing Member States into two categories, the smaller and less powerful States being subject to safeguards, while the Great Powers are above them. This will increase rather than decrease international tension.[45]

In short, the Indians were publicly opposing bilateral safeguards throughout international negotiations at the very same time that the CIRUS agreement was being finalized. In addition, these pronouncements were being made several months before the eventual signing of the CIRUS contract.

India: RAPP I, 1963

Canada was right to assume in 1956 that providing India with a research reactor would lead to future sales of the more expensive power reactors. In 1963, Canada exported its first power reactor, the 100 megawatt Rajasthan Atomic Power Plant (RAPP I), to India. The AECL was elated, especially because the Indians chose it over a competing bid from the powerful U.S. firm General Electric. In addition, GE, which was trying to secure its own share of the nuclear market, had offered financial terms for its light-water reactor that were 'extraordinarily favourable.'[46] When India announced its decision, it led AECL president Lorne Gray to exclaim that the selection of the CANDU 'above the systems being developed in other countries would have a considerable impact on world thinking.'[47] With the RAPP I case, commercial interests were again the dominant variable, but not to the extent evident in CIRUS. This evolution in Canada's concern with nuclear proliferation was manifest in the safeguards agreement that was reached because the safeguards were more stringent this time.

In 1962, China invaded India in the northeast corner of its shared 3,200-kilometre border. The Indian troops were no match for the Chinese and were easily overrun. Although the war was brief, and the territorial losses minor, India was deeply humiliated by its defeat. This brought a whole new angle into the security issues of the Indian subcontinent as India now felt compelled to prepare for a potential two-front war against Pakistan and China. In addition, it was known that the Chinese were actively working on a nuclear weapons program, perhaps with Soviet assistance, and would succeed in testing a device in 1964. This provided India with an obvious need to acquire its own bomb. As a result of the 1962 war, as well as the continuing Indo-Pakistani conflict, Canadian officials had started to 'express anxiety' about India's nuclear aspirations, and there were concerns that India might eventually 'divert to military purposes the plutonium obtained from CIRUS.'[48] Official statements from the Indians did nothing to calm Ottawa's anxiety. Homi Bhabha, at an international disarmament conference following the 1962 war, declared that a 'country with a huge population, such as China, must always present a threat to its smaller neighbours, a threat they can only meet either by collective security or by recourse to nuclear weapons to redress the imbalance in size.' Bhabha went on to remind his audience that 'any knowledge of operating a reactor for peaceful purposes can be employed later for operating a reactor for military purposes.'[49] Although Canadian officials wanted 'reassurances' from the Indian government, they realized that they could not withdraw from the CIRUS program 'so long as India did not violate the letter and spirit of the bilateral agreement.'[50]

To prevent this possible military application of CIRUS, Canadian officials attempted to use the negotiations on RAPP I 'as a lever,' arguing that 'we can say we won't go ahead unless the Indians safeguard CIRUS.'[51] However, Ottawa was met with India's outright condemnation of nuclear safeguards. In addition, there was pressure from inside Canada. In particular, the Canadian domestic nuclear industry, and its allies in the Department of Industry, Trade, and Commerce (ITC), prevented renegotiation of the CIRUS deal. According to one RAPP I negotiator, 'we knew that reactor was naked. Here was a chance to do something about it. But the commercial people kept saying that if we didn't give the Indians what they wanted, they'd get it elsewhere.'[52] Thus, CIRUS remained without adequate safeguards. Canadian insistence on tougher safeguards, as Robert Bothwell has noted, was again 'postponed until a later and presumably better day, when the advantages of the Canadian reactor would be manifest to the Indians, or until the Indians were so far committed to the Canadians and so far behind in negotiations with anyone else, that they would swallow the safeguards without wincing.'[53]

With the battle now lost over retroactively securing CIRUS, the agenda shifted towards negotiating a safeguards agreement for RAPP I. The IAEA had been created in the years between the CIRUS export and the negotiations over RAPP I. This indicated a greater awareness of the problem of nuclear proliferation. However, India was widely recognized as the IAEA's strongest critic. Nehru constantly referred to the objectives of the IAEA as constituting 'atomic colonialism.'[54] Canada obviously knew about India's dissatisfaction with the emerging nonproliferation regime. For example, Nehru had sent a strongly worded letter to the Canadian high commissioner in 1960 outlining India's attitude towards the IAEA's proposed nuclear safeguards. Nehru maintained that India would 'exert every effort to assist in the evolution of a system to prevent the diversion of fissionable materials to military purposes,' but any safeguards policy had to take into account certain 'basic considerations.' For example, 'it must be consistent with the honour and dignity of every nation,' and 'it must be universally applied.' Finally, safeguards 'must take into account the fact that atomic energy has become an absolute necessity' for developing countries, and therefore it is 'the responsibility of nations to cooperate in arrangements for the most rapid exchange of technical knowledge and materials required to put the atom to its most beneficial use.' However, Nehru noted that the proposed safeguards model – which did not apply to indigenous nuclear programs – would have the 'least effect in the highly industrialised countries, while it would be most effective in under-developed countries.' In Nehru's mind this was 'highly discriminatory,' and it would also lead to 'a loss of independence' for developing countries.[55]

In response, Nehru developed an alternative approach to safeguards. First, 'no conditions should be attached to the supply of plant and equipment, including nuclear reactors or components.' Safeguards on these facilities, which have 'other non-atomic industrial purposes,' would 'result in interference with national sovereignty.' Second, there should be no safeguards on 'the supply of unprocessed source material, such as uranium.' This would give special status to those countries that had these source materials as a natural resource. Third, 'the only system of safeguards which would be practicable and effective would be one which envisaged world-wide controls applicable to all nations without discrimination.' Thus, safeguards should only apply to 'special fissionable materials' that could be used for bomb production.[56]

Although, ITC was clearly concerned about the loss of a sale to a competitor, the Department of External Affairs had its own concerns if the Indians got their reactor elsewhere. It was not worried about the United States, because the Americans had made it clear that it would attach bilateral safeguards on any nuclear transaction with India. The question marks were France and the Soviet Union. The DEA knew that neither the Soviet Union nor France would 'apply safeguards' to any reactor it sold to India.[57] Ottawa also feared that the British 'would not feel bound to maintain their present policy' if France or the Soviet Union would not attach safeguards.[58] These developments led DEA to conclude that there would be great international ramifications 'should reactors be supplied to India without safeguards.' In particular, it might lead other governments, that is, China, to believe that India was developing nuclear weapons. Ottawa also made the linkage between the extent of Canadian government subsidies with the RAPP I project and nuclear non-proliferation. In one department memo, a DEA official realized that 'agreeing to derogation in context of a transaction involving Canadian financial assistance would ... make it even less possible to hold the line on safeguards in normal commercial transactions.'[59] Thus, Ottawa was determined that it, or the U.S., had to be the supplier for India's nuclear reactors because Canada and the U.S. were the only ones who would attempt to attach safeguards.

Ottawa may have been unsuccessful in its efforts to use RAPP I to attach adequate safeguards to CIRUS, but it was successful in achieving a tougher safeguards agreements for RAPP I. First, a 'peaceful purposes only' clause was inserted in the preamble. Although entirely symbolic, the preamblatory clause did capture Canada's desire that the reactor not be used for military purposes. Second, the agreement mentioned 'fissile materials' by name, emphasizing the fact that the agreement was concerned with the fuel question that had been ignored in the earlier CIRUS deal. Third, the agreement allowed for Canadian inspections of the reactor to ensure that the 'peaceful purposes only' guarantee was being met. This was a big improvement over the CIRUS agreement that had contained no provisions for onsite inspections. To make this clause more palatable for the Indians, the agreement was reciprocal with India being entitled to inspect the Douglas Point Station in Canada. Fourth, there were to be no third-party transfers of nuclear materials, equipment, and technology without Canadian approval. In this way, Canada could maintain firmer control of its product even after it left its territory. Fifth, Canada would be informed of any fuel being removed from the reactor. Finally, a reliable accounting system would be established to ensure proper accountability for all fuel and fissionable materials.[60]

The RAPP I safeguards agreement reflected the development of international nuclear safeguards concepts and mechanisms that had emerged out of the IAEA. It also illustrated the growing importance of Canada's proliferation concerns vis-à-vis its commercial interests. While RAPP I did contain additional safeguards, it was not as protected as the Canadians would have liked. The inspections were only bilateral; the IAEA was still not involved. Also, the safeguards applied to first-generation use only, taking account only of Canadian uranium exports. This meant that any indigenous uranium supplied by the Indians would be free from any safeguards. There were two reasons why the safeguards on RAPP I were not stronger. First was the fact that the IAEA did not approve its safeguards system until 1965, two years after the RAPP II safeguards agreement was signed.[61] Second was the pressure that AECL and the private sector component companies were placing on DEA.

Pakistan: KANUPP, 1965

In 1965, Canadian General Electric (CGE) sold a 137 megawatt CANDU unit – the Karachi Nuclear Power Plant (KANUPP) – to Pakistan. This deal was on a turnkey basis. This meant that Canada would build the reactor on its own and then hand the finished product over to the Pakistanis who would simply 'turn the key' to start the energy production. With this type of arrangement, Canada maintained firm control over the design and construction of the reactor. CGE officials noted that 'essentially all manufactured equipment was imported into Pakistan.'[62] As a result, it allowed Canada to transfer only a minimal amount of its nuclear technological capability to Pakistan. A significant feature of the KANUPP sale was that it was CGE's only reactor export. In 1968, CGE withdrew from the export market after failed bids in Argentina and Finland. With CGE's departure – it remained in the industry as a nuclear components supplier – AECL was left as the sole domestic exporter of nuclear reactors.

The origins of the KANUPP sale go back to the 1959 treaty for cooperation in the peaceful uses of atomic energy between Canada and Pakistan. This agreement, which was a precursor of any possible nuclear transfer, contained numerous safeguards. First, there was a clause in both the preamble and in the body of the text that stated that all nuclear materials would be 'used for peaceful purposes only.' In order to ensure that Pakistan lived up to this promise, there was a provision in the treaty for Canadian onsite inspections. There was also a proscription on third-party transfers without Canadian approval. Similarly, Canada would be informed of any fuel being removed from the reactor. To ensure that fuel could not be covertly removed, a reliable accounting system for all fuel and fissionable material would be established. Finally, a sanctions clause was inserted into the treaty which allowed Canada, 'if it has determined that identified material is furthering a military purpose,' to 'suspend or cancel' all nuclear transfers.[63] The 1959 nuclear cooperation treaty formed the basis of the safeguards provisions for KANUPP. However, due to the evolution in Canada's position on nuclear safeguards as well as the establishment of the IAEA safeguards system, the 1965 KANUPP agreement would include additional protections against nuclear proliferation.[64] A second safeguards agreement was reached in 1969. This was a trilateral treaty between Canada, Pakistan, and the IAEA, which called for IAEA inspections of KANUPP and included sanctions for non-compliance.[65]

In assessing the safeguards agreements between Canada and Pakistan, it appears at first glance that Canadian non-proliferation concerns appeared to be very influential. No Canadian reactor on Pakistani soil would be left unprotected (unlike CIRUS in the case of India). In addition, Canada was able to obtain these safeguards from Pakistan without being forced to 'pull teeth' as had occurred in the previous Indian cases. However, one cannot merely take these bilateral agreements at face value and argue that all non-proliferation concerns were satisfactorily put to rest. Since a treaty is just a promise between governments, one must look at how trustworthy a country is. In the case of nuclear energy, one must examine the stability of a regime and the nature of its regional relations because unstable situations may result in the military application of nuclear energy by a country despite its commitments on a piece of paper.

The Pakistani–Indian conflict had been a constant source of instability since the partition of the subcontinent in 1947. In 1949, Pakistan invaded the Indian province of Kashmir, the control of which had been in dispute between the two countries since partition. Pakistan's actions resulted in the United Nations being called in to police a ceasefire in Kashmir between the two warring countries. The Kashmir issue continued to simmer until, finally, the two countries went to war again in 1965.[66] Although Pakistani–Indian relations were relatively cordial in 1961, when the negotiations for nuclear export began, it would have been naive of Canada to consider that the situation was stable. For Canada to be involved in a nuclear relationship with both Pakistan and India required great delicacy, and it must be judged that Canada was quite possibly *adding* to the instability of the region by providing nuclear technology to both sides.

The reliability of the Pakistani government must also be assessed. In stark contrast to India, Pakistan abandoned democracy soon after gaining independence. Autocratic military regimes have ruled Pakistan for most of its existence, except for a brief period in the 1970s when civilian rule was restored following Pakistan's humiliation in the 1971 war, and for short periods of time in the late 1980s and late 1990s. During the KANUPP negotiations, Pakistan emphasized that it would be responsible, but it must have been difficult for Canadian officials to take the government solely at its word.

Speculations about India's nuclear aspirations provided Pakistan with a perfect rationale for developing its own weapons. In particular, Islamabad must have been concerned after 1964 when India started nuclear reprocessing. While a reprocessing plant can be used for the fabrication of enriched fuel, it can also accommodate the procedure for processing plutonium for bombs. This explains why Pakistan had tried to obtain a French nuclear reprocessing plant in the mid-1960s. Although its bid was deflected by American and Canadian pressure, this episode did indicate some of the policy debates that were occurring in the Pakistani government.

This view about Pakistan's nuclear weapons aspirations is strongly opposed by a prominent Canadian specialist on nuclear proliferation: Ashok Kapur. Kapur has argued that Pakistan's nuclear program was 'entirely peaceful' in the 1960–71 period and that Pakistan's decision to pursue nuclear weapons only emerged in the aftermath of its military defeat to India in 1971.[67] Nevertheless, Kapur does acknowledge that a 'minority view' existed in Pakistan among the Foreign Office, Ali Bhutto, the press, and select academics, which 'favoured Pakistani nuclearisation to manage the Indian threat by matching India's nuclear potential.'[68] Those who favoured developing nuclear weapons might have been in the minority, but Kapur underplays the fact that it was a very influential minority. In particular, it is difficult to ignore the influence, or at least the potential influence of, Bhutto who was a minister in the Ayub Khan government throughout most of the 1960s. Bhutto may have been viewed as an outsider, and, in fact, left the Ayub government in 1966, but he clearly had elements of support, both popular and elite, within Pakistan, and was obviously jockeying for the top job. It is notable that it was only when Bhutto was able to assume full control of the Pakistani government in 1972 that its nuclear weapons program blossomed. Thus, contrary to the view outlined by Kapur, there were important elements of the Pakistani government that did want a nuclear weapons capability. Even if the pro-nuclear forces were not currently in power at the time of the KANUPP negotiations, given the nature of succession in the Pakistani political system, Canadian officials should not have ignored them.

By allowing a reactor sale to such an unstable government, which had clear designs on building a nuclear weapon, it is evident that Canada's proliferation concerns were not particularly influential in the decision to export a nuclear reactor to Pakistan. After all, a military dictatorship that was involved in a regional battle with a larger and wealthier country ruled Pakistan. Pakistan's continual losses to India in conventional wars were probably leading its rulers to consider a different approach, the capacity to threaten and/or use nuclear weapons.

Notwithstanding the safeguards negotiated, Ottawa's neglect of the proliferation considerations noted above suggests that commercial influences remained the dominant factor in the Pakistani reactor export. Many of the same economic arguments that led to the CIRUS export were evident in this case. However, there were additional impetuses in the KANUPP sale. First, was the necessity for Canada to establish more than one market for its nuclear reactors. Showing potential customers that there were several countries that favoured its nuclear reactors would constitute the greatest form of advertisement – word of mouth. In this respect, acquiring a second customer, even if it was Pakistan, was seen as being critical to the Canadian nuclear industry. A second incentive was that Pakistan was willing to import heavy water from Canada. This would necessitate the building of a second heavy-water facility in Canada.[69]

KANUPP was important because it established a second purchaser of Canadian reactors, but it was also important because it established, with CGE, a second Canadian seller of nuclear technology. Ottawa wanted to see CGE succeed and, in fact, greatly assisted it with the KANUPP sale, because this would increase competition in Canada by giving credibility to a second supplier.[70] As industry minister C.M. Drury commented, 'I am sure that an aggressive [CGE], employing a very sharp pencil, and encouraged by AECL, should be able to look to markets abroad in the nuclear field in the years immediately ahead.'[71] Even AECL supported CGE's efforts at selling a nuclear reactor to Pakistan. CGE's Civilian Atomic Power Division (CAPD) was a competitor to AECL because it was the only other Canadian company with the ability to design and manufacture a nuclear reactor. Nevertheless, AECL wanted to ensure the survival of CAPD because it was not just its competitor, it was also a major supplier to AECL of fuel bundles, refuelling machines, and other nuclear materials and equipment. However, CAPD was in trouble. It had been one of the chief contractors (with AECL and Ontario Hydro) of the NPD reactor, but by 1961 construction was almost finished. Unless more nuclear work was obtained, CAPD would have to start laying off workers at its headquarters in Peterborough, Ontario, and since CAPD employed most of the high-tech workers in that city, it would be quite a blow. If it was forced to lay off its workers, it was likely that CAPD would lose its nuclear ability and disappear from the industry. This would hurt AECL and the rest of the nuclear industry. The desire to keep CAPD employed and in the nuclear game explains why both Ottawa and AECL, its erstwhile rival, strongly supported the Pakistani project. In fact, AECL president Gray even lobbied Ottawa to provide concessionary financing and to prevent overly stringent nuclear safeguards from killing the deal.[72]

There were also political factors that facilitated a CANDU export to Pakistan. Pakistan, like India, was a Commonwealth partner, and it was part of Canadian foreign policy to aid members of the Commonwealth. In addition, Canada had already exported reactors to India, and it was important to the government that Canada assume a balanced role in the region. Ottawa did not want to appear that it was choosing sides in the dispute between India and Pakistan. Finally, Pakistan, unlike India, was a firm member of the Western alliance and played a strategic role in the containment of communism in Asia. Ottawa bowed to New Delhi's demands for minimal nuclear safeguards because India was showing interest in establishing closer relations with the Soviet Union. Why should Pakistan be held to a higher standard because it remained unambiguously in the Western camp?

The final element of the KANUPP export that needs to be assessed is the financial terms under which the deal was made. Similar to CIRUS, the KANUPP export could more accurately be referred to as an aid package rather than an actual commercial transaction. KANUPP was valued at $63 million, and of this amount, the Canadian government financed $47.2 million.[73] Half of Canada's financial commitment was a low-interest loan (at between 3 per cent and 4 per cent interest), with a grace period of ten years and then a thirty-year repayment schedule. The other half was an export credit at 6 per cent with a grace period of five years and then a ten-year repayment schedule. Here is how the 1982 *Nuclear Policy Review* described KANUPP's financing arrangements: 'Between 1966 and 1978 a total of $12.4 million was provided in export credits, and $29.4 million was loaned through the EAO/CIDA account. (Grants of about $1.5 million, which covered supervision, training and the financing of spare parts, were also extended by CIDA.) The EAO/CIDA loan was concessionary. Its terms included a 10-year period of grace followed by a 50-year repayment schedule with no interest charges.'[74] These generous terms reflect the urgency which both the government and the Canadian nuclear industry attached to obtaining an export, any export, even to a country that could obviously not afford it – Pakistan.

After examining the clash of foreign policy objectives in the KANUPP deal, it can be concluded that fears of nuclear proliferation did not constrain Canada. The Canadian government was satisfied by Pakistan's willingness to accept written safeguards agreements; it did not look beyond these treaties and assess the intentions of Pakistan. Pakistan was a country that was ruled by a military dictatorship that was involved in a seemingly never-ending dispute with India, which often erupted into military conflict, and where there was an influential element in its government that desired to obtain a nuclear bomb. The fact that Canada basically gave the reactor away illustrates the pressure that the nuclear industry placed on the government to consummate the deal.

India: RAPP II, 1966

Almost immediately after construction began on RAPP I, India started asking for another CANDU. So, in 1966, Canada exported a second power reactor, the Rajasthan Atomic Power Plant (RAPP II), to India. RAPP II's capacity, at 200 megawatt, was twice as much as the first RAPP unit. The growing security concerns of Canada are in clearer evidence in this case. To assess fully the role that the competing foreign policy goals had on RAPP II, an examination of two safeguards agreements must be undertaken. The original safeguards agreement was signed in 1966, but there were two amendments to this agreement, with the more relevant one being concluded in 1971.

It was clear from the beginning that the safeguards negotiations for RAPP II would be just as difficult as they were for CIRUS and RAPP I. The Indians, in contrast to the Canadians, firmly believed that they had accepted stringent safeguards on RAPP I. Homi Bhabha made it clear that, this time, India would be much tougher during the safeguards negotiations. According to Bhabha, Canadian officials 'had beaten him down over RAPP I,' but the negotiations over RAPP II would be different. India's opening gambit was that it would only accept safeguards on 'the reactor core, uranium fuel, and heavy water' and would not allow restrictions on 'items of equipment' that were 'normal items of commerce.'[75] AECL, reflecting Canadian commercial interests in the nuclear field, sympathized with Bhabha, asserting that 'it would be a great pity if Canadian industry were denied the opportunity to participate in this work by reason of the application of a political decision on safeguards of doubtful merit.'[76] Countering these commercial interests were the security concerns of the Department of External Affairs. External Affairs Minister Paul Martin Sr. was 'adamant in his view that the price for RAPP II should be Indian acceptance of IAEA safeguards.'[77] A typically Canadian compromise was reached: a safeguards agreement identical to RAPP I would be signed for RAPP II, but negotiations would continue on the upgrading of these safeguards.

Canada was able to maintain identical safeguards on RAPP II as on RAPP I, despite Indian opposition, for two reasons. First, Bhabha had tragically died in a plane crash in January 1966. This left India without its most experienced, and toughest, negotiator. Second, Lorne Gray, president of AECL, convinced Bhabha's successors that Canada considered RAPP I and RAPP II to be 'two units of the same station.' Therefore, the safeguards that existed on RAPP I must also be applied to RAPP II. Gray also emphasized that any efforts by India 'to escape Canadian safeguards by procuring only the conventional parts of the reactor in Canada while making the rest in India were not acceptable' to Canada.[78]

Nevertheless, Canada could not be satisfied with the status quo on the safeguards issue. It needed to push for the tougher IAEA safeguards. Canada had been earlier constrained in its desire to attach agency safeguards to RAPP I by the fact that the IAEA had not yet established its safeguards system. But by 1966, the IAEA had come to an agreement on its safeguards system. How could Canada leave RAPP II unprotected? India represented a test case. If Canada could not convince India to accept IAEA safeguards, what other countries in the future would allow their sovereignty to be opened up for onsite inspections of its nuclear facilities? What would be the ramifications on the emerging nuclear non-proliferation regime?

Canada was also deeply concerned about the changing security environment in south Asia. There was strong evidence that India was working on a nuclear weapons program. China had successfully tested its first nuclear bomb in 1964, and this event, combined with its defeat in the 1962 border war with China, gave ample incentive for India to develop its own nuclear bombs. The Chinese bomb, as K.K. Pathak has noted, 'created a grave security threat to India and provoked a national debate in the country. The Government of India came under heavy pressure to abandon its policy of peaceful uses of atomic energy and to immediately start a nuclear weapons programme.'[79] The reaction of the Indians can best be seen by the person who was best positioned to direct India's nuclear direction: Homi Bhabha. Bhabha initially asserted that India could match China's nuclear feat within eighteen months. A few days later, in a speech to the United Nations eight days after the Chinese test, Bhabha commented that 'atomic weapons give a state possessing them in adequate numbers a deterrent power against attack from a much stronger state. Indeed, the importance of nuclear weapons is that they enable a country possessing them in adequate measure to deter another country also possessing them from using them against it.'[80]

There was also significant political support for a change in Indian nuclear policy. For example, the governing India Congress Party passed a resolution in Parliament calling for the re-examination of the country's policy on nuclear weapons.[81] In addition, recently declassified documents show that British and American intelligence services were warning Canada in 1965 that India wanted to use Canadian technology to develop nuclear weapons.[82] Finally, Canadian technicians stationed at CIRUS in the 1960s knew that India was diverting plutonium, but accepted the official explanation that the fuel was being removed because of problems with the cladding (an aluminum covering for the uranium fuel rods). A retired AECL senior manager has suggested that the cladding story was accepted because it was what they wanted to hear. "We were just interested in the science. Nobody really wants to rock the boat. Its quite obvious there was not enough vigilance. Certainly more could have been done.'[83]

As a result of this worrisome change in direction in Indian nuclear policy, Canada was determined to upgrade the safeguards applicable to RAPP I and II. What Canada wanted was a safeguards agreement that met guidelines established by the NPT. The NPT had been drafted in 1968, and Canada had signed and ratified it in 1970. India, however, was deeply opposed to the NPT, calling it an imperialistic, discriminatory agreement, and refused to sign it. India, obviously, was not about to allow the new NPT safeguards policy to be applied to its nuclear program. The adoption of NPT full-scope safeguards would mean that it was not just RAPP I and II that would be subject to IAEA rules and inspections. Instead, India's entire nuclear program – research reactors, power reactors, all fissile material, and so on – would be safeguarded. In addition, the NPT/IAEA did not care where the nuclear technology came from because full-scope safeguards did not discriminate based on rules of origin.

In the course of its safeguards negotiations with Canada, India once again threatened to buy its future reactors from France. India calculated, as it had in the past, that this would result in the Canadian nuclear industry pressuring the Canadian government to ease up on its safeguards demands in order to preserve its sales to India.[84] Canadian commercial interests did have some effect on the government as less-stringent IAEA safeguards replaced the demand for NPT safeguards. However, the security concerns that existed in Canada were powerful enough to withstand the demand that the RAPP agreements did not need to be amended and that bilateral inspections were enough.

In the agreement that was reached on 9 June 1971, safeguards were toughened on both RAPP I and II. IAEA safeguards, which would include Agency inspections and sanctions for non-compliance, would now apply to the CANDUs. In addition, Canadian fissile materials as well as 'all subsequent generations of nuclear material produced' would be under safeguards.[85] Even the use of Indian uranium was now safeguarded on the Canadian reactors. Canadian officials seemed content with the strengthened safeguards agreement that it negotiated. However, it is safe to assume that commercial interests still played the superior role in the negotiations because Canada did not make its initial insistence on NPT safeguards a deal-breaker.

It is true that the influence of non-proliferation concerns on Canadian policy steadily increased. In 1956, the lone safeguard was a 'peaceful purposes only' pledge, but by 1971 IAEA safeguards had been applied to all Canadian nuclear reactors exported to India except for CIRUS.

Canada's safeguards may have been slowly increasing, but its concerns about India's intentions with nuclear technology were increasing exponentially. India's 1962 war with China, the 1964 Chinese nuclear test, and the 1965 and 1971 wars with Pakistan contributed to a greater volatility in the region and the concurrent likelihood of India developing nuclear weapons. This meant that Canada's attitude towards Indian nuclear proliferation had also changed from a 1950s naivety to a 1960s desperate hope that the intelligence reports it was receiving were wrong.

Taiwan: TRR, 1969

On 16 September 1969, Canada concluded an arrangement to export an NRX-type research reactor to Taiwan. The Taiwan Research Reactor (TRR) constituted an almost perfect export for Canada. The Taiwanese paid $30 million in cash; the construction of TRR was completed on time as the reactor went critical by September 1973; and there were no problems with negotiating safeguards as Taiwan easily concluded an agreement with the IAEA. However, a little more than a year later, on 12 October 1970, Canada terminated all nuclear cooperation with Taiwan when Taiwan officially was recognized the People's Republic of China (PRC). As a result of this recognition, Ottawa severed all diplomatic relations with Taiwan.

The original decision to supply the TRR was made for commercial reasons, and proliferation concerns did not act as a constraint on the Canadian government. Taiwan, although ruled by an authoritarian government, was stable. However, the issue was not so much the internal stability of Taiwan as the instability of the region, for the conflict between the PRC and Taiwan resulted in a very unsettled situation. Following the communist revolution on mainland China in 1949, which sent Chiang Kai-shek and his followers retreating to Taiwan, both the PRC and the Republic of China (Taiwan) claimed rightful ownership of Taiwan and the mainland. As a result, the two 'countries' have been in a state of civil war since 1949, with only the Taiwan Strait and the Seventh Fleet of the U.S. Navy separating them. Under these circumstances, supplying Taiwan with a *potential* nuclear capability could be seen as contributing to an already tense situation. In 1964, China secured the bomb, and this made Taiwan fearful. In addition, China had a population advantage of almost a billion people. As former U.S. Department of Defence director George Rathjens said in 1976, 'if mainland China made a determined effort to take Taiwan, the Taiwan government could only effectively respond with nuclear weapons.'[86]

It can be clearly stated that Taiwan was originally supplied with the TRR for commercial reasons. The fact that Taiwan was able to pay the entire cost for the reactor, rather than having the Canadian government subsidize it either through CIDA grants or ECIC loans, meant that Taiwan was a valuable customer. Also, Taiwan possessed a growing economy and was expected to require additional reactors. Canada could thus become a major nuclear supplier. The potential for conflict with China was not taken into consideration, and this is indicative of the lack of concern with proliferation issues. The possible argument that the export resulted from Cold War considerations can also be discounted. It is true that Taiwan was a staunch anti-communist ally in a region where the domino theory was in clear evidence, but Canada, especially after the 1968 election of Pierre Trudeau, was not as committed to military-style containment as its American ally. Canada was also moving to normalize its relations with mainland China. Therefore, containing communism was not a factor in Canada's conclusion of this reactor sale.

If the export of TRR was based on commercial interests, the decision to terminate nuclear assistance was clearly done for political reasons. When Canada started the formal negotiations in 1970 that eventually led to full recognition of China, it decided to terminate nuclear assistance to Taiwan. Once Canada had ended official recognition of the Taiwanese government, it would have been 'impossible to sell such a sensitive item as a nuclear reactor to a government which no longer had any legitimacy in official Canadian eyes.'[87] Although the commercial interests in Canada objected, the political arguments dominated. AECL contended that it had assured Taiwan in 1969 that Canada's negotiations with the PRC would not jeopardize the TRR project in any way, but the Canadian government was not moved by AECL's appeals to this effect.[88] Also hurting AECL's case was the view that closer ties with the PRC held the possibility of great long-term economic benefits to Canada. In 1969, Canada held a trade surplus of $100 million with the PRC largely due to wheat sales. Canadian trade officials, as John Holmes wrote at the time, also saw the potential of 'raw and semi-finished materials, industrial machinery and transport equipment.'[89] In essence, Ottawa was able to rebut AECL's commercial arguments regarding nuclear relations with Taiwan by pointing to the possibility of even greater economic benefits with the substantially larger market on mainland China. AECL never forgot the lost sale, or forgave Ottawa for costing it a valuable customer. AECL was again prompted to blame Ottawa for a lost opportunity when Taiwan later purchased six reactors from the Americans.[90] AECL even began negotiations in the early 1980s with Taipower (Taiwan's nuclear company) to sell a CANDU to Taiwan but, once again, the deal was blocked by Ottawa for fear of offending the PRC.[91]

It has been suggested that the termination of nuclear assistance to Taiwan actually *contributed* to instability in the region. Gordon Edwards has argued that 'supplying Taiwan with the means to make nuclear weapons, and then joining in its international abandonment, might be said to invite the spread of the atomic bomb.'[92] This is debatable considering the influence that the United States had, and has, on Taiwan. Taiwan was, and is, dependent on the U.S. for its protection, and the U.S. would not allow Taiwan to develop nuclear weapons. Despite better Sino-American relations since the official American recognition of China, the U.S. is not yet prepared to abandon Taiwan and continues to exert control over the government's military policy. For example, U.S. pressure has twice stopped the Taiwanese from operating a small plutonium reprocessing plant designed to produce weapons-grade uranium.[93] Rather than contributing to instability in the region, cutting off nuclear assistance to Taiwan actually helped stabilize the situation. Appeasing China, which was a nuclear power, was a more important political goal than running the slim risk of terminating sales to Taiwan or of the latter developing nuclear weapons to defend itself from Chinese aggression.

Argentina: Embalse, 1973

When Canada sold the Embalse CANDU reactor to Argentina in 1973, its economic interests were of paramount importance. By 1972, it had become clear that foreign sales of the CANDU were critical to the future of the Canadian nuclear program. As AECL president Lorne Gray noted, 'we were getting pretty tired' of the search for exports and 'were really concerned about the future of the Canadian nuclear power programme if we did not get something.'[94] Canadian opposition parties placed additional pressure on the government to generate nuclear exports. The opposition Progressive Conservatives, in questioning the government's commitment and ability to conclude foreign sales, asked whether ITC was 'on the job, attempting to sell this country another plant, or do they have some doubts about our capacity to build these plants, keep them up-to-date and equal to atomic energy plants in the rest of the world?'[95]

These pressures resulted in AECL hiring a sales agent named Shaul

Eisenberg. Eisenberg, an Israeli citizen who called himself an international industrial salesman, came to AECL in 1968 and declared, 'I can
sell that sleeping beauty of yours. You fellows will never sell it, [as] you
don't know the market.'[96] AECL justified the hiring of agents by asserting that 'we are going to need agents in future to do our business. AECL
simply is not equipped to provide the kind of marketing organization
that is needed to sell the Candu reactor abroad.'[97] AECL also entered
into a partnership with an Italian firm, Italimpianti, in its Argentine bid.
Italimpianti had told AECL that they were 'babes in the woods' who
would 'never sell in South America,' and although AECL had 'a good
system, we think it is going to go around the world, but if you want to
sell in South America you better let us do it for you.'[98] In addition to the
use of sales agents and international partners, the Canadian Export
Development Corporation (EDC) provided a $130-million loan at a
very low interest rate.[99] This was a very generous financial package.

It is obvious that Argentina, at the time, must have been considered a
fairly serious candidate for nuclear proliferation. It was not a party to
either the NPT or the Treaty of Tlatelelco, which attempted to maintain
Latin America as a nuclear free zone. One reason why Argentina might
have been viewed as a potential nuclear weapons candidate was its
regional rivalry with Brazil.[100] These two countries were battling for
economic, political, and military hegemony in South America. In this
rivalry, 'nuclear technology was a source of pride, unity, and status with
the continent,'[101] but it had not yet led to war because both countries
seemed to be preoccupied with internal threats rather than external
enemies.

If the security concern of regional conflict can be largely discounted,
regime stability cannot. Argentina had had a history of unstable military dictatorships, and even though free elections were to be held in
March 1973, one could not be sure how long the government would
last. In the elections that occurred, Argentina elected a Peronist president in Hector Campora, but Juan Peron continued to exercise real
power in Buenos Aires. However, Peron was in his late seventies and
could not live much longer, and the Argentine military was waiting in
the wings. The situation in Argentina during the CANDU negotiations
was one where civil war between left- and right-wing forces was ready
to erupt at any moment, and the only thing preventing an outbreak of
hostilities was an old man. It is clear that Argentina was very unstable
and this was demonstrated when an undeclared civil war did, indeed,
break out in 1974.

South Korea: Wolsung I, 1973

In 1973, Canada also sold a 600 megawatt CANDU – the Wolsung I – to South Korea. This was an unexpected sale because, four years earlier, in 1969, Canada had failed in its efforts to sell a CANDU to South Korea. An additional unusual aspect of this case was that it was not AECL approaching Seoul, in fact the South Koreans did not even bother with holding an international tendering process, instead, it was Seoul that asked Ottawa about the possibility of a CANDU export. The Canadian government claimed that South Korea had purchased the CANDU without calling for international bids because it was impressed with the Canadian system. However, this seems a bit too pat. There must have been other reasons why South Korea would approach Canada to sell it a nuclear reactor. A more convincing explanation is that the CANDU's use of natural uranium would allow the South Koreans to decrease their dependency on American supplies of enriched uranium.

A second possibility involves the 'persuasive' ability of AECL's new sales agent Shaul Eisenberg. What exactly was Eisenberg's role in securing the Wolsung I contract? During a heated debate during question period, Maurice Dupras, the parliamentary secretary to the minister of energy, mines, and resources, took on the responsibility of explaining what Eisenberg was doing on behalf of AECL. He is worth quoting at length:

> First, assistance in getting AECL's office and personnel established in Korea; second, assistance with the entry and handling of all goods imported for the job ... third, assistance, as necessary, with local subcontracts for labour, material and ervices; fourth, advice on Korean laws and regulations affecting the execution of the main contract; fifth, commercial assistance to AECL in respect of dealing with the customer concerning changes in the scope of the work and the provision of spare parts; sixth, provide experienced staff in Korea and elsewhere as necessary to perform these functions.[102]

Eisenberg may, indeed, have performed the tasks enumerated by Dupras. However, that does not explain why only $5.1 million of Eisenberg's total commision of $18.5 million went towards paying his fee. The remaining $13 million was for expenses. It was these expenses which the Auditor General viewed as inadequately documented. According to the Auditor General, Eisenberg's commission included fees to 'three agent consultants,' which did not give any details of the services which these agents had performed.[103] These were clearly payments by Eisenberg to high-level Korean nuclear officials to procure the reactor contract.

The financial terms of the CANDU deal were consistent with other large-scale industrial projects rather than most past Canadian reactor exports, which often typified aid projects. The EDC committed $330 million to finance the Korean sale, and a consortium of Canadian and British banks added another $60 million.[104] Although Ottawa did provide significant loan guarantees, Wolsung I was not an aid package like in the Indian and Pakistani cases.

A tight nuclear safeguards agreement was negotiated, alleviating Canada's proliferation concern. Since the negotiations occurred after the Indian nuclear explosion, the safeguards agreement is assessed in chapter 5 (rather than here). However, the issue of South Korea's regional conflict needs to be explored in order to address the issue of why, irregardless of formal safeguards arrangements, Canada was willing to conclude any type of nuclear transaction. Although there had been a ceasefire since the end of the Korean War in 1953, no formal peace treaty had been signed, thus South Korea remained technically in a state of war with North Korea. South Korean president Syngman Rhee had even refused to sign the ceasefire agreement. Therefore, South Korea maintained a security incentive to acquire nuclear weapons, as they could provide a relatively cheap and effective deterrent to invasion from the north.

However, any possible military action that Seoul might have wished to take against Pyongyang was constrained by the United States. The U.S. had provided the South Koreans with a security guarantee, and backed it up with over 30,000 American troops stationed in South Korea. The Canadian government believed that the U.S. maintained a strong enough presence to prevent South Korea from producing nuclear weapons. It has been suggested that if for any reason the U.S. were to weaken its guarantee, even going so far as to withdraw its forces, then this would result in a substantial motivation for South Korea to develop a nuclear weapons capability. Nevertheless, Ottawa was satisfied that this risk was minimal and that South Korean nuclear ambitions would continue to be constrained by the United States.

The issue of South Korea's human rights record must also be examined. At the time, South Korea was a military dictatorship led by civilian president Park Chung-Hee. However, its internal stability had been maintained by South Korea's rapid industrial growth in the post–

Korean War era. Numerous human rights groups, including Amnesty International and the International Commission of Jurists, stated that the South Korean regime was corrupt, repressive, and relied on torture and false confessions to remain in power.[105] Monique Begin, the parliamentary secretary for external affairs, in response to some heavy questioning during parliamentary debates, in particular from Progressive Conservative member Doug Roche, tried to distance herself from discussions about the nature of the South Korean regime by asking, 'Who are we to pass judgement on political systems under which other people choose to live?'[106] Clearly, Canada was concerned more about South Korea's stability – even if that stability was maintained through governmental repression – than human rights. In fact, Ottawa could argue that it was actually preserving stability in South Korea by assisting it with its energy needs via Wolsung I.

In the 1945–74, period Canada's economic and political incentives clearly prevailed over its security concerns. It could be argued that commercial interests were even more important in 1974 than they were in 1956 because of the substantial investment that Canada had already made in the nuclear industry. Canada was clearly prepared to abandon, or minimize, its demands for nuclear safeguards if the customer, as India often did, threatened to go elsewhere. In fact, of the four constraining foreign policy objectives that were developed in chapter 2, only one – the threat of nuclear proliferation – was even considered by Ottawa. During this time period, human rights, environmental concerns, and government subsidies did not even appear on the government's radar screen.

Even nuclear proliferation was not much of a constraining influence. There was some upgrading of its nuclear safeguards policy during this time period, such as the inclusion of IAEA safeguards, but there were still some huge cracks in Canada's non-proliferation policy. NPT safeguards which came into force in 1970 were not included in any of the relevant cases: RAPP II, Embalse, and Wolsong I. As well, Canada was not overly concerned about whether countries were engaged in regional conflicts. In fact, each of the purchasers of the CANDU during this time period were involved in either a regional conflict (India–Pakistan, Taiwan–PRC, and South Korea–North Korea), or a potential regional conflict (Argentina–Brazil). It was likely that Canada's CANDU export policy would probably have remained intact as it stood at the end of this period for many years to come if it had not been for the 18 May 1974 Indian nuclear explosion.

5 Strengthening Safeguards, 1974–1976

On 18 May 1974, India exploded a nuclear device in the Rajasthan desert. The Pokhran test made India the sixth member of the world's 'nuclear club,' despite the Indian government's official position that its nuclear initiative was for peaceful purposes only. India was able to explode this device using plutonium that had been diverted from the CIRUS nuclear research reactor. As a consequence of its actions, both the international non-proliferation regime and Canada's nuclear export policy were challenged.

The reaction in India to the explosion was euphoric. There was a feeling that it had joined the ranks of the great powers. Raja Ramanna, the architect of the nuclear test, later wrote that the explosion 'came as a surprise to the world. They hadn't expected such an achievement from a developing country ... their criterion for measuring success was different in the sense that they judged the success of a country by its material acquisitions and its overt proof of development ... India didn't conform to any of these, and in this context alone it seemed somewhat relevant when the Western world expressed bewilderment, coupled with fear and panic at the success of Pokhran.'[1] While there was jubilation in India, the explosion came as a catastrophic jolt to the world's nuclear non-proliferation regime. Not only was India the first new member of the 'nuclear club' since China's 'admittance' in 1964, but there were also great fears that the Indian explosion would result in the floodgates opening with many of the near-nuclear-weapons states rushing to develop the bomb. A continuation of the 'nuclear domino theory,' this time in the developing world, was prophesied. That India was the first country to develop the bomb from a civilian nuclear program and that it had acquired both the fuel and the technological capability through transfers from Western nuclear suppliers added to the negative effects on the non-proliferation regime.

The explosion also caused an immediate crisis in Canada, and AECL attempted some damage control. John Foster, vice-president of AECL, was quoted in the *Times of India* as saying that 'some people in Canada seem to have a guilty complex about what happened in India, which they should not have. Many countries contributed to India's nuclear development.'[2] However, there was little doubt Canadians believed that Canada had played a significant role in enabling India to test a nuclear device. The *Globe and Mail* proclaimed that while ultimate responsibility lies with the Indians, Canada 'should not be let off the hook.' With the sale of CIRUS, Canada must bear 'continuing responsibility for expansion of the nuclear club.'[3]

The Canadian public was also unhappy. One letter to the editor of the *Globe and Mail* asked why would 'Canada, which has assiduously advocated non-proliferation of nuclear weapons, allow India to acquire steadily over two decades Canadian technological skills, funds, training and equipment to become a nuclear power?'[4] George Quester, an academic writing in *Foreign Affairs*, observed that 'Canada's reaction was indeed openly and righteously angry perhaps it reflects ... a certain embarrassment at having failed to draft a more airtight agreement with the Indians eight or ten years ago.'[5] Robert Morrison and Edward Wonder added to this sentiment by writing that Canada's reaction stemmed from the fact that it 'had contributed to nuclear proliferation and world insecurity, not through cynical arms sales or manipulative power politics, but through sheer naivete.'[6] Canada's self-flagellating approach to the Indian explosion was matched by the public finger-pointing of its American friends. U.S. Secretary of State Henry Kissinger, while denying that the United States had contributed any nuclear material for the bomb, quickly placed the blame on the Canadians.[7] Ashok Kapur has noted that 'Kissinger's open criticism of Canada's nuclear assistance program to India added to the Canadian dilemma.'[8]

What was the basis for Canada's guilt? Basically, Canadian assistance had been essential for India's military aspirations in two principal ways. The first was through the production of plutonium by CIRUS. In order to produce a nuclear weapon, a supply of plutonium was needed; India had obtained this necessary ingredient by extracting irradiated fuel from CIRUS. The reason that the Indians chose to use CIRUS for their supply of plutonium, and not one of their other reactors, was because CIRUS was not governed by any nuclear safeguards. The second involved Canada's technical transfers and assistance to India's nuclear program during the 1950s and 1960s that helped to create India's self-sufficiency in reactor technology. As a result of its role in the Indian explosion, Canada's nuclear reactor export policy would be dramatically altered. Concern with nuclear proliferation would ascend to the top of its foreign policy objectives. From 1974 to 1976, the Canadian government introduced changes that strengthened its non-proliferation policy and took significant steps to enforce these changes.

Changes to Canada's Non-Proliferation Policy

Before analysing the consequences of Canada's new safeguards policy for individual situations, an assessment of the evolution of this policy is necessary. Following the May 1974 Indian explosion, Canada's non-proliferation policy was reviewed. This review revealed a number of deficiencies in Canada's existing safeguards agreements, which included

- no coverage for nuclear equipment or material produced with Canadian supplied technology; equipment or material produced with Canadian know-how could therefore be used for the production of nuclear explosive devices
- ambiguity as to whether there was coverage of subsequent generations of nuclear material produced with Canadian supplied equipment or material
- inadequate control over the retransfer to third countries of Canadian supplied nuclear material and equipment
- lack in most cases of any Canadian hold over the reprocessing of spent fuel (and over storage of any extracted plutonium) and the enrichment of nuclear material, and
- the ability to legally withdraw from safeguards obligations before the end of the operating life of Canadian supplied nuclear equipment; an agreement needed to remain in force for the life of Canadian supplied material, including subsequent generations[9]

To remedy these deficiencies, on 20 December 1974, the minister of energy, mines, and resources, Donald Macdonald, announced a more stringent nuclear safeguards policy that contained the following conditions:

1   A binding assurance that Canadian-origin items would be used exclusively for peaceful, non-explosive purposes.
2   A binding assurance that Canadian-origin items would be covered by international (IAEA) safeguards for their lifetimes.
3   A binding assurance that any nuclear material produced by or with Canadian-supplied items would be subject to conditions (1) and (2).
4   A binding recognition of Canada's right of prior consent over the retransfer beyond the recipient's jurisdiction of any Canadian-origin items or of any nuclear material used with or produced by those items.
5   A binding recognition of Canada's right of prior consent over the reprocessing of Canadian-origin nuclear material irradiated in a Canadian-origin facility as well as over the subsequent storage of any plutonium produced.
6   A binding recognition of Canada's right of prior consent over the enrichment beyond 20 per cent and the subsequent storage of Canadian-origin uranium.
7   A binding recognition of Canada's right to apply fall-back safeguards should IAEA safeguards cease to be applied for any reason.
8   A binding commitment that adequate physical protection measures would be applied.[10]

In order to implement this policy, Macdonald announced that Canada would also renegotiate its 1973 reactor sales to both Argentina and South Korea. A time limit of one year was originally placed on these negotiations, but it was later extended to two years.

Canada's non-proliferation policy continued to evolve, and at the Non-Proliferation Treaty (NPT) Review Conference in May 1975, the government announced that 'future Canadian bilateral official development-assistance commitments for the financing of nuclear projects will be undertaken solely to NPT party states.'[11] Since most reactor exports involve a great deal of government financing, the withholding of this financing arrangement would clearly limit AECL's ability to sell the CANDU. Therefore, the limiting of financing and other forms of assistance from the Export Development Corporation (EDC) to NPT states represented a significant toughening of Canada's non-proliferation policy. An additional incremental step was also made in 1975 when the cabinet decided to prohibit all sales to the unstable region of the Middle East.

On 22 December 1976, the minister of external affairs, Don Jamieson, announced further changes in Canada's policy. In addition to the requirements of the December 1974 announcement, he stated that 'shipments to non-nuclear-weapons states under future contracts will be restricted to those which ratify the Non-Proliferation Treaty or otherwise accept international safeguards on their entire nuclear program. It follows from this policy that Canada will terminate nuclear shipments to any non-nuclear weapon state which explodes a nuclear device.'[12] In making this announcement, Jamieson also stated that the Canadian government was 'determined to do everything within its power to avoid contributing to nuclear weapons proliferation.' Pointing out that Canada was strengthening its non-proliferation policy 'unilaterally,' Jamieson emphasized that Canada was 'prepared to accept the commercial consequences of being clearly ahead of other suppliers.' This, he said, was the price Canada had 'to pay to curb the threat to mankind of nuclear proliferation.'[13] The assertion that Canada was prepared to accept the 'commercial consequences' of its non-proliferation policy, meant the subordination of Canada's commercial interests in exporting nuclear reactors.

With any new policy, the implementation stage is the most important. For example, a confidential cabinet document warned that the future of Canada's nuclear export policy 'may to a large extent hinge on decisions relating to Korea and Argentina which have to be taken under considerable pressure of time and relate largely to safeguards and the political situation of these two countries.'[14] To assess whether the 1974–6 changes in Canada's non-proliferation policy really brought about a shift in priorities, an analysis of the implementation of the new policy must be undertaken. Some critics have suggested that the only thing that changed after the Indian explosion was the 'level of anti-proliferation rhetoric' and that 'while there was an increase in the numbers and type of commitments required of recipients of Canadian-supplied nuclear material and technology, the system was not altered.'[15] However, a close examination of the specific steps that Canada took to implement its non-proliferation policy shows clearly that there was a significant strengthening of the safeguards attached to its CANDU export policy.

India: Suspension of Nuclear Assistance

Canada responded very quickly to the Indian nuclear explosion. On 22 May 1974, four days after the explosion, Canada suspended all nuclear assistance to India and all non-food bilateral aid. Non-nuclear aid was resumed to India within several months, but because of the time lag, India, which was supposed to have received $127 million in aid, instead received only $96.4 million, resulting in a loss of over $30 million.[16] However, nuclear assistance remained suspended until its formal termination in 1976.

It is important to examine the implications of the explosion in order to clearly understand the role competing foreign policy goals had in the suspension decision. In particular, there are two interrelated issues that need to be considered. The first concerns the difference, if any, between a peaceful nuclear explosion and a military explosion. Second, is the question of whether or not India broke either the letter or the spirit of any multilateral or bilateral safeguards agreements.

The question of whether India's nuclear explosion was peaceful or military was raised at the time. In its official announcement of the event, the Indian Atomic Energy Commission described it as 'a peaceful nuclear explosion [PNE] experiment using an implosion device. As part of the programme of study of peaceful uses of nuclear explosions, the Government of India has undertaken a programme to keep itself abreast of developments in this technology, particularly with reference to its use in the field of mining and earth-moving operations.'[17] However, the Indian government never indicated precisely how it planned to use PNEs for economic development.[18] The research on this subject suggests two possibilities for PNEs: earth-moving for building canals and harbours, and underground blasts that would make it easier to extract natural gases, oil, and minerals.[19] Yet, by 1974, these possible uses had been ruled out because they were either uneconomical or impractical. For its part, Canada made it clear that it saw no distinction between the development of nuclear explosions for 'so-called peaceful purposes' and explosions for military purposes. As External Affairs Minister Mitchell Sharp pointed out in 1974, 'there can be no distinction between peaceful and potential military applications. For all intents and purposes ... India now has developed the capability of producing a nuclear weapon.'[20]

Prior to 1974, international opinion had already reached the conclusion that there was no difference in essence between a 'peaceful' and a 'military' explosion.[21] This view was affirmed in the 1970 Non-Proliferation Treaty which specifically emphasized the inseparable link between the two. Article II of the NPT states that 'each non-nuclear-weapon State Party to the Treaty undertakes not to receive the transfer from any transferor whatsoever of *nuclear weapons or other nuclear explo-*

sive devices or of control over such weapons or explosive devices directly, or indirectly; not to manufacture or otherwise acquire *nuclear weapons or other nuclear explosive devices*; and not to seek or receive any assistance in the manufacture of *nuclear weapons or other nuclear explosive devices.*' In addition, in 1974, the UN General Assembly stated that it had not yet been proven possible to differentiate between the technology of nuclear weapons and that of nuclear explosive devices for peaceful purposes. It is clear, then, that, despite India's contrary stance,[22] there was an international consensus that PNEs were the same as military nuclear explosions.

The most important aspect of the nuclear explosion from a Canadian standpoint was the legality of India's actions. Did India break any multilateral or bilateral agreements in the process of conducting its explosion? The answer to the above question would determine, accordingly, whether or not Canada's suspension of nuclear cooperation with India could be legally justified. It was important for Canada to find legal justification for its decision, otherwise, its reputation as a reliable nuclear supplier could have been damaged. In fact, Ashok Kapur has suggested that perhaps it was Canada which 'broke its nuclear supply contracts with India ... when it first suspended supplies in May 1974 and then terminated the agreement in May 1976.'[23] K.K. Pathak, an Indian nuclear specialist, has similarly argued that it was the Canadians who 'unilaterally abrogated their contractual obligations entered into under international agreements between the two countries.'[24] Canada needed to find a legal justification for its actions, not only to deal with the criticism that it was singling out India but also to protect its commercial and political dealings with other countries, and not just in the realm of nuclear materials.

It is clear that India's action violated the two most crucial elements of the NPT: the prohibition against non-nuclear-weapons states developing a nuclear explosive device and the application of international safeguards on civilian nuclear programs. However, since the NPT had never been signed or ratified by India, the question of India's legal obligations vis-à-vis the NPT rested on whether or not the NPT 'represents customary international law to such an extent that its provisions are binding even upon states that are not a party to the treaty.' For a treaty to create a new legal principle, there must be a 'high level of adherence' before that treaty can be considered representative of customary international law.[25]

However, India had not just failed to sign or ratify the NPT; it was also its harshest critic. India's opposition to the NPT was based on three major criticisms. First, was the discriminatory nature of the treaty. The NPT created two classes of states: nuclear-weapons states (the United States, the Soviet Union, China, France, and the United Kingdom) and non-nuclear-weapons states (everybody else). For India, this violated the principle of sovereign equality of all states. During and after the negotiations that led to the formulation of the NPT, India publicly denounced the treaty as discriminatory and unfair. The Indian minister of foreign affairs, M.C. Chagla, stated that 'this treaty on the face of it is discriminatory, whereas, the non-nuclear powers are expected to subject themselves to inspection and supervision, the nuclear powers will not be subject to supervision.'[26] Second, it also wondered why other countries could detonate a PNE – the United States had already conducted fourteen PNEs and the USSR seventeen[27] – but India could not. Therefore, it repeatedly declared that it reserved the right to conduct its own nuclear explosions for peaceful purposes.

Its third complaint centred on the obligations of the nuclear weapons states. While the non-nuclear-weapons states had specific obligations under the treaty, such as foregoing nuclear weapons and accepting safeguards inspections, the nuclear weapons states had only made vague promises to reduce their nuclear weapons stocks. Therefore, it appeared to the Indians, that the NPT was, in fact, condoning vertical proliferation at the same time that it was condemning horizontal proliferation. As K. Subrahmanyam, a prominent Indian nuclear specialist, wrote, '[T]he Indian objection was mainly against the unequal nature of the treaty and the misuse of international public opinion to subserve a policy of vertical proliferation by a few powers and obfuscation of the dangers of nuclear first use. In India's view this was not a non-proliferation treaty but a measure designed to disarm the unarmed.'[28] Given India's strident opposition, the NPT, under the state practices component of customary international law, could not be considered binding on India.

Despite India's position on the NPT, it could, however, still be considered bound by its provisions *if* there were widespread adherence to it by strategically important states. By 1974, over eighty-two states had either signed or ratified the treaty, suggesting that it had been met with worldwide support. However, neither France nor China, two of the nuclear weapons states, had ratified it. More importantly, many of the other non-adherents to the NPT were the so-called near-nuclear-weapons states. In addition to India, countries like Argentina, Brazil,

South Africa, Pakistan, and Israel had all refused to sign. The position of these near-nuclear states is crucial, because the NPT was dependent upon near-unanimity among nuclear-capable countries to be viewed as part of customary international law.[29] In addition, many countries, particularly those in the developing world, considered that the Indian explosion was, in fact, peaceful.[30] Two nuclear powers, France and the Soviet Union, even congratulated India on advancing the peaceful uses of nuclear energy.[31] These points, taken with India's refusal to sign the treaty, meant that India did not breach a binding custom of international law.

If India did not break an obligation under customary international law, did it break any bilateral agreements that had been made with Canada? More specifically, did it violate either the letter or the spirit of the 1956 CIRUS agreement? The first facet that needs to be investigated is whether the CIRUS agreement explicitly banned PNEs. As has been stated earlier, the principal safeguards measure was Article III, which stated that 'the reactor and any products resulting from its use will be employed for peaceful purposes only.' Since the term 'peaceful purposes' was never defined, Indians could argue that its PNE did not break Article III, and it could also argue that since the uranium used to produce the plutonium for the device was Indian uranium – albeit derived from CIRUS – and not Canadian uranium, it was not technically in violation of the agreement.[32] It can be concluded, then, that India did not break the letter of any agreement with Canada.

The question of whether India violated the spirit of any agreements with Canada rests on whether Canada sufficiently articulated its position on PNEs. It is indisputable that India was aware of Canada's position that there is no difference between a nuclear explosive device and a nuclear weapon. Following the signing of the NPT in 1968, Canada stated that it 'strongly supported the provision that will prohibit non-nuclear states from conducting nuclear explosions for peaceful purposes, since it maintains that military and civil nuclear explosive technologies are indistinguishable and that the development of the latter would inevitably accord a non-nuclear state a nuclear-weapon capability.'[33] Canada's position was also made perfectly clear in a letter from Prime Minister Trudeau to Prime Minister Gandhi in 1971:

The use of Canadian supplied material, equipment and facilities in India, that is, at CIRUS, RAPP I or RAPP II, or fissile material from these reactors, for the development of a nuclear explosive device would inevitably

call on our part for a reassessment of our nuclear cooperation arrangements with India, a position we would take with any other non-nuclear-
weapons state with which we have cooperation arrangements in the
nuclear field.[34]

Prime Minister Gandhi's reply did not dispute Canada's position on
PNEs:

> You have referred to the question of peaceful nuclear explosions. I entirely
> agree that the basis of the dedication of our two Governments in conclud-
> ing nuclear cooperation agreements has been the development and appli-
> cation of nuclear energy for peaceful purposes. Nuclear cooperation
> agreements between India and Canada emphasize the mutual advantage
> of development and application of nuclear energy for peaceful purposes
> and it is my sincere hope that our nuclear cooperation would not only
> continue but increase with the passing of time.
>
> My Government reiterates its commitment to the provisions contained
> in the nuclear cooperation agreements between India and Canada to
> which your Government is also committed. Our two Governments have
> acted in conformity with these agreements for the past several years. The
> obligations undertaken by our two Governments are mutual and they
> cannot be unilaterally varied. In these circumstances, it should not be
> necessary nor in our view, to interpret these agreements in a particular
> way based on the development of a hypothetical contingency.[35]

On the basis of this exchange, it can be concluded that India *did*
violate the spirit of its bilateral agreement with Canada. Therefore,
when External Affairs Minister Sharp announced the suspension of
nuclear cooperation, he was correct in stating that 'we have made it
clear in international discussions and in bilateral exchanges with India
that the creation of a nuclear explosion for so-called peaceful purposes
could not be considered as a peaceful purpose within the meaning of
our cooperative arrangements.'[36] India's violation of the spirit of a
bilateral agreement thus provided the justification the Canadian government required for the suspension of nuclear cooperation.

It is obvious that it was Canada's proliferation concerns that led to
this suspension of nuclear cooperation with India, but commercial interests still had some influence on the Canadian government at this
time. If the Canadian government had been preoccupied exclusively
with the security risk of nuclear proliferation, logically it would have

terminated rather than suspended cooperation with India in 1974. However, commercial interests apparently ruled out an outright cessation of cooperation at this time. The government hoped that it could negotiate a new safeguards agreement with India. This new agreement would have India renounce its nuclear explosion, place CIRUS under the RAPP safeguards agreement, and have India sign the NPT. This was, however, a vain hope in that Canada had been trying for twenty years to accomplish these objectives, and it was very unlikely that India would now capitulate to Canada's demands.

How would Canada's commercial interests have been affected by a termination of nuclear assistance with India in 1974? Obviously, there were the immediate economic losses: $12 million worth of heavy-water sales; a $6-million turbo generator export; and $1 million in spare parts for the RAPP program. By ending its nuclear cooperation, Canada also lost out on the opportunity to secure future nuclear exports to India. In particular, it forfeited additional supplies of heavy water and spare parts for the two RAPP reactors. Canada also gave up the possibility of supplying heavy water and spare parts for India's first indigenous power reactor, the Madras, whose design was based on the CANDU.

In addition to these immediate financial costs, Ottawa was concerned about the effects that ending nuclear assistance to India would have on Canada's ability to export reactors to other states, raising the issue of its reliability as a supplier. As Morrison and Wonder have suggested, 'the cut-off of shipments probably did more immediate harm to the Canadian nuclear industry than to India's nuclear programme.' This was primarily because the cessation may have led 'potential third world customers to question Canada's reliability as a supplier.'[37] This point cannot be overstated because, while supplier reliability is an important component in any major industrial project, it is critical in the nuclear industry. As the Canadian government's *Nuclear Policy Review* later noted:

The long lead times needed to cultivate the market, prepare bids, negotiate contracts, obtain regulatory approval, and build and commission plants require long-term, economic and political commitments to nuclear cooperation. Even after they are in service, the reactors will involve the two countries in a continuing relationship to ensure safe and efficient operation. Perceptions of the strength and stability of the vendor government's commitment to the project are essential components of the decision to purchase a nuclear reactor.[38]

In sum, while proliferation concerns were clearly the reason why nuclear cooperation was suspended with India, Canada's commercial interests did constrain it from pursuing a stronger immediate action: outright termination of assistance. Canada's commercial interests resulted in only a suspension of cooperation in 1974, with the hope that cooperation could eventually be resumed. This commercial factor prompted Canada and India to negotiate for two years in an effort to come up with a solution.

South Korea's Safeguards Agreement

When Donald Macdonald announced changes to Canada's 1974 non-proliferation policy, he stated that Canada would renegotiate its safeguards agreement with South Korea. Although a sales agreement had been signed for the CANDU export, a safeguards agreement had yet to be signed. It was assumed at the time the sale was concluded that the only applicable safeguards on Wolsung I would be the facility-specific ones monitored by the IAEA, but the Indian explosion led Canada to seek more substantial safeguards. In fact, there were some in Ottawa who wanted to stop the CANDU sale completely. However, this option was discounted for both economic and security reasons. First, it was acknowledged that the 'CANDU sale to Korea represents a significant export opportunity which would enhance Canada's reputation as an exporter of manufactured goods to the Pacific rim.' There was also a concern that 'the termination of the CANDU negotiations could damage present as well as future Canadian commercial negotiations with the ROK. The resultant loss of contracts for Canadian companies would result in severe criticism from' the Canadian nuclear industry. On the security side, it was argued that if Canada were to obtain a sale based on a stringent safeguards agreement, this 'might provide an impetus to nuclear suppliers' efforts to arrive at a more stringent international safeguards regime.' Moreover, if Canada 'refus[ed] to sell a CANDU even with stringent safeguards it could put into question the efficacy of international safeguards.'[39]

Canada decided to continue with the CANDU sale, but it terminated negotiations on the proposed sale of a clone of the NRX nuclear research reactor. In 1973, the South Koreans had inquired about purchasing an NRX clone to further its nuclear research, but the Indian explosion which relied on plutonium from CIRUS, another NRX clone, convinced Ottawa to cancel the negotiations.[40] Ottawa also presented the South

Koreans with two major safeguards demands: that they ratify the NPT and that they forego any nuclear reprocessing. South Korea had signed the NPT in 1968, but it had never ratified it. With its change in policy, Canada made NPT ratification a non-negotiable condition for continuing with the CANDU export. After a period of negotiations, and with the assistance of the Americans, the South Koreans finally ratified the NPT in March 1975. The first Canadian condition was met with some resistance, but it was achieved. However, the second condition, regarding nuclear reprocessing, proved to be even more difficult for Canadian negotiators to achieve.

In 1974, it became known that South Korea was planning to purchase a French nuclear reprocessing plant. Reprocessing separates the fission products (including plutonium) from the uranium. In this way, much of the original nuclear waste can be recycled back as fuel for the reactor. This is a great economic benefit. In addition, there are environmental benefits because reprocessing reduces the amount of nuclear waste produced by a reactor. Seoul claimed that there would be great economic savings by reprocessing its spent fuel and that the reprocessing facility would ensure greater economic security by providing South Korea with an independent source of fuel.[41] Unfortunately, reprocessing, despite its economic and environmental advantages, can also be used to develop nuclear weapons. This is because reprocessing also separates plutonium from the spent fuel rods. Since plutonium is the key ingredient for nuclear weapons, reprocessing has an obvious proliferation concern. Thus, there were grave fears in both Ottawa and Washington that the Koreans wanted this plant for military purposes. Both countries felt that there was little economic justification for the plant and so they placed strong pressure on Seoul to cancel the deal. In particular, Canada told the Koreans that despite the economic necessity of making the Wolsung I sale, Ottawa was prepared to break the deal over the issue of the French reprocessing plant.

The belief that South Korea was attempting to develop a nuclear military capability through the purchase of a reprocessing plant was given additional credibility by Korean actions during 1974–5. According to American intelligence sources, 'in 1975 the Koreans were running all over the world picking up material and equipment for a nuclear-weapons program. The reprocessing plant was practically the last thing on the list of things they needed.'[42] Furthermore, during a trip to Washington in June 1975, South Korean president Park Chung-Hee told reporters that his country was capable of building nuclear weapons.

He pointed out that while Korea was honouring the NPT, it did have a nuclear weapons potential. He later added that 'if the U.S. nuclear umbrella were to be removed, we would have to start developing our nuclear capability to save ourselves.'[43] The United States greatly aided Canada's efforts by warning the South Koreans that purchase of the reprocessing plant would damage the bilateral security relationship.[44] In the end, Seoul was forced to acquiesce and cancel plans to obtain the reprocessing plant, because it relied upon the American security blanket to protect it from the larger North Korean army.

Even though Seoul had ratified the NPT and cancelled the reprocessing plant, there were still some doubts about its commitment to nonproliferation. In both of the two incidents highlighted above, South Korea was forced to change its position because of significant outside pressure. It is true that the North Koreans represented a security threat that might have led Seoul to initiate a nuclear weapons program, but there were many other political factors that would have constrained it from pursuing that policy. First, if Seoul violated its safeguards agreements with Canada, the United States, and the IAEA, it would have resulted in the termination of all nuclear cooperation – similar to what happened to India – and its civilian nuclear program would have been devastated. Not only would the energy sector have been damaged, the entire South Korean economy would have been severely affected by the development of nuclear weapons. In addition, South Korea would have antagonized its principal economic trading and investment partners – Japan and the United States. It is likely that even if there were no economic sanctions, at the very least, there would have been some resistance in Washington and Tokyo to further assist the South Koreans by providing easy access to their economic markets. Third, it would have damaged, perhaps irreparably, its security relationship with the United States. If Washington pulled out its troops before South Korea had a fully functioning nuclear weapons system, it would be more vulnerable, particularly if it led the North Koreans to ponder a preemptive invasion. Thus, for a variety of domestic and foreign policy reasons, it was unlikely – despite some threats by senior South Korean officials – that Seoul would have pursued nuclear weapons in the mid-1970s.[45]

Now that its proliferation concerns had been resolved, Canada gave the go-ahead to sign the safeguards agreement. The agreement for the Wolsung reactor was signed on 26 January 1976, and it was the most stringent of all safeguards agreements to that time, containing several important conditions. For instance, the agreement affirmed that nuclear cooperation was for peaceful purposes only. However, Ottawa had learned its lesson from the Indian explosion and therefore ensured that all nuclear explosive devices, whether intended for peaceful uses or not, were strictly prohibited. In addition, Canada insisted upon a requirement of prior consent for retransfers of all nuclear equipment, material, facilities, fuel, or technology. It also attached its prior consent requirement for the reprocessing of all generations of fuel. To make sure that its position was well-known on this issue, Canada sent an appended diplomatic note to the agreement in which South Korea was informed that the 'Government of Canada would not be prepared, at this time' to agree to reprocessing. The agreement also contained provisions for full-scope safeguards. Finally, it stated that in the event of noncompliance, all nuclear cooperation would cease and all nuclear items provided by Canada would be returned.[46]

Argentina's Safeguards Agreements

In addition to the renegotiations with South Korea, Canada also re-opened negotiations with Argentina regarding nuclear safeguards on the Embalse nuclear reactor project. The original contract to sell a CANDU to Argentina had been signed in December 1973, and the only safeguard put in place at the time was the understanding that Argentina would sign an acceptable agreement with the IAEA. Immediately following India's nuclear explosion, however, the Canadian government began to demand that the safeguards agreement be strengthened. Canada wanted a safeguards package that would extend beyond the IAEA's normal attention to nuclear equipment and fissile material to include Canadian technology as well.[47] The first Canada–Argentina accord concerning new and improved nuclear safeguards for Embalse was completed with an exchange of notes in September 1974. The first Canadian demand was met when Argentina guaranteed that it would not use Canadian technology, material, or expertise to produce any nuclear explosive devices, peaceful or otherwise.[48]

Reaching the second accord over nuclear safeguards took much longer, and the negotiations were more difficult, because of Canada's intention to also renegotiate the Embalse's commercial contract at the same time. Argentina was going through a period of hyperinflation, and the 'escalation ceilings' provided in the original contract between AECL and its Italian partner Italimpianti and the CNEA, were found to be grossly inadequate. Ottawa determined that 'proceeding under the present terms of the contract without renegotiation would likely involve unacceptably high losses.'[49]

It was felt that renegotiation was Canada's only acceptable option because of the negative repercussions that unilateral termination of the contract would entail. First, CNEA would launch a legal suit in the hundreds of millions against AECL. Lawyers from external affairs believed that it was highly likely that Canada would lose such a suit. Second, it would hinder the efforts of Canadian firms in Argentina from obtaining future nuclear orders. Future contracts for Embalse's spare parts, technical upgrades, and spin-off projects would all be jeopardized. Officials were also concerned that non-nuclear areas of Canadian investment – 'a major hydroelectric project, an iron pelletizing plant, and other projects' – might 'be affected by Argentina retaliatory action.' Third, it would affect Canada's efforts at developing closer bilateral and multilateral links with Latin America. Would Mexico and Venezuela, countries currently being wooed by AECL, still be interested in the CANDU system after Canada terminated the Argentine contract? Fourth, Canada's nuclear components suppliers might start to withdraw from the industry. If, for example, Babcock and Wilcox and Sulzer Bingham Pumps decided to leave the nuclear industry, where would the steam generators, pressure tubes, and pumps for future CANDUs – for either the domestic or foreign market – come from? Would these have to be imported? Moreover, these companies also exported their nuclear-related products. This meant that, in the event of a massive exiting by Canadian component suppliers as a result of a unilateral abrogation of AECL's contract with CNEA, Canada's balance of payments would face a double whammy – higher imports of nuclear components and lower exports of nuclear components. This was a particular worry for Canadian officials because the cancellation of Embalse would come so soon after the cancellation of nuclear cooperation with India and Pakistan.[50]

There were, indeed, important economic reasons for requiring a renegotiation of Embalse's commercial contract. The problem was, despite Canadian efforts at divorcing the commercial and security issues, there were 'some Argentinian officials' who regarded the 'insistence on stringent safeguards in part as an effort to exert leverage on the commercial renegotiation.'[51] Although, a renegotiated commercial contract was achieved between AECL, Italimpianti, and CNEA on 12 March 1976, the perceived linkage with the safeguards agreement likely meant that Canada did not obtain an optimal result.

The other reason why reaching the second safeguards accord was so difficult was Canada's intention to upgrade its non-proliferation policy as expressed in the December 1976 announcement referred to earlier. Ottawa's principal demand was for a veto over any fuel reprocessing in Embalse, whether the fuel was of Canadian origin or not. The reprocessing issue was a major point of contention between Canada and Argentina, but finally on 30 January 1976 a strengthened safeguards agreement was signed. It proclaimed that nuclear cooperation would be for peaceful purposes only, and that provision included a prohibition on nuclear explosive devices derived from Canadian-supplied items. Canada would hold a veto on any attempts by Argentina to retransfer nuclear equipment, material, facilities, fuel, or technology. This veto would also hold for the reprocessing of all generations of fuel. The agreement established that the nuclear safeguards on Embalse would be administered by the IAEA. Finally, in the event that Argentina did not comply with the requirements contained in the agreement, Canada would cease all nuclear cooperation.[52]

This safeguards agreement was based on the one reached with the South Koreans, but there were some notable differences. First, Buenos Aires had not been forced, as Seoul was, to sign and ratify the NPT. Second, the 'no nuclear explosive devices' clause was restricted to items of Canadian origin only. Conceivably, Argentina could use its other reactors, like the Atucha I which had been purchased from West Germany in 1968 and had become operational in 1974, to develop and test nuclear weapons. Finally, in the event of non-compliance, Argentina was not required to return all Canadian supplied nuclear items. This meant that even if Argentina violated its safeguards agreement, it could still keep the reactor.

Why was the Argentina agreement weaker than the one reached with the South Koreans? This did not make much sense. Was it not logical that the safeguards agreement with Seoul, because it came first, would be the template for any future agreements, including with Buenos Aires? Canada was in the process of strengthening its nuclear non-proliferation policy as a consequence of the Indian explosion, so why was it downgrading its standards only months later? What message would this send to the countries with which it was still negotiating, notably India and Pakistan?

One possible explanation was the role of the United States. The United States had greatly assisted Canada in convincing South Korea to strengthen the safeguards on its nuclear program. Washington was successful in this instance because of the bilateral security relationship it had with Seoul. However, in the case of the Argentineans, the United States lacked such an influential bargaining tool. In short, Canada was on its own when it tried to renegotiate the Embalse safeguards agreement. Another possibility was that the international nuclear non-proliferation regime was still evolving. The NPT came into force in 1970, but five years later, the nuclear suppliers still did not adhere to a common standard. The Nuclear Suppliers Group started off in 1975 as informal meetings in London between the world's major nuclear suppliers: Canada, France, Japan, the United Kingdom, the United States, and the USSR, and West Germany. However, its guidelines for nuclear exports were not agreed to until 1977. This meant that there would be different safeguards applied to every reactor export depending upon who the buyer was and who the seller was.

The lack of U.S. pressure on Argentina and the fluctuating international non-proliferation regime may indeed have played a role in Canada's decision to accept a nuclear safeguards agreement with Argentina that was less stringent than the one reached with South Korea. However, recently declassified Privy Council documents reveal that there was one factor that dominated Ottawa's decision-making: Canadian efforts at strengthening its nuclear safeguards agreement with Argentina were greatly hindered by its concurrent efforts at renegotiating Embalse's commercial contract. For example, during a 1975 cabinet meeting, the minister of external affairs, Allen MacEachen, emphasized that 'Canada must not be seen to be holding up safeguards for commercial reasons.' Don Jamieson, the minister of industry, trade, and commerce, 'agreed that we can't use safeguards to get out of bad commercial deals.'[53] It was this fear that Canadian motives might be misconstrued that allowed Argentina to negotiate a less stringent safeguards agreement. For example, in a 1975 cabinet document explaining why Argentina was refusing Canada's tougher safeguards proposal, it was admitted that the perception of the commercial/safeguards linkage 'no doubt may have influenced' the refusal by Buenos Aires to accept the 'safeguards requirements.'[54]

The strengthening of the Embalse safeguards agreement, even if it was weaker than the one reached with the South Koreans, illustrated the increased awareness of nuclear proliferation in Canada. However, the presence of commercial interests was still lurking in the background of the deal. In many respects, it is remarkable that the Argentina sale went ahead at all, for there was substantial pressure on the government to announce a moratorium on all CANDU exports (in the wake of the Indian explosion), especially to Argentina. Critics wanted to cancel the Embalse sale for three reasons.

First, was the extent that Embalse benefited from Canadian government subsidies. In trying to make the sale, Ottawa included a very generous financial package with a $130-million EDC loan at a very low interest rate. However, a ceiling of 25 per cent was placed on the inflation that Argentina would have to take into account when paying AECL, and, therefore, when Argentina suffered hyperinflation of 300 per cent, the resulting loss to Canada was in the tens of millions. In the end, despite the renegotiation of the commercial contract, Canada lost over $130 million on the 'sale' of the CANDU to Argentina.[55] The Canadian nuclear industry justified the loss of money by portraying Embalse as a 'loss-leader.' AECL argued that the Argentine sale would depict Canada as a 'viable reactor exporter' to potential purchasers thus ensuring that there would be opportunities for Canadian component suppliers in the future.[56] In looking at these commercial arguments, one cannot help but think back to the earlier deals with India and Pakistan, when the same arguments were made. Had nothing changed in twenty years that Canada still had to use loss-leaders to export the CANDU?

The second issue was the AECL sales agent scandal that erupted in 1975. This scandal had been brewing for a year, but came to a head when the Auditor General tabled his year-end report in the House of Commons on 22 November 1976. In his report, he brought to the attention of the government that there had been payments by AECL's foreign sales agents to the Argentineans, which the report described as inadequately documented. In the case of Embalse, the auditor general had questions about the authorization of a $2.4-million payment to 'a commercial agent' relating to services rendered during negotiations over an extended period. This payment, which was made on the instructions of Ita-limpianti, AECL's Italian partner in the sale, was not supported by any agreement or invoice on the part of the agent.[57] At the time, nobody in Canada seemed to know who the agent was, but subsequent information revealed that José Ber Galbard, then Argentine minister of economic affairs, was the recipient of the $2.4-million payment, plus an additional $1.4-million worth of payments.[58] This scandal led to investigations by both the Parliamentary Standing Committee on Public Accounts and the RCMP to determine why Canadian taxpayers' money was being used in this fashion. While the investigations did not reveal anything new, and no criminal charges were laid, it did give the scandal additional prominence, as both AECL and the Trudeau government faced much public criticism. The AECL sales agent scandal led to an organizational shake-up at AECL, and seriously damaged the reputation of Canada's nuclear export program. As *Maclean's* magazine so aptly pointed out, 'if we have to loan people money at subsidized interest rates to buy CANDU at prices below cost and then bribe them to do it, how great is the accomplishment?'[59]

The third issue was related to Argentina's internal crisis compounded by the undeclared civil war that hit its peak in 1974–6. Canada had concerns about Argentina's internal stability, even before the Embalse contract was signed in 1973, and these fears were eventually realized when the fighting started in earnest in early 1974. Although the state of terror hit its peak following the 24 March 1976 military coup – several months after the Embalse safeguards agreement was signed – there was much extrajudicial killing during 1974 and 1975. In particular, the military junta targeted left-wing political activists and labour leaders for repression.

Despite the calls for a cancellation of the Embalse sale particularly because of the political situation, it did go through, largely as a result of Canada's commercial interests in concluding the transaction. Canada was willing to settle for the minimum level of safeguards upgrading rather than pushing, as it did in the cases of South Korea, India, and Pakistan, for full-scope NPT safeguards. This was because the economic necessities that originally justified the export of the CANDU in 1973 were still present during the safeguards negotiations. As the president of AECL, Lorne Gray, explained:

Some of us (at AECL) came to the conclusion that if we did not sell a CANDU system to a recognized country in direct competition with somebody, other than the deal in India and the deal in Pakistan, the last one was mainly a CIDA deal which the world did not really recognize as being a competitive programme, that the system we had developed, the CANDU system, would finally fall by the wayside. It could not be supported on a Canadian programme alone. We in the staff were absolutely sure of this. We might have six plants running in Canada and there would be 600 light water reactors around in the world, and when you get out to the Western utilities they were more likely to go American than they were to stay Canadian. Whereas if we had some countries – *we did not like Argentina, but it happened to be the only game in town*. It is an advancing country. It would be much better to sell in the United States, or Germany, or France, or Italy. These are the ones we looked at, but Argentina came along and became convinced that a natural uranium reactor was the right thing, so we concentrated on it because we thought it was essential to maintain the CANDU system in the future. We may have been wrong.[60]

India: Termination of Nuclear Cooperation

On 18 May 1976, two years to the day after the Indian nuclear explosion, Secretary of State for External Affairs Allan MacEachen stood up in the House of Commons and announced that the government had terminated all nuclear cooperation with India.[61] In doing so, he acknowledged that Ottawa's efforts to renegotiate a safeguards agreement with India had failed. Starting in 1975, there had been intense Canadian–Indian negotiations over the possible resumption of nuclear assistance in order to finish construction on the RAPP reactors. New Delhi threatened that if Canada terminated nuclear assistance, it would result in a cancellation of safeguards on the RAPP reactors. While obviously concerned about India's threats, Canada's objectives in negotiating were to place strengthened safeguards on India's entire nuclear program, including CIRUS and the indigenous Madras reactors (based on the CANDU design), and to obtain a pledge from India to refrain from further PNEs. In response to Canada's demands, India remained consistent with its policy on nuclear safeguards and refused to place additional safeguards on CIRUS and its other reactors. Instead, India promised that it would not set off another PNE while work continued on RAPP II (over the next eighteen months) and that it would not develop a PNE using plutonium from the RAPP reactors.[62]

It seemed apparent that the Canadian and Indian positions were miles apart and an acceptable safeguards agreement could not be reached. This is why it was such a surprise when, in March 1976, a tentative agreement was reached between the negotiators, led on the Canadian side by Prime Minister Trudeau's special foreign policy adviser, Ivan Head. An initialled draft agreement was submitted to the Canadian cabinet. However, despite this hopeful development, on 18 May 1976, the government announced the termination of nuclear assistance to India. What happened in the eight weeks between March and May to explain this reversal? Ashok Kapur has suggested several possible hypotheses, two of which seem most likely.[63]

The first possibility is that the Head delegation may have overstepped its authority in initialling an agreement in which Canada's major positions had not been met. Although the initialled agreement covered most of the guidelines stipulated in the December 1974 nuclear policy, it did leave out the requirement that safeguards would cover 'all nuclear facilities and equipment using Canadian supplied technology.' This had not been included in the Head agreement because the 'Indians claimed that Indian-built reactors were no longer Canadian even though the original technology had been Canadian.' In other words, India would not accept the fact that, because its Madras reactors were based on the CANDU design, Canada could demand that they be subject to international nuclear inspections. But the Canadian cabinet would not agree to this exception. When MacEachen told the House of Commons that Canada had terminated its nuclear assistance with India, he reiterated that 'the Canadian Government ... could agree to make new nuclear shipments only on an undertaking by India that Canadian supplies, whether of technology, nuclear equipment or materials, whether past or future, shall not be used for the manufacture of any nuclear explosive devices ... this undertaking would require that all nuclear facilities, involving Canadian technology, in India be safeguarded.'[64] Since MacEachen was simply adhering to the guidelines established in the December 1974 statement, it is possible that the Head delegation overstepped its mandate when it agreed to India's demands concerning the Madras reactors.

The second hypothesis is that the government feared a massive outcry, both by the opposition and the public, if nuclear assistance were resumed. The Head agreement certainly did generate a reaction within Canada. The opposition Progressive Conservatives attacked the government in Parliament during a memorable House debate on 23 March 1976. Allan Lawrence, PC critic for external affairs, put forward the following motion: 'That this House condemns the government for increasing the threat posed to mankind by the proliferation of nuclear weapons, and in particular by its present negotiations to resume nuclear assistance to India.'[65] A longer transcript of Lawrence's speech in the House of Commons reveals the depth of the vehement opposition to any further nuclear cooperation with India. In opening the debate on the resumption of nuclear assistance with India, Lawrence attempted

> to drag out of the minister, if we can, for the first time some rational explanation, if one exists, for the intended resumption of nuclear assistance to India; and finally if, as I suspect, there is no rational explanation,

to embarrass those government members who are either unthinking enough or partisan and disciplined enough to vote willy-nilly for the government's resumption of nuclear aid to India, the timing of which, the circumstances of which and the merits of which are simply incomprehensible to the people of Canada and to the ations of the western world.[66]

Opposition to the resumption of nuclear cooperation with India extended to many members of the Liberal caucus and even the cabinet. In their foreign policy memoirs, Trudeau and Head wrote that there were 'several cabinet ministers who remained either outraged or deeply disappointed at what they regarded as duplicity on the part of the Indians.'[67] The government also had to consider public opinion if it were to resume nuclear cooperation with India. There had been widespread anger in Canada at India's 1974 explosion. It was this sense of anger and betrayal, which was one of the reasons for Canada's original decision to suspend all nuclear assistance with that country. To have recommended further nuclear cooperation without at least achieving all of its goals for safeguards would undoubtedly have set off a strong public reaction and that could have contributed to the government's decision to back away from the initialled agreement and terminate cooperation.

The factors that Kapur identified quite certainly played a role in Canada's decision, but there were further factors that led to the cessation of cooperation, in particular, the evaporation of trust of India among Canadian officials. There were many inside external affairs who went by the maxim 'Once bitten, twice shy.' Some of the top officials in the 1974–6 period, including Minister Mitchell Sharp and Under-Secretary Gordon Ritchie, had been involved in the Indian reactor sales of the 1950s and 1960s and there was among them a sense of having been betrayed.[68] Many external affairs officers who had served with the Indians on the three Indo-China International Commissions felt further 'anti-India feeling.' A 1965 interview between Marcel Cadieux, the Under-Secretary for External Affairs, and the Indian High Commissioner revealed the growing distance between Canada and India: 'a whole generation of Cdn officials had served in Commissions and ... their experience had affected Cdn-Indian relations. Their views on Indian policy had become much more concrete and detailed and this process had had a very sobering effect. Quality of relationship between Indian and Cdn officials had changed as a result of experience in IndoChina.'[69] Ten years later, according to Ivan Head, many external affairs officers still 'distrusted their Indian counterparts.'[70]

This distrust of Indian officials extended right to the top of the Indian political system when Prime Minister Indira Gandhi declared a state of national emergency in 1975. Gandhi set aside the civil and political rights of the world's largest democracy in the wake of violent street demonstrations after a state high court had found her guilty of corrupt electoral practices. Gandhi's actions were widely condemned throughout most of India and the international community as an arbitrary exercise of power. The general election was postponed until 1977. More importantly, for over a year and a half, fundamental freedoms were suspended as Gandhi heavily censored the domestic press, ousted most foreign correspondents, suspended civil liberties, and sent thousands of political opponents to jail without trial. Numerous opposition members of Parliament, including a man who would later become prime minister, Atal Vajpayee, were among those who were incarcerated for standing up to Gandhi's illegitimate actions. Thus, when Canada was negotiating with India over the future of their nuclear relationship, it was hard to picture a fellow parliamentary democracy in the British Commonwealth tradition. Instead, Canadians must have viewed the Gandhi government as a personalized dictatorship.

The final rationale for terminating nuclear cooperation with India was that it might serve as a deterrent to other near-nuclear-weapons states from exploding their own nuclear devices. Canada's concern about the effect India's test would have on other states was a key component of its decision to suspend its nuclear cooperation immediately. In the suspension announcement, External Affairs Minister Mitchell Sharp stated:

> Canada was concerned as to the effect that India's action – whatever its motivation – would have on international efforts to limit and control the proliferation of nuclear exploration technology, for which there can be no distinction between peaceful and potential military applications. For all intents and purposes ... India now has developed the capability of producing a nuclear weapon ... The development of this technology by India is bound to have serious and widespread repercussions throughout Asia and the world.[71]

After taking such a strong stand in 1974, how could Canada reverse its position in 1976? If Canada had resumed nuclear assistance to India, then other near-nuclear-states could have pointed 'to the resumption of Canadian aid as Canadian condonation of India's explosion.'[72]

Although the arguments in favour of terminating nuclear assistance to India were persuasive, there were some plausible security concerns which pointed to the desirability of a resumption of nuclear assistance. In the 23 March 1976 debate in the House of Commons, External Affairs Minister Allan MacEachen outlined these arguments. The first issue was the RAPP II reactor that was still under construction. As MacEachen explained, 'under the agreement with India that we entered into, we have an obligation to complete the shipment to the reactor, both of material and fuel.' If Canada cancelled the construction of RAPP II, India might react by allowing 'the safeguard system at that reactor to disappear entirely.' This was important because RAPP I, when operating at full capacity, could produce enough plutonium for five nuclear bombs a year, while RAPP II could produce 11 bombs.[73] The argument was also raised that continuing nuclear cooperation might act as a restraint on further Indian explosions. This argument seems a bit naïve and ridiculous given that nuclear cooperation prior to 1974 had not constrained India from making its first nuclear explosion. Nevertheless, MacEachen raised this possibility by asking rhetorically, 'Would the completion of our particular project with India be an inhibiting or delaying factor regarding a further explosion in India? Would we have any effect or, indeed, would a second explosion be delayed or be out of bounds in India?'[74]

In the end, these arguments were discounted. First, Ottawa contended that the Indians had already violated the nuclear agreements when they exploded their nuclear device, and therefore Canada was not bound by the RAPP agreements. Second, the government took the view that India's threats to forswear IAEA safeguards on the RAPP reactors were a bluff. Third, Ottawa was sure that the United States, which was the supplier of India's TARAPUR light-water reactors, would be able to deter India from both renouncing its nuclear safeguards and exploding additional PNEs. Ottawa knew that Washington was just as outraged by the Indian nuclear explosion, particularly because of the unauthorized role that American heavy water had played in the explosion. Ottawa's belief in the Americans was well founded because, in 1978, the United States passed the Nuclear Non-Proliferation Act, which significantly strengthened its nuclear export controls. Finally, Ottawa was also convinced that the Soviet Union, which had become India's sole supplier of heavy water after Canada terminated its nuclear exports, would assist the United States in ensuring that India's nuclear program remained peaceful. In fact, the USSR was able to attach indefinite safeguards to both RAPP I and II.[75] In short, Canada believed that India's nuclear program was not yet self-sufficient enough that it 'could act with complete impunity.'[76]

In a 1999 article, Louis A. Delvoie wrote that the 'ineffectiveness' of Canada's response to the 1974 Indian test was 'eloquently demonstrated by the latest series of tests' in 1998.[77] However, Delvoie's logic is severely flawed in that there was a twenty-four-year gap between tests. Where is the ineffectiveness in substantially slowing down the rate of Indian nuclear proliferation? In fact, contrary to Delvoie's assertion, Canada's actions did have an adverse effect on India's nuclear program. By terminating its nuclear cooperation, Canada forced India to pay a hefty admission fee for joining the nuclear club. Canada's nuclear sanctions can be measured through its effects on both the RAPP projects as well as on India's indigenous nuclear industry. RAPP II was originally scheduled to be operational by 1975, but due to the suspension and eventual termination of nuclear assistance, it was not completed until 1981 – six years behind schedule. India may have been able to finish RAPP II, but there have been lingering effects on RAPP II's performance as a result of Canadian nuclear sanctions. Both RAPP units, as Richard Cronin has commented, have 'suffered repeated breakdowns due to deficient engineering quality control, a shortage of heavy water that has prevented the units from reaching their design capacity and inefficient operations.'[78]

The industry standard for measuring nuclear reactor efficiency is through its capacity load factor percentage. This is the reactor's actual electricity production divided by what the reactor would produce if it always operated at its design rating. Use of this device highlights the problems that the RAPP reactors have encountered as a result of the ending of Canadian nuclear cooperation. RAPP II has had a lifetime load factor of 20.3 per cent. This makes it, according to the rankings put out by the *World Nuclear Industry Handbook*, a dismal 334 out of the world's 349 nuclear power reactors.[79] RAPP I, which went online in 1973, a year before the imposition of Canadian nuclear sanctions, has fared marginally better. Its lifetime load factor is 50.6 per cent. However, even RAPP I's efficiency is significantly lower than the median for power reactors which is 68 per cent.[80]

In addition to the effects on the reactors that they bought from Canada, the rest of India's civilian nuclear energy program has suffered as a result of the 1974 explosion. When Canada announced its sanctions, some observers replied that it did not matter because India had developed an indigenous nuclear capability, but evidence has been presented since that the Indian nuclear program continues to need foreign support. There are indications that India is dissatisfied with the domestic power reactor technology that it has developed, which is far behind the state of the art available from the major suppliers.[81] Further confirmation that India's nuclear program has suffered since Canada's termination of assistance comes from Indian writers. Dhirendra Sharma, in *India's Nuclear Estate*, has written that 'the Pokharan explosion ... led to India's nuclear technological debacle when all external cooperation was withdrawn. The post-Pokharan fall out delayed India's nuclear projects by 10 to 15 years.'[82] The efficiency of all the 'CANDU-clones' has been quite weak. Five of the six Madras reactors have performed under 50 per cent.[83] The inefficiency of the Indian nuclear industry – due in good measure to the termination of Canadian nuclear cooperation – explains why it provides only 1.89 per cent of India's electricity.[84]

A further complication was the fact that, because the RAPP and Madras reactors were CANDU-designed, they needed heavy water to work. This forced India to import heavy water from the Soviet Union. Ironically, while India had consistently refused to increase safeguards on its nuclear program during its negotiations with Canada, when they were forced to go to the Soviets for heavy water they had to accept strict safeguards. The Soviet Union insisted that a stringent IAEA safeguards agreement be attached to Indian facilities and material exposed to Soviet-supplied heavy water, including the Madras reactors, thus forcing expanded safeguards coverage that India had originally tried to avoid.[85]

Pakistan: Termination of Nuclear Cooperation

In implementing its strengthened nuclear non-proliferation policy, Canada terminated its nuclear cooperation not only with India but also with Pakistan. In announcing the revised policy on 22 December 1976, External Affairs Minister Don Jamieson stated that 'for all practical purposes the nuclear co-operation between Canada and Pakistan is effectively at an end.'[86] This announcement signalled the termination of two years of unsuccessful safeguards negotiations with Pakistan that had begun soon after the Indian nuclear explosion.

In 1971, Islamabad attempted to crush a secessionist movement in East Pakistan. In the ensuing bloodbath, millions of Bengali refugees fled to India. This led India to launch a military intervention in East

Pakistan against the government forces. The result was a humiliating defeat for Islamabad. Not only were its armed forces shown to be grossly inadequate but it also lost East Pakistan, which declared its independence as Bangladesh. As the British historian Hugh Trevor-Roper wrote, 'in December 1971, Pakistan was divided, defeated, demoralized, and in the eyes of the world, disgraced.'[87] Pakistan's continual losses to India in conventional wars provided a very strong incentive for it to consider developing nuclear weapons.

In the aftermath of its defeat, Ali Bhutto assumed the presidency of Pakistan. Bhutto had been the strongest proponent for Pakistan to develop a nuclear weapons capability during the 1960s, and now he was in a position to ensure that this was indeed done. According to Steve Weissman and Herbert Krosney, two well-respected investigative journalists who wrote *The Islamic Bomb* in 1981, it was during a meeting at Multan in January 1972, a month after taking power, that Bhutto announced that 'Pakistan would begin a national crash program to get the bomb.'[88] Pakistan proceeded to conduct secret meetings with Libya, Saudi Arabia, and the Gulf States in its search for the 'Islamic Bomb.' One direction that Pakistan was pursuing was the diversion of plutonium from KANUPP.[89] It is estimated that KANUPP, at full capacity, can produce enough plutonium for six nuclear bombs a year.[90]

The activities of Pakistan post-1972 did not go unnoticed by the international community. For example, J.G. Hadwen, Canada's ambassador to Pakistan in 1974, had admitted that Ottawa knew 'that nuclear weapons research was being conducted at a heavily protected facility on the outskirts of Islamabad.'[91] Now that India had broken through the nuclear glass ceiling, these fears about the extent of Pakistan's nuclear weapons program were magnified. Ottawa doubted that the safeguards agreement that had been signed with Pakistan over the KANUPP reactor would be sufficient to prevent it from following India's lead and exploding its own nuclear device. Pakistani leaders heightened this concern through the public statements they made in the aftermath of the Indian explosion. On 19 May 1974, Prime Minister Ali Bhutto called the explosion a 'fateful development,' a 'threat' to Pakistan's security, and said that 'a more grave and serious event ... has not taken place in the history of Pakistan. The explosion has introduced a qualitative change in the situation' between Pakistan and India. Bhutto also stated that Pakistan would not succumb to 'nuclear blackmail,' and that it would not accept Indian domination of the subcontinent or of the Kashmir situation. In closing, Bhutto asserted that Pakistan could never sign a non-war pact with India because of its recent nuclear explosion. Such a pact would mean capitulation on the part of Pakistan.[92] These inflammatory statements by Bhutto echoed his earlier, more famous, quote that 'if India builds the bomb, we will eat grass or leaves, even go hungry, but we will get one of our own.'[93] This type of reaction from Islamabad, combined with the tragic history of Pakistani–Indian relations gave pause to the Canadian government.

In 1973, Canada had reached an agreement with Pakistan for the purchase of a fuel fabrication plant. A $1.7-million interest-free loan for the $3.5-million plant was to be supplied, but the Indian explosion of 18 May 1974, changed that situation.[94] In November of that year, Canada informed Pakistan that it would not negotiate a new fuel contract for the KANUPP reactor until a strengthened safeguards agreement which precluded PNEs was arranged. When Pakistan refused, Canada suspended shipments of spare parts for KANUPP and cancelled the export of the fuel fabrication plant.

Negotiations between Canada and Pakistan continued throughout 1975, but a new and more serious issue then emerged: Pakistan's intention to purchase a French reprocessing plant. Islamabad had signed contracts with the French engineering firm Saint-Gobain Techniques Nouvelles (SGN), which would provide the Pakistanis with the basic design of the nuclear reprocessing plant. SGN would also conduct most of the start-up procedures for the facility. As with the South Koreans, Ottawa felt that a reprocessing plant was uneconomical for Pakistan, and that its real interest in acquiring the plant lay in its military applications. If the Canadian government was not already uneasy about Pakistan, the reprocessing deal with France certainly made it so. During its negotiations with Islamabad, Ottawa's position was that it would have to retain its veto over KANUPP's spent fuel being reprocessed and have that veto extended to Pakistan's entire nuclear program. In addition, Pakistan would have to renounce the option of termination written into the original 1959 Nuclear Cooperation Agreement, and instead would have to accept whatever new safeguards were agreed upon throughout KANUPP's lifetime. Finally, Canada required that there would be yearly reviews, with IAEA participation, of its nuclear safeguards arrangements with Pakistan.[95]

Pakistan agreed with the Canadian proposal for mandatory reviews of nuclear safeguards, since these would make the agreement renegotiable and allow for new conditions each year. However, it was not prepared to renounce its option to terminate the 1959 agreement without an accompanying removal of Canada's veto over KANUPP fuel reprocessing. Further, Pakistan wanted assurances of continued supply of spare parts and fuel for KANUPP and the delivery of the fuel fabrication plant from Canada.[96]

It appeared that Pakistan and Canada were at a deadlock in their safeguards negotiations, but there was hope that during Prime Minister Bhutto's visit to Canada in February 1976 an agreement could be reached. During his visit, Bhutto indicated that Pakistan would allow stronger safeguards on KANUPP, and conceded that Canada would have the right to terminate all bilateral assistance, even foreign aid, if Pakistan ever exploded a nuclear device.[97] However, he rejected all attempts to place safeguards on non-Canadian items. In particular, Pakistan would not allow Canadian safeguards on its proposed French reprocessing plant or on its proposed second reactor, the CHASMA, which it had purchased from China.

On 4 December 1976 Canada presented Pakistan with an ultimatum in the form of three options:

1 Canada would provide fuel and other support services for KANUPP for ten years and supply the fuel fabrication plant under two conditions – Pakistan must not acquire the French reprocessing plant, and must improve the existing safeguards to ensure that all nuclear materials provided by Canada would be used for peaceful purposes only.
2 Canada would provide fuel for KANUPP for five years, if Pakistan acquired the reprocessing plant, but did agree to strengthened safeguards. However, neither the fuel fabrication facility would be shipped, nor would KANUPP's spent fuel be reprocessed.
3 Canada would provide fuel for KANUPP for two years if Pakistan acquired the reprocessing plant and refused to grant Canada the desired veto over the reprocessing of Canadian origin spent fuel, but agreed to more stringent safeguards. Again, the fuel fabrication plant would not be shipped under this option.[98]

Pakistan was given only a week to decide. On 13 December 1976, it responded to Canada's demands. On certain issues, Pakistan was willing to accede to the Canadian position. For example, Pakistan would give an 'explicit assurance' that it would refrain from all nuclear explosions. It would also allow strengthened Canadian safeguards on all nuclear items of Canadian origin. Pakistan also recognized that all of

KANUPP's spent fuel, after reprocessing, would remain under Canadian safeguards.[99] However, on other issues, the Pakistanis would not budge. Islamabad emphatically rejected Ottawa's demands for Canadian safeguards over Pakistan's entire nuclear program and that those safeguards remain in force throughout KANUPP's lifetime, even if Canada terminated its nuclear cooperation.[100] Given Canada's strengthened position on nuclear non-proliferation, it could not agree to Pakistan's proposals and on 22 December 1976 nuclear cooperation was terminated.

It was probably inevitable that Canada would terminate its nuclear cooperation with Pakistan following India's detonation of its nuclear device. Given the rising importance of Canada's proliferation concerns, it was unlikely that it would allow cooperation to continue without additional and stronger nuclear safeguards. It was also just as likely that Pakistan would never allow new safeguards to be applied to its nuclear program. As Robert Morrison and Edward Wonder point out, 'it was inconceivable that Pakistan would bind itself with all-encompassing safeguards while India remained free to proceed along the nuclear weapons path.'[101]

Of all the cases that have been studied in this chapter, Canada's commercial interests played the least role in the Pakistan termination. It might be possible to argue that, as in the Indian situation, it was commercial interests that persuaded the Canadian government to at least negotiate with Pakistan for two years rather than terminate all cooperation in 1974. However, while there were some economic benefits that could accrue from continued nuclear cooperation with Pakistan – supplies of fuel and spare parts, the fuel fabrication facility, and the possibility of being the supplier for CHASMA – these were not the main reasons why Ottawa was prepared to go through the labourious process of attempting to negotiate new safeguards. The principal reason, besides a possibly naive belief that Canada would convince Pakistan to accept strengthened nuclear safeguards, was that Pakistan had not broken any agreement, bilateral or otherwise, as was the case with India. Thus, Ottawa lacked clear ground for terminating the Pakistani–Canadian nuclear cooperation agreement.

Indeed, Pakistan argued passionately that Canada's actions were not justified. Following Canada's decision to terminate nuclear cooperation, Minister of State for Defence and Foreign Affairs Aziz Ahmed stated that the Canadian decision was 'arbitrary' and constituted the 'violation of its three bilateral agreement[s] for cooperation with Pakistan in peaceful uses of atomic energy.' Ahmed also said that these agreements 'envisaged termination of cooperation by Canada only if Pakistan were to violate its undertaking not to use Canadian supplies and assistance to further a military purpose.' Finally, Ahmed pointed out that Pakistan had 'scrupulously honoured' all of its nuclear arrangements with Canada, and that Canada's actions were 'totally unwarranted.'[102]

Pakistan argued that it was being punished for India's crime. As the *Pakistan Times* editorialized, 'Canada, betrayed by India and publicly acknowledging its inability to influence her ... unaccountably sought to bill all that to Pakistan with interest.'[103] Even the Canadian government itself seemed to acknowledge that perhaps it was not entirely justified in terminating its nuclear cooperation with Pakistan. The external affairs minister, in his 22 December 1976 announcement regarding safeguards policy stated that 'with regard to retroactivity, the question becomes one of legality in terms of the contracts which are already in place and the like. It was not deemed by the Government of Canada to be in the best interests of the country to abrogate or in any way change contracts which in some instances had been entered into a long time ago with, of course, the exception of the Pakistan one.'[104] Despite the complaints of the Pakistanis, Canada did have the legal right, under its 1959 nuclear cooperation agreement with Pakistan, to end its cooperation by giving the Pakistanis six months notice.[105] It thus appears to have been this need to give notice that led to Canada's attempts at bilateral negotiations.

However, to focus on whether or not the termination was legal would be to miss the central point. Canada's rationale for cancelling the agreement was its fear that Pakistan would develop a nuclear bomb in response to India's nuclear explosion and this illustrates the increasing impact of proliferation concerns on Canada's CANDU export policy. In effect, Canada terminated what had previously been a mutually beneficial arrangement because of fears of what Pakistan *might* do, not what it had done.

Canada's termination of nuclear cooperation with Pakistan, just as in the Indian case, has seriously damaged Pakistan's nuclear program. In fact, because KANUPP was Pakistan's only operational power reactor, Canada possessed a much greater ability to inflict pain through its nuclear sanctions. When KANUPP became operational in 1972, the Pakistan Atomic Energy Commission (PAEC) suggested that because of the 'exhaustive training' of their nuclear scientists and engineers that 'the KANUPP operating team is fully capable of running the plant efficiently.'[106] Since 1977, KANUPP has consistently performed very poorly. As Richard Cronin has noted, KANUPP 'has been operating at a sharply reduced level due to [the] cutoff in Canadian fuel supplies.'[107] According to the IAEA, KANUPP's lifetime load factor percentage has been only 28.3 per cent,[108] and it has supplied less than 1 per cent of Pakistan's electricity.[109] As PAEC now acknowledges, KANUPP must be judged as unsuccessful given the 'inadequate training of operators' and the frequent 'equipment failures.'[110]

The period 1974–6 saw a significant shift in Canada's CANDU export policy. Prior to the May 1974 Indian nuclear explosion, Canada's economic and political interests dominated all other foreign policy objectives, but by December 1976, proliferation concerns were clearly dominant. This shift did not happen immediately, rather there was an increasing focus on proliferation issues over this period. This shift in emphasis was apparent in the evolution of Canada's non-proliferation policy in the two years between December 1974 and December 1976. Not only did Canada strengthen its policy, it also made retroactive changes in its safeguards arrangements with countries where CANDU exports had already been concluded. Canada pressured both Argentina and South Korea into accepting more stringent nuclear safeguards on reactors that had been sold only months before the Indian explosion. Canada also attempted to strengthen nuclear safeguards on reactors it had previously sold to India and Pakistan, and when these countries refused, Canada terminated all of its nuclear cooperation. By taking these concrete steps to enforce its new non-proliferation policy, the Canadian government showed the increased importance attached to security concerns in its CANDU export policy.

It is important, however, to acknowledge that while proliferation concerns increased in importance during this period, the same cannot be said for Canada's other foreign policy objectives. For example, the AECL's sales agent scandal did not lead to renegotiation or cancellation of CANDU contracts in either South Korea or Argentina. Likewise, the 1974 military coup in Argentina did not lead Canada to consider suspension, or even termination, of nuclear cooperation. There was no spillover from nuclear non-proliferation to Canada's other foreign policy considerations. In short, if a country accepted Canada's new safeguards policy, then Canada's economic and political arguments would continue to dominate issues like human rights, environmental considerations, and the role of government subsidies.

6 Suffering the Consequences, 1977–1989

By the end of 1976, it was evident that Canada's security concern over the threat of nuclear proliferation had become the dominant foreign policy goal related to CANDU exports, overriding any commercial interests. The measures that Canada had taken between 1974 and 1976 to strengthen its nuclear non-proliferation policy thus had a major impact during the 1977–89 period. Canada was obliged to face the economic consequences for its unilateral actions during the preceding three years. Throughout this period, Canada had to confront the question of whether or not CANDU exports were compatible with a stringent nuclear non-proliferation policy.

From an exporter's point of view, Canada's 1976 non-proliferation policy was implemented at probably the worst possible time because, starting in the late 1970s and continuing throughout the 1980s, a worldwide recession occurred in nuclear reactor exports. For example, the period 1975–9 saw only a third of the reactor sales that had taken place in 1971–4.[1] This recession, which lasted well into the 1990s, was the result of the twin influences of supplier overcapacity and lower-than-expected electricity demand. The combination of the nuclear recession with Canada's nuclear non-proliferation policy resulted in few sales opportunities and even fewer actual sales. The lack of CANDU exports that Canada experienced in the 1977–89 period meant that the Canadian nuclear industry was on 'life support systems' throughout those years. At several stages, the Canadian government had to make a conscious decision whether to continue with a domestic nuclear industry. It would not be overstating the case to declare that had exports not picked up in the 1990s, Ottawa would probably have pulled the plug on it.

Romania: Cernavoda I, 1978

Canada had been negotiating with Romania since the 1960s for a CANDU sale. Nothing concrete came out of these early discussions, but contacts with Romanian nuclear officials were established. In 1975, however, Romania approached AECL to purchase a 600 megawatt CANDU. Instead of a turnkey project, as had been discussed earlier, it wanted AECL to provide a licensing and service agreement while Romania itself would handle the project management function. The first step was a nuclear cooperation agreement with Romania, signed in 1977. Within the non-proliferation framework established by the safeguards agreement, AECL signed three agreements with the Romanian foreign trade office ROMENERGO in December 1978: (1) a licensing agreement, which allowed ROMENERGO to build between one to four CANDU reactors, with a 'significant amount of components and services being provided by Canadian industry'; (2) an engineering services agreement, which saw AECL provide ROMENERGO with design information for a CANDU modified to meet Romania's electrical grid; and (3) a procurement agreement under which AECL agreed to act as ROMENERGO's agent for the purchasing of components for the reactor.[2]

Romania was an original signatory to the Nuclear Non-Proliferation Treaty (NPT), but that did not eliminate all of Canada's proliferation concerns. At the top of the list was the undesirability of transferring sensitive nuclear technology to a Warsaw Pact country. The mid-1970s had seen some thawing in relations between NATO and the Warsaw Pact through the process of détente, but, make no mistake, the Cold War was still on. Observers wondered why Romania, when it decided to construct a nuclear reactor, ignored its Soviet ally, which had its own nuclear industry and which had already exported reactors to all of the other Eastern European countries. There were, in other words, questions about the ulterior motives of the Romanian government. Romania had previously tried to operate its economy free of foreign interference, but now it was committing 'itself to Canadian technology on such an essential part of its economy.'[3] In short, would Canada be aiding Soviet bloc attempts at nuclear espionage with a CANDU export to Romania?[4]

A second concern was over the issue of inspections on the nuclear facilities. Since inspections were at the heart of Canada's nuclear safeguards system, a failure to ensure that adequate inspections were allowed to take place unfettered and without restriction would undermine all of its efforts at non-proliferation. Several critics, particularly Flora MacDonald, the external affairs critic for the Progressive Conservatives, pointed out that Romania was a satellite of the Soviet Union, which had refused IAEA inspections on its civilian nuclear facilities, despite the fact that it had signed the NPT. MacDonald suggested that Romania would also refuse inspections on its nuclear facilities.[5]

Finally, there were concerns that Romania might resell CANDU technology to undesirable countries. What was the point of Canada's export controls if third parties like Romania could retransfer sensitive nuclear technology to prohibited regions? The possibility of retransfers was particularly strong with respect to Romania. As critics pointed out, 'Romania has a long history of trading without regard to morality,' and 'its economic partners include dictatorships of all political stripes.'[6] For instance, Ion Pacepa, the former head of the Romanian foreign intelligence services, who defected in 1978, later alleged that Romania was cooperating with Pakistan in using CANDU technology to develop the bomb.[7]

However, Ottawa discounted these proliferation risks for a couple of reasons. First, Romania had signed the NPT and had agreed to its safeguards. It was noted that the USSR was not required to allow IAEA inspections under the NPT because it was a nuclear-weapons state (NWS), but Romania was a non-nuclear-weapons state (NNWS) and therefore it had to allow inspections. Furthermore, in the Canada–Romania nuclear cooperation agreement, both sides had agreed to IAEA inspections as well as to a 'prior written agreement' from both countries before retransfers could be completed.[8] Thus, Canada felt that it had a number of multilateral and bilateral guarantees from Romania that addressed all possible security concerns. In addition to these formal guarantees, Canada was confident that the USSR would act as a constraint on Romania. The last thing the Soviets wanted was a country with an independent nuclear weapons capability along its borders. This was the case even if it was one of its 'friendly' Eastern European allies. Therefore, while the USSR would not allow inspections of its own nuclear facilities (its right as an NWS), it nevertheless enforced strict nuclear safeguards requirements on the other members of the Warsaw Pact. As the minister of external affairs, Don Jamieson, pointed out 'Romania is clearly within the Soviet orbit, certainly a country in a sense that is involved, if I can use appropriate language, in terms of the Soviet influence ... In other words, it is not very likely – if I can be diplomatic about it – that there would be any development of nuclear weapons in a country such as Romania.'[9]

There were also political considerations that facilitated the CANDU export to Romania. In particular, there was, at the time, the growing belief in the Western bloc of 'peaceful coexistence' with the Soviet bloc. The United States and the USSR had already taken a series of steps towards détente in the 1970s. Starting in 1972, there had been three major summits between President Richard Nixon and Premier Leonid Brezhnev. President Gerald Ford, Nixon's successor, met an additional two times with his Soviet counterpart. The results of these summits included cultural exchanges, technical cooperation, and a growth in American–Soviet trade. Even more important to détente was the signing of the Strategic Arms Limitation Treaty (SALT I) in 1972 which limited stockpiles of nuclear warheads. SALT II, which was being negotiated at the same time as Canada was considering nuclear exports to Romania, would have gone even further in reducing the nuclear weapons capability of the superpowers.

Like the Americans, Canada also believed in reducing East–West tensions. This was particularly the case with Prime Minister Trudeau, who during the 1968 election campaign had promised to revisit Canada's commitment to NATO. Trudeau lived up to this electoral promise when, in 1969, half of Canada's NATO forces were withdrawn from Europe. According to Thomas Axworthy, the prime minister's former principal secretary, Trudeau believed that the communist bloc countries needed 'to be encouraged, enticed or cajoled into becoming full participants in the community of nations. The way to reduce their revolutionary zeal was to bind them to the world, not to cast them beyond the pale. Trade, scientific exchanges, tourism and culture were all threads to be spun into a web.'[10] In a sense, then, Canada felt that it could make a contribution to détente, in its own unique fashion, through nuclear cooperation with Romania.

A second factor was the nature of Romania's foreign policy and of President Nicolae Ceausescu. Ceausescu was considered the 'maverick' of Eastern Europe because of his attempts at creating an independent foreign policy for Romania. In April 1967, Romania was the first communist state to establish diplomatic relations with West Germany. A year later, it refused to join in the USSR's invasion of Czechoslovakia. These events made Ceausescu, notwithstanding his own domestic oppression, the 'darling' of the West. In later years, this image was reinforced by Romania's condemnation of the USSR's invasion of Afghanistan and by its violation of the Soviet-led boycott of the 1984 Olympics in Los Angeles. Thus, Ottawa felt that Romania was different from the rest of Eastern Europe. In fact, there were those in external affairs who thought that Romania could be turned into another Yugoslavia, an independent communist country, and cooperating with it in the nuclear domain was seen as one way of achieving this objective.[11]

The issue of the human rights record of Eastern European countries was becoming a feature of international relations in the late 1970s. This was best symbolized by the signing of the Helsinki Accords in 1975. In exchange for the West formally accepting the European territorial boundaries created by the Second World War (especially the recognition of East Germany), the Helsinki Accords provided for the protection of human rights by all signatory groups across Europe and North America. Civilian human rights monitoring groups, such as Helsinki Watch, sprung up to try to ensure that the Eastern Europeans adhered to these commitments. Nevertheless, there is absolutely no evidence that the issue of Romania's human rights record was ever raised during the Cernavoda I negotiations. Canada may have felt that forging economic ties would improve Romania's human rights record, but as Aurel Braun later pointed out, 'political oppression kept increasing, so the motivation of moderation made no sense.'[12]

The Canadian government also heavily subsidized the Cernavoda project. After the Argentinean and South Korean scandals of two years earlier, AECL did the deal directly with the Romanians and without the use of an outside sales agent. However, financing from the Export Development Corporation was a major component of this CANDU export. In 1978, EDC provided a $860-million loan, and followed that up a year later with a line of credit of over $1 billion.[13] This second EDC loan was based on Romania's decision to expand the Cernavoda project to five reactors, rather than only one. However, the idea of building five CANDUs was a ruse perpetrated by the Romanians. There may have been five outer shells, but only one reactor was actually being built. Trying to explain this discrepancy provides great insight into the type of regime that Canada was dealing with. Jennifer Wells, a *Globe and Mail* reporter, has suggested several possibilities. 'That Ceausescu fumbled in a speech, and said there would be five, and so there had to be. Or that he viewed a hole in the limestone bed along which the reactors were being built and immediately ordered the pouring of a fifth concrete pad. Or, most probably, that he determined that the bigger the project, the greater the political impact, both at home and abroad.'[14] This confusion about the number of reactors that Canada was actually building in

Romania was symbolic of the fact that the financial arrangements for Cernavoda would be a constant source of irritation throughout the nuclear relationship between Canada and Romania.

Argentina: Atucha II, 1979

Although the Romanian case appeared to suggest that CANDU exports could be reconciled with a stringent nuclear non-proliferation policy, other events soon suggested that Canada's commercial interests in nuclear exports and its security interests in avoiding proliferation were incompatible. The prime example of this, and the only case where even the Canadian government openly acknowledged that it lost a sale due to its safeguards requirements, was the deal to provide Argentina with the Atucha II reactor in 1979. AECL, despite having the better bid, lost the contract to build Atucha II to the West German firm Kraftwerk Union (KWU). In addition, it also lost the contract to build a heavy- water plant to KWU's partner Sulzer of Switzerland. Canada lost this contract as a result of Argentina's unhappiness over Canada's retroactive strengthening of safeguards on the Embalse reactor in 1975 and because West Germany's nuclear safeguards requirements were not as stringent.

Since the earlier CANDU sale to Argentina, public opinion had become disenchanted with Canada's export of nuclear reactors. A 1976 study on elite opinion on nuclear energy – which interviewed over two hundred business executives, politicians, civil servants, academics, and environmentalists – registered wide disapproval with 'the sale of CANDU reactors to other nations by AECL.'[15] The opposition Progressive Conservatives had enthusiastically supported the Canadian public's rejection of CANDU exports. In 1979, however, Joe Clark and the rest of the PCs were elected into government, which meant that the new government now had to reconcile its harsh rhetoric from its time in opposition with the greater responsibilities of being in power. In particular, the PCs would have to confront their past opposition to CANDU exports in general, and specifically the 1973 sale to Argentina. A typical statement against the earlier Embalse sale to Argentina that emanated from Conservative opposition benches in the House of Commons was: 'We have supplied a reactor to Argentina, one of the most unstable countries in the world, and I want to debate this point as a moral issue and not as a commercial one. It is interesting to note that we not only supplied a reactor to Argentina but we did it at enormous cost to

Canadian taxpayers.'[16] Clearly, the Clark government must have felt constrained by its reaction to the earlier Embalse sale when it came time to consider a second CANDU sale.

Although AECL was responsible for CANDU exports, final approval for any foreign sale remained in the domain of the political leadership. This meant, as P.R. Johannson has noted, that 'bureaucratic politics' was 'a feature of nuclear policy-making.'[17] The Atucha II export was no exception. Joe Clark's cabinet, which was deeply divided over the Atucha II sale, was characterized as a clash between 'those who wanted to put the reactor on the next plane and never ask for payment, and those who didn't want to sell it at all, even if they paid us in advance, in gold.'[18] Those ministers who were most against the sale were External Affairs Minister Flora MacDonald, Communications Minister David MacDonald, and Health and Welfare Minister David Crombie. Of these three, only the two MacDonalds were part of Prime Minister Joe Clark's 'inner' cabinet. Those ministers who were most in favour of giving approval for the sale were Minister of Industry, Trade and Commerce and Minister of State for Economic Development Robert de Cotret and International Trade Minister Michael Wilson. Only de Cotret was a member of the 'inner' cabinet.[19]

The opponents in cabinet listed several reasons why the government should not allow AECL to sell reactors to Argentina. First, Canada did not want a repeat of 1974, when India, exploiting Canadian technology, exploded a nuclear device. Canada's own domestic view of itself, as well as its international prestige, had taken a severe beating with the 1974 Indian explosion, and it had vowed never to make a similar mistake again. In this vein, Argentina was seen as an India in waiting. The similarities between India and Argentina were indeed striking: both were involved in regional conflicts with nuclear rivals (Pakistan/ China and Brazil); both had the technological wherewithal to produce a nuclear bomb; and both had refused to sign the NPT.[20]

It was argued that, at a minimum, Argentina had to sign and ratify the NPT. Since 1976, it had been Canadian policy to apply the NPT's full-scope safeguards to all exports. Although Argentina had yet to sign the NPT, it had agreed to facility-specific safeguards on Embalse, and would have done similarly had it purchased another CANDU. However, Flora MacDonald, and her cabinet supporters, were demanding that Argentina go all the way and actually sign and ratify the NPT. This meant that Argentina's entire nuclear system – its indigenous research reactors as well as Atucha I (which had been purchased from West

Germany in 1968) – would be under international nuclear safeguards. In addition, Argentina's ratification of the NPT held deep symbolic value for the Canadians. This was because it would have been easier to convince the Canadian public about the Atucha II sale if the government could point to a concrete change in Argentina's nuclear policy. Finally, ratification of the NPT could be taken as a stronger commitment by Buenos Aires not to develop nuclear weapons.

Forcing an additional political commitment was felt necessary because Ottawa still possessed significant doubts about the extent of Argentina's peaceful intentions, especially since the Argentine military junta had come to power in a coup in March 1976. Although this effectively ended the civil war in Argentina, it meant that the military had exclusive control over Argentina's nuclear program, with no political counterbalance. Canada, in fact, had been exposed to some pieces of evidence that Argentina was trying to produce nuclear weapons. On many occasions, Argentina's military leaders had indicated that their interest in nuclear technology extended beyond electricity production to nuclear bombs.[21] In fact, in 1982 Miguel Ussher, a high level official of the Argentine Nuclear Energy Commission (CNEA) confirmed both the existence of a reprocessing plant and that Argentina was, and had been, pursuing the bomb.[22] Thus, *Maclean's* was right to ask, following the 1976 coup, 'Who are the people behind this bloody self-destruction, who many believe capable of making a nuclear explosive if they could obtain the needed material from a reactor?'[23]

Argentina's atrocious human rights record was also cited as a reason to stop the Atucha II export. Starting in 1976 with the coup and lasting until 1983, when democracy again returned to Argentina, the military cracked down on left-wing groups using methods such as arrests, torture, killings, and perhaps the most insidious method, 'disappearances.'[24] Responding to the stories of human rights violations in Argentina, an interest group called No CANDU for Argentina was formed in the summer of 1977 on the premise that 'Canada [was] selling a potential weapon of mass destruction to a regime that represses, tortures, and murders its own citizens.'[25] No CANDU was an umbrella group which had the support of over fifty individual organizations, such as the Canadian Labour Congress, seven provincial federations of labour, the major unions in Canada's nuclear industry, the Latin American Working Group, the Group for the Defence of Civil Rights in Argentina, a number of church groups, and the New Democratic Party. It called for the halt of all exports of Canadian nuclear technology and equipment to the Argentine military junta of General Jorge Videla. Besides lobbying Ottawa, No CANDU also organized a demonstration at the port in Saint John, New Brunswick, that temporarily prevented an Argentina-bound freighter from being loaded with heavy water.[26] Although human rights were only just starting to emerge as an issue in Canadian foreign policy at this time, it did have an influential supporter in the new external affairs minister, Flora MacDonald. During the cabinet discussions on Atucha II, MacDonald continued to make the case that Argentina's deplorable human rights record should make it ineligible for importing Canadian nuclear technology.

Ottawa also needed to ensure that all CANDU sales could survive public scrutiny. In using this type of argument, the anti-Atucha II faction were reminding their colleagues of the previous AECL sales agent scandal, and the public statements that PC members of Parliament gave on that issue. The fact that AECL was proposing another sale to Argentina provided this line of argument with additional ammunition.

The cabinet members in favour of the sale responded to this internal criticism by listing several reasons why the proposed sale should go ahead. First, the CANDU was Canada's technological showpiece. As the *Globe and Mail* wrote, '[T]he CANDU reactor stands almost alone as a shining example of what, when we put our minds to it, we can do by ourselves in achieving new frontiers in sophisticated energy-producing high tech.'[27] The legacy of the Avro Arrow was ever present in the minds of the political decision-makers and the Canadian public. The Diefenbaker government withstood a lot of pressure when it cancelled the Arrow in 1959, and even today the thing that many Canadians remember most about Diefenbaker's time in office is that he killed the Arrow. This public outcry warned future governments of the political price to be paid for the cancellation of a high-profile scientific project. The pro–Atucha II members clearly viewed Canada's nuclear technology as an asset not to be squandered.[28] Did the Clark government want to be known as the killers of the CANDU? For Joe Clark, who was an expert on the history of the PC Party, these fears had particular connotations: John Diefenbaker, PC leader, prime minister, Avro Arrow; Joe Clark, PC leader, prime minister, CANDU. The political imagery must have been too frightening for Clark to handle.

CANDU exports also provided an excellent opportunity to improve Canada's balance of trade. The Atucha II sale was worth over $300-million, and it would be accompanied by the sale of a $300-million

heavy-water plant. In addition, there were the potential spin-off benefits of a natural uranium fuel fabrication plant and sales of uranium
mining and exploration technology and equipment. There was also the
hope that a successful sale could lead Argentina to purchase two or
three additional CANDUs.[29]

The pro–Atucha II faction warned that the very survival of the Canadian nuclear industry was at stake if further exports were not obtained.
AECL emphasized that it needed one CANDU sale annually in order to
keep Canada's nuclear power infrastructure intact. AECL's view was
supported by two major reports that were critical of the future of the
Canadian nuclear industry. The Ontario government's 1978 Porter Report on electric power planning, suggested that Ontario cut back on
building nuclear reactors.[30] Since Ontario was the largest domestic
purchaser of nuclear reactors, this was devastating news to the industry. A second report from the Federal Task Force on Canadian Nuclear
Export Marketing warned that 'if no new orders are obtained, which is
probable ... thousands of jobs will be lost.'[31] The Canadian nuclear
industry undoubtedly contributed to this sense of urgency. For example, once the Atucha II deal had been lost, AECL official Ken Jones
noted that this would 'definitely create problems for the domestic industries.' In fact, 'several companies were already considering whether
they will stay in the nuclear industry.'[32]

Pro–Atucha II supporters emphasized that CANDU R&D meant
35,000 jobs and 90 per cent of those jobs were in Ontario. This was an
important political argument given the electoral importance of Ontario.
The PCs were in a precarious situation due to their minority government status, and the key to the Clark government's 1979 electoral
victory was winning fifty-six of Ontario's ninety-five seats. Obviously,
the Clark government did not want to undertake policies that might
damper its support in such a voter-rich region.

Finally, there was a feeling that if Canada did not sell a nuclear
reactor to the Argentines, the West Germans would. Aiding this argument was a view that West Germany would also apply full-scope
safeguards. However, as the eventual Atucha II contract revealed, this
proved to be a mistaken opinion. In fact, there has been some speculation that the West Germans may have intentionally misled the Canadians on the issue of full-scope safeguards.[33]

The government's decision-making process was complicated by the
fact that Prime Minister Clark was widely believed to be a foreign
policy 'lightweight.' As opposition leader, he had undertaken a disas-

trous foreign trip in 1978 where he had lost his luggage and was almost impaled by a bayonet while reviewing a Thai honour guard. Clark contributed to this image with an ill-fated foray into Middle East politics. During the 1979 election campaign, Clark promised to move Canada's embassy in Israel from Tel Aviv to Jerusalem.[34] Well-known political commentator Jeffrey Simpson characterized Clark's announcement as the product of 'a numbing mixture of unforgivable stupidity and crass politics.'[35] It was a promise that was given in the context of a tight election campaign, and nobody really expected him to keep it. Yet Clark used his first press conference as prime minster to confirm that he was, in fact, keeping his promise and moving the embassy. The announcement generated threats of economic sanctions from the Arab countries. It also created a public uproar in Canada as Bell Canada, the Royal Bank, ATCO, Bombardier, the Canadian Council of Churches, and Canadian farmers lobbied the government for a policy reversal. Powerful cabinet ministers like External Affairs Minister MacDonald and Finance Minister John Crosbie opposed the embassy move. So did the bureaucrats in the Department of External Affairs. Eventually Clark was forced to backdown, appointing an investigative team headed by former PC leader Robert Stanfield as political cover. The embassy episode seemed to confirm that Clark lacked sufficient foreign policy experience and knowledge, and might also be in over his head as prime minister.

The flip-flop over the Israeli embassy move affected the cabinet discussions on the proposed Argentine reactor sale. The prime minister was silent during the 'pulling and hauling' in cabinet over Atucha II. Joe Clark did not have a strong opinion one way or another, but, this time, he wanted to ensure that he had a consensus in cabinet. Thus, while the final decision would indeed rest with the prime minister, Clark would stay out of the bureaucratic political infighting, and wait until a survivor was present, and then he would make his decision based on the cabinet's decision. What resulted was a political 'gang-up' on Flora MacDonald. Although MacDonald was the fiercest opponent to the sale, she lacked sufficient allies, both in numbers and in political clout. When contrasted with the pro side, which possessed both a majority in cabinet as well as its most important (save for MacDonald herself) members, MacDonald was outmatched.

MacDonald was also betrayed from inside her own Department of External Affairs.[36] The proposed Atucha II sale led to a heated, and very personal, battle between MacDonald and her ostensible deputy

Alan Gotlieb, the Under-Secretary of State. Although, 'MacDonald opposed the reactor sale,' it was Gotlieb, while 'sympathiz[ing] with her revulsion of an odious regime, nonetheless believed that Canada had committed itself to a deal.' In fact, the department had initially drafted a memo for cabinet which 'essentially supported the sale.' However, Gotlieb agreed to a compromise whereby the memo would simply outline the potential consequences of Canada's decision 'without recommendations.'[37]

Further evidence that MacDonald was being opposed by her own bureaucrats can be deduced from a DEA briefing paper which was leaked to the *Ottawa Citizen* in April 1982.[38] This paper outlined the possible courses of action, including ending all nuclear cooperation, that the Trudeau government could take against Argentina in the wake of the Falklands Island crisis. It is reasonable to assume that the viewpoints expressed by DEA in 1982 would be similar to those that were expressed privately to ministers in other departments in 1979. In this document, DEA acknowledged that Argentina was close to developing an indigenous nuclear fuel cycle that was 'completely free of safeguards.' The immediate concern was that 'the Argentines may be tempted to exploit their power reactor programme which is now under safeguards.'

Despite this situation, the DEA paper outlined the consequences of ending the nuclear relationship, even though it did admit that there were domestic consequences to maintaining nuclear cooperation with Argentina. For instance, it stated that 'the media has already begun to focus on the nuclear dimension to our relationship with Argentina and if the situation drags on, a highly visible anti-CANDU lobby can be expected.' Nevertheless, DEA felt that, on balance, it was more important not to terminate its nuclear cooperation as this might 'provoke Argentina to denounce its nuclear co-operation agreement with Canada and related safeguards agreements' that 'would have profound consequences for Canadian policy and the international non-proliferation regime.' Additionally, DEA noted that since Argentina had 'proven to be extremely difficult on non-proliferation and safeguard matters' and 'the suspension of co-operation, even if temporary, could negatively affect our non-proliferation position' and the ability of the IAEA to safeguard the reactor. DEA recommended that the government had little choice but to live up to its CANDU contract and hope that Argentina did not produce nuclear weapons.

In the end, the Canadian government decided on a compromise that would satisfy nobody and would, if the decision-makers had been completely honest with themselves, not work. Ottawa decided that it would allow AECL to continue to try to obtain the Atucha II contract, but it would not weaken Canada's nuclear non-proliferation policy. Argentina would still be required to accept full-scope safeguards. Ottawa knew that its position on non-proliferation might damage its chances of winning the bid for Atucha II because of Argentina's repeated vows that it would not be pressured into signing the NPT. Carlos Castro Madero, the head of CNEA, stated that 'the Canadian government is prohibiting the export of technology to Argentina because we have not signed the Nuclear Non-Proliferation Treaty. We have not signed the NPT because it's discriminatory. It does not treat all states fairly. We fully support the NPT effort, but disagree with the fairness of the treaty.'[39]

Given the position of Buenos Aires, it was really no surprise when it selected KWU's bid for Atucha II, despite the fact that AECL's bid of $1.075 billion was 30 per cent lower than KWU's $1.579 billion.[40] Argentina listed two official reasons for its rejection of the Canadian bid. First, Argentina was disappointed with AECL's construction timeline. The Embalse reactor, Madero asserted, was 'originally slated for completion by 1980, its start-up has since been pushed back to 1982 at a swollen cost of about $1 billion after a succession of contract negotiations.' KWU, on the other hand, had built Atucha I 'in six years at the price specified in the contract.'[41] Second, Argentina wanted to maintain competition among all potential nuclear suppliers. More specifically, Argentina did not want its reactor and heavy-water plant to be supplied by the same country, as Canada was pressing for; rather, it wanted to be able to split the contracts, something that the joint German–Swiss bid allowed.

However, despite these official reasons for rejecting the Canadian bid, a consensus emerged that Argentina had turned to West Germany to supply Atucha II principally because of its apprehension over Canada's non-proliferation policy. Argentina considered Canada to be an unreliable nuclear supplier after Ottawa successfully pressed to reopen the safeguards agreement on Embalse. There were additional concerns in Buenos Aires that, given the division that existed inside of the cabinet over the issue of nuclear safeguards, Ottawa might again seek to strengthen safeguards once Atucha II was signed. The Canadian government attempted to reassure Argentina that it would operate in good faith, even sending International Trade Minister Wilson to Buenos Aires at the eleventh hour to calm Argentine concerns. However, even this attempt backfired on Ottawa because at the same time that Wilson was wooing and coaxing the Argentine generals, External Affairs Minister Flora MacDonald was in New York plotting revenge against her cabinet colleagues and DEA officials who had succeeded in trumping her in the cabinet room.

MacDonald was in New York to deliver Canada's yearly address to the United Nations. She used her platform at the UN's General Assembly to censure Argentina for its human rights violations and to emphasize that Canada demanded that 'stringent safeguards be applied to countries buying Canadian nuclear power facilities or materials. We want to ensure that the continued recourse to nuclear power is undertaken in the most stringent conditions possible, guaranteeing against any non-peaceful use.'[42] To ensure that her message was heard in both Ottawa and Buenos Aires, MacDonald had granted an exclusive interview with the *Toronto Star* the day before her speech. During this interview, she stated that Canada would not have 'any further extension of facilities to them unless they come under' the NPT 'umbrella and agree to full investigation of everything they have.' MacDonald further emphasized that a country's 'political stability' and 'goals' should 'be part and parcel of any condition of export.' Finally, she promised that 'even stricter safeguards' would soon be recommended by a parliamentary review on nuclear exports.[43] This last point was not only a direct contradiction of what Wilson was telling the Argentine generals but it also violated the cabinet compromise decision. Clearly, by openly discussing the possibility of a further unilateral strengthening of Canada's nuclear non-proliferation policy, MacDonald was using her opportunity on the global stage to reverse her defeat in cabinet by publicly playing on Argentina's fears of Canadian unreliability. In later years, MacDonald bragged about how she 'scuttled' the proposed CANDU export to Argentina 'with one speech.'[44]

Members of Canada's nuclear industry were understandably furious with MacDonald. Ross Campbell, vice-president of AECL in charge of CANDU exports, asserted that 'Argentina seemed ready to buy the reactor until Ms. MacDonald's U.N. speech stating that Argentina is one of the few countries responsible for significant violations of human rights.'[45] Campbell extended his criticism to the entire Clark government by blaming it for its waffling over the issue of nuclear safeguards. 'Argentina was so nervous about the indecision of successive governments here they felt they could not put the monopoly in Canada's hand.

Through our own indecision we have created a competitor that wasn't there before.'[46]

In addition to the concerns that Argentina had over potential shifts in Canada's policy, it also wanted to acquire Atucha II under less stringent safeguards than Ottawa demanded. Madero was worried that Canada's full-scope safeguards requirements would affect 'Argentina's capacity to develop an independent program with a minimum of possibilities of outside interference.'[47] Since the German requirements only pertained to the Atucha II reactor itself rather than Argentina's entire nuclear program, as Canada demanded, the former safeguards were less stringent than those of Canada.

The Atucha II case is a very good example of Canada's competing foreign policy objectives at work. In the end, Canada's concerns over nuclear non-proliferation and human rights prevailed over its economic interests in securing the sale. Commercial interests were not totally neglected, since Ottawa was willing to proceed with negotiations despite its fears about the nature of the Argentine junta and its human rights record. However, it retained its requirement of full-scope nuclear safeguards. More importantly, by publicly embarrassing Argentina at the United Nations, Flora MacDonald was able to get through the back door what she could not get at the cabinet table. It is not clear whether AECL would have secured the Atucha II contract had it not been for MacDonald's intervention, but her speech surely made the decision by Buenos Aires easier.

Export Failures in the 1980s

After Canada's mixed record of CANDU exports in the late 1970s – a sale to Romania but not to Argentina – several attempts were made in the 1980s to export the CANDU. Canada pursued a variety of countries in order to conclude a sale, but was unsuccessful throughout the 1980s. In some cases, it was the inability of the purchasing country to come up with the funds needed for a CANDU, but in other cases Canada's non-proliferation policy was an important factor in the loss of the sale.

Canada's first significant export defeat was its attempt to make a sale to Japan in 1979. Canada had placed a great deal of emphasis on obtaining this sale because Japan was, for a variety of reasons, a very attractive market. Most obviously, Japan was an economic powerhouse. This meant that a CANDU sale would not have to rely upon significant financing from Ottawa. In addition, Canada had been very eager to penetrate the Japanese market with high-tech manufactured goods rather than simply supplying it with primary resource products like wood and fish. The CANDU would provide this opportunity. Japan was also the only industrialized country that would actually import nuclear reactors. Canada had never sold a CANDU to an industrialized country because the nuclear markets in places like the United States and France were closed to foreign suppliers. Selling a CANDU to Japan was also desirable because the Japanese were very influential with other Pacific Rim countries. If Japan found the CANDU technologically sound, perhaps its neighbours would as well. Finally, Japan did not have to be convinced about the benefits of nuclear power. In fact, Japan has always been a firm believer: it currently has over 33 per cent of its electricity needs being met by its fifty-one nuclear reactors.[48]

In addition to the economic attractiveness of Japan, the Canadian government did not feel constrained by any of its other foreign policy objectives, especially nuclear non-proliferation. Japan was a signatory of the NPT and had agreed to full-scope safeguards. Moreover, Japan had been at the forefront of the international campaign against nuclear weapons. Since Japan was the only country to experience the military application of the atom, it had a unique moral authority to ensure that nuclear power remained peaceful. In fact, the Japanese constitution specifically prevented any application of nuclear power for military purposes. Thus, it could be concluded that Japan was probably the least likely country in the world to utilize nuclear power for military ends.[49] It is thus ironic that it was Canada's implementation of its non-proliferation policy that played an important role in Japan's decision not to purchase a CANDU.

Although Canada had engaged in nuclear cooperation with Japan since 1959 and there were sporadic attempts at making a sale from the mid-1960s onward, Canada did not undertake a serious marketing effort until the mid-1970s. Included in this effort were state visits by both Prime Ministers Trudeau and Clark to flog reactors to the Japanese. Unfortunately, the CANDU became a victim of internal battles inside Japan's byzantine bureaucratic political structure. The Japanese Ministry of International Trade and Industry (MITI) and the semi-governmental Electric Power Development Company favoured the purchase of the CANDU, while the Japanese Atomic Energy Commission (JAEC) and the Science and Technology Agency suggested that, instead, Japan should continue developing its domestic FUGEN reactor. A decision was made in August 1979, when the JAEC ruled that 'at the present stage, it is difficult to find positive reasons for introducing the CANDU reactor.' In an attempt at softening the blow, the report added that 'should the situation change, calling for a review of Japan's nuclear reactor development line, [the JAEC] would at that point reconsider the situation including the CANDU reactor.'[50]

The Canadian nuclear industry complained that Japan's decision was based on overarching political considerations contained in the Japanese–American bilateral relationship. Mark MacGuigan, who was then Canada's Secretary of State for External Affairs, maintained that 'we were not able to consummate a sale to Japan ... because it was more in the political interests of Japan to enter into an arrangement with U.S. suppliers.'[51] While political considerations undoubtedly played a role in Japan's decision – what megaproject in any country is completely devoid of political considerations? – there were other, more persuasive, explanations. In assessing Japan's decision, Mike Donnelly noted that 'the fundamental explanation surely is that CANDU does not fit easily into the country's over-all nuclear strategy, which aims at maximum self-sufficiency and national autonomy.'[52] However, a second factor emerged which gave CANDU critics in Japan a crucial advantage in the bureaucratic infighting: the unilateral implementation of Canada's non-proliferation policy in 1977–8. Japanese opponents of the CANDU option pointed to Canada's safeguards policies, alleging that 'Canada is not always a totally reliable partner, citing export policies, which have sometimes been arbitrary, erratic and, on occasion, subject to change without prior notice.'[53] The incident that most damaged Canada's reputation was the temporary suspension of uranium shipments to Japan following the 1974 Indian explosion.

On 1 January 1977, as part of its implementation strategy for the 1976 nuclear non-proliferation policy, Canada suspended uranium shipments to Japan as well as to the European Community (EC), pending renegotiation of all safeguards arrangements with these countries. In particular, Canada wanted a formal guarantee that prohibited all nuclear reprocessing. Although there might have been some justification for this action with respect to the EC countries (in particular, Ottawa wanted guarantees from France that it would not use uranium of Canadian origin as part of its nuclear weapons program), there was no logical justification for the suspension of uranium shipments to Japan. Even 'Canadian officials admitted that they knew Japan had no intention or likelihood of engaging in a weapons program, but the sanction was levied anyway.'[54] The only reason for the Japanese suspension was the need for Canada to be consistent between Europe and Japan. However, the timing of the suspension of uranium shipments to Japan was not very politically astute. The ban occurred just after Prime Minister Trudeau had signed a Framework for Economic Cooperation agreement with the Japanese, souring relations at the very moment when Canada was seeking closer economic ties. The situation was eventually resolved, and uranium shipments were resumed in January 1978 after a new bilateral nuclear safeguards agreement was reached.

It is apparent that Canada's implementation of its non-proliferation policy was an influential factor leading to the Japanese decision not to purchase a CANDU. Canada could doubtlessly have reached a safeguards agreement with Japan without resorting to the extreme measure of a unilateral suspension of the uranium trade. While that move did allow Ottawa to demonstrate the rising importance of nuclear non-proliferation, the effect of its seemingly irrational action was to undermine efforts at exporting the CANDU to Japan. Canada's exaggerated foreign policy concerns in this instance prevailed over the significant economic interest in selling Japan a CANDU, and contributed to the loss of what might have been the most commercially beneficial CANDU export ever.

A second region in which Canada was starting to show interest during the 1980s was the Middle East. In early 1982, Energy Minister Marc Lalonde discussed the possibility of selling CANDU reactors to Kuwait and Saudi Arabia.[55] This denoted a potential shift in Canada's non-proliferation policy because, at the time, neither country was a signatory of the NPT. Canada later maintained that the discussions were conditional on the acceptance of full-scope safeguards. However, as William Walker and Mans Lönnroth point out, 'the mere fact that the discussions were held' was 'a departure from the former practice of regarding the Middle East as a "no-go area"for Canadian nuclear exports.' In 1975, the Canadian cabinet had placed a blanket prohibition on all CANDU sales to the Middle East, but the Lalonde visit indicated that a revision of this policy had taken place to allow for country-by-country negotiations.[56]

Although Canada failed to convince Kuwait and Saudi Arabia to purchase nuclear reactors, its attempt to do so raised questions about Ottawa's commitment to its non-proliferation policy. Why was Canada initiating discussions with countries that were bound to insist on the alteration of the policy if cooperation agreements were to be successfully concluded? Why would Kuwait or Saudi Arabia, two of the largest oil exporters in the world, even want or need access to civilian nuclear power? Why was Canada pursuing sales in the volatile Middle East region at all? Even though these negotiations did not progress, the fact that they even took place demonstrates the continuing presence of economic considerations in CANDU exports at the time when non-proliferation concerns were at their apex.

In the end, the only Middle Eastern country with which Canada signed a nuclear cooperation agreement, which is a necessary precursor for exports, was Egypt.[57] By completing a cooperation agreement with that country in 1982, Canada was acknowledging that it believed that the security risks with Egypt had largely disappeared. Egypt was a signatory of the NPT and would accept full-scope safeguards on any nuclear supplies from Canada or other countries. Moreover, as a result of the 1979 Camp David Peace Treaty with Israel, Egypt had become the only Arab country that did not have an all-encompassing motivation for developing nuclear weapons. Although no CANDU sales have come out of Canada's agreement with Egypt, it has not been because of any security concerns on Canada's part but because of Egypt's financial difficulties.

Canada's dealing with the Middle Eastern region illustrates the growing commercial imperative to produce a CANDU export at the time. These pressures forced Canada to revise a previous ban on nuclear exports to the Middle East, but they were not strong enough to lead Canada to lessen its full-scope safeguards requirements. In the end, by completing an agreement with Egypt – the sole Middle Eastern state to meet all of Canada's safeguards requirements – Canada signalled that nuclear non-proliferation remained the cornerstone of its CANDU export policy.

A third region to which Canada tried to export a CANDU was Mexico. Canada had lost two earlier contracts in Mexico to the United States in 1975, but was hopeful of a Mexican sale by 1982. Mexico was considered to be a perfect recipient of nuclear technology. First, it was one of the very few developing countries with an industrial infrastructure that was capable of handling nuclear power. Second, Canada had a chance to compete fairly against the other nuclear suppliers. Since Mexico did not have any existing reactors, no supplier held a pre-existing advantage. In addition, Mexico was not dependent upon the Americans for its security like the South Koreans or the Taiwanese. This meant that Washington could not use military aid as a lever to help guarantee a reactor contract for either Westinghouse or General Electric. Third,

Ottawa did not fear the potential of nuclear proliferation. Mexico was a signatory of the NPT and would agree to full-scope safeguards, and it was unlikely to become engaged in conflict with any of its neighbours. Finally, Ottawa considered Mexico to be a stable country with a relatively good human rights record, albeit only when compared with the standard set by other developing countries.

Since Mexico was such an attractive market both economically and politically, the Canadian nuclear industry put together an enhanced marketing plan to gain the sale. AECL, in partnership with the nuclear components firms, 'launched a full-scale marketing effort' which was 'equivalent to that of its most serious competitors.' AECL was also aided by the Canadian government, which 'supported the efforts through the full cooperation of its embassy and through several visits of senior Cabinet ministers and by the Prime Minister.'[58] Indeed, when Prime Minister Trudeau visited Mexico City in January 1982, he tried to link CANDU exports to the expansion of overall trade relations between the two countries.

In addition to AECL's marketing efforts, Ottawa came up with numerous financial inducements. A $6-billion loan was proposed, with the EDC supplying $1.5 billion, and with Canadian government revenues, funnelled through the EDC, adding an additional $4.5 billion. Moreover, Canada was also willing to provide preferential interest rates. The current interest rates in Canada were at 16 per cent, but the loan to Mexico would be at rates between 7 and 8 per cent. This 'difference between borrowing and lending costs represents the subsidy Canada is prepared to make to sell nuclear reactors to foreign buyers.' A final financial inducement was a proposition from Ottawa that Canada would import an amount of oil from Mexico equal to the amount of nuclear equipment that it exported to Mexico.[59]

Despite Canada's efforts, Mexico decided in June 1982 not to purchase any nuclear reactors. The financial problems of Mexico, in particular its foreign debt crisis, precluded a project of the size of a nuclear reactor. The Mexican case illustrates the problems that Canada faced in its CANDU exports program during the 1980s; even when all its foreign policy objectives were synchronized, a sale was not always forthcoming.

It was during the period 1977–89 that Canada faced the consequences of its enhanced preoccupation with nuclear security in the preceding period. Except for the exports to Romania, Canada was unable to make a single CANDU sale during this period. In several instances, most notably the Atucha II bid, but probably in the Japanese case as well, countries refused to purchase a CANDU because of Canada's reputation as an unreliable supplier.

While AECL was marketing its CANDU, external affairs officials were working on a variety of multilateral fronts to obtain an international consensus on nuclear non-proliferation. Canada was motivated to reach a stronger agreement on nuclear non-proliferation in two ways. First, by reducing the possibility of the proliferation of nuclear weapons, Canada would be contributing to a safer world. Second, CANDU exports would no longer be disadvantaged if all nuclear suppliers and purchasers accepted the same safeguards. This led Canada to campaign for tougher international safeguards standards. In 1971, the Nuclear Exporters Committee of the IAEA attempted to develop a uniform standard on export controls of nuclear materials. The Zangger Committee, named after its first chair, Claude Zangger a Swiss professor, was charged with interpreting Article III, paragraph 2 of the NPT that established safeguards on 'equipment or material especially designed or prepared for the processing, use or production of special fissionable material.' In 1974, obviously spurred on by the Indian nuclear explosion, the Zangger Committee published a 'Trigger List' of specific materials that required IAEA safeguards.[60] The 'Trigger List' included six major components: complete nuclear reactors, pressure vessels, reactor control rods, fuel reprocessing plants, fuel fabrication plants, and isotope separation plant equipment. The Zangger Committee also established three conditions for the supply of exports to NNWS that were not signatories of the NPT: a non-explosive use assurance, an IAEA safeguards requirement, and a retransfer provision that required the receiving state to apply the same conditions when re-exporting these items.

Another effort was soon launched to better prevent the potential of nuclear technology being diverted for military uses. In 1975, major nuclear suppliers like the U.S., Canada, the UK, France, West Germany, Japan, and the USSR started meeting in London.[61] The London Club, which later became more formally known as the Nuclear Suppliers Group (NSG), established its own trigger list of nuclear materials, equipment, and technology.[62] The NSG guidelines also adopted a requirement for physical protection measures, agreement to exercise particular caution in the transfer of sensitive facilities, technology and weapons-useable materials, and strengthened retransfer provisions.

The safeguards established by the Zangger Committee and the NSG were an improvement, but ultimately they were weaker than what the Canadians wanted in several respects. First, Ottawa wanted a complete ban on all nuclear material to any unsafeguarded plant. Second, it wanted to ban the export of reprocessing and enrichment plants. The French and the Germans blocked both of these proposals because they saw them as unfair infringements on their ability to sell nuclear materials. Both countries had recently concluded sales to South Korea, Taiwan, Pakistan, Iraq, and Brazil and did not want to see them cancelled.[63] As a result, the language of the NSG guidelines was marred by phrases like 'suppliers should exercise restraint in the transfer of sensitive facilities, technology and weapons-usable materials.' The frequent use of the word 'should' throughout the NSG guidelines revealed the fact that, in the final analysis, they were only voluntary. The United States, with its 1978 Nuclear-Non-Proliferation Act, was the only other state to adopt nuclear safeguards that were as stringent as Ottawa desired. Despite this gap among nuclear suppliers, Canada could not weaken its non-proliferation policy because, as the 1982 *Nuclear Industry Review* noted, 'it is likely that the Canadian public would demand the termination of all nuclear exports.' Thus, the review concluded that 'significant modifications to nuclear safeguards policy should not be considered as an option.'[64] Although Canada tried to wiggle out of its commitment to nuclear non-proliferation, that is, in Argentina and the Middle East, at the last minute it stuck to its principles.

As a result of AECL's inability to sell CANDUs in the 1980s, the Canadian nuclear industry saw its high level of government subsidies gradually reduced. In 1985, the newly formed Progressive Conservative government announced that over a five-year period it would gradually reduce by $100 million the level of parliamentary appropriations to AECL for nuclear R&D. In 1984, parliamentary appropriations to nuclear R&D stood at $184.4 million, which was 87 per cent of AECL's total R&D expenditures. By 1990, parliamentary appropriations had been reduced to $154 million, and this amount constituted only 53 per cent of the R&D total.[65]

The nuclear industry responded by having its friends at the Department of Energy, Mines, and Resources (EMR) produce a study – *AECL and the Future of the Canadian Nuclear Industry* – which once again spelled out the benefits of a nuclear industry and also highlighted the costs that would befall Canada if its nuclear industry disappeared. EMR asserted that 'while Canada could, in theory, do without the CANDU, it is much better off in practice to retain this option.'[66] EMR's paper was designed to nudge the government towards action that would ensure the survival of the nuclear program until such time as the export market improved. *AECL and the Future of the Canadian Nuclear Industry's* major component was a plea for increased nuclear R&D spending. The study noted that Canada's R&D efforts had been 'remarkably cost-effective' when compared with other nuclear suppliers. EMR claimed that importing light-water reactors was the only alternative to maintaining a domestic nuclear program. However, this situation would not eliminate 'the need for R&D spending.'[67] In its recommendations to secure the survival of the Canadian nuclear industry, EMR stated that the government must 'ensure that the R&D program is maintained at a level which retains confidence of present and prospective Candu customers.' EMR suggested that a turn around in the market for the CANDU was right around the corner. All that the federal government had to do to ensure that AECL was ready when that time came was to make a strong commitment in the form of increased R&D spending and 'direct federal risk-sharing.'[68]

The EMR study, in part, led to the Mulroney government's 1990 decision to increase R&D spending and, just as importantly, transfer funding responsibilities to the three provinces which benefited from nuclear power. The 1990 initiative entailed a seven-year plan of increased funds for nuclear R&D, provided by a consortium of governments and government agencies, including the federal government, Ontario Hydro, Quebec, and New Brunswick. In total, the increased funding would result in an additional $66 million annually for nuclear R&D.[69] It was assumed by members of the nuclear industry that this was a seven-year trial period, and if no new sales emerged, in particular foreign sales, then the program would be terminated.[70] The ability of AECL to re-acquire substantial nuclear R&D investments shows that by 1990 the commercial objective of exporting nuclear reactors and technology was again beginning to assert itself. In the 1985 decision, it appeared that the federal government could accept the loss of the domestic nuclear industry, but the 1990 decision is evidence of a reversal in thinking.

The period 1977–89 shows that Canada was willing to sacrifice its economic interests to nuclear non-proliferation. However, Canada's other foreign policy goals were still subordinate. With the notable exception of the Atucha II case, human rights did not factor into the government's decision-making process. Even in the Atucha II case, human rights took on a higher profile because of its linkage with nuclear proliferation and because it was being championed at the cabinet table and in international forums by Flora MacDonald. The issues of the potential environmental consequences of nuclear power, even after the 1979 Three Mile Island accident, were almost completely ignored by Ottawa. Finally, government subsidies for the nuclear industry were largely maintained. This was despite the fact that AECL had been unable to sell a CANDU, with the exception of the Romanian deal, for almost two decades. Ottawa was still propping up an industry where domestic sales had dried up and where the export market appeared to have collapsed. In addition, the government, as its financial package for the proposed CANDU export to Mexico showed, was still willing to heavily subsidize individual reactor sales. This is very convincing evidence that the economic and political arguments mustered by the Canadian nuclear lobby remained influential in Ottawa, at the expense of other foreign policy objectives.

7 Nuclear Renaissance, 1990–1996

The 1980s were dark times for AECL and the rest of the Canadian nuclear industry. The nuclear market had dried up. Opportunities for new reactor sales were scarce. To make matters worse, Canada's sales efforts in Argentina, Japan, and other countries were being hindered by its nuclear safeguards policies. There were growing indications that Ottawa was going to pull the plug on its continued support of nuclear research and development. Supporters and critics could finally agree: the future of an independent Canadian nuclear industry was in serious jeopardy.

However, the arrival of the 1990s brought a nuclear renaissance. In 1990, AECL ended its decade-long slump with a CANDU sale to South Korea. The following year, Canada signed a contract to finish construction on the stalemated Cernavoda nuclear reactor project in Romania. In 1992, AECL followed up its earlier success in South Korea with the sale of two more CANDUs. Finally, in 1996, AECL landed its first new reactor customer in over twenty years when it sold two CANDUs to China. This chapter examines the changing fortunes of the Canadian nuclear industry and assesses the influence of Canada's competing foreign policy objectives.

South Korea: Wolsung II to IV, 1990–2

On 27 December 1990, South Korea decided to purchase a second CANDU from Canada, the Wolsung II. Two years later, in 1992, South Korea added Wolsung III and IV. As with previous CANDU exports, the sales of Wolsung II, III, and IV provided immediate financial and employment benefits. The Wolsung II reactor was worth $1.2 billion with the Canadian contribution accounting for $400 million going to AECL and its Canadian component manufacturers. This would provide more than 7,000 jobs over a four-year period.[1] Wolsung III and IV netted an additional $500 million for AECL and Canadian suppliers.[2] What made the sales even more attractive was the fact that they were straight cash deals. No loans from the Export Development Corporation (EDC) or other types of Canadian government financing were involved. This was in stark contrast to the vast majority of CANDU exports that were facilitated with plenty of Canadian government money.

There were also high hopes that AECL's success in South Korea would spread to other parts of Asia. Robert Gadsby, vice-president and representative for AECL in South Korea, stated at the time, 'I'm optimistic we will see Candu exports to other parts of Asia ... This is one of the key areas in the world to be.'[3] Indonesia was considered the prime candidate for future sales. It had signed a nuclear cooperation agreement with and purchased a nuclear laboratory from Canada. As well, AECL had allowed Indonesian nuclear personnel to gain experience by working on CANDUs in both South Korea and Canada.[4] AECL officials were absolutely convinced that Indonesia would eventually purchase a CANDU.[5]

Finally, it was hoped that the sale of CANDUs would strengthen Canada's overall trading relationship with South Korea. In the early 1990s, and prior to the 1997 Asian financial crisis, economic views towards South Korea were very positive. As one of the 'Asian tigers,' South Korea had maintained double-digit economic growth rates for years. Some even predicated that it could seriously challenge Japan's position in Asia by the next century. Thus, securing ties in that market, especially in high-tech products like nuclear reactors, was of vital importance to Canada. In 1992, South Korea was Canada's fifth largest trading partner worldwide and its second largest market, behind Japan, in all of Asia, with two-way trade exceeding $4 billion.[6] AECL was Canada's largest business in South Korea, and its former chair, Robert Ferchat, presided over the Canada–Korea Business Council. Canada's ambassador in Seoul, Len Edwards, stated that 'the sales of the Candu reactors have done much to build awareness of Canada in Korea.'[7]

Despite these inticing economic incentives, the real motivation behind the CANDU sales was not optimism, but fear – the very real fear for the future of the Canadian nuclear industry. Wolsung II to IV were critical sales not only because they were the first exports of CANDUs in over a decade but also because, in many respects, they could be credited with saving the Canadian nuclear industry. In 1990, Ottawa had unveiled a seven-year plan of increased funding for nuclear R&D, which would pump an additional $66 million into the nuclear industry, but this decision was based on the assumption that the Wolsung II sale was imminent.[8] If Canada had failed to close the deal, it could very well have been the end of Canada's reactor export program as well as government support for the domestic nuclear industry.

Due to its desire to 'save' the Canadian nuclear program, Ottawa downplayed any constraining foreign policy objectives. However, these issues were not insignificant and need to be explored. South Korea, although a signatory to the Nuclear Non-Proliferation Treaty (NPT), continued to maintain a strong security incentive to acquire nuclear weapons because it remained technically at war with North Korea. However, by the time of the Wolsung II to IV sales in 1990 and 1992, there were strong reasons for external affairs officials to believe that South Korea was 'not a proliferation risk.'[9] Noteworthy was the fact that efforts to clandestinely develop nuclear weapons, which had worried Canadian and American officials throughout the 1970s, had ended with the assassination of President Park Chung-Hee in October 1979.[10] As proliferation expert David Fischer commented, 'were it not for the history of violent relations between the two Koreas there would be no reason to doubt Seoul's continuing attachment to the NPT.'[11]

Even in that respect, it appeared that a nuclear thaw was occurring between the two Koreas. The North Koreans, relying heavily on Soviet training, had begun work on a nuclear program in the 1950s. By the late 1980s, North Korea had over a 100 different nuclear facilities, including a uranium mine, a nuclear fuel rod fabrication plant, and a number of small research and power reactors. There was also no doubt that by the 1970s North Korea was trying to develop nuclear weapons. However, by the late 1980s, it appeared that North Korea, 'because of various economic, financial, and scientific difficulties' that were exacerbated by the changing international political climate, was forced to abandon 'the military aspect of the nuclear program.'[12] Once this decision was made, North Korea took a number of significant steps to show the international community that it had decided to stop its development of nuclear weapons.[13] In 1985, North Korea finally acceded to the NPT. Seoul and Pyongyang later signed a 1991 joint declaration on the denuclearization of the Korean peninsula. For its part, the United States also removed all of its nuclear weapons from South Korea. A year later, North Korea signed a nuclear safeguards agreement with the International Atomic

Energy Agency (IAEA) and international inspectors started arriving at North Korea's nuclear facility at Yongbyon.

By 1990 there was strong evidence that Ottawa's fears over South Korea's development of nuclear weapons had dissipated. Ottawa, as part of the Wolsung II negotiations, was considering allowing the Koreans to reprocess the spent fuel from the CANDU reactors. During the nuclear safeguards negotiations over Wolsung I in 1974–6, Canada had placed a great deal of emphasis on preventing South Korea from purchasing a French reprocessing plant (as discussed in chapter 4), but by 1990, Canada's position had changed. The reason for this shift in policy was the promise of tandem fuel cycles. The development of this type of advanced fuel cycle technology was one of the major reasons why South Korea agreed to purchase Wolsung II.[14] Tandem fuel cycles give the CANDU a technical advantage over its light-water reactor (LWR) competitor because the process increases uranium utilization by allowing the spent fuel from an LWR to be reused in a CANDU. In addition, this can be done without separating the plutonium, thus reducing its vulnerability to diversion for weapons purposes. While the use of tandem fuel cycles removes some proliferation risks, unfortunately, it opens the door for other ones. The fact that Canada was willing to compromise on a historically sensitive issue was an indication not only of the commercial imperatives to make the sale but also of the diminishing threat of nuclear proliferation from South Korea.[15]

Unfortunately, this optimism towards the South Korean nuclear program was jeopardized in 1993 by concerns over North Korea's nuclear intentions. 'Suspicion that [North Korea] had a nuclear weapons program was aroused when the results of the inspection of the reprocessing facility were inconsistent with North Korean claims: The characteristics of the plutonium samples analyzed did not match North Korean claims of their production.'[16] The IAEA's request to conduct 'special inspections' of nuclear waste areas was refused and its inspectors were ejected from the country. Pyongyang subsequently announced that it would withdraw from the NPT. This crisis, which at several stages looked like it would turn hot, was only resolved through heavy U.S. diplomatic pressure. U.S. President Bill Clinton dispatched former president Jimmy Carter to Pyongyang as a special envoy to negotiate an end to the North Korean nuclear weapons program.[17] Carter used a number of negotiating techniques including public condemnation and threats of political, economic, and military sanctions. Ultimately, however, the Americans relied on carrots rather than sticks. The result was the Agreed Framework of October 1994. Under this agreement, North Korea agreed to freeze its weapons program and eventually to comply with IAEA safeguards obligations in return for the provision by an American-led international consortium (the Korean Peninsula Energy Development Organization) of two 1,000 megawatt light-water reactors to meet its electricity needs.

The 1994 nuclear crisis did not end concerns about North Korea. Most notably, it tested a long-range missile in 1998 that greatly upset the South Koreans and the Japanese.[18] The United States has continued to officially cite North Korea as a terrorist state and has even referred to it as a member of the 'Axis of Evil.' On 10 April 2003, North Korea became the first country to officially withdraw from the NPT.[19] While there is no doubt that North Korea has a weapons program, in the absence of a nuclear test, experts are divided over whether they actually have workable nuclear weapons (and, if so, how many do they have) or are close to developing them (and, if so, how far along they are).[20] The United States has been reluctant to take the lead in negotiations with the North Koreans as it did in 1994, preferring instead to use a multilateral framework involving China, Russia, Japan, and South Korea.[21] The possibility cannot be ignored that North Korea's military provocations may yet provide South Korea with the justification to pursue its own nuclear option.

South Korea's human rights record had previously been a constraining influence on CANDU exports. This is because South Korea used to be run by a series of military dictators who were not adverse to widespread violations of human rights in order to maintain civic order. This started to change when, in 1988, South Korea began a successful transition to democracy. Today, international observers refer to South Korea as one of the great success stories of the third wave of democratization. In contrast to those countries that have either stalled or reversed their democratic transition, South Korea has successfully consolidated its democracy. For instance, Freedom House – a well-respected think tank that monitors civil and political rights around the world – has for the last decade placed South Korea in its 'free' category of states for political rights and civil liberties.[22] The election of Kim Dae-Jung, who had been imprisoned under the Park Chung-Hee regime, as South Korea's president in 1998 was a symbol of the changed role of human rights in that country.

Like human rights, Canadian government subsidies were no longer a constraining variable in the case of South Korea. Wolsung I may have benefited from a large EDC loan, but the sales in 1990 and 1992 were free of concessionary financing. A bigger concern, however, was the fact that the corruption associated with Wolsung I did not end in the 1970s but continued into the 1990s with the sales of Wolsung II, III, and IV. In 1994, a scandal involving the Korean Electric Power Corporation (KEPCO) and AECL's Korean agency, Samchang Corporation, resulted in South Korea charging, convicting, and incarcerating Park Byon-chan (Samchang) and Ahn Byong-wha (KEPCO) for bribery and corruption. AECL responded by firing Samchang Corporation as its agent in South Korea.[23]

Romania: Increasing Nuclear Cooperation, 1991

Even as it was celebrating the Wolsung exports, Ottawa had to deal with the 'problem child' of the CANDU export program. In 1978, Romania signed a contract to build five CANDU reactors at the Cernavoda site, a project that would turn out to be nothing less than a fiasco. Financial difficulties, design flaws, technical mishaps, safety problems, and construction delays continually plagued the project. Jennifer Wells described the site as 'a hazardous, ill-lit disaster. The workmanship was faulty, quality and safety standards non-existent. Many labourers would die here.'[24] The Cernavoda project was a microcosm of the mismanagement, corruption, and political repression of Nicolae Ceausescu's communist regime.

The fall of 1989 was one of the most stunning periods in world history. The people of Eastern Europe, in an ironic twist on the old domino theory of communist expansion, overthrew their communist states one by one. After decades of armed confrontation in Europe, which threatened to explode into a third world war, it was startling to see the Iron Curtain fall with a whimper, not a bang. Governments were toppled by large-scale peaceful demonstrations, not by the use of force. An exception was Romania, where street battles between pro-democracy groups and embattled government troops killed several hundred people. Included in the death toll were Ceausescu and his wife who were both executed on Christmas Day in 1989.

After the fall of Ceausescu, Ottawa was faced with a request from the new Romanian government to reinforce its nuclear assistance by helping it finish Cernavoda I. Despite over a decade of construction, Cernavoda I was still only 45 per cent completed and the other units were little more than holes in the ground. Canada decided in September 1991 to further assist the non-communist Romanian government by providing technical assistance and $315 million in additional funds to complete the reactor.[25] There were some economic interests that favoured improved nuclear cooperation. First, the level of Canadian content in the reactor would be substantially increased from the 1978 agreements. Second, AECL would operate the reactor for the first eighteen months. Third, much of the money that Canada would supply to finish Cernavoda I would be used to purchase Canadian goods and services and would be paid back with interest. Finally, Romania agreed to lease, with an option to purchase, heavy water from the Bruce heavy-water plant in Ontario.[26]

Canada also had an important political interest that favoured further nuclear cooperation with Romania. It was expected that the Cernavoda reactors would supply over 30 per cent of Romania's electricity needs. Romania was desperate for electricity, and if the project were not finished soon it could push a country already close to the edge into a state of collapse. In short, the economic conditions in Romania could act as a catalyst for a return to an authoritarian dictatorship. Canadian officials believed that allowing the Romanians to 'freeze in the dark' would only add to that potential.[27] Canada also felt a duty, after years of combating communism, to reward a people who had just thrown off their communist yoke.

In 1991, the threat of nuclear proliferation, rather than acting as a brake, facilitated Canada's decision to further assist the Romanians. Ottawa believed that the threat of nuclear proliferation would increase even more so if Canada withdrew its support from Cernavoda. If Canada withdrew its support, Romania would be left with the blueprints for Canadian nuclear technology at a time when the former Soviet Union was in no position to ensure that Romania would use its nuclear power only for peaceful purposes. By placing Canadian officials in charge (which could occur only if Canada pledged additional funds), the Canadian government would be in a position to take over the role played in the past by the Soviet Union. Department of External Affairs officials asserted that 'the current regime has taken on all obligations of the former regime and has informed on discrepancies of the past.'[28]

The influence of human rights on Canada's nuclear cooperation with Romania was insignificant despite the fact that Canadian officials knew about Romania's disgraceful human rights record during Ceausescu's reign. Moreover, even as Ottawa was debating further nuclear cooperation, External Affairs Minister Joe Clark was acknowledging that there were still 'widespread and systematic human rights violations in Romania.'[29] Forced labour had even been used at the Cernavoda site,[30] where over 14,000 workers 'received starvation wages and little food, and lived in appalling conditions in unheated, poorly serviced barracks.'[31] When confronted with these allegations, AECL officials first tried to justify this practice by referring to the workers as military conscripts and even contended that Cernavoda was considered a 'preferred posting' because it was better than a 'gulag.'[32] In the end, however, the evidence was just too damning. This led Donald Lawson, president of AECL's CANDU operations, to acknowledge that 'we knew that people had very limited food rations. We knew they had limited heat.'[33]

Ottawa claimed that Romania's human rights violations were simply a reflection of the former Ceausescu communist regime.[34] Nevertheless, Romania, of all the former Warsaw Pact members, was widely considered to be lagging behind in its path to democracy with its Hungarian and Gypsy minorities still subject to state-sponsored persecution.[35] By 1996, Freedom House was scoring Bulgaria, the Czech Republic, Hungary, and Poland as 'free' countries, but Romania (as well as Russia) remained only 'partly free.'[36] Aurel Braun has argued that by assisting with Romania's nuclear program, Canada was 'contributing to the maintenance of a proto-communist regime in power.'[37]

International environmental concerns were irrelevant during the original CANDU transaction in 1978, but during the 1991 decision over renewed nuclear assistance they were an important factor. If Canada left the reactors half built, Romania might attempt to finish them, using substandard materials and guidelines, thereby creating the potential for another Chernobyl. Romanian nuclear engineers at Cernavoda were later to remark that, in the years just prior to the 1989 revolution, 'a lot of work was performed without being checked in an appropriate way.'[38] The IAEA reported that Cernavoda was not even close to meeting minimum safety standards. It noted that the nuclear components – the calandria, pressure tubes, steam generators, and so on – were all adequate, but the equipment was not clean, there was poor lighting, and the reactor lacked sufficient safety features.[39] By continuing with the project, Canada could help ensure that the Cernavoda reactor remained safe. Indeed, once the renewed commitment was made, 'the Canadian technical advisory team on-site strictly supervised completion of repair work to piping wielding: which had previously been done by the Romanians, evidence of the safety advantages stemming from Canada's continuing cooperation.'[40]

In the years immediately following the signing of the original

Cernavoda contracts, the extent to which the Canadian government had previously subsidized the project had become an issue. The Cernavoda project benefited from EDC loans totalling over $1.8 billion in 1978 and 1979. When Romania was forced into massive financial restructuring in the early 1980s because of its high foreign debt, Ottawa suspended all EDC loans, but, unfortunately, over $320 million had already been disbursed. The Ceausescu government also insisted that Canadian suppliers of CANDU components buy Romanian products equal in value to their selling price in Romania. Canadian critics of Romania's countertrade demands labelled it 'CANDUs for strawberries.' However, AECL defended the provisions by asserting that 'it was a countertrade deal or no deal at all,' and that if Canada did not 'take the business,' there were 'plenty of countries' that would.[41] Ultimately, a number of Canadian suppliers made barter arrangements with the Romanians. Over $700-million worth of steel, textiles, and tractors were sent to Canada in exchange for nuclear components.[42] Finally, there was a question of the amount of content actually produced by Canada. In order to clinch the deal, AECL had sold much of its nuclear technology, allowing the Romanians to act as their own contractors. This resulted in many of the non-nuclear components, and all of the administrative responsibilities, being handled by non-Canadian firms.[43]

The government subsidies issue resurfaced during the negotiations in the early 1990s, when the opposition in the House of Commons asserted that Canada would be 'throwing good money after bad in helping to complete the CANDU reactor project in Romania.'[44] Nevertheless, Canada decided to supply Romania with $315 million in additional loans so that Cernavoda I could be completed. This meant that by the time all of the Canadian subsides were tallied up, the cost of the Cernavoda project to Canada reached over $2.2 billion. As Jennifer Wells has commented, 'no business case' can be made for Cernavoda.[45]

The decision-making process that led to further cooperation with Romania is an anomalous case. Variables that had traditionally tended to facilitate nuclear exports, like economic considerations, were actually constraints. There was no real economic benefit to providing Romania with additional loans to finish construction of Cernavoda I. Canada would never recover enough money to justify the $2.2 billion worth of loans. Meanwhile, variables that had traditionally tended to constrain nuclear exports, like nuclear non-proliferation and environmental protection, actually promoted additional cooperation. Canada could simply not risk the consequences of the Romanians trying to operate a fundamentally unsafe nuclear reactor.

China: Qinshan I and II, 1996

After winning the 1993 election, Canadian prime minister Jean Chrétien, in a flip-flop of traditional Liberal policy symbolized by its opposition to the Canada–U.S. Free Trade Agreement during the 1988 federal election, decided that, in fact, Canada needed to increase international trade. Now in office, the Chrétien government not only accepted the Free Trade Agreement with the Americans, but also quickly ratified the North American Free Trade Agreement that extended the trade pact to Mexico. It was also decided that Canada needed to increase trade in non-traditional regions, that is, outside the United States and Western Europe. Chrétien came up with the idea of Team Canada trade missions. The prime minister, federal cabinet ministers, senior bureaucrats, provincial premiers, and Canadian business executives would board a couple of jets, arrive in a country and negotiate millions (perhaps even billions) of dollars worth of deals. The Team Canada idea held a number of benefits: it illustrated Ottawa's support of Canadian exporters, won some major contracts, generated a major media splash, and improved global diplomacy. The destination of the first mission in November 1994 was the People's Republic of China.

Since the early 1980s, Canadian nuclear officials had dreamed about selling CANDUs to China. It would be considered a major coup if the world's most populated country could be established as a nuclear customer. Canadian government politicians and officials believed the same thing and arrived in China hoping to convince Beijing of the benefits of Canadian nuclear power. They were rewarded when Chrétien and Chinese premier Li Peng signed a Nuclear Cooperation Agreement on November 8, 1994. This agreement was widely viewed as the centrepiece of the Team Canada trade mission. The next two years involved serious negotiations between AECL and China's National Nuclear Corporation (CNNC). Ottawa continued to support AECL's bid by sending Canadian cabinet ministers, including Roy MacLaren and Anne McLellan, to Beijing to negotiate directly with the Chinese government. Finally, on 26 November 1996, two years after the signing of the Nuclear Cooperation Agreement, contracts were formally signed for the construction of two 700-megawatt CANDUs at Qinshan. High-level diplomacy was a necessary ingredient in AECL landing the contract. AECL vice-president Gary Kugler remarked that 'the fact that there was good political support really helped. Canada and China had an excellent relationship ... and you can't underappreciate the significance of that. We depended on it a lot.'[46]

China was an interesting location for Canada to export a CANDU. Like every other foreign customer of AECL, it was a developing country. However, China was also recognized by the NPT as a nuclear weapons state. Canada had exported nuclear reactors to countries in the past that were clandestinely pursuing nuclear weapons, but this was the first time that Canada had sold a nuclear reactor to a country that was legally allowed to possess and produce nuclear weapons. In addition, China was an exporter of enriched uranium, heavy water, research reactors, and other aspects of nuclear technology. It may be true that China still required 'Western civilian nuclear technology for its nuclear energy program,'[47] but it was still quite rare for Canada to sell nuclear materials to a competing supplier state.

Strong economic interests drove Canada to sell nuclear reactors to China. Canadian officials frequently cited a number of the immediate economic benefits of the $4-billion Qinshan project. Minister of Natural Resources Anne McLellan pointed out that 'the Canadian component of the contract will be worth $1.5 billion over the next six to eight years, providing a major boost to our economy. As a result of this sale, 27,000 direct and indirect jobs will be generated by AECL and the more than 100 Canadian private-sector firms that will provide goods and services to the project.'[48] China agreed that, once the reactors became operational, it would purchase heavy water from Canada for the next fifteen years. This would generate an additional $450 million for Canada.[49]

These direct and immediate economic benefits of the Qinshan project were important, but an overarching objective was Canada's need to penetrate the huge Chinese market. With over a billion people and a dramatically accelerating growth rate, China remains the world's largest and last untapped market. Foreign Minister André Ouellet stated in 1994 that a central pillar of Canada's China policy was 'to build an economic partnership with China that will create jobs and prosperity in Canada and will also benefit the people of China.'[50] AECL president Reid Morden described the sale of two CANDUs as a 'beachhead ... in the fastest growing economy in the world.'[51] Ottawa hoped to use CANDU exports beyond China, as it had previously tried with the Wolsung sales, and to expand its relations throughout the entire Asian Pacific region. While in Shanghai in November 1996 to finalize the Qinshan project, both Prime Minister Chrétien and International Trade Minister Art Eggleton linked the sale of the reactors with Canada's emerging role in the region. Chrétien stated that 'Canadians are experiencing a profound change in the way we see ourselves and our place in the world. Canada is proud to be a Pacific nation. I can tell you there is a growing sense of excitement about our connection to the Asia Pacific region.'[52] Eggleton noted that 'as China's economy expands, Canada is determined to participate in its growth. Recent years have demonstrated the potential of our relationship, with trade between us growing at a dramatic rate – averaging 22 per cent in each of the last four years.'[53]

Canada's commercial interests provided it with an incentive to export CANDUs to China, but would Canada contribute to nuclear proliferation with the Qinshan reactors? It was possible that the Qinshan project could have an effect on vertical proliferation if China were to complement Canadian nuclear technology with its indigenous variety to expand or enhance its weapons arsenal. This remains one of the reasons why the United States has prevented its nuclear industry from trading with China.[54] When it comes to horizontal proliferation, it appears, on the surface, that CANDU exports would have no effect since China was and continues to be an NPT-recognized nuclear weapons state. However, concern was raised about China's nuclear export policy. At the time of Qinshan, China was not a member of the Nuclear Suppliers Group or the Zangger Committee and, 'unlike other nuclear suppliers, China [had] no atomic energy statute in place, nor specific regulation about nuclear export control.' Not only was it outside of internationally accepted multilateral export-control guidelines, but it viewed such safeguards as impediments to technology transfers to developing countries. As Weixing Hu has written, '[I]n the area of technology transfer, Beijing often view[ed] itself as a victim both of the Western countries' refusal to share technology and of their economic sanctions for exporting technology itself.'[55] China included among its nuclear clients such proliferation-risky countries as Algeria and Iran.

Ottawa was particularly concerned about China's practice of selling nuclear exports to Pakistan. Since Canada had terminated its nuclear cooperation with Pakistan, it did not want to see China engage in retransfers of CANDU technology to assist the KANUPP reactor. Chinese assistance had been of great benefit to Pakistan's nuclear program, particularly after the Canadians departed in 1976. The best example of Chinese–Pakistani nuclear cooperation was the 1991 contract for the CHASMA nuclear reactor. CHASMA, which is not protected by full-scope safeguards because Pakistan is not a party to the NPT, was 'designed, manufactured, and constructed by the Chinese.'[56]

Ottawa downplayed the proliferation risk by highlighting the fact that China has, in the last decade, taken some important steps in improving its non-proliferation policy: joining the IAEA in 1984 and ratifying the NPT in 1992. Nevertheless, China has remained absent from most other aspects of the non-proliferation regime and continues to view export controls and safeguards with suspicion. As Hu has commented, 'although China has embraced the norms and principles of nonproliferation, there is still a gap between its general nonproliferation posture and its export practice.'[57] Foreign affairs officials believed that it was unrealistic to assume that CANDU exports, or the lack thereof, would alter that policy.[58] They also remained 'fully confident that our nuclear trade with China [would] be for peaceful purposes only' because the nuclear safeguards agreement included provisions for IAEA inspections.[59]

It was also possible that China's human rights practices could constrain the export of nuclear reactors. 'Trade and human rights,' as one commentator has written, are 'the broad parameters defining the space in which Canada's China policy is formulated and implemented.'[60] China has been one of the world's worst violators of human rights since the Second World War. Millions of innocent Chinese were killed during the forced collectivization of the 1950s and the Cultural Revolution of the 1960s. Despite these and other events, Canada remained officially quiet about China's human rights policy. With no domestic anti-Chinese lobby group and little news coverage, it was easy for Ottawa to concentrate on the growing bilateral linkages and ignore China's human rights record. For years, as one official admitted, 'the Canadian government, media and many sections of the public had looked at China with rose-coloured glasses.'[61]

Canada's benign view of China was shaken in June 1989 when Chinese troops, in front of the world's media, brutally repressed thousands of pro-democracy demonstrators. The Tiananmen Square massacre was notable for its timing, savagery, and availability of ample visual proof. Pressured by unprecedented public outrage, Ottawa was forced to confront the reality of the Chinese government and to join its allies in applying a package of economic sanctions. Yet, once again, Canada's human rights objectives were trumped by economic and political considerations. Ottawa's rhetoric may have been tough, but the sanctions were in place less than three years and many of the 'initiatives were relatively inconsequential.'[62] Five years after Tiananmen Square, the Team Canada trade mission arrived in Beijing to promote stronger economic ties, including nuclear reactors.

Post-Tiananmen China has continued to stifle democracy and repress political and religious dissidents. All international human rights organizations have China at the head of the class when it comes to states violating human rights. Human Rights Watch noted that 'in its campaign to eradicate Falungong, Chinese officials imprisoned thousands of practitioners and used torture and psychological pressure to force recantations.'[63] Amnesty International reported that Chinese

> authorities continued to show willingness to adhere on a pro-forma level to the international human rights regime, but pursued domestic policies which resulted in serious human rights violations on a large scale, undermining efforts by some groups and institutions to strengthen the rule of law and the protection of human rights. Faced with growing social unrest and public criticism of official corruption and economic inequalities, the government responded with both containment and reforms. It imposed new restrictions on the media and cracked down on groups and individuals deemed a threat to the 'stability' or 'unity' of the country.[64]

Freedom House has consistently given China its lowest possible grades for political rights and civil liberties and has labelled the country as 'not free.'[65] The Canadian government has also acknowledged China's poor human rights record. In the midst of the CANDU negotiations, Canada's Secretary of State (Asia-Pacific) Raymond Chan, on the occasion of the sixth anniversary of the Tiananmen Square massacre, asserted that 'the human rights situation with regard to human rights advocates in China has not improved significantly since 1989 ... China continues to violate international standards of human rights.'[66] Chan later wrote that he has 'pointed out to Chinese officials that they are in violation of international standards on human rights, that China lacks the rule of law, and that this has hindered China's economic development and contributed to the corruption of government officials.'[67]

Although Canada is fully cognizant of the character of the Chinese regime, it believes that constructive engagement, not diplomatic isolation or economic sanctions, is the proper strategy for stopping human rights violations. As one analyst noted, 'business was the best way to open up China, especially since human rights pressures by themselves produced no visible change.'[68] For his part, Prime Minister Chrétien argued that 'isolation is the worst recipe in my judgement for curing human rights problems.'[69] Raymond Chan noted in a speech that 'trade is also a powerful tool. It encourages co-operation, and co-operation leads to understanding and appreciation, with which we can better manage concerns such as human rights development.'[70] Thus, Canada's official position is that international trade, such as CANDU exports, can be used as leverage to improve China's human rights record.

The episode of the environmental impact study for the Qinshan project illustrates that international environmental considerations were becoming an increasingly important variable in CANDU exports. However, it also shows that while environmental considerations may have increased in importance, they still do not carry sufficient weight to prevent a CANDU export. The Canadian Environmental Assessment Act states that before any federal project can be authorized it must undergo a comprehensive environmental impact assessment. For foreign projects, the Projects Outside of Canada Environmental Assessment Regulations require additional studies to ensure that Canadian environmental standards will be met. However, in a move clearly aimed at the imminent Qinshan sale, the cabinet issued an Order in Council on 7 November 1996, exempting all overseas megaprojects from Canadian environmental assessment requirements.[71] Cabinet ministers confirmed that the regulations were passed 'to clarify the law for the peace of mind and benefit of the Chinese buyers.'[72] These new regulations were not publicly disclosed until November 27, 1996: the day after the formal signing of the Qinshan contracts.

Canadian anti-nuclear groups strongly opposed Ottawa's last-minute decision to waive its environmental requirements. Elizabeth May, the executive director of the Sierra Club, asserted that 'the government has violated its own Environmental Assessment Act. By passing regulations in cabinet, in the middle of the night, the government has shanghaied the democratic rights of Canadian citizens. In the process of trying to sell CANDU reactors at any cost to China, the government has jettisoned parliamentary procedure and public accountability in Canada.'[73] The Sierra Club subsequently launched a court challenge against the Chrétien government in January 1997.[74] Environmental regulations, according to the Sierra Club, were triggered when the federal cabinet authorized EDC financing for the reactor sale. The federal ministers of finance, international trade, foreign affairs, and the Attorney General were named as respondents in the case. The Sierra Club also requested the full disclosure of all agreements and documents pertaining to the sale of the two CANDUs to China. Andrew Chisholm, a policy adviser to the Sierra Club, argued that 'Canada has a legal obligation to conduct an environmental review under the Canadian Environmental Assessment Act, which has a special section applying to publicly funded projects outside Canada. From an ethical standpoint as well, we have an obligation to enforce the environmental standards we would use in our own country.'[75]

The government commissioned Marbek Resource Consultants to determine whether an environmental assessment was necessary for the Qinshan project. Marbek recommended that public hearings in Canada be held because of a dearth of scientific data and a lack of cooperation from the Chinese authorities. However, the government decided to ignore the report, and even tried to bury it and pretend that it never existed. Only through an Access to Information request by the environmental watchdog group Energy Probe did the truth come out.[76]

Ottawa was clearly worried about the anti-nuclear movement's court challenge. If the government lost, it would open up the Qinshan contract for public examination. This could jeopardize the completion of the reactors and possibly effect future nuclear exports to China. In addition, the Sierra Club wanted to use the Environmental Protection Act to open up the Qinshan deal to examine not just the environmental impact but also its commercial aspects. This would affect not only the Qinshan sale but *all* future CANDU sales. At the time, AECL was in the midst of negotiations for the sale of two CANDUs to Turkey and was eyeing possible sales in South Korea, Thailand, Australia, and Indonesia. In addition to its potential impacts on CANDU exports, other economic sectors, like mining and forestry would be affected. In fact, all export projects that received significant EDC financing (which required cabinet approval) would be subject to Canadian environmental regulations even though the projects receiving assistance were in another country. This raised the spectre of extraterritoriality and possible infringements on state sovereignty. This was not just hypothetical worrying, because there was a good chance that the government could lose the case. According to a confidential cabinet document prepared by the Privy Council Office, 'Justice has advised that its case is not strong and that the Federal Court may well rule in favour of the Sierra Club. If the government loses, Justice expects that the court could issue an order directing' DFAIT and Finance 'to conduct an environmental assessment which satisfies the Projects Outside Canada Environmental Assessment Regulations.'[77]

The federal government prepared its court defence on a number of different levels. It pointed out that AECL and EDC are Crown corporations and therefore exempt from the provisions of the Environmental Assessment Act. A full environmental review was not required because the federal cabinet played only a minor role in the Qinshan deal. International Trade Minister Art Eggleton maintained that 'the act was never intended to apply to Export Development Corporation's commercial financing operations in foreign countries.'[78] It also noted that China had completed an environmental impact study and that this met the Canadian legal requirements. The Third Qinshan Nuclear Power Company, in conjunction with AECL, which participated in and monitored the Chinese review, found that 'there [would] be no unfavourable environmental impact from the nuclear plants.'[79] These arguments, regardless of their persuasiveness, did not guide Ottawa's decision-making, instead they acted as a legal fig leaf to cover its economic motivations to conclude the Qinshan sale. The Department of Foreign Affairs and International Trade (DFAIT), in briefing notes prepared for the cabinet, argued that requiring environmental assessments would put Canada at a great disadvantage with other nuclear suppliers.[80] That is the real reason why cabinet waived the requirements contained in the Canadian Environmental Assessment Act.

AECL had a vested interest in the Sierra Club's court challenge, so it requested that it be added as a respondent. When this was denied, AECL requested, and was granted, intervener status. AECL argued that its Qinshan documents should remain secret on the grounds of commercial confidentiality. An AECL official also maintained that many crucial documents were, in fact, the property of the Chinese government, and Canadian courts did not have the jurisdiction to force the disclosure of foreign documents.[81] The federal government had previously supported AECL on these points. Paul Zed, Chrétien's parliamentary secretary, told the House of Commons that 'loan agreements in support of CANDU sales abroad are commercially confidential documents to which AECL is not party. Therefore, AECL cannot provide information with respect to the terms and conditions of eventual loans to China ... nor can it provide comparative information in relation to past loans to Argentina, Romania and South Korea.'[82] In 1999, a Federal Court judge refused AECL's efforts to keep the Qinshan documents secret. Mr Justice Denis Pelletier ruled that 'I am not satisfied that the need for confidentiality exceeds the public interest in open justice. The issue of Canada's role as a vendor of nuclear technology is one of significant public interest with animated positions being taken on both sides of the question. The burden of justifying a confidentiality order in such circumstances is very onerous.'[83] A subsequent appeal to the Federal Appeals Court was also rejected. That left the matter up the Supreme Court of Canada.

The Sierra Club has charged that AECL's purpose in intervening was not to offer a legitimate legal defence of the Qinshan project but to create delays, thereby lengthening the legal process. If the reactors came onstream prior to a final court decision, then the case would be ruled moot. Timothy Howard, the lead attorney for the Sierra Club, said that AECL's role in the case – which included challenging the Sierra Club's legal standing and introducing thousands of pages of very technical Chinese-language documents – was designed simply to bog things down in motions and document filings.[84] Larry Shewchuk, a spokesperson for the AECL, defended his company's legal tactics, '[W]e're not dragging out the matter, but at the same time, there's a lot of legal mileage that has to be done here.'[85]

The Sierra Club suffered a major legal setback when, on April 26, 2002, the Supreme Court of Canada overturned the previous Federal Court rulings. In a unanimous 7–0 decision, the Court ruled that AECL could keep over thirty volumes of commercial documents secret. This allowed AECL, as part of its intervention in the court challenge against the federal government, to tender court documents dealing with the environmental assessment done by the Chinese in perfect confidence. This honoured a request made by the Chinese government and protected AECL's trade secrets. In handing down the ruling, Mr Justice Frank Iacobucci wrote that 'although the exact contents of the documents remain a mystery, it is apparent that they contain technical details of a nuclear installation ... and there may be a substantial public security interest in maintaining the confidentiality of such information.' Opening up AECL's documents for public scrutiny would cause it to 'breach its contractual obligations and suffer a risk of harm to its competitive position' and 'impose a serious risk on an important commercial interest of AECL.'[86]

AECL's court victory regarding commercial confidentiality resulted in the Sierra Club reluctantly dropping its court challenge of the Qinshan project.[87] Nevertheless, the case has had an impact on Canada's environmental assessment policy. EDC, which is exempt from the Canadian Environmental Assessment Act, has been under pressure for years to adopt more stringent environmental protection for the projects that it supports with export credits. Environmentalists have criticized EDC investments in the Three Gorges Dam in China, the Urra hydroelectric dam in Colombia, the Omai mine in Ghana, and other megaprojects. In response to this pressure, EDC adopted a voluntary Environmental Review Framework in April 1999. EDC president Ian Gillespie stated that the Framework 'strives to create a balance between ensuring environmental integrity and encouraging sustainable development for [emerging] countries to grow and create their own economic and social development.'[88] However, the Gowlings Report, a DFAIT-sponsored study, advised that the review process was insufficient. It recommended that EDC meet the environmental standards set by the World Bank and decline any project that failed to meet those guidelines. The Gowlings Report was followed up when the House Standing Committee on Foreign Affairs and International Trade (SCFAIT) issued its own report in December 1999. Some of SCFAIT's major recommendations were that:

- an ombudsman position be set up to respond to the negative environmental and human rights effects of EDC projects
- a provision be made that EDC financing should be contingent on an environmental impact assessment
- EDC should submit its forthcoming disclosure policy and Environmental Framework to a full public consultation, and
- consistency with international environmental and human rights conventions must be assured through the purpose clause of EDC's governing statute[89]

In response to these recommendations, EDC introduced a new Environmental Review Directive in December 2001,[90] which established three categories of projects. Category A included all projects 'likely to have significant adverse environmental effects that are sensitive, diverse, or unprecedented.' Those projects that included nuclear reactors and other megaprojects would require an environmental impact assessment before EDC funding was provided. The Directive specified that the EDC would meet the environmental standards established by the Export Credits Group of the OECD. This may have been a major improvement from the previous environmental policy, but critics still noted a number of deficiencies: EDC was still exempt from the Canadian Environmental Assessment Act; it still did not meet World Bank guidelines; the disclosure guidelines were not retroactive; and the language was too flexible and open for interpretation.[91]

These changes to the operating procedures of EDC, which were sparked, in part, by the Sierra Club's court challenge of the Qinshan reactor deal, could undoubtedly affect future CANDU exports. EDC financing was a crucial component of virtually every CANDU export. The sales to India, Pakistan, Argentina, South Korea, Romania, as well as China, all received EDC loans. Without EDC assistance, it is highly unlikely that the nuclear sales could have been completed. This is going to continue because, as Robert Morrison reminds us, 'AECL's most likely markets are in the emerging industrial economies, many of which require financing in order to manage the purchase of such large items.'[92] The establishment of EDC's Environmental Review Directive will consequently have a number of major effects on future CANDU exports. Greater attention will be placed on the possible environmental impact of nuclear reactors. Environmental impact assessments will have to be completed, their procedures more exacting, and their results more closely scrutinized. There will need to be greater public transparency of the contracts and agreements that make up a CANDU sale, in order to increase public awareness and knowledge about nuclear reactor exports.

As the above section makes clear, an important linkage to the controversy over environmental protection was the extent of Ottawa's subsidization of the Qinshan project. The commercial contract signed between AECL and the China National Nuclear Corporation has not been publicly disclosed. Nevertheless, an examination of public statements made by AECL, EDC, and Canadian government officials allows us to get a basic idea of what it contains. The two years between the signing of the 1994 Nuclear Cooperation Agreement and the November 1996 Order in Council was a period of intense negotiations over the price and financing of the Qinshan project. In the initial period of the negotiations, AECL speculated that its revenues from a Chinese reactor deal would be $200 to $800 million and that the Canadian component suppliers might receive up to $2.7 billion in business.[93] However, by the spring of 1996, AECL president Reid Morden was complaining that 'the Chinese terms are onerous' and the Canadian consortium was forced to reduce its bid by an additional 15 per cent.[94] With such tight margins, it is doubtful whether AECL will ever see a profit from Qinshan.

Given the history of CANDU subsidies and the negotiations with the

Chinese, a reasonable question to ask is, To what extent did Ottawa subsidize the Qinshan project? National Resources Minister Anne McLellan claimed that the sale 'would not be subsidized by Canada, but would have to proceed on the basis of fair market costs.'[95] Yet the entire Canadian component of the project, $1.5 billion, was financed through EDC. The Chinese would not put up one cent of their own money, but borrowed the entire amount from Canada. EDC provided a $1.5-billion loan with a fifteen year repayment schedule at an interest rate of 7.3 per cent.[96] EDC later added another $350 million in U.S. currency.[97] This loan was EDC's largest ever. As a result, EDC was unable to place the loan on its own books, but instead placed it on its 'Canada Account' that is carried by foreign affairs. Canada Account loans are used in cases where the loan is extremely large or there is an extreme risk to the project. Moreover, there is no political risk insurance – covering currency fluctuations, expropriation, breach of contract, war, and civil disturbance - on the loan. Canada's business press, which tends to support Canada's export efforts, was outraged by the Qinshan deal. The *Globe and Mail*'s business columnist Terence Corcoran blasted the deal as 'a high-order abomination, a dishonest flouting of Canadian principles and possibly Canadian laws, carried out behind a screen of deceptive information.'[98]

In sum, the Qinshan project was a further example of Canada's economic interests outweighing any of its other foreign policy considerations in the export of CANDUs. Clearly, Ottawa was staying the course set by previous sales when it exported CANDUs to China. Gaining a nuclear toehold in the world's most populated country was the most important foreign policy objective. That Canada was negotiating with a repressive dictatorship was largely irrelevant. The fact that Ottawa heavily subsidized the project and, in the process, was forced to amend its own environmental protection laws further indicates the significant economic interests Canada had in securing the nuclear sale.

The first half of the 1990s saw a renaissance in the export of CANDUs. After suffering the consequences for its nuclear non-proliferation policy in the 1980s by failing to make a single foreign sale, AECL was able to sell three CANDUs to South Korea and another two to China. In addition, Canada's renewed nuclear cooperation with Romania paved the way for Cernavoda I to come onstream in 1996 and offered the potential of even more business. The period 1990–6 was one of excellent news for AECL and Canadian nuclear component suppliers.

What do AECL's successes in South Korea and China, and its efforts in Romania, reveal about the foreign policy priorities of the Canadian government? As the case studies show, Canada's economic and political interests clearly predominated over nuclear non-proliferation, human rights, environmental protection, and government subsidies. This was a reversal of Canada's policy established in the wake of the 1974 Indian nuclear test when non-proliferation considerations came to the forefront. In a sense, Canada was now operating as it did back in the 1950s and 1960s. Yes, there was a greater awareness of new foreign policy objectives, like human rights and environmental protection, but the strength of economic arguments still managed to prevail.

When it comes to nuclear non-proliferation, Canada continues to rely solely on the written guarantees contained in the NPT and the physical inspections conducted by the IAEA. While this should be a necessary condition for all nuclear exports, it is not a sufficient safeguard against proliferation. Canada needs to ensure that regional threats – like those that exist in the Korean peninsula – do not provide a CANDU recipient with a rationale for developing nuclear weapons. In addition, the Chinese case shows that Canada also needs to consider the potential fallout from retransfers of nuclear materials.

On the issue of human rights, Canada continued to trade in nuclear materials with major human rights violators. In the case of China, Ottawa could claim that it was dealing with a stable country, although it had one of the worst human rights records in the world. However, it would be difficult to classify Romania as stable. A more significant policy shift in the area of human rights occurred during this time period as Canada began to embrace the concept of constructive engagement. Stronger bilateral relations, especially trade, were seen as a way to produce changes in human rights violators. This meant that Ottawa transformed the variable of human rights from a constraint to a facilitator of CANDU exports.

Similarly, when it came to environmental matters, the Canadian government only used them when they supported reactor exports. For example, if environmental arguments could facilitate greater nuclear cooperation (Romania), then their role in the decision-making process was heightened. However, when they constrained CANDU sales (China), Ottawa changed, some would say violated, its own environmental protection laws to ensure that the export was not jeopardized.

The first half of the 1990s showed that Ottawa was not hesitant, despite significant financial losses in the past, to continue generously subsidizing CANDU exports. EDC was the key ingredient in all CANDU transactions because the risk was too great for commercial lending institutions. However, even the EDC had to rely on its 'Canada Account,' because CANDU sales were too risky for its ordinary 'Corporate Account.'

8 New Challenges and New Opportunities, 1997–2005

How will the clash between Canada's economic and political interests and its normative foreign policy objectives play out in future CANDU exports? The historical record, as described in chapters 4 to 7, has shown that Canada's economic and political interests have tended to strongly outweigh any other considerations. Only in very rare circumstances have Canada's other foreign policy objectives determined an important decision over CANDU exports. For example, fears over nuclear proliferation rose in ascendancy only in the immediate aftermath of the 1974 Indian nuclear test. The human rights record of potential recipient regimes acted as a constraining influence only in the case of Canada's efforts at exporting a CANDU to Argentina in 1979. Some foreign policy objectives were almost completely absent from the decision-making process. For example, in only one previous case, the sale of two CANDUs to China in 1996, did Ottawa seriously consider the negative effects of nuclear safety and environmental protection. At other times, these other normative foreign policy objectives, instead of constraining a CANDU export, were actually used to facilitate the nuclear transaction. For example, China's human rights record was used to justify the sale of two CANDUs through the concept of constructive engagement. Similarly, a concern over environmental protection and nuclear safety was a major incentive for renewing nuclear cooperation with Romania in 1991.

Will Canada's economic and political interests continue to prevail? This chapter assesses the future of CANDU exports by revisiting both the arguments in favour of CANDU exports (outlined in chapter 2) and those opposed (outlined in chapter 3). In addition, it traces the effect of Canada's competing foreign policy objectives on CANDU exports by focusing on four major recent events: (1) Ontario Hydro's 1997 decision to temporarily shut down seven of its twenty reactors; (2) the nuclear tests conducted by India and Pakistan in May 1998; (3) AECL's unsuccessful attempt to sell two CANDUs to Turkey in the late 1990s; and (4) the decision to provide additional financing to complete Romania's Cernavoda II reactor.

Nuclear Non-Proliferation

The impact of nuclear proliferation on CANDU exports had reached its peak in the period immediately following India's 1974 nuclear test. However, the issue regained its primacy when, on May 11, 1998, India conducted another nuclear weapons test at a site in Pokhran. Within a week, India had exploded a total of five nuclear devices. Unlike in 1974 when it claimed that its tests were for peaceful purposes, India justified the 1998 tests purely on national security grounds. Prime Minister Atal Behari Vajpayee declared after the tests that 'India is now a nuclear weapon state.' Defence Minister Abdul Kalam added that the tests have provided 'critical data for the validation of [India's] capability in the design of nuclear weapons of different yields for different applications and different delivery systems.'[1]

New Delhi's actions were a direct warning to China and Pakistan. China had attacked India along its Himalayan border in 1962 and had tested its own nuclear weapons in 1964. Indian–Pakistani relations had included three major wars and periodic fighting in the contested Kashmir region. Jaswant Singh, the senior adviser on defence and foreign affairs to Vajpayee, claimed that India's nuclear weapons are 'of self-defence, to ensure that India ... is not subjected to nuclear coercion.'[2] Vajpayee asserted that India's nuclear tests were due to 'an atmosphere of distrust' with China. 'To add to the distrust,' China 'has materially helped' Pakistan 'to become a covert nuclear weapon state.'[3]

There were other factors that seemed to motivate India's desire to test nuclear weapons. There was a sense that India desired greater world prestige. In praising the tests, the *Times of India* wrote that 'India is a large country demanding its place in the world. It has come to the conclusion, if you do not have the bomb the world will not take you seriously.'[4] This helps to explain why there were people dancing in the streets of Indian cities after reports of the tests were released. The tests can also be viewed as an explicit protest against what New Delhi saw as the discriminatory nature of the Nuclear Non-Proliferation Treaty (NPT).[5] Jaswant Singh wrote:

If the permanent five's possession of nuclear weapons increases security, why would India's possession of nuclear weapons be dangerous? If the permanent five continue to employ nuclear weapons as an international currency of force and power, why should India voluntarily devalue its own state power and national security? Why admonish India after the fact for falling in line behind a new international agenda of discriminatory nonproliferation pursued largely due to the internal agenda or political debates of the nuclear club? If deterrence works in the West – as it so obviously appears to, since Western nations insist on continuing to possess nuclear weapons – by what reasoning will it not work for India? Nuclear weapons powers continue to have, but preach to the have-nots to have even less. India counters by suggesting either universal, nondiscriminatory disarmament or equal security for the entire world.[6]

Indian domestic politics also appeared to play a role in the decision to test nuclear weapons. The Bharatiya Janata Party (BJP) is a right-wing Hindu nationalist party that is 'the most enthusiastic advocate of India becoming a full-blown nuclear weapons state. In the defence of a Hindu India, the BJP made clear its "resolve to give nuclear teeth to the Indian armed force."'[7] In May 1998, the BJP had been in power for only a couple of months and had only been able to form a government based upon a fragile coalition of twelve parties in the Indian Parliament. There had been speculation about whether the BJP government would fall in a non-confidence vote. Instead, the nuclear tests helped to provide some short-term political support as more than 90 per cent of Indians approved of the tests.[8]

India's nuclear tests were widely condemned throughout the West, although its actions were supported by a number of south-east Asian states. The United States and Japan, India's two largest aid donours, cut off over $2-billion worth of non-humanitarian aid.[9] Canada also condemned the tests. Foreign Minister Lloyd Axworthy stated that he was 'deeply concerned and very disappointed' by India's actions.[10] Canada then immediately applied the following sanctions:

- recalled its High Commissioner
- cancelled CIDA consultation, trade policy talks, and the Joint Ministerial Committee
- banned all military shipments
- opposed non-humanitarian loans to India by the World Bank
- stopped non-humanitarian Canadian development assistance to India[11]

Axworthy later explained to the Standing Committee on Foreign Affairs and International Trade that 'India's recent nuclear tests constitute a clear and fundamental threat to the International Security regime and, thus, to Canada's security.' Consequently, Canada must 'step forward and take a leading role' to 'preserve the integrity of the non-proliferation regime so critical to international security.'[12]

In the immediate aftermath of the Indian tests, there were fears that the tests would set off a nuclear arms race in south Asia between China, India, and Pakistan. Two weeks later, on May 28, 1998, these fears were realized when Pakistan, despite the pleading of much of the international community, exploded six nuclear devices at the Chagai test site in Baluchistan province. The six explosions were explicitly intended to match India's 1974 explosion and its five in 1998. In announcing the tests, Prime Minister Nawaz Sharif asserted that 'we have settled the score with India. As a self-respecting nation we had no choice left to us. Our hand was forced by the present Indian leadership's reckless action.'[13] As they did with India, Canada and the rest of the Western world responded with condemnations and sanctions.[14]

Canada was quick to claim that it was not responsible, in any way, for the nuclear tests. After all, Canada had terminated nuclear assistance to both India and Pakistan following India's 1974 nuclear test. In addition, the plutonium and enriched uranium that fuelled the 1998 tests, unlike the 1974 explosion, came from indigenous reactors. Thus, Prime Minister Chrétien was largely correct when he stated that 'that was 25 years ago. Since then technological evolution has been such that the technology of 1974 is completely *passé*. They have their own scientists, and the old technology doesn't mean anything now.'[15] The IAEA similarly confirmed that no materials from the three facility-specific safeguarded reactors in India (RAPP I and RAPP II) and Pakistan (KANUPP) were used in the 1998 tests.[16]

Nevertheless, there is some evidence, as Kristen Ostling, national coordinator of the Campaign for Nuclear Phaseout, has argued, that 'Canada bears special responsibility for the current nuclear escalation between India and Pakistan by beginning the nuclear programs of both countries.'[17] Canada's original sales of nuclear reactors in the 1950s and 1960s established the facilities for the development of India and Pakistan's indigenous nuclear capability. In addition, much of India's indigenous nuclear program is based on Canadian technology, the so-called CANDU clones. Thus, even if the plutonium and tritium (used in thermonuclear devices) for its 1998 tests came from its own reactors, these reactors were still based on Canadian technology. Finally, and most importantly, the first generation of Indian and Pakistani nuclear scientists, the backbone of any nuclear program, were trained in Canada. It is estimated that 260 Indian nuclear scientists and engineers, and another fifty from Pakistan, were given training at Canadian nuclear facilities.[18] Since it is impossible to separate the civilian and the military applications when you educate people about the scientific nature of the atom, Canada was also undoubtedly contributing to the body of knowledge that would lead to the development of nuclear weapons programs in India and Pakistan. For example, P.K. Iyengar, who would eventually head India's nuclear weapons research centre and who played a vital role in the 1974 Indian nuclear test, was trained at Chalk River.[19] In the case of Pakistan, J.G. Hadwen, Canadian ambassador to Pakistan from 1972–4, has written that 'of course Pakistani scientists and engineers were in many cases trained in Canada and Pakistan's experience in the operation of KANUPP formed the basis of whatever program the country decided to develop outside Karachi.'[20]

There have been additional signs that, perhaps, Canada should share some of the blame for the nuclear arms race on the Indian subcontinent. Canada, in recent years, had appeared to be downgrading its nuclear sanctions against India and Pakistan. In 1988, India and Pakistan had been allowed to join the CANDU Owners Group (COG). COG was formed by AECL and Ontario Hydro in 1984, but it also included CANDU operators in Romania, South Korea, and Argentina. The decision to include India and Pakistan in COG's information exchange program was seen as the first step in restarting full nuclear cooperation. Nevertheless, Ottawa still prevented India and Pakistan from purchasing Canadian spare parts or uranium for their reactors. Ottawa would not approve, for example, Pakistan's 1993 request to purchase 'replacement of neutron power monitors and power regulation instrumentation.'[21] This was the reason that COG was pressuring Ottawa to allow full nuclear cooperation with India and Pakistan. Its 1994–5 Annual Report stated that COG 'will continue to encourage the Canadian Government to review their export policy with the ultimate objective of reducing the current restrictions on cooperation among CANDU stations.'[22] AECL officials had also been secretly visiting India to discuss the possibility of exporting CANDUs to them.[23] Finally, there was a significant level of 'back-door' nuclear cooperation with Indian nuclear scientists touring Canadian nuclear plants and Canadian experts visiting Indian reactors (including those that were free of IAEA safeguards).[24]

The shock value of the 1998 nuclear tests did not approach that of the 1974 test, but its impact on CANDU exports should not be underestimated. If the purpose of the unofficial visits of Canadian and Indian nuclear scientists was, in the words of P.K. Iyengar, former chair of India's Atomic Energy Commission, 'to rebuild ties,'[25] then that had surely ended. There was no way that Canada would dare renew nuclear cooperation with either India or Pakistan. In fact, Canadian sanctions against India and Pakistan have been some of the toughest in scope and duration.[26] This can be traced, just as it could in 1974, to Canadian guilt over its role in the testing. In addition, it could be expected, just as it could in 1974, that there would be a period of heightened concern about the potential link between nuclear exports and nuclear weapons proliferation. In the aftermath of India's nuclear tests, Foreign Minister Axworthy felt it necessary to reaffirm Canada's commitment 'to preserv[ing] the integrity of the non-proliferation regime so critical to international security.'[27]

Do Canada's considerations of nuclear non-proliferation extend beyond India and Pakistan? What about other potential purchasers of CANDUs? An examination of the unsuccessful attempt to sell Turkey two CANDUs offers a test of whether the Indian and Pakistani nuclear tests have renewed the importance of non-proliferation considerations. Ankara announced in 2000 that it was shelving its plans to purchase nuclear power plants, nevertheless this case is still worth examining because of Canada's willingness to sell the reactors to Turkey. It was only due to its own financial problems that Ankara decided to cancel the proposed project. The question is, How did Canada assess the risk of nuclear proliferation in its decision to pursue the sale?

AECL had been trying to sell a CANDU to Turkey since the mid-1980s. In 1985 a nuclear cooperation agreement was signed between Canada and Turkey because both sides believed that a CANDU sale was imminent. However, because of Turkey's proposal that BOT financing (build, own and operate, transfer) be applied to the reactor, the sale fell through. This procedure would have seen the reactor's ownership divided between AECL holding a 60 per cent share and a privately owned Turkish consortium holding the remaining 40 per cent. In order for AECL to recoup its substantial investment, it would have to sell the electricity generated by the CANDU back to the Turkish government. Within a few years, AECL would then sell its share of the reactor to the Turkish government for what Ankara considered a fair market price. Ottawa believed that this arrangement would leave AECL with too much financial risk for too long a period of time. According to Canadian officials, Ottawa wanted a sovereign guarantee of payment before it would allow the sale to proceed, but this was not forthcoming.[28]

In the mid-1990s, Turkey's state-owned electrical utility TEAS called for international bids to build two nuclear reactors. There were three finalists in this multibillion dollar project: AECL, a consortium led by Siemens (Germany) and Framatome (France), and a partnership between Westinghouse (U.S.) and Mitsubishi (Japan). Turkey's renewed interest in nuclear power was prompted by the surging growth in its demand for energy. According to the Turkish government, '[O]ne of the stumbling blocks in Turkey's economic development [was] the lack of reliable, diversified and low-cost energy.'[29] The Canadian Embassy in Ankara estimated that, by the year 2000, Turkey's power consumption would increase by 44 per cent, which would result in an energy shortfall of 50.6 million oil-equivalent tonnes.[30] Lacking adequate oil and natural gas reserves, an insufficient hydroelectric capacity, and with only low-grade heavily polluted coal, Turkey felt that nuclear power was its best energy option. In addition to alleviating its energy needs, Turkey's desire for nuclear power can be traced to other factors. For example, the Turkish government wrote:

> Building a nuclear power plant implies utilization of the technology of the twenty-first century. This technology comprises not only energy technology but also most modern clean methods and system relating to agriculture, that is use of nuclear energy to improve the agricultural output, technology relating to medicine such as utilising nuclear system in cancer and other diseases' therapy and upgrading industry. Therefore, opting for nuclear technology is opting for modern and contemporary technology in many areas of our lives.[31]

These are the stated reasons for Turkey's desire to acquire civilian nuclear reactors. Is it also possible that Turkey wanted the technology to produce nuclear weapons? In most respects, there is no reason to doubt Turkey's contention that its desire for a nuclear reactor was for civilian power purposes. After all, Turkey ratified the NPT in 1980 and it also ratified the Comprehensive Test Ban Treaty that outlaws all nuclear testing. Nevertheless, it is true that there are countries that, on the one hand, have ratified the NPT, but on the other hand have secretly pursued nuclear weapons. The experiences of countries like Iraq, North Korea, and Iran have shown that if a country is insecure, it will try to acquire nuclear weapons regardless of whether or not it has ratified the NPT. However, Turkey's security is also provided for under Article V of the North Atlantic Treaty, which establishes that an armed attack against any NATO member is an attack against all, and therefore would be met with the full force of the Alliance. This means that, just as non-nuclear-weapons states like Canada and Germany are protected under NATO's nuclear umbrella, so is Turkey. Why would Turkey feel insecure inside the world's most powerful military alliance?

Despite these facts, there is, unfortunately, some evidence that puts some doubt on Turkey's commitment to refrain from pursuing a nuclear weapons capability. Over the last thirty years, Turkey has made serious efforts to acquire a substantial civilian nuclear power program, but it has been consistently rebuffed because of fears concerning its plans for weapons production. In the late 1980s, AECL officials acknowledged that Turkey had withdrawn its bid for a nuclear reactor contract, in part, because of 'pressure from Western countries,' which feared that 'Turkey may build a nuclear bomb based on CANDU technology.'[32] Senior members of both the Turkish military and the Turkish Atomic Energy Authority (TAEK) have also periodically openly supported an independent nuclear weapons capability. This pro-nuclear weapons option was reflected in a 1998 report drafted by former TAEK chair Mehmet Ergin, which stated that 'nuclear technology ... makes the country honourable and powerful, and it allows the country to advance one step further because nuclear technology has scientific, technological, strategic and economic components.' In a more worrisome passage, the report identifies India as a model for Turkey to follow. 'India constructed reprocessing plants by itself. Only a few countries have these plants that reprocess nuclear fuel, the transfer of which is strictly forbidden. In the last years, India has been in a race with developed countries. In addition to this, on the one hand it is aiming to double its nuclear power capacity, and on the other hand to continue to test atomic bombs and endeavouring to develop hydrogen bombs.'[33]

Why would Turkey consider developing nuclear weapons? Turkey's historical dispute with Greece offers a nice incentive. Greek officials are understandably leery about Turkey's acquisition of nuclear technology. In 1995, Thanos Dokos, a Greek foreign ministry official, publicly stated concerns about 'nuclear cooperation between Ankara and Islamabad ... and reports that Turkey might try to acquire nuclear weapons material and technology and recruit nuclear scientists from the Muslim republics of the former Soviet Union.'[34] Given the historical animosity between Greece and Turkey, an analyst is understandably cautious when assessing Greek allegations about Turkey. But in this situation, Dokos's charges follow a well-established pattern of behaviour. Allegations of Pakistani–Turkish nuclear cooperation go back to the early 1980s. In 1981, a high-ranking Turkish diplomat named Omer Ersun confirmed that the U.S. administration intervened in Turkish efforts, via a textiles firm, to assist Pakistan's uranium enrichment program.[35] U.S. senator John Glenn demanded in 1992 that foreign aid be cut off to Turkey because it was shipping Pakistan technology designed to be used in uranium enrichment.[36] In May 1998, following the Indian nuclear tests, an unnamed Turkish cabinet minister, noting that many of Turkey's neighbours (Israel, Iraq, Iran, India, Pakistan) either had nuclear weapons or were actively pursuing them, stated that Turkey must also 'acquire these technologies in the next ten years. The necessary investments are unavoidable.'[37] When Pakistan retaliated with its own nuclear tests in May 1998, there were more reports that Islamabad would assist Ankara in developing nuclear weapons. Before he was deposed in an October 1999 coup, Prime Minister Nawaz Sharif of Pakistan went on record as offering to 'work together on nuclear weapons' with Turkey.[38]

The most visible example of the Greek–Turk dispute is the seemingly intractable conflict in Cyprus. The battle between Turk Cypriots and Greek Cypriots has frequently involved their patrons in Ankara and Athens. Most notably in 1974, when Turkey, in a major military campaign, invaded Cyprus and claimed the northern half of the island. Turkey's intervention occurred after the National Guard, under the direction of Greek officers, conducted a coup d'état against the Cypriot government. The potential for renewed fighting in Cyprus, which would likely bring in Greece and Turkey, remains a possibility.[39]

Human Rights

There is little indication that the issue of human rights violations will constrain CANDU exports in the future any more than they have in the past. For example, the list of countries that AECL is currently wooing to buy CANDUs – China, Turkey, and Indonesia – all have substantial problems with their human rights records. Turkey, for instance, has been a frequent target of human rights activists. Amnesty International has condemned Turkey for its 'gross violations' of human rights and has pointed out that 'torture of political and criminal detainees in police stations was routine and systematic.'[40] In 1996, Amnesty International felt compelled to launch a worldwide campaign against Turkey called No Security Without Human Rights.[41] The European Union had previously cited Turkey's human rights record as one of the reasons for its continued exclusion from that entity.[42] Former German foreign minister Klaus Kinkel was recorded as saying that Turkey was rejected for membership in the EU because of 'human rights, the Kurdish question, relations with Greece, and of course, very clear economic questions.'[43]

In addition, while Turkey may be considered a formal democracy, its armed forces have frequently intervened in the political process, with successful military coups occurring in 1960, 1971, and 1980. Former prime minister Necmettin Erbakan discovered first-hand the role that the Turkish military continues to play in domestic politics. Erbakan, leader of Refah (the Islamic Welfare Party), formed a coalition government in June 1996. This was the first time that an Islamic government had taken power since Kemal Ataturk's creation of the modern Turkish state in 1923. Erbakan made a number of moves that made more secular Turks, especially in the military, believe that he was trying to establish an Islamic Republic: for example, he met with Moammar Ghaddafi in Libya, proposed bringing back veils and scarves for women in the civil service, urged the construction of new mosques in Istanbul, and encouraged the establishment of religious schools.[44] Finally, in spring 1997, the Turkish military forced the resignation of Erbakan by threatening a military coup,[45] an episode which has been referred to as a 'soft coup.'[46]

Particular targets of Turkey's oppression have been its minority Kurds. The Kurds are a disadvantaged ethnic group with a population in excess of 25 million, spread across three Middle Eastern countries: Iran, Iraq, and Turkey. They have faced repression in all three countries. Iraqi president Saddam Hussein famously used gas attacks against the Kurds in the 1980s and brutally crushed a Kurdish uprising in the aftermath of the 1991 Gulf War. A humanitarian safe area, protected by American and British military flights, was later established in northern Iraq. Following the defeat of Saddam in the 2003 Gulf War, the Kurds have been able to establish a degree of autonomy in Iraq. However, because the majority live in the territory of Turkey, it is there that the repression is best organized. The Kurdish Workers' Party (PKK) is the largest and most militant political organization of Turkish Kurds. The PKK has demanded either an independent Kurdish state or, at a minimum, the establishment of an autonomous region in Turkey. In response to this secessionist movement, the Turkish government outlawed the PKK through its anti-terror law. Although intended for the PKK, this law has also been used 'to prosecute and imprison innocent Kurds.'[47] There have been atrocities on both sides as the two groups battle in a virtual civil war that closely resembled Argentina's 1974–6 'dirty war.' The Turkish government, which has the upper hand against the PKK because of its superior military resources, has, at times, initiated major military campaigns against PKK strongholds. Ankara, in both March 1995 and May 1997, launched major military attacks – involving tens of thousands of troops backed by tanks, heavy artillery, and fighter jets – on PKK bases across the border in northern Iraq. Despite the 1999 capture of Kurdish rebel leader Abdullah Ocalan and his subsequent conviction for treason, the Kurdish independence movement has not been weakened and relations between the Turkish government and the Kurds remain violently tense.[48]

Nuclear Safety and Environmental Protection

By the late 1980s, Ottawa had become very concerned about the nuclear safety of the reactors that it had exported to India and Pakistan in the 1960s. After building the reactors, and then withdrawing all nuclear cooperation, Canada feared that another Chernobyl was possibly brewing on the Indian subcontinent. Without Canadian assistance, Pakistan was unable to produce enough properly trained and experienced operators for KANUPP. This led to at least one serious incident when KANUPP's operators lost access to the control rods because 'the operator forgot to transfer control of the reactor control rods to the controlling computer before allowing maintenance of the computer.'[49] KANUPP was also 'suffering from a range of woes that included condenser tube leaks, bellows leaks, heat-exchange tube leaks, flow blockage and ruptures in the refuelling machine.'[50] Pakistan's Atomic Energy Commission reported in 1996 that 'signs of normal ageing and obsolescence are becoming apparent. Many critical components are reaching the end of their designed life and need to be replaced.'[51] However, the necessary spare parts could not be obtained because the key suppliers for CANDUs are in Canada, and Ottawa still maintained nuclear sanctions against Pakistan. The situation was the same in India. Donald Lawson, former president of AECL's CANDU division, wrote to the IAEA to warn it about the safety problems associated with India's reactors. Lawson advised that 'conditions are such that there is a real potential for a pressure-tube rupture to occur at any time.'[52]

Because of these concerns over nuclear safety, Canada allowed India and Pakistan to join the CANDU Owners Group in 1988. Barry Collingwood, Manager of COG, noted that the 'initiative is consistent with the COG mandate of promoting co-operation and mutual assistance in the safe operation of CANDU reactors and is a positive step towards re-establishing technical co-operation with Pakistan.'[53] The IAEA also urged Canada to provide safety-related technological assistance to the two countries. In 1990, under the auspices of the IAEA, Canada authorised limited technical assistance, but not the sale of nuclear materials like spare component parts, to address safety concerns at the Canadian-supplied safeguarded reactors in Pakistan and India. This assistance was 'largely diagnostic in nature' and was 'aimed at identifying any serious and urgent safety concerns.'[54] AECB ultimately advised PAEC to permanently stop its operation of KANNUP. Pakistan rejected this advice, preferring that Canada end its sanctions and provide KANNUP with the necessary nuclear components to keep the reactor operational. PAEC has written that 'KANNUP is one major window for acquiring from the West the technology required to build nuclear power plants in the country.'[55]

Nuclear safety is a good rationale for reinstating some form of dialogue on nuclear matters. The problem, as Canadian officials have admitted, is that, in addition to addressing environmental concerns, Canada may also have been improving India's and Pakistan's nuclear programs. This is because 'you cannot clearly delineate between operational efficiency and safety with a nuclear reactor.'[56] By increasing the efficiency of a civilian nuclear program, one may also be increasing technical expertise that could spill over into the area of nuclear weapons. Pakistan ignored AECB's advice and continued to operate KANNUP because, as Zia Mian and A.H. Nayyar have asserted, it 'provided a fig leaf for a range of activities that were key elements of the nuclear weapons program.'[57] Thus, the decision to increase nuclear cooperation, as a result of environmental arguments, could actually jeopardize a second foreign policy objective: maintaining nuclear non-proliferation. Finally, the apparent willingness of Canada to renew nuclear cooperation with India and Pakistan was very reminiscent of its 1991 decision to renew nuclear cooperation with Romania. Ottawa would take into account environmental arguments only if they facilitated, rather than constrained, further nuclear cooperation.

It was one thing for CANDUs to be having technical problems in India, Pakistan, or Romania, but the issue of nuclear safety was really brought home to Canadians on 12 August 1997. It was on that day that Ontario Hydro, the largest domestic CANDU customer, announced that it had temporarily shut down seven of its twenty reactors. AECB had identified a number of significant problems with the performance of the nuclear reactors in Ontario and, in 1996, decided to renew the license for the Pickering plant for only six months, as opposed to the normal two years. This convinced Ontario Hydro to hire American consultants to perform an 'independent integrated performance assessment' (IIPA) of its nuclear operations. The IIPA report, issued in early August 1997, recommended a recovery plan that involved shutting down a number of reactors. Ontario Hydro complied because the IIPA report was a scathing indictment of the safety culture that existed in Ontario's nuclear plants.[58] It stated that Ontario Hydro's safety standards were only 'minimally acceptable.' 'Minimally acceptable' is a ranking substantially below industry standards and was the lowest grade that could be given to a reactor before revoking the utility's nuclear license. It put the cause of Ontario Hydro's problems squarely on 'a lack of authoritative and accountable managerial leadership.' For example, the nuclear plants were portrayed as being operated by poorly trained workers with a blatant disregard for safety. Numerous instances were documented of unqualified radiation safety technicians, unauthorized ad hoc modifications to the CANDU design, unsafe storage of dangerous chemicals, and alcohol and drugs in the workplace.[59] The IIPA report took pains not to criticize the technology of the CANDU. In fact, they stated that Ontario Hydro had done an excellent job in the 'design and construction phase,' but it had failed in the second stage of 'operating and maintaining' its nuclear reactors.[60]

Ontario Hydro's decision likely had a major impact on the importance of environmental consequences in relation to CANDU exports. 'The performance of CANDUs in Canada,' as Bruce Doern, Arslan Dorman, and Robert Morrison have noted, 'is an important determinant in the development and maintenance of an international market.'[61] Potential foreign customers could have had doubts about the CANDU's safety and reliability. AECL's competitors could have attempted to capitalize on Ontario Hydro's decision to shut down one-third of its reactors, telling potential customers that 'Canadians are shutting down their own CANDUs because they are unsafe. Why should you buy one from them?' AECL recognized that Ontario Hydro's announcement could have significantly compromised its ability to secure future exports. In a notable understatement, Gary Kugler, AECL vice-president of commercial operations, said at the time: 'It's certainly not great advertising for us.'[62] There was little doubt that AECL would launch a public relations campaign, at home and abroad, to seek to minimize the damage caused by the disaster in its CANDU showroom. Kugler articulated one of their strategies when he stated that 'if our international partners do show concern, they can look at the Ontario Hydro report which shows that it was a management problem which caused the problems.' He emphasized that AECL would concentrate on the fact 'that the CANDU technology is basically sound.'[63]

The federal government also suggested ways the nuclear industry could alleviate the public's concern about the environmental consequences of nuclear power. There were three elements to this strategy:

1 Communicating clearly the benefits of the technology from an environmental and energy-supply perspective.
2 Proving we, Canadians, can build and operate our plants safely and efficiently.
3 Effectively managing radioactive waste.[64]

Ralph Goodale, the former minister of natural resources, was quick to point out that

the best way to do that, of course, is to demonstrate to Canadian[s], demonstrate to the world, that CANDU technology is robust, reliable and cost-competitive throughout its economic life. Ontario Hydro's ability to improve the management of its nuclear assets will be integral to the industry's future, both in Canada and in international markets. Quite simply, we need to demonstrate that we can manage our technology – Canadians and the international community are watching very closely.[65]

However, there were significant limitations with AECL and the federal government's spin-doctoring. As Gordon Edwards, the president of the Canadian Coalition for Nuclear Responsibility, pointed out, 'here you have people [at Ontario Hydro] who are the best-placed in the world to understand and maintain the CANDU and they can barely do it. How do we expect these other countries to be able to run these plants safely?'[66] There was also increased public opposition to any attempt to export the CANDU. Ontario Hydro's shutdowns, as a Senate committee on nuclear safety reported, 'also reawakened public concern about the safety of nuclear reactors.'[67] The pro-nuclear lobby inside of the government recognized this. For example, Goodale warned the Canadian Nuclear Association that the industry had 'lost credibility' with the Canadian public. He added that, 'without public support, nuclear power has only a limited future.'[68] In addition, the anti-nuclear movement, which had been previously disdained for its lack of scientific knowledge, was given immense credibility since it was proven to be correct about the problems at Ontario's nuclear sites. Thus, it looked as though the expansion of the Canadian nuclear industry was at an end, and even its maintenance was in doubt. For example, Ontario Hydro estimated that it would cost the utility between $5 billion and $8 billion in upgrades and replacement energy costs for it to adhere to the IIPA report's recommendations. If nuclear energy had been proven to be unsafe for Canadians, how could it morally justify exporting it to other, primarily developing nations? What politician would want to be as closely linked to future CANDU exports as Team Canada was to the sale to China?

Despite the attention paid to the shutting down of reactors in Ontario, Ottawa showed, at the very first opportunity, that it would not necessarily be dissuaded by environmental factors in its efforts to export CANDUs. A case in point was the effort to sell CANDUs to Turkey. Canada had planned, in a repeat of its decision in the Chinese sale, to exempt Turkey's purchase of CANDUs from Canada's environmental assessment rules.[69] This move by the Canadian government was a direct acknowledgment that environmental protection laws should not be an obstacle to multibillion dollar commercial export projects. The biggest environmental concern with regards to the proposed Akkuyu Bay reactor was the possibility of an earthquake hitting the site and creating a nuclear catastrophe that would inevitably spread throughout the eastern Mediterranean region. Turkey, according to Karl Buckthought, president of Earthquake Forecasts Inc., is 'one of the most earthquake-prone areas on the face of the earth.'[70] The devastating Izmit earthquake of August 17, 1999 – which killed more than 18,000, injured over 42,000, and left over 600,000 homeless – brought the fear of earthquakes into the open. Nevertheless, Ottawa continued with its efforts to sell the CANDU. Prime Minister Chrétien, on a trip to Turkey, even tried to minimize the earthquake risk by saying that 'Turkey is a very big country.'[71] The Turkish government echoed this sentiment by pointing out that 'Akkuyu is located in the least seismically hazardous area in the current earthquake zones map of Turkey.'[72]

AECL defended itself by arguing that 'CANDU rectors are designed and have been proven to withstand earthquakes and operate safely.' In the event of an earthquake, the CANDU's safety features would engage and the reactor would shut down. 'For example, if an earthquake were to cause a change in the performance of the reactor – such as loss of pressure in a pipe – this would be detected by the safety systems and the reactor would be automatically and safely shut down.'[73] AECL president Allen Kilpatrick asserted that CANDU reactors had already withstood two earthquakes: Gentilly 2 in November 1988 and Point Lepreau in 1983.[74] AECL also incorporated some Japanese techniques into making sure that its CANDUs were earthquake resistant.[75] Japan has relied heavily on nuclear power for its electricity and is the most advanced country in the world when it comes to dealing with earthquakes. Since Japan's reactors have functioned safely through earthquakes, it only makes sense that AECL would have consulted them. AECL engineers modified the design of its CANDU to withstand the higher earthquake risks associated with the Akkuyu Bay seismic area. These changes included 'changes to civil engineering; process equipment and piping; control and instrumentation; and reactor fuel channels and fuel handling equipment.' The most novel feature of the CANDU redesign plans was through 'seismic isolation – essentially floating a foundation pad using alternating steel and rubber disks to absorb the energy of an earthquake.'[76]

The Turkish government, TEAS, AECL, and the IAEA conducted numerous studies on the seismic risk of the Akkuyu Bay region. This did not satisfy critics who alleged that these studies were flawed. They argued that the early studies, completed in the 1970s and 1980s, contained methodological problems, and the more recent studies had not been released to the public for proper scrutiny. Thus, earthquake specialists, like Attila Ulug, head of the Geophysics Department at the Institute of Marine Science and Technology at Dokuz Eylül University, demanded that the Turkish government 'conduct further investigations of the Akkuyu Bay area to determine the threat posed by the Ecemis Fault. To go ahead and build a reactor at Akkuyu Bay without further study would be a totally irresponsible, if not criminal, decision.'[77] Akkuyu Bay, which is over 500 kilometres from the site of the Izmit earthquake, is only 25 kilometres from another major fault line that runs through southern Turkey. Thus, earthquake experts like Buckthought have contended that 'it's very irresponsible to build a nuclear reactor in Turkey.'[78] He also asked, 'Can you possibly design a nuclear reactor which would be safe under any circumstances anywhere in Turkey? The answer is no, you can't.'[79]

Another example of Canada considering environmental concerns is Romania. An agreement was reached in 1998 between AECL, its Italian partner Ansaldo Nucleare, and Romania' state-owned nuclear company Societatea Nationala Nuclearelectrica (SNN) to finish construction of Romania's Cernavoda II reactor. Chapter 7 described the controversies over both AECL's decision to re-establish nuclear cooperation with Romania and the environmental assessment process for the Chinese reactor sale. As a result, AECL felt compelled to conduct a brand new environmental assessment for Cernavoda II. AECL's environmental assessment concluded that the effects of the construction, operation, and decommissioning of the Cernavoda II reactor would 'not be significant, unlikely to occur or beneficial under normal operating conditions. ... AECL, its partners and SNN ... are committed to applying mitigative measures such that significant adverse environmental effects are not likely to occur.'[80] SNN also wrote that 'an argument in favour of Unit 2 completion is the fact that Unit 1 operation has proved to be safe and in agreement with the environmental permit that was issued.'[81]

The Sierra Club drafted a report, endorsed by over seventy international non-governmental organizations, responding to AECL's environmental assessment and outlining a number of deficiencies with the assessment:

- the lack of an adequate public process, including the failure to provide complete versions of the environmental assessment documents
- the failure to consider alternatives to completing Cernavoda reactor 2
- the failure to assess the consequences of a catastrophic nuclear accident
- the failure to disclose details of the nuclear emergency plan
- the failure to conduct an adequate Probabilistic Risk Assessment
- the failure to assess the security provisions at the Cernavoda nuclear plant and the ability to defend against a terrorist attack
- the failure to disclose the complete nature of seismic risks near the site and the ability of Cernavoda 2 to withstand these risks
- the failure to present details of additional pollution control options which would reduce harm to health from ongoing radioactive pollution from the plant
- the failure to identify the full range of decommissioning activities required to rehabilitate the site and manage associated nuclear wastes in perpetuity

- the failure to define the hazards that may have resulted from past labour practices and faulty equipment at the partially-constructed nuclear reactor, and
- the failure to discuss safety-related financial matters, including possible problems obtaining sufficient funds to support ongoing operations and maintenance work and to pay qualified staff[82]

The Canadian government accepted AECL's environmental assessment and largely ignored the critique of the NGO community. This is because, while the Sierra Club's response may have included a number of valid points, its argument was lost in many of its 'over-the-top' criticisms. For example, the report required that AECL conduct a full examination of worst-case scenarios, like a catastrophic nuclear accident or a terrorist attack. In addition, while the report demanded that AECL contemplate alternatives, such as the environmental impact of *not* building Cernavoda II, the report did not compare the potential environmental impact of Romania's current electricity source: coal-fired plants. Oddly, the report did address Romania's fossil-fired capacity, but only in the context of financial cost, not environmental impact.[83] Nevertheless, the Cernavoda II case illustrates that environmental considerations, like nuclear safety, were beginning to play a larger role in Ottawa's foreign policy decision-making process. As the Sierra Club report remarked, 'the environmental assessment on the proposed Cernavoda 2 project is precedent-setting. This is the first time that AECL has ever invited public comment on an environmental assessment of a reactor export. To the best of our knowledge, it is also the first time that the Export Development Corporation (EDC) has ever invited public comment on an environmental assessment of a project for which it has provided financing.'[84]

Government Subsidies

Although AECL failed in its efforts to sell CANDUs to Turkey, the case demonstrates that the Canadian government was still willing to heavily subsidize nuclear exports. In December 1993, the newly elected Liberal government was asked to consider a request by AECL for $1 billion in financing for a potential nuclear sale to Turkey. The Cabinet Committee on Economic Development (which included Natural Resources Minister Anne McLellan) estimated that EDC could finance $250 million from its Corporate Account and that another $100 million could come from Canadian commercial banks. However, the remaining $650 million was too much for EDC's Canada Account because it would 'likely put a severe strain on the resources available for Canada Account financing of export projects generally, and would unbalance EDC's portfolio.'[85] Nevertheless, four years later the cabinet reversed its position and approved a $1.5-billion EDC loan to help finance the two proposed CANDUs for Turkey.[86] This change of policy was most likely a result of continued AECL lobbying. AECL president Reid Morden had been emphasizing that a large financing package was essential to winning the contract in Turkey. Morden wrote that Turkey's call for bids was 'the first time in living memory' that AECL would be 'in a true, competitive international competition,' and that 'price [would] be a critical element.' Thus, AECL was 'working hard to maximize the amount [of financing] that we obtain in Canada.'[87]

The loan that Ottawa was being asked to approve, as had been the case with the Chinese project, would have come from EDC's Canada Account. In other words, Canadian taxpayers could have been on the hook for the entire loan if the Turkish state-owned electrical utility TEAS had defaulted because Ankara would not offer a hard sovereign guarantee of payment. In fact, at the time of the Turkish decision to cancel the project, AECL and Westinghouse (another bidder on the project) were both giving serious consideration to beginning the project without a sovereign guarantee of payment.[88] There were several realistic scenarios that could have seen TEAS default on its loan. A substantial downturn in Turkey's economy might have made it difficult for TEAS to make its loan payments. Canadian cabinet documents reveal that there was serious concern expressed over 'several structural problems that could ultimately affect [Turkey's] creditworthiness over the long term.'[89] Construction delays might have caused TEAS to unilaterally renegotiate its repayment schedule, or the reactor might have been damaged beyond repair by an earthquake or through PKK sabotage.[90]

In the aftermath of Turkey's decision to cancel its proposed purchase of a nuclear reactor, stories started to circulate over AECL's bribery of Turkish energy officials. Once again the issue of the use of bribes to secure CANDU contracts – an issue which first reared its head in the 1970s with regards to the reactor sales to Argentina and South Korea – was in the news. Muzaffer Selvi, a senior official with TEAS, made a number of startling allegations during a major Turkish inquiry into the possibility of corruption in the tendering of energy megaprojects. Selvi testified that Bayindir Holding Inc, AECL's Turkey's consortium partner, had offered him $1 million to grant AECL the contract to build Turkey's nuclear reactors. He also alleged that over $50 million in bribes, including to Turkey's former energy minister Cumhur Ersumer, were paid out by the AECL-led consortium to ensure that it would win the reactor bid over its competitors from Germany and the United States. AECL did not appear before the inquiry, but fiercely disputed the allegations.[91]

As this study has shown, almost every sale, or attempted sale, of CANDU reactors has been accompanied by stories of payments to secure sales. There have been bribery investigations and convictions for accepting or offering bribes on behalf of AECL, its subsidiaries, or its international partners in Canada, South Korea, and Turkey. Canada's auditor general has repeatedly slammed AECL for making illegal bribes since the 1970s. Therefore, it is no wonder that Canada passed the Corruption of Foreign Officials Act in 1998 with crown corporations like AECL in mind.[92] AECL's behaviour in the last thirty years has shown that the CANDU often cannot be sold without payments to the buyer accompanying the transaction. The Turkish episode confirms, for the nth time, that government subsidies like research and development dollars, loans, and bribes are an essential ingredient of CANDU sales, and even non-sales.

The view that Ottawa was still willing to subsidize the export of CANDUs was further proven when the federal government increased, once again, its nuclear cooperation with Romania. In 1991, following the collapse of communism in Romania, Canada provided $315 million in financing to finish construction on the first unit of the Cernavoda nuclear project. After Cernavoda I came onstream in 1996, the Romanians requested that Canada finish construction on the partially built second unit.[93] In 1998, a consortium headed by AECL was awarded a $200-million contract for work on Cernavoda II.[94] AECL and EDC (through its Corporate Account) provided some of the financing. However, Romania's nuclear utility suggested that another US$750 million in financing was required to ensure that Cernavoda II was completed.[95] During a state visit to Ottawa in May 1998, Romanian president Emil Constantinescu formally asked the Canadian government to provide an additional $1 billion in financing for Cernavoda II. Constantinescu also requested that the following concessions be attached to the loan: release from the sovereign guarantee of 100 per cent of Canadian loans, a longer payback period for the loans, and a four-year holiday before loan repayments started.[96]

In July 2000, a contract was signed between SNN and AECL and its Italian partner Ansaldo to finish building Cernavoda II, which is expected to come onstream in 2007. SNN still needed another US$750 million in financing, so EDC provided an additional $390 million from its Canada Account as opposed to its regular Corporate Account. (All currency is in Canadian dollars unless otherwise specified.) For the remaining amounts, Romania has applied for a loan of $350 million from Euratom and hopes to raise additional funds from electricity countertrades or direct export contracts.[97] In late December 2002, International Trade Minister Pierre Pettigrew announced that the federal government had guaranteed, through EDC's Canada Account, an additional $329 million for the construction of Cernavoda II.[98] In total, EDC loaned SSN $719 million to finish the reactor. This is in addition to the original $1.860 billion loaned in 1978–9 and the $315 million loaned to finish Cernavoda I. In total, the Cernavoda project has received a staggering $2.897 billion in government-guaranteed EDC loans since 1978. Much of this money will never be paid back.

The contract to finish Cernavoda II does not end the possibility of Romania receiving further subsidies from Ottawa. This is because John Saroudis, the marketing director for AECL in Bucharest, wants to go even further and finish construction on the remaining three CANDU shells at the Cernavoda site. Saroudis has noted that the addition of these three reactors, combined with Cernavoda I and II, would give Romania five CANDUs making it AECL's 'biggest export market.'[99] The current state of completion of the three remaining Cernavoda units are as follows: Cernavoda III is 14 per cent completed; Cernavoda IV 5 per cent, and Cernavoda V, 4 per cent.[100] Bucharest is keeping this area of the Cernavoda complex preserved while it awaits financing.

Canada seems to be willing to continue to subsidize the Cernavoda project because it anticipates future sales in Romania.[101] This is ignoring the fact that the Romanian government is so short of financing that even the construction workers who are building Cernavoda often go months without being paid.[102] AECL, as John Saroudis has stated, views Romania as 'a very important market for us, which is why we've hung in here for so long. We've been very patient.'[103] Beyond the reactor construction, there are also contracts for spare parts. AECL appears to have some powerful friends as it lobbies Ottawa for further financial assistance. For example, Prime Minister Chrétien travelled to Romania in 1996 to be part of the official opening of Cernavoda I.

In addition to financing requests for specific CANDU exports, there is also the question of AECL's R&D subsidies, which have been slowly declining. In 1998–9, the federal government's contribution to AECL's research and development had dropped to $100 million, down from the $150 to $170 million that it had received during the rest of the 1990s.[104] A 1995 independent review of AECL by Nesbitt Burns had specified that it would need to sell ten reactors in ten years to remain viable with only $100 million worth of government subsidies each year.[105] Because the AECL has failed to win the Turkish contract, it seems highly unlikely that it will be able to hit the 'ten in ten' requirement. It is also doubtful that AECL will be able to maintain a high level of nuclear R&D without vast government support. Natural Resources Canada has been conducting an internal review of AECL's subsidies.[106] This will erode its innovation ability in nuclear technology and will make it that much harder for AECL to compete with the other nuclear suppliers (General Electric, Westinghouse, Framatome, and Siemens).

Economics

While the two principal political interests associated with past CANDU sales – economic development and anti-communism – have lost their influence, it would be unwise to assume that other foreign policy goals will not emerge to take their place. There will always be some type of political interest that will facilitate, or constrain, exports, and Canada still possesses a commercial interest in pursuing them. This section examines the state of these economic arguments as well as evaluating the likely future market for the CANDU.

Canada's efforts to sell two nuclear reactors to Turkey showed that there remain important economic benefits derived from CANDU exports. A successful sale to Turkey would have extended AECL's global presence by establishing it in a brand new market. In addition, it would have established it in a brand new region: Western Europe. This could have been very significant if Turkey, as expected, enters the European Union. After years of being shunned by the EU, Turkey is now a candidate for membership. A large-scale nuclear project in Turkey, combined with its existing partnership with the Italian firm ANSALDO, would have made it easier for AECL to finally penetrate the coveted European market.

There would also have been some immediate economic benefits if AECL had successfully sold the CANDU to Turkey. AECL had estimated that the project would result in the creation of 125,000 person-years worth of work in Canada.[107] These jobs, as Larry Shewchuk, the manager of corporate media relations for AECL, reminded *Toronto Star* readers in an op-ed piece, 'are well-paying jobs for highly educated Canadians, which generate substantial consumer spending and taxation revenue.' Shewchuk also reiterated the traditional economic argument that 'Canada earns both profit and wealth on CANDU exports.'[108]

Table 8.1. Lifetime reactor efficiency, by country, 1991

Country*	Number of reactors	Load factor %
Canada	19	74.9
Germany	21	72.2
Japan	56	67.6
France	40	62.7
United States	109	60.0
United Kingdom	29	49.5

*Data for the Soviet Union were unavailable.
Source: Compiled from data in Nuclear Engineering
International, World Nuclear Industry Handbook 1992
(Surrey, UK: Reed, 1991), 18–20.

Table 8.2. 1999 efficiency by reactor model

Model*	Load factor (%)
Boiling water reactors	81.4
Pressurized water reactors	79.8
Advanced gas-cooled reactors	76.9
Pressurized heavy-water reactors (CANDU)	72.8

*Data for the Russian style reactors are unavailable.
Source: 'Load Factors to End December 1999,' Nuclear
Engineering International (June 2000), 36.

One of the major selling points, as presented by AECL and its patrons in Ottawa, has been the safety and reliability of the CANDU. Former energy minister Anne McLellan used to brag that 'the CANDU 6 reactor is acknowledged to be among the safest and best performing designs in the world.'[109] Unfortunately, as the CANDU has aged, its efficiency rating has greatly decreased and has fallen behind those of other reactor designs. As recently as 1988, seven of the top ten most efficient nuclear reactors in the world were Canadian, but by 1996 there were only three in the top ten.[110] In addition, in 1991, the CANDU was the most efficient reactor model in the world (see table 8.1), but by 1999 the CANDU had become the most inefficient reactor design in the world (see table 8.2). It is important to note that these decreasing efficiency ratings are not because international customers were dragging down the model's rating. The Canadian CANDU efficiency rating was 73.09 per cent, while the international CANDU efficiency rating was very close at 72.24 per cent (see table 8.3).[111]

Ontario Hydro has taken much of the blame for the poor performance of Canada's nuclear reactors. An AECL official said that the

Table 8.3. 1999 CANDU reactor efficiency

Country	Reactor	Load factor (%)
Canada	Bruce 'B'	69.74
Canada	Bruce 'B'	91.15
Canada	Bruce 'B'	84.19
Canada	Bruce 'B'	54.86
Canada	Darlington	93.80
Canada	Darlington 2	84.53
Canada	Darlington 3	73.74
Canada	Darlington 4	81.13
Canada	Pickering 'B' 5	56.26
Canada	Pickering 'B' 6	74.97
Canada	Pickering 'B' 7	98.77
Canada	Pickering 'B' 8	78.19
Canada	Gentilly 2	68.49
Canada	Point Lepreau	73.58
Argentina	Embalse	98.93
India	RAPP 1	50.00
India	RAPP 2	70.64
Pakistan	KANUPP	6.49
Romania	Cernavoda 1	99.46
South Korea	Wolsong 1	82.84
South Korea	Wolsong 2	89.21
South Korea	Wolsong 3	80.33

Source: 'Nuclear Electricity Generation for December 1999,'
Nucleonics Week, 10 February 2000.

seven reactors were shut down in Ontario because of the 'management problems at Ontario Hydro' not the 'CANDU technology.'[112] However, the recent experience of the Point Lepreau nuclear plant in New Brunswick provides evidence that perhaps it was not Ontario Hydro's entire fault. Point Lepreau has confirmed that as the CANDU has aged, its safety and performance have become questionable. In November 1999, the AECB put Point Lepreau under a special watch because its quality assurance program needed to be strengthened. According to Ken Pereira of AECB's performance evaluation division, 'the program at Point Lepreau is no longer appropriate for conditions of the plant, the age of the plant and the experience of the plant.'[113] Point Lepreau raises some serious concerns that as the CANDUs age, their safety, reliability, and efficiency are decreasing. For years, Point Lepreau consistently ranked in the top ten most efficient reactors in the world, but after sixteen years of operation, its efficiency has dramatically dropped. For example, while Point Lepreau's lifetime efficiency rating in 1996 was a very high 88.4 per cent, in 1999 its efficiency rating dropped to 73.58 per cent.[114] More worrisome was that in 1997 and 1998, Point Lepreau 'suffered two major shutdowns and has had a dozen serious reportable nuclear incidents.'[115]

There has also been some debate over the number of people employed in the nuclear industry. It has been alleged that the employment figures have been inflated in order to present a stronger economic justification for CANDU exports. For example, AECL, through Ernst and Young, has estimated that almost 30,000 people are employed in the nuclear industry. However, Martin and Argue have suggested that the real number is closer to 18,000. They claim that this discrepancy is due to

- double-counting
- counting total employee levels at some or all companies, instead of just the nuclear-related employment
- overestimating the number of companies in the nuclear manufacturing private sector, and
- using overly optimistic assumptions for the extrapolation of employment among the estimated number of companies[116]

There has also been growing scepticism over the view that Canada has economically benefited from CANDU exports. Even some of its former advocates have disavowed their earlier claims. For example, in 1987, George Lermer wrote a monograph for the Economic Council of Canada in which he argued that, although each CANDU sale had lost money, Canada had still received a modest benefit from its investment in the CANDU.[117] However, as a result of the steadily decreasing efficiency rate of the CANDU and the future costs of decommissioning old reactors, Lermer, less than a decade later, dramatically reversed his position and argued that 'the federal expenditure on CANDU has been a financial disaster.'[118]

What is the future market for CANDU sales? Doern, Dorma, and Morrison, have suggested that AECL is entering into a period of 'precarious opportunity.' They have identified 'two main scenarios' for the future of nuclear power. 'On the one hand, some offer the view that the nuclear energy industry can prosper and make an important contribution to energy and the environment in this age of climate change policy ... On the hand, there are some who perceive the nuclear energy industry as economically in decline and environmentally questionable.'[119] Not surprisingly, the first scenario greatly attracts the pro-nuclear lobby. 'Nuclear technology,' as David Torgerson, a vice-president of AECL, has asserted 'has an important role to play in meeting future national and international energy demands.'[120] The second scenario is supported by the anti-nuclear lobby, typified by the Campaign for Nuclear Phaseout's book entitled *Nuclear Sunset*.

There is little possibility of new CANDU sales in Canada in the foreseeable decade. Ontario Power Generation is spending its time and money repairing its existing nuclear reactors to make them competitive in a restructured electricity market.[121] Therefore, the export market remains the only possibility for future CANDU sales. AECL's organizational restructuring in the 1990s reflected the importance of foreign sales. With Reid Morden (1993–8) and Allan Kilpatrick (1998–2001) at the helm, AECL was able to draw on the extensive international experience and contacts of two former foreign service officers. In addition, Morden, as a former deputy minister at DFAIT, 'knew the internal channels of influence in the federal government much better than some of his immediate predecessors, and was more comfortable using them.'[122]

Despite periodic attention, it is unlikely that AECL can make inroads into Canada's largest trading partner: the United States. The conditions of the nuclear market at the beginning of the twenty-first century are not that different from what was described in chapter 2. As Doern and his colleagues have written '[A] small handful of reactor supply countries and firms are bidding for reactor sales in a few larger, fast-industrializing countries; these countries are in turn making their own choices about power in the context of energy needs, national security, local environmental concerns, and global climate change strategies and pressures.'[123] Price, reliability, and environmental costs are the factors that will determine which suppliers win out. However, as has always been the case, the international market for nuclear reactors is not a pure economic market and is fraught with political interference. To quote Doern, Dorman, and Morison once again:

> *Price* is important, but price here refers to the cost of reactors as well as possible industrial development incentives to build a local supply industry. *Reliability* certainly includes uninterrupted power supply, but it also includes the long-term reliance of the buying country on the supplier country's nuclear expertise. And the internalization of *environmental* costs is an even larger game of political and economic influence, with newly industrializing countries being pressured into accepting climate change rules and regimes that are still being defined, and with trade-offs that are even wider than for the developed OECD countries, which are now rich enough to be able to use competitive electricity markets.[124]

AECL has already lost a number of contracts that it thought it could have secured: a research reactor for Australia (June 2000), two power reactors for Turkey (July 2000), and a power reactor for South Korea (March 2001). AECL still sees itself selling additional reactors to China, and it has kept its traditional wish list of new markets (Bulgaria, Indonesia, and Thailand), but one new possibility has recently emerged. British Energy has submitted a $23-billion proposal to its government to replace its gas-cooled reactors with up to ten new nuclear power plants.[125] Even though other suppliers are expected to bid on the project, most notably Westinghouse, AECL is considered a front-runner. This is because British Energy is very familiar with CANDUs – it has a long-term lease on the Bruce nuclear plants in Ontario. As British Energy chair Robin Jeffrey pointed out, '[W]e have gained a wealth of knowledge about these reactors. We are delighted with their performance.'[126] AECL president Robert Van Adel remarked that 'it would be an important breakthrough for us if we were to be selected for all or a portion of the U.K. solution.'[127]

Examining these economic arguments shows that some of the benefits are not as powerful as they have historically been, but they still remain strong incentives to pursue foreign sales. Exports, although not to the same degree that they once did, still maintain and create employment in the nuclear sector. In the absence of continued sales, job losses will occur. For example, AECL cut 12 per cent of its workforce between 1996 and 1999. Moreover, as parliamentary appropriations decline, AECL's commercial operations, especially exports, are to a greater degree funding its nuclear research and development.[128]

The revenue earned in nuclear components and uranium continues to be generated by exports. Figure 8.1 shows that Canada sells around $40 million in nuclear reactor components every year, and table 8.4 shows the destination of these exports. The market is incredibly concentrated, only a handful of countries have purchased nuclear equipment in the last five years, and since 1999, over 95 per cent of annual nuclear component exports have gone to China. This concentration can be explained by the fact that the Qinshan reactors are still being built. This also means that the market for spare parts is not even close to being large enough to sustain the Canadian nuclear component suppliers. Additional CANDU sales are still necessary. Figure 8.2 shows that Canada continues to have annual uranium exports in the $700 to $800 million range. A closer examination of uranium exports reveals, however, that there is little linkage between reactor exports and uranium exports. Figure 8.3 identifies the top markets for Canadian uranium.

Figure 8.1. Canadian nuclear reactor components exports, 1997–2001

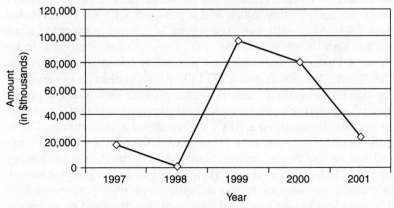

Source: Statistics Canada, 'Canadian Trade Balances – Nuclear Reactors and Parts of Nuclear Reactors,' *Canadian Trade Balances – by Sector* (Ottawa: Statistics Canada, 2002).

Table 8.4. Destination of nuclear reactor component exports, by percentage, 1997–2001

	1997	1998	1999	2000	2001
China	0	0	98.4	98.1	95.3
South Korea	89.4	17.1	1.3	1.5	2.8
Romania	0.7	49.8	0	0.2	1.8
Argentina	0.2	5.8	0.2	0	0
Others	0.7	27.3	0.1	0.2	0.1

Source: Statistics Canada, 'Canadian Trade Balances – Nuclear Reactors and Parts of Nuclear Reactors,' *Canadian Trade Balances – by Sector* (Ottawa: Statistics Canada, 2002).

Over 70 per cent of all uranium exports go to the United States, and it does not operate a single CANDU. In fact, none of the top three markets – U.S., France, and Britain – that make up over 90 per cent of total Canadian uranium sales operate a CANDU. Table 8.5 lists all foreign recipients of CANDUs and shows the level of their purchases of Canadian uranium. These seven countries combined make up approximately 2 per cent of total uranium sales. Uranium exports continue to be a major source of foreign exchange for Canada, but they are not dependent on CANDU exports.

Figure 8.2. Canadian uranium exports, 1997–2001

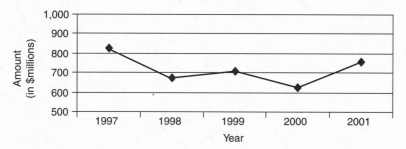

Source: Statistics Canada, 'Canadian Trade Balances – Uranium,' *Canadian Trade Balances – by Sector* (Ottawa: Statistics Canada, 2002).

Figure 8.3. Destination of uranium exports, 1997–2001

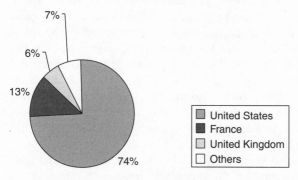

Source: Statistics Canada, 'Canadian Trade Balances – Uranium,' *Canadian Trade Balances – by Sector* (Ottawa: Statistics Canada, 2002).

Table 8.5. CANDU operators and uranium exports, 1997–2001

	Uranium exports	Percentage of total exports
South Korea	$60,680,220	1.69
Argentina	$9,085,716	0.25
India	$6,257,062	0.17
China	$4,024,680	0.11
Taiwan	$1,570,616	0.04
Pakistan	$882,640	0.02
Romania	$377,877	0.01
Total	$82,878,811	2.3

Source: Statistics Canada, 'Canadian Trade Balances – Uranium,' *Canadian Trade Balances – by Sector* (Ottawa: Statistics Canada, 2002).

9 Explaining CANDU Exports

This book has provided the most comprehensive account of the history of CANDU exports to date. Every CANDU sale, and even some unsuccessful attempts, from 1956 to the present has been examined in great detail. It has also traced the changes that have occurred in the international environment throughout the history of CANDU exports. For example, the book has charted the development of the international nuclear non-proliferation regime through the creation of institutions and treaties such as the International Atomic Energy Association (IAEA), the Nuclear Non-Proliferation Treaty (NPT), and the Nuclear Suppliers Group (NSG). It has also illustrated the increasing importance of human rights and environmental protection on world politics.

The arguments for and against CANDU exports might have changed over the last half century, but there has also been a certain level of consistency. The market for reactor exports remains concentrated in a handful of middle-power states and large developing countries. The great powers, which have their own indigenous nuclear industries and protectionist lobbies, do not import nuclear technology. In addition, Canada continues to compete for nuclear exports against large American multinationals and western European consortiums. Canada's share of the international nuclear market has remained largely unchanged over the years, fluctuating between 10 and 15 per cent.

The Canadian government also remains substantially involved in the entire CANDU export process. This is despite the fact that reactor contracts are signed through Crown corporations such as Atomic Energy Canada Limited (AECL) and the Export Development Corporation (EDC), and constructed and supplied by private sector firms like Babcock and Wilcox and Canatom. Ottawa, as a precondition for any nuclear export, must negotiate a bilateral Nuclear Cooperation Agreement. In addition, it continues to use high-level diplomacy to support CANDU exports. In India in 1956, External Affairs Minister Lester Pearson met face to face with India's prime minister Jawarharlal Nehru over CIRUS. Four decades later, Prime Minister Jean Chrétien negotiated directly with Chinese premier Li Peng in support of the Qinshan nuclear project. Finally, Ottawa continues to heavily subsidize CANDU exports. These subsidies range from parliamentary appropriations to AECL for nuclear research and development to giving cabinet authorization for EDC to use its Canada Account to finance reactor sales. CANDU exports could not have been concluded without Ottawa's money. The very first export, to India in 1956, was part of the Colombo Plan's foreign aid package, and Canada's most recent export in 1996 saw EDC finance the entire Canadian contribution to the Qinshan project in China.

An organizational framework was used to determine the influence of different foreign policy objectives on Canada's decision-making process with regards to CANDU exports. The first three chapters of this book identified a series of variables that clashed in the foreign policy decision-making process. Variables that favoured CANDU exports included economic factors such as the benefits that would accrue to Canada through the export of nuclear reactors, as well as the economic consequences of insufficient exports. Other facilitating factors included the containment of communism and assisting the developing world. Variables that opposed the export of CANDUs included the fear of nuclear proliferation, human rights abuses, environmental protection and nuclear safety, and government subsidies.

This organizational framework was used to sift through the historical record of Canada's nuclear export policy. Chapter 4 examined the initial period, 1945–74, of CANDU exports. Table 9.1 summarizes the variables that facilitated, constrained, or were absent in the decision-making process. It also identifies the dominant variable, the one that would, ultimately, determine the decision. An examination of this time period shows that it was largely a debate between Canada's economic and political interests and its concern with nuclear proliferation. Since nuclear proliferation concerns were in their infancy at the time, it was not much of a debate. The economic imperative of establishing markets for nuclear exports, when combined with Canada's political interests in fighting communism and promoting economic development, easily overwhelmed any fears that recipient countries would develop nuclear

Table 9.1. Key variables in CANDU exports, 1945–74

Case	Facilitating variables	Constraining variables	Absent variables	Dominant variable
CIRUS	Economics development Anti-communism	Non-proliferation	Human rights Environment Subsidies	Economics
RAPP I	Economics development Anti-communism	Non-proliferation	Human rights Environment Subsidies	Economics
KANUPP	Economics Development Anti-communism		Non-proliferation Human rights Environment Subsidies	Economics
RAPP II	Economics	Non-proliferation	Development Anti-communism Human rights Environment Subsidies	Economics
TRR	Economics Anti-communism		Non-proliferation Human rights Environment Subsidies	Economics
Taiwan Termination	Economics Anti-communism	PRC recognition	Non-proliferation Human rights Environment Subsidies	PRC recognition
Embalse	Economics		Development Anti-communism Non-proliferation Human rights Environment Subsidies	Economics
Wolsung I	Economics		Development Anti-communism Non-proliferation Human rights Environment Subsidies	Economics

weapons. The period 1945–74 was also marked by the absence of many constraining variables. There was no attention paid to the human rights records of recipient states, considerations about the reactor's environmental impact, or the extent of Ottawa's subsidies of the sale.

India's test of a nuclear weapon in 1974 marked the beginning of a new period in the history of CANDU exports. For the next two years,

Table 9.2. Key variables in CANDU exports, 1974–6

Case	Facilitating variables	Constraining variables	Absent variables	Dominant variable
India suspension	Economics	Non-proliferation	Development Anti-communism Human rights Environment Subsidies	Non-proliferation
Embalse safeguards	Economics	Non-proliferation	Development Anti-communism Human rights Environment Subsidies	Non-proliferation
Wolsung I safeguards	Economics	Non-proliferation	Development Anti-communism Human rights Environment Subsidies	Non-proliferation
India termination	Economics	Non-proliferation	Development Anti-communism Human rights Environment Subsidies	Non-proliferation
Pakistan termination	Economics	Non-proliferation Development Anti-communism	Human rights Environment Subsidies	Non-proliferation

Canada took steps to design and implement a strengthened nuclear non-proliferation policy. This was the high-water mark for Canada's concern with nuclear proliferation and, logically, it was the dominant variable in Canada's foreign policy decision-making (see table 9.2). There were economic incentives to maintain nuclear relations with India and Pakistan, but these were trumped by Canada's security considerations. As was the case with the earlier time period, Canada's other foreign policy considerations remained absent.

Canada's commercial interests continued to be subordinate to its nuclear non-proliferation policy from 1977 to 1989 (see table 9.3), as Canada was willing to suffer commercial loses in order to maintain its strong stance on nuclear non-proliferation. There may have been some wavering at times, but in the end, Ottawa would not weaken its security position for the sake of a successful sale. A potential sale to Argentina was lost, in large part, to Canada's position on NPT ratification and nuclear safeguards. In addition, it was in this time period that human

Table 9.3. Key variables in CANDU exports, 1977–89

Case	Facilitating variables	Constraining variables	Absent variables	Dominant variable
Cernavoda	Economics Anti-communism	Anti-communism	Development Non-proliferation Human rights Environment Subsidies	Economics
Atucha II	Economics	Non-proliferation Human rights Subsidies	Development Anti-communism Environment	Human rights
1980s export attempts	Economics	Non-proliferation Subsidies	Development Anti-communism Human rights Environment	Non-proliferation

rights started to emerge as a constraining variable on CANDU exports. The most notable example was when Argentina's horrible human rights record motivated Flora MacDonald to spike the proposed Atucha II sale.

The period 1990–6 was notable for a couple of reasons (see table 9.4). First, it saw the return of the dominance of economic considerations in Canada's nuclear export policy. This was most evident in the sales to South Korea and China. Second, it saw the emergence of many variables which had been absent for most of the previous sales. Environmental considerations, government subsidies, and human rights were all influential variables in the decision-making over CANDU exports in the early to mid-1990s. Third, many traditional constraining variables were reframed as facilitating variables. For example, concerns about the safety of the Cernavoda reactors became a reason to increase nuclear cooperation with Romania. Likewise, China's human rights record was viewed as an incentive, rather than a constraint, to sell it nuclear reactors. The reasoning was constructive engagement over diplomatic isolation and/or economic sanctions.

The final time period, 1997–2005, has continued the process of a much more multifaceted debate over CANDU exports (see table 9.5). Ottawa has had to consider all of the identified variables in its foreign policy decision-making process. In the case of renewing nuclear cooperation for Romania's Cernavoda II project, there were three facilitating variables (development, environment, and non-proliferation) and three

Table 9.4. Key variables in CANDU exports, 1990–6

Case	Facilitating variables	Constraining variables	Absent variables	Dominant variable
Wolsung II to IV	Economics		Non-proliferation Human rights Environment Subsidies	Economics
Cernavoda I Renewed cooperation	Development Environment Non-proliferation	Human rights Subsidies Economics		Environment
Qinshan I and II	Economics Human rights	Non-proliferation Subsidies Environment Human rights		Economics

Table 9.5. Key variables in CANDU exports, 1997–2005

Case	Facilitating variables	Constraining variables	Absent variables	Dominant variable
Cernavoda II Renewed cooperation	Development Environment Non-proliferation	Economics Human rights Subsidies		Environment
Failed Turkey export	Economics	Non-proliferation Human rights Environment Subsidies		Economics

constraining variables (economics, human rights, and government subsidies). Meanwhile the decision, ultimately unsuccessful, to pursue a CANDU sale with Turkey saw the interplay of economics, non-proliferation, human rights, environmental protection, and government subsidies.

Table 9.6 identifies the dominant variable for CANDU exports in each time period. It shows that economic incentives for securing exports have been the most important variable in Ottawa's decision-making process. The only exceptions were the periods where Canada reformulated (1974–6) and implemented (1977–89) its nuclear safeguards policy. In these two time periods, nuclear non-proliferation was the guiding principle behind exports. Table 9.6 reflects the fact that the traditional debate over CANDU exports was between Canada's commercial interests and its security concerns.

Table 9.6. Dominant variable for CANDU exports
by time period, 1945–2004

Time period	Dominant variable
1945–74	Economics
1974–6	Non-proliferation
1977–89	Non-proliferation
1990–6	Economics
1997–2004	Economics

Figure 9.1. The changing debate over CANDU exports

Traditional debate

PLANE #1   Economic benefits ⟺ Fear of nuclear proliferation

New debate

PLANE #1   Economic benefits ⟺ Economic costs

PLANE #2   Environmental benefits ⟺ Environmental costs

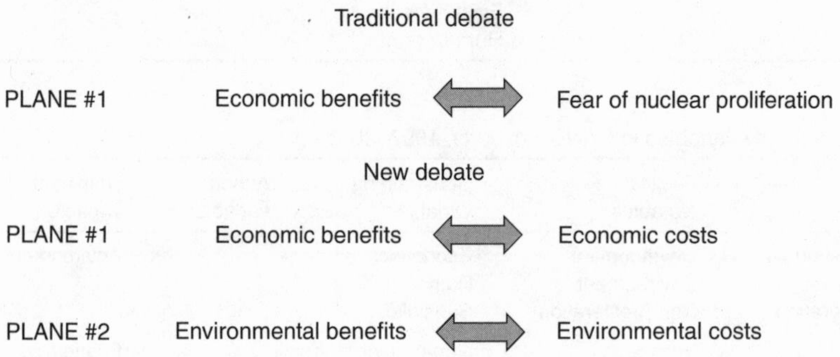

The last two time periods (1990–6 and 1997–2005) indicate that the debate over CANDU exports has gone beyond the simple economic benefits versus nuclear non-proliferation dilemma. This new debate centres on two separate planes of arguments (see fig. 9.1). The first is between Canada's economic benefits in exporting the CANDU contrasted with the economic cost. The economic benefits argument stresses revenue and employment and warns about the economical consequences of failing to acquire sufficient reactor sales. The economic costs argument highlights the role of the extensive government subsidies that accompany most CANDU exports. It also argues that the economic benefits of exports are not as great as its advocates proclaim. The second plane is between the environmental benefits of CANDU exports contrasted with the environmental costs of building or promoting nuclear power. The environmental benefits argument emphasizes the clean air aspect of nuclear power and compares the emissions produced by nuclear power with that of other energy sources (natural gas, coal, and so on). The environmental costs argument stresses the dangers of reactor safety, radiation, and nuclear waste. The debate over CANDU exports has thus become much more comprehensive than the traditional dilemma over economics and security.

Clashing Nuclear Actors

This book has been organized around a set of competing foreign policy variables, but a subtheme of its analysis relied upon a more actor-centric model. Chapters 2 and 3 introduced the concept that Canada has both a pro-nuclear lobby and an anti-nuclear lobby. The pro-nuclear lobby is made up of AECL, the component suppliers, provincial utilities, and interest groups like the Canadian Nuclear Association. The anti-nuclear lobby is largely made up of environmental groups like the Sierra Club and Energy Probe and specific interest groups like the Canadian Coalition for Nuclear Responsibility and the Campaign for Nuclear Phaseout. As the history of CANDU exports has shown, it is not just the competing variables that clash in decisions about CANDU exports, but also the competing actors.

More research on the exact role and influence that the pro-nuclear lobby and the anti-nuclear lobby have on CANDU exports is necessary. However, the evidence so far suggests that a modified version of Cranford Pratt's dominant-class theory might provide great insight into the decision-making process surrounding CANDU exports.[1] Pratt argues that an examination of dominant-class interests provides the best explanation of Canada's foreign policy. The pro-nuclear lobby, given its collective economic and political power in Canada, can be viewed as constituting Canada's dominant class. Pratt writes that 'the literature on the role of interest groups and lobbying in Canada frequently acknowledges that business interest groups have a much more intimate and influential access to policy-makers than do public interest groups or other economic interest groups such as consumer associations and the trade unions.'[2] When policy issues touched 'the economic interests of the dominant class and had relevance to Canada's perceived geopolitical interests,' decision-makers would 'guard against pressures that would shift the primary focus away from important commercial and geopolitical objectives.'[3] This provides a powerful explanation for why Canada's economic interests and political interests in, say, anti-communism have been significantly more influential in the history of CANDU exports than the other foreign policy objectives of human rights, environmental protection, and government subsidies. The fact that the only powerful constraining variable has been the fear of nuclear proliferation confirms this view. This is because nuclear proliferation is a security concern as opposed to an ethical concern.

Foreign policy decisions, like CANDU exports, are not always made on the basis of *what* the arguments are, but on *who* is making the arguments. 'The Canadian system,' as Pratt has argued, is 'responsive in particular to business interests in ways that are haphazard, unintegrated, and a product primarily of lobbying and of political bargaining.'[4] The role of behind-the-scenes lobbying is heightened because government departments and agencies, ostensibly neutral in clashes between different societal groups, may conceive of the national interest in the same way as the dominant class. In the case of CANDU exports, these would include Natural Resources Canada, the Department of Foreign Affairs and International Trade (DFAIT), and the Canadian Nuclear Safety Commission (CNSC). As Pratt writes, 'many governmental departments and divisions within those departments have developed close links with the sectors of the Canadian economy that directly relate to their responsibilities ... It is even the case that close relationships often develop between government regulatory agencies and the industries they are intended to regulate.'[5]

Pratt's dominant-class theory provides great insight into Canadian foreign policy because it is much more nuanced than a purely doctrinaire Marxist approach. Pratt acknowledges that an examination of Canadian policies towards foreign aid and apartheid South Africa 'demonstrates that there are particular moments in which major policy initiatives ignore those interests and respond instead to humanitarian values. ... It is thus reasonable to conclude that when there are strategic conjunctures of circumstances that open decision-making to a wider range of options, the efforts of ethically motivated citizen organizations can make important contributions to the shaping of foreign policy.'[6] In the case of CANDU exports, we can point to the Atucha II decision in 1979 that was greatly influenced by Ottawa's abhorrence of Argentina's human rights record.

Nevertheless, Pratt's theory needs to be modified to make it more relevant to the case of CANDU exports. A major strength of the pro-nuclear lobby, beyond its economic power and political connections, is its scientific knowledge. The Canadian nuclear industry has a virtual monopoly on the science behind the atom. Thus, a major asset of the pro-nuclear lobby is not its business personnel but the nuclear scientists at Chalk River.[7] A complete understanding of nuclear technology requires years of education and training. It is no wonder that politicians and bureaucrats can be intimidated by the experts when it comes to nuclear issues. Knowledge, especially very technical and specialized knowledge, is power. For example, William Farlinger, the former chair of Ontario Hydro, explained the decision to shut down the reactors by referring to the nuclear scientists and engineers as a 'nuclear cult' that had bamboozled the board.[8] Nuclear scientists do not place government officials under a 'trance,' but when they explain safety features and risk analysis, their arguments tend to be accepted.

Robert Morrison and Edward Wonder wrote in 1978 that 'those opposed to nuclear exports are likely to be the most visible in the domestic political scene. However, those who favour exports have greater economic clout and more technical expertise. The entrenched position of the pro-export interests within the government suggests that policy will tend to be dictated more by economic than security considerations. It is only when the nation's vital political interests are perceived to be at stake in international activities that the prime minister's advisors and External Affairs will dominate the policy process.'[9] More than twenty-five years later, it is difficult to argue with their conclusions.

When it comes to CANDU exports, then, the anti-nuclear movement has had limited influence. They can sue over the environmental assessment in China and campaign against a CANDU sale to Turkey. These are very public protests that get the attention of the Canadian media. Nevertheless, the protestors themselves lack the influence with government because they do not have the money, political connections, and, especially, the scientific knowledge of the pro-nuclear lobby. AECL has former deputy ministers, like Reid Morden, in its head offices, while the anti-nuclear lobby is filled with activists, academics, and lawyers. The pro-nuclear lobby, although at times feels it necessary to get into a debate with the anti-nuclear lobby, does not need public campaigns. It works its political magic behind closed doors because it has much greater access to government officials. For example, while AECL and other firms were part of the Team Canada trade mission to China, the Campaign for Nuclear Phaseout and the Sierra Club were not invited.

This final chapter has summarized the empirical findings contained in chapters 4 to 8. It has argued that the arguments in favour of CANDU exports – economic benefits, fighting communism, and assisting developing countries – have greatly outweighed the arguments opposed to CANDU exports – nuclear non-proliferation, human rights, nuclear safety and environmental protection, and government subsidies of the nuclear industry. Will this trend continue? What will be the future role of each variable in Ottawa's decision-making process? What is likely to be the future of CANDU exports?

Nuclear proliferation appears to have regained its importance as a constraining variable on CANDU exports. In the early to mid-1990s, Ottawa seemed to diminish the threat of nuclear proliferation. This was because of the tighter controls that Canada had attached in the 1970s and the increasing global adherence to the international nuclear non-proliferation regime. The NPT had been extended in 1995, and today there remain only three hold-out states (India, Pakistan, and Israel). The 1990s witnessed a number of successful stories of states abolishing their nuclear weapons programs: South Africa, Brazil, Argentina, Ukraine, Belarus, and Kazakhstan. Moreover, IAEA inspections proved their usefulness when they detected the diversion of spent fuel in North Korea. However, the 1998 nuclear weapons tests by India and Pakistan have, once again, raised the spectre of nuclear proliferation. These nuclear tests were joined by a number of important international events in 2002–4 that have refocused the international community's awareness of the dangers of nuclear proliferation.

In March 2003, the United States and the United Kingdom attacked Iraq and forcibly replaced the regime of Saddam Hussein. This decision was driven by the belief that the Iraqi dictator was developing weapons of mass destruction (biological, chemical, as well as nuclear). A second prominent episode involved North Korea's decision to withdraw from the NPT and its claims that it either had, or could quickly assemble, nuclear weapons. Finally, as a consequence of the 11 September 2001 terrorist attacks on the United States, there has been significant public discussion about terrorist groups acquiring nuclear weapons. These incidents will increase the attention of international and Canadian decision-makers on nuclear proliferation. Thus, while Canadian officials may have been lulled to sleep in the immediate post–Cold War environment, they are now wide awake in considering the potential proliferation impact of CANDU exports.

In the case of environmental protection and nuclear safety, there is now much greater public awareness of the risks surrounding nuclear power. In particular, Ontario Hydro's 1997 decision to suspend operations of a third of its nuclear reactors showed Canadians, who may not follow nuclear issues closely, the complexity of nuclear power technology. Even though Ontario Hydro's decision was based on performance issues, and not directly related to reactor safety, it reminded the Canadian public that nuclear power is a high maintenance, and perhaps unforgiving, technology. Accidents can happen. This led to the greater public scrutiny over the proposed projects in Turkey and Romania. If, in the final analysis, environmental protection and nuclear safety have so far been unable to prevent a CANDU export, it has acted as a constraining influence. Its importance is also rising. It is conceivable that a future CANDU export could be blocked solely because of environmental concerns.

It is hard to predict the future impact of human rights on CANDU exports. Since the mid-1970s, there has been an increasing focus of many countries and international organizations on the need to promote human rights. The rhetoric emanating from Canadian political leaders similarly stresses the importance of human rights in the conduct of Canadian foreign policy. Nevertheless, as the Chinese and Turkish cases demonstrated, the human rights records of recipient states will not prevent CANDU exports from being concluded. Even a foreign minister like Lloyd Axworthy, with his commitment to human security, was unwilling to try to block the proposed sale to Turkey. A poor human rights record may present some challenges to the export of CANDUs, but, by itself, will unlikely stop the transaction. That being said, if critics of a CANDU sale could couple a poor human rights record with other constraining variables, say nuclear proliferation, then they could block the transaction.

It has also become evident that the economic arguments put forward by AECL and its supporters in government, which have historically swayed the decision to export CANDUs, are now being scrutinized more heavily. There has been a noticeable weakening in the perceived economic benefits of nuclear power exports. After all, if the CANDU is not an economically viable source of energy, why pursue the technology? If the CANDU is not very efficient, who will buy it? If Ottawa has to heavily subsidize the sale, why do it? If the spin-off benefits are negligible, like spare parts or uranium sales, why push it?

It would, however, after almost fifty years of effort of the CANDU export program be extremely premature to sound the death knell. A new argument in favour of CANDU exports has emerged, and the idea that nuclear power is a solution to climate change could help to prolong the industry. The pro-nuclear lobby is clearly pushing the case of CANDU exports as the 'environmentally clean' energy choice. This position is already starting to take hold in the government departments of natural resources and foreign affairs. If the nuclear industry can convince the media and the public to compare its environmental record to fossil-fuel-based industries, it is possible that a reconsideration of nuclear power could take place. Some environmental groups are slowly starting to see nuclear power in a new light. They still do not see nuclear as 'green,' but some are starting to see nuclear as, to paraphrase Winston Churchill's view of democracy, the best of a bad lot. In the future, it is a distinct possibility that environmental protection may become a facilitating variable to CANDU exports.

Appendix: Basics of Nuclear Energy

This book is not designed to be a technical manual on nuclear energy. Nevertheless, some basic understanding of the nuclear process and an introduction of key terms and concepts is necessary.[1] To understand nuclear energy, you need to examine the atom, the basic building block of all matter. A substance that is composed entirely of the same atoms is called an element. Common elements are carbon, oxygen, iron, and uranium. Atoms are so small that if you lined them up on a table, it would take tens of millions to reach just one centimetre. An atom is composed of a nucleus that is made up of protons (positive charged particles) and neutrons (uncharged particles). Electrons that carry a negative electric charge surround the nucleus. One way of comparing atoms is through their atomic number and atomic mass number. The number of protons and electrons measures the atomic number. As the periodic table familiar to every high-school chemistry student shows, every element has a different atomic number, for example, uranium has ninety-two protons. The atomic mass number, obtained by the total number of protons and neutrons, is used to distinguish isotopes. Isotopes are different kinds of the same element. In the case of uranium, U-235 has an atomic mass of 235 and U-238 has an atomic mass of 238.

Nuclear power comes from the fission, or 'splitting,' of uranium. Nuclear fission occurs when a uranium atom, on absorbing a neutron, splits into two equal parts and emits further neutrons. This releases a tremendous amount of energy. To give the reader an indication of the power generation of nuclear fission, the fission of one atom of uranium releases about 50 million times as much energy as does the burning of one atom of carbon. The emission of neutrons also creates a chain reaction of further fission. A nuclear bomb has a very fast chain reaction, while a power reactor has a much slower and controlled chain reaction. In a nuclear power reactor, the heat from the fission process is used to boil water and the resulting steam turns large turbines that drive the generators to produce electricity.

In addition to nuclear fission, there is another source of energy from atoms: nuclear fusion. Fusion is a form of nuclear power with the potential to generate massive amounts of power by forcing atomic nuclei together (fusing), rather than splitting them apart. This creates much heavier nuclei. Nuclear fusion is the power source for the hydrogen bomb, but as a commercial energy source it is still at a highly developmental stage.[2]

An essential part of the process of producing nuclear energy is the fuel cycle.[3] The fuel cycle refers to the steps involved in the preparation and disposal of fuel for nuclear power reactors (see fig. A.1).

1 Mining and milling the uranium.
2 Conversion. This is the process of refining and purifying the uranium.
3 Enrichment. This is the process of increasing the amount of U-235. This is an unnecessary step for the CANDU.
4 Fuel fabrication. This creates fuel rods for use in reactors.
5 Heavy-water production. Necessary for the CANDU, but unnecessary for reactors that use natural water.
6 Spent fuel management. In an 'open' fuel cycle, like in Canada, spent fuel is kept in storage pending eventual disposal as nuclear waste. In 'closed' fuel cycles, like in France or Japan, the spent fuel is reprocessed into new fuel elements.

There are three main distinguishing features for comparing nuclear reactors: moderator, coolant, and fuel. The moderator is a material that surrounds or permeates the reactor core and is used to slow down the neutrons. Neutrons in a nuclear reactor do not usually travel very far. They get produced from the fission in the fuel, bounce around a lot in the moderator and lose most of their energy. Once this occurs, two other possibilities remain. They can either cause further fission, which will create more energy, or they can get absorbed in the support structure or the fuel, in some cases producing a more energized uranium isotope. Moderators can be ordinary water, heavy water, or graphite.

The second feature is the coolant. The purpose of the nuclear fission process is to produce a tremendous amount of heat in order to move the

Figure A.1. The nuclear fuel cycle for a light-water reactor

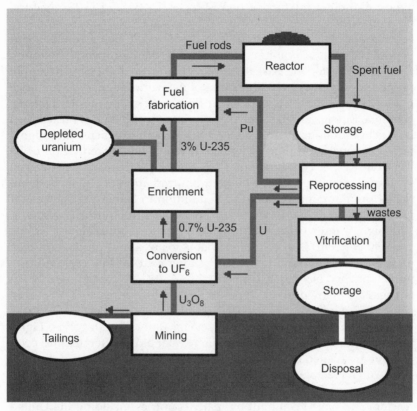

Source: World Nuclear Association, *Nuclear Fuel Cycle*, www.world-nuclear.org/info/inf03.htm

turbines. Typical coolants include water, heavy water, or gases like carbon dioxide and helium. Coolants are used to remove the heat and maintain the temperature of the fuel within acceptable limits. Sometimes the coolant is used to cool the moderator which, in turn, can be used to cool the fuel. Sometimes the coolant cools the fuel by passing around the rods containing the fuel.

The third distinguishing feature is the type of fissile material used to fuel the reactor. The fissile material's nuclei, when hit by neutrons, split and release energy as well as releasing additional neutrons, which can result in a chain reaction. There are three types of fissile material:

natural uranium, enriched uranium, or plutonium. Natural uranium is almost entirely a mixture of two isotopes, U-235 and U-238. Natural uranium is 99.3 per cent U-238 and 0.7 per cent U-235. Natural uranium is a mineral that exists naturally in the world. Canada contains rich deposits of natural uranium with mines in the Northwest Territories, northern Ontario, and Saskatchewan. Today, it is the largest uranium producer, providing over 30 per cent of the world's supply. Other large pockets of uranium are located in South Africa, Australia, Nigeria, Namibia, Russia, and the United States. The second type of nuclear fuel is enriched uranium that is created through an expensive and highly technical separation process, which increases the concentration of U-235 from 0.7 per cent to about 4 per cent. Plutonium, or PU-239, is a synthetic mineral produced by neutron irradiation of U-238. Both enriched uranium and plutonium, in addition to being fuel sources for nuclear reactors, are also the key ingredients for nuclear weapons. Although, it must be said that highly enriched uranium (enriched beyond 90 per cent) is even more suitable for weapons production than mere enriched uranium (enriched to 4 per cent) or low enriched uranium (enriched beyond 20 per cent).

There are many different types of nuclear power reactors. However, using the key distinguishing features of coolant, moderator, and fuel they can be largely grouped into several umbrella categories. Light-water reactors (LWRs) utilize ordinary water as a moderator and coolant, but are fuelled by enriched uranium. There are two main types of light-water reactors: pressurized-water reactors (PWR) and boiling-water reactors (BWR). LWRs are the most common form of nuclear reactors and have been built by many countries including the United States, France, Germany, and Japan. Heavy-water reactors (HWRs) are fuelled by natural uranium, but are moderated and cooled by heavy water. In heavy water, the hydrogen atoms (H_2) have been replaced by deuterium (D_2), a heavy isotope of hydrogen. It is called heavy water because the nucleus contains one neutron and one proton which makes it about twice as 'heavy' as the nucleus of normal hydrogen. The Canada Deuterium Uranium reactor (CANDU) is the major type of HWR. A gas-cooled reactor (GCR) is a reactor in which a gas, such as carbon dioxide, is the coolant. In such a reactor, graphite is often used as the moderator. Britain's Magnox reactor and Russia's RBMK are examples of GCRs. The fast-breeder reactor (FBR) is a reactor with little or no moderator, so that the neutrons from the reaction are not slowed down. It produces more fissile material than it consumes by 'breeding' fissile

Table A.1. Comparing the types of nuclear reactors

	CANDU	LWR	GCR	RBMK
Moderator	Heavy water	Ordinary water	Graphite	Graphite
Coolant	Heavy water	Ordinary water	Carbon dioxide	Ordinary water
Fuel	Natural uranium	Enriched uranium	Natural uranium with magnesium	Natural uranium

Table A.2. World nuclear power capacity by reactor type, 2000

Reactor type	Main countries	Number	GWe
Pressurized-water reactor (PWR)	U.S., France, Japan, Russia	252	235
Boiling water reactor (BWR)	U.S., Japan, Sweden	93	83
Gas-cooled reactor	UK	34	13
CANDU	Canada	33	18
Light-water graphite reactor (RBMK)	Russia	14	14
Fast-breeder reactor (FBR)	Japan, France, Russia	4	4
Other	Russia, Japan	5	0.2
Total		435	364

Source: World Nuclear Association, *Nuclear Power Plants in Commercial Operation* (August 2000), www.world-nuclear.org/education/ne/ne3.htm

material in a blanket of fertile material. Unlike conventional reactors that use U-235, the FBR uses the much more common U-238. However, the FBR is still in the experimental stage. Table A.1 provides a comparison of the different reactor types, while table A.2 provides the nuclear power capacity of each reactor type.

The CANDU[4]

The CANDU is a pressurized-heavy-water, natural-uranium power reactor. How does the CANDU convert natural uranium into electricity? Every CANDU reactor has a core that consists of fuel bundles (containing the uranium), fuel channels, moderator, and a calandria (a low-pressure tank). The fuel bundles are placed in a number of fuel channels that pass through the calandria containing the heavy-water moderator. Since the fission process produces so much heat, the heavy water coolant is circulated throughout the fuel channels. The steam generator transfers heat from the pressurized heavy water to low-pressure ordinary water which it then boils to produce steam to turn the turbine. The turbine is what creates the electricity. After this steam has expanded through the turbine it is condensed, by a large flow of cooling water, and the condensate is returned to the steam generator. Figure A.2 illustrates the basic schematic of the CANDU.

The CANDU's two most attractive features are its use of natural uranium and its online refuelling capability. Using natural uranium as its fuel source is desirable to those states which either do not own enrichment facilities or do not wish to become dependent on states which do have enrichment facilities, that is, the United States or France. Online refuelling also has a number of advantages: it reduces core excess reactivity, increases fuel burnup, increases the availability of the reactor, allows the fine-tuning of the power distribution, allows the operators to detect and remove defective fuel, and minimizes any power perturbations due to refuelling.

AECL, the CANDU's designer, has proclaimed a variety of technical advantages that its model has over the LWR:

- lower lifecycle generating costs
- higher utilization of uranium
- the ability to use natural uranium (which provides greater independence of fuel supply)
- high plant availability of CANDU stations
- design features which enhance inherent safety
- ease of manufacture
- ease of maintenance
- ease of handling and storing fuel (fresh or irradiated)
- secure supply of heavy water from Canada
- obsolescence-resistant fuel cycle options that can be introduced in the future without major change of reactor design and manufacturing concepts
- Canadian experience of industrial application of nuclear heat[5]

There are also technical disadvantages with the CANDU design. Since heavy water is used as the coolant and the moderator, a country needs access to a reliable supply of heavy water. In the early years of

Figure A.2. The basic schematic of the CANDU

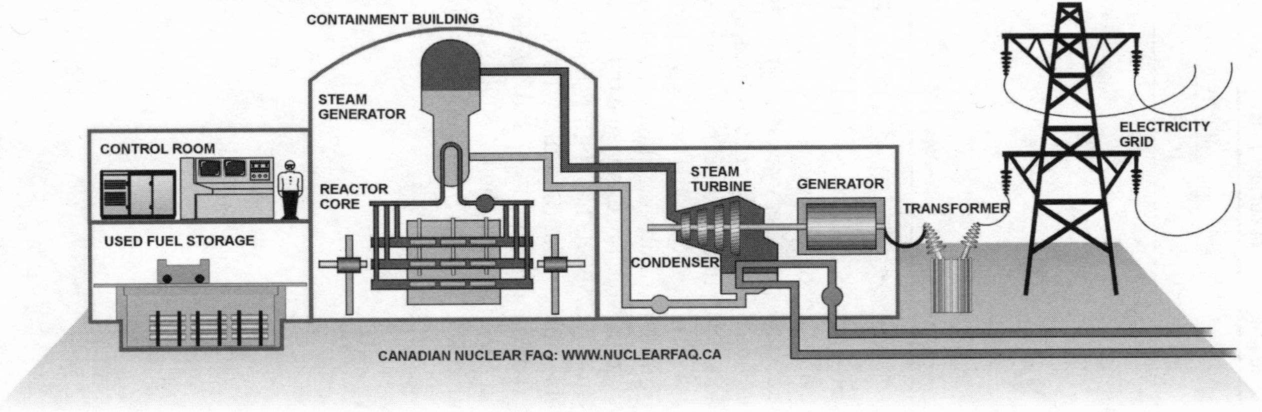

CONTAINMENT BUILDING

STEAM GENERATOR

REACTOR CORE

CONTROL ROOM

USED FUEL STORAGE

STEAM TURBINE

GENERATOR

CONDENSER

TRANSFORMER

ELECTRICITY GRID

CANADIAN NUCLEAR FAQ: WWW.NUCLEARFAQ.CA

Source: Jeremy Whitlock, *The Canadian Nuclear FAQ*, www.nuclearfaq.ca

Table A.3. Advantages of specific types of nuclear reactors

	Heavy water	Light water	Gas cooled	
	CANDU	PWR	BWR	RBMK
Online refuelling	Yes	No	No	Yes
Lower capital costs	No	No	Yes	No
Lower worker radiation exposures	Yes	Yes	No	No
Containment	Yes	Yes	Yes	No
Lowest operating costs (equivalent labour costs)	Yes	Yes	Yes	No

Canada's nuclear program, Canada was dependent upon American heavy water. However, Canada became one of the world's largest suppliers of heavy-water thanks to a heavy-water separation tower located at Bruce Point.[6] The Bruce Heavy Water Plant was shut down in 1997, so Canada relies on an accumulated stockpile of heavy water to fuel all of the CANDUs. Using this process, the heavy water is extracted from the quantity that is found naturally in ordinary water rather than manufactured. Heavy water is also more expensive than ordinary water, and this is one reason why the CANDU has slightly higher capital costs than other reactor models. This is balanced out by the lower fuelling cost – due to the use of natural uranium – of the CANDU. Most nuclear experts agree that in the long term the CANDU is cheaper, but it does have more up-front costs. Table A.3 outlines the advantages of each type of reactor.

Notes

1. Introduction

1 Three major scholarly works have examined CANDU exports: Robert Morrison and Edward F. Wonder, *Canada's Nuclear Export Policy* (Ottawa: Norman Paterson School of International Affairs, 1978); Ron Finch, *Exporting Danger: A History of the Canadian Nuclear Energy Export Program* (Montreal: Black Rose Books, 1986); and Robert Bothwell, *Nucleus: The History of Atomic Energy of Canada Limited* (Toronto: University of Toronto Press, 1988).

2 'Chrétien Government Pro-nuclear,' *Nucleonics Week*, 11 Nov. 1993, 15.

3 Bruce Doern, 'The Politics of the Canadian Nuclear Industry,' in Doern and Robert W. Morrison, eds., *Canadian Nuclear Policies* (Montreal: Institute for Research on Public Policy, 1980), 47.

4 A model Nuclear Cooperation Agreement Treaty is available online at www.dfait-maeci.gc.ca/nndi-agency/nuclear_agreement-en.asp

5 Quoted in Bothwell, *Nucleus*, 22. For a more in-depth history of Canada's nuclear program, see Wilfrid Eggleston, *Canada's Nuclear Story* (Toronto: Clarke, Irwin, 1965); Gordon H.E. Sims, *A History of the Atomic Energy Control Board* (Hull: Supply and Services, 1981); Robert Bothwell, *Eldorado: Canada's Natural Uranium Company* (Toronto: University of Toronto Press, 1984); Finch, *Exporting Danger*; Bothwell, *Nucleus*; Ruth Fawcett, *Nuclear Pursuits: The Scientific Biography of Wilfrid Bennett Lewis* (Montreal: McGill-Queen's University Press, 1994); and Brian Buckley, *Canada's Early Nuclear Policy: Fate, Chance, and Character* (Montreal: McGill-Queen's University Press, 2000).

6 The Americans, despite the fact that it was being manufactured in Trail, BC, controlled the heavy water for all of the allied labs.

7 Eggleston, *Canada's Nuclear Story*, 67.
8 Buckley, *Canada's Early Nuclear Policy*, 26.
9 Ibid., 28.
10 The entire text of the Quebec Agreement has been reproduced in Margaret Gowing, *Independence and Deterrence: Britain and Atomic Energy, 1939–1945*, vol. 1, *Policy Making* (London: Macmillan, 1974), 439–40.
11 Quoted in Buckley, *Canada's Early Nuclear Policy*, 34.
12 Fawcett, *Nuclear Pursuits*, 61.
13 Bothwell, *Nucleus*, 171.
14 Quoted in Finch, *Exporting Danger*, 27.
15 Quoted in Bothwell, *Nucleus*, 204.
16 Fawcett, *Nuclear Pursuits*, 102.
17 Bothwell, *Nucleus*, xiv.
18 Further evidence that the early years of Canada's nuclear development were non-partisan was the fact that Tommy Douglas, the leader of the NDP, would support the construction of the Pickering A reactor in 1964. I would like to thank one of the anonymous reviewers for this interesting tidbit.
19 Quoted in Bothwell, *Nucleus*, 223. Emphasis added.
20 Quoted in ibid., 407.
21 Department of Energy, Mines, and Resources, *Nuclear Policy Review: Background Papers* (Ottawa: EMR, 1981), 259.
22 Canada, House of Commons, *Debates*, 3 September 1958.

2. Justifying CANDU Exports

1 The Canadian nuclear industry has commissioned two major studies that have highlighted the economic benefits of nuclear power: Ernst and Young, *The Economic Effects of the Canadian Nuclear Industry* (Toronto: Ernst and Young, 1993) and Leonard and Partners Ltd., *Economic Impact of the Nuclear Energy Industry in Canada* (Toronto: Leonard and Partners Ltd., 1978).
2 Canadian Nuclear Association, 'Benefits of Nuclear Industry,' retrieved 20 September 2005 from cna.ca/english/files/Benefits.pdf
3 Ernst and Young, *Economic Effects*, 22.
4 Natural Resources Canada, *Speech* 96, 116 (26 November 1996).
5 CNA, 'Benefits of Nuclear Energy.'
6 Ernst and Young, *Economic Benefits*, 52.
7 Minister of Industry, Science and Technology and Minister for International Trade Michael Wilson, 'Address to the Canadian Nuclear Association,' *Statement* 92/04 (11 February 1992), 3.

8 EMR, *Nuclear Policy Review: Background Papers*, 259.

9 Ernst and Young, *Economic Effects*, 53.

10 Wilson, 'Address to the Canadian Nuclear Association,' 3.

11 Atomic Energy of Canada Limited, *Annual Report*, 1999–2000 (Ottawa: AECL, 2000), 49

12 Canadian Nuclear Society, *Canada's Nuclear Export Industry*, retrieved 5 September 2005 from www.cns-snc.ca/Publications/Canadas _Nuclear_Export_Industry.pdf

13 Ernst and Young, *Economic Effects*, 83.

14 Ibid., 50.

15 Ibid.

16 Atomic Energy of Canada Limited, *Annual Report*, 2001–2002 (Ottawa: AECL, 2002), 45.

17 Atomic Energy of Canada Limited, *Annual Reports, 1951–1952* to *2001–2002* (Ottawa: AECL 1951–2, 2001–2).

18 Ernst and Young, *Economic Effects*, 23.

19 G.C. Hanna, 'Basic Research: An Introduction,' in Atomic Energy of Canada Limited, *Canada Enters the Nuclear Age: A Technical History of Atomic Energy of Canada Limited as Seen From its Research Laboratories* (Montreal: McGill-Queen's University Press, 1997), 113.

20 T.A. Eastwood, 'Chemistry and Materials Science,' in AECL, *Canada Enters the Nuclear Age*, 117–36.

21 J.C.D. Milton, 'Physics,' in AECL, *Canada Enters the Nuclear Age*, 137–68.

22 Brian Buckley, *Canada's Early Nuclear Policy*, 100–101.

23 B. Ullyett, 'Radioisotopes,' in AECL, *Canada Enters the Nuclear Age*, 97–116.

24 AECL sold off its cobalt-60 business in 1991, but there continues to be brisk sales of isotopes.

25 Jeremy Whitlock, *The Canadian Nuclear FAQ*, retrieved 5 September 2005 from www.nuclearfaq.ca

26 Ruth Fawcett, in her biography of W.B. Lewis, paid particular attention to 'his inflexible insistence on "neutron economy." Lewis devoted a great deal of time and effort to ensuring neutron economy, performing elaborate calculations of expected burn-up and supervising an increasingly wide range of experimental programs aimed at providing more complete and accurate input data for the calculations.' Illustrative of Lewis's commitment to neutron economy was his championing of the ultimately doomed intense neutron generator (ING) project during the 1960s. See Fawcett, *Nuclear Pursuits*, 50 and chap. 7.

27 For an examination of research conducted on accelerators see G.C. Hanna, 'Accelerators and Fusion,' in AECL, *Canada Enters the Nuclear Age*, 169–90.

28 Ernst and Young, *Economic Effects*, 59–61.
29 The nuclear industry, like all other industries, has undergone a significant process of mergers, acquisitions, and joint ventures. In 1998, British Nuclear Fuels Limited (BNFL) purchased Westinghouse's nuclear division. Despite the ownership change, Westinghouse's nuclear manufacturing, engineering services, and research and development remains concentrated in the United States. Framatome (now part of the Areva group) has formed a strategic partnership with Siemens to design the European EPR reactor.
30 Russia, which used to be one of the largest exporters, is no longer a serious competitor to Canada because it has lost its primary export market in Eastern Europe.
31 Mark MacGuigan, *An Inside Look at External Affairs during the Trudeau Years: The Memoirs of Mark MacGuigan*, edited by Whitney Lackenbauer (Calgary: University of Calgary Press, 2002), 69.
32 EMR, *Nuclear Policy Review*, 261.
33 Department of Energy, Mines, and Resources (EMR), *Nuclear Industry Review: Problems and Prospects, 1981–2000* (Ottawa: EMR, 1982), 27.
34 Fatih Birol, 'Nuclear Power in the World Energy Outlook,' in Organization for Economic Cooperation and Development, *Business as Usual and Nuclear Power* (Paris: OECD, 2000), 19–30.
35 For more information on the major suppliers, see Joseph Pilat, 'The Major Suppliers: A Baseline for Comparison,' in William C. Potter ed., *International Nuclear Trade and Nonproliferation: The Challenge of the Emerging Suppliers* (Lexington, MA: Lexington, 1990).
36 Wendy Stueck, 'Candu Officials Hope for Sale to Britain,' *Globe and Mail*, 1 October 2001, A14.
37 For a good description of the infrastructure requirements needed for nuclear power see Renzo Tavoni, 'Infrastructure Needs for Nuclear Power,' in OECD, *Business as Usual and Nuclear Power*, 99–105, and International Atomic Energy Agency, *Financing Arrangements for Nuclear Power Projects in Developing Countries*, Technical Reports Series No. 353 (Vienna: IAEA, 1993). There is a fourth factor that affects the export market: the pursuit of nuclear power primarily for its military applications. This is assessed in chapter 3.
38 International Atomic Energy Agency, Power Reactor Information System, *Nuclear Power Plants Information: Number of Reactors in Operation Worldwide*, retrieved 5 September 2005 from www.iaea.org/programmes/a2/index.html
39 Peter Wilmer, 'Nuclear Power in the Electricity Market,' in OECD, *Business as Usual and Nuclear Power*, 31–5. For a comprehensive analysis of nuclear

power in the developed world see Organization for Economic Co-operation and Development, *Nuclear Power in the OECD* (Paris: OECD, 2001).

40 Jean Daudelin, 'Trapped: Brazil, Canada and the Aircraft Dispute,' in Norman Hillmer and Maureen Appel Molot, eds., *Canada among Nations 2002: A Fading Power* (Don Mills, ON: Oxford University Press, 2002), 261.

41 World Trade Organization, 'Canada: Export Credits and Loan Guarantees for Regional Aircraft – Request for Consultations by Brazil,' Case Number DS222 (25 January 2001). This document can be accessed online at docsonline.wto.org

42 George Lermer, *Atomic Energy of Canada Limited: The Crown Corporation as Strategist in an Entrepreneurial, Global-Scale Industry* (Ottawa: Economic Council of Canada, 1987), 59.

43 Birol, 'Nuclear Power in the World Energy Outlook,' 19–30.

44 William Walker and Mans Lönnroth, *Nuclear Power Struggles: Industrial Competition and Proliferation Control* (London: George Allen 1983), 51.

45 EMR, *Nuclear Industry Review*, 36.

46 EMR, *Nuclear Policy Review*, 251.

47 Ernst and Young, *Economic Effects*, 47–8.

48 Leonard and Partners, *Economic Impact*, 13–14.

49 Natural Resources Canada, *Quarterly Report on Canadian Nuclear Power Programme* (March 1999).

50 Canadian Nuclear Association, 'Economic Benefits of Canada's Nuclear Industry.'

51 Ernst and Young, *Economic Effects*, 51–2.

52 Ibid., 48.

53 Margaret Gowing, *Independence and Deterrence: Britain and Atomic Energy, 1945–1952*, vol. 2, *Policy* Execution (London: Macmillan, 1974), 328.

54 For a comprehensive examination of Canada's role during these nuclear disarmament negotiations see Joseph Levitt, *Pearson and Canada's Role in Nuclear Disarmament and Arms Control Negotiations, 1945–1957* (Montreal: McGill-Queen's University Press, 1993).

55 Lermer, *Atomic Energy of Canada Limited*, 13.

56 Editorial, 'The Jilted Candu,' *Toronto Star*, 3 October 1979, A8.

57 Atomic Energy of Canada Limited, *Annual Report, 1998–1999* (Ottawa: AECL, 1999), 1.

58 AECL has, since 1961, also maintained a sizable research facility at the Whiteshell Laboratory in Pinawa, Manitoba. The laboratory, however, is in the process of being decommissioned.

59 AECL does not maintain offices in either India or Pakistan, despite selling

both of them CANDUs, because Canada no longer has a nuclear relationship with them.

60 Ernst and Young, *Economic Effects*, 26–7.

61 Canadian Nuclear Association, 'About the CNA,' retrieved 5 September
2005 from http://www.can.ca/english/about.asp

62 Canadian Nuclear Society, 'About the Society,' retrieved 5 September 2005
from www.cns-snc.ca/home_eng.html

63 The Organization of CANDU Industries, 'Who We Are,' retrieved 5 September 2005 from www.oci-aic.org/who.asp

64 Robert W. Morrison and Edward F. Wonder, 'Canada's Nuclear Export
Policy,' in Doern and Morrison, eds., *Canadian Nuclear Policies*, 105.

65 Quoted in Bothwell, *Nucleus*, 407.

66 AECL, 'Reid Morden Speech' (June 1997), retrieved 25 May 2002 from
www.aecl.ca/english/news/news_f.html

67 See, for example, the 'Letters to the Editor' section of the Canadian
Nuclear Association's web page at www.cna.ca/english/letters.asp

68 AECL, 'Reid Morden Speech.'

69 Cranford Pratt, 'Competing Rationales for Canadian Development Assistance,' *International Journal* 5, no. 2 (Spring 1999), 306–23.

70 Andrew Cooper, *Canadian Foreign Policy: Old Habits and New Directions*
(Toronto: Prentice-Hall, 1997), 210–46.

71 In the first couple of decades after the Second World War, the Common-
wealth was quite an important component of Canadian foreign policy. See
John W. Holmes, *The Better Part of Valour: Essays on Canadian Diplomacy*
(Ottawa: Carleton Library Series #49, 1970), 89–122.

72 Quoted in Iris Heidrun Lonergan, 'The Negotiations Between Canada and
India for the Supply of the N.R.X Nuclear Research Reactor, 1955–56: A
Case Study in Participatory Internationalism' (MA thesis, Carleton Univer-
sity, 1989), 29.

73 Fawcett, *Nuclear Pursuits*, 74.

74 Prime Minister Pierre Trudeau, 'Canada's Obligations as a Nuclear Power,'
Statements and Speeches 75/22 (17 June 1975), 3.

75 Although the Trudeau government took steps to diversify Canadian
development assistance, for example to the francophone countries of West
Africa, Commonwealth members remained the principal destination. See
Robin S. Gendron, 'Educational Aid for French Africa and the Canada–
Quebec Dispute over Foreign Policy in the 1960s,' *International Journal* 56,
no. 1 (Winter 2000–2001), 19–36.

76 J.G. Hadwen, 'A Foreign Service Officer and Canada's Nuclear Policies' in
David Reece, ed., *Special Trust and Confidence: Envoy Essays in Canadian
Diplomacy* (Ottawa: Carleton University Press, 1996), 160.

77 Quoted in Buckley, *Canada's Early Nuclear Policy*, 44.
78 It is true that a number of Canadian and British scientists and officials with access to classified nuclear information, most notably the British nuclear physicist Alan Nunn May, had assisted the Soviets spy effort. However, the Americans were themselves not immune as Alger Hiss and the Rosenbergs would illustrate.
79 Quoted in Escott Reid, *Envoy to Nehru* (Toronto: Oxford University Press, 1981), 22.
80 Quoted in Cooper, *Canadian Foreign Policy*, 213.
81 Escott Reid, 'Canada and the Struggle against World Poverty,' *International Journal* 25, no. 1 (Winter 1969–70), 145–6.

3. Constraints on CANDU Exports

 1 Quoted in George Perkovich, 'Nuclear Power and Nuclear Weapons in India, Pakistan, and Iran,' in Paul L. Leventhal, Sharon Tanzer, and Steven Dolley, eds., *Nuclear Power and the Spread of Nuclear Weapons: Can We Have One without the Other?* (Washington, DC: Brassey's, 2002), 194.
 2 Ibid., 196.
 3 William Epstein, *The Last Chance: Nuclear Proliferation and Arms Control* (New York: The Free Press, 1976), 147.
 4 Mitchell Reiss, *Without the Bomb: The Politics of Nuclear Nonproliferation* (New York: Columbia University Press, 1988), 247.
 5 International Atomic Energy Agency, *The Structure and Content of Agreements between the International Atomic Energy Agency and States Required in Connection with the Treaty on the Non-Proliferation of Nuclear Weapons (NPT Model Safeguards Agreement)* (Vienna: IAEA, 1971), para. 28.
 6 International Atomic Energy Agency, *IAEA Safeguards: An Introduction* (Vienna: IAEA, 1981), 12.
 7 Mitchell Reiss argues that one of the most significant factors in explaining nuclear restraint is the existence of multilateral or bilateral disincentives. Reiss, *Without the Bomb*, 251–60.
 8 Board of Consultants to the Secretary of State's Committee on Atomic Energy, *A Report on the International Control of Atomic Energy*, U.S. Department of State Publication 2498 (Washington, DC: U.S. Government Printing Office, 1946).
 9 Quoted in Gordon Edwards, 'Myth of the Peaceful Atom,' in Ernie Regehr and Simon Rosenblum, eds., *Canada and the Nuclear Arms Race* (Toronto: Lorimer, 1983), 139.
10 Lawrence Scheinman, 'The Nonproliferation Regime and Fissile Materi-

als,' in Leventhal, Tanzer, and Dolley, *Nuclear Power and the Spread of Nuclear Weapons*, 204.

11 Richard Kokoski, *Technology and the Proliferation of Nuclear Weapons* (Stockholm: SIPRI, 1995), 6.

12 Quoted in Canada, House of Commons Standing Committee on Foreign Affairs and International Trade, *Canada and the Nuclear Challenge: Reducing the Political Value of Nuclear Weapons in the Twenty-first Century* (December 1998).

13 David H. Martin, *Nuclear Threat in the Eastern Mediterranean: The Case against Turkey's Akkuyu Nuclear Plant* (Uxbridge, ON: Nuclear Awareness Project, 2000), 74.

14 Ibid.

15 Edwards, 'Myth of the Peaceful Atom,' 166.

16 Jeremy Whitlock, 'How Easily Can an Atomic Bomb Be Made with Spent CANDU Fuel?' *Canadian Nuclear FAQ*, retrieved 5 September 2005 from www.nuclearfaq.ca

17 Stockholm International Peace Research Institute (SIPRI), *Internationalization to Prevent the Spread of Nuclear Weapons* (London: Taylor and Francis, 1980), 30–1.

18 Kokoski, *Technology and Proliferation of Nuclear Weapons*, 77.

19 Brad Roberts, 'Proliferation and Nonproliferation in the 1990s: Looking for the Right Lessons,' *Nonproliferation Review* 6, no. 4 (Fall 1999), 72.

20 EMR, *Nuclear Industry Review: Problems and Prospects*, 29.

21 Canada, House of Commons, *Debates*, 5 December 1945, 2959.

22 Buckley, *Canada's Early Nuclear Policy*, 43.

23 William Epstein, 'Canada,' in Jozef Goldblat, ed., *Non-Proliferation: The Why and the Wherefore* (Stockholm: SIPRI, 1985), 171.

24 Buckley, *Canada's Early Nuclear Policy*, chap. 11.

25 Other studies of nuclear-capable countries who have abstained from acquiring nuclear weapons have emphasized that the key variables in the decision whether to acquire nuclear weapons are security threats and national prestige. In the case of Sweden, see Paul M. Cole, *Sweden without the Bomb: The Conduct of a Nuclear-Capable Nation without Nuclear Weapons* (Santa Monica, CA: Rand, 1994). For an examination of the motivations of potential proliferates, see John Arquilla and Paul K. Davis, *Modeling Decisionmaking of Potential Proliferators as Part of Developing Counter-proliferation Strategies* (Santa Monica, CA: Rand, 1994). For comparative studies of both proliferators and abstainers, see T.V. Paul, *Power versus Prudence: Why Nations Forgo Nuclear Weapons* (Montreal: McGill-Queen's University Press, 2000); Reiss, *Without the Bomb*; and Mitchell Riess, *Bridled*

Ambition: Why Countries Constrain Their Nuclear Capabilities (Washington, DC: Woodrow Wilson Center Press, 1995).

26 Quoted in Buckley, *Canada's Early Nuclear Policy*, 134.
27 Canada Treaty Series, Declaration on Atomic Energy made by the President of the United States of America, the Prime Minister of the United Kingdom, and the Prime Minister of Canada, 1945 No. 13 (Washington, 15 November 1945), Article 2.
28 Canada, House of Commons, *Debates*, 3 June 1946, 2106.
29 Address by Mr. Dwight D. Eisenhower, President of the United States of America, to the 470th Plenary Meeting of the United Nations General Assembly (8 December 1953).
30 Quoted in Buckley, *Canada's Early Nuclear Policy*, 10.
31 Minister of National Health and Welfare Paul Martin, 'International Co-operation in Developing the Peaceful Uses of Atomic Energy,' *Statements and Speeches* (5 November 1954), 9.
32 IAEA, *Statute of the International Atomic Energy Agency* (Vienna: IAEA, 1956). Available online from www.iaea.org/About/statute_text.html
33 The IAEA's safeguard system has been extended twice to cover large reactor facilities, reprocessing plants, conversion plants, and fabrication plants. See: IAEA 'The Agency's Safeguards System (1965, as Provisionally Extended in 1966 and 1968),' *Information Circular* INFCIRC/66/Rev.2 (Vienna: IAEA, 16 September, 1968). Available online from www.iaea.org/Publications/Documents/Infcics/Others/inf66r2.shtml
34 These were not easy negotiations. Both the Soviets and the Indians wanted to restrict the agency's ability to conduct onsite inspections.
35 Quoted in Bothwell, *Nucleus* 241.
36 Quoted in Finch, *Exporting Danger*, 77.
37 United Nations, *Treaty on the Non-Proliferation of Nuclear Weapons* (New York: United Nations, 1968). Available online from www.iaea.org/Publications/Documents/Infcircs/Others/infcirc140.pdf
38 Article IX defines a nuclear weapons state as one 'which has manufactured and exploded a nuclear weapon or other nuclear explosive device prior to 1 January 1967.'
39 IAEA, 'The Structure and Content of Agreements Between the Agency and States Required in Connection with the Treaty on the Non-Proliferation of Nuclear Weapons,' *Information Circular* INFCIRC/153 (corrected) (Vienna: IAEA, June 1972). Available online from www.iaea.org/Publications/Documents/Infcircs/Others/infl53.shtml
40 'Nuclear Non-Proliferation Treaty: The Canadian Position,' in Arthur E. Blanchette, ed., *Canadian Foreign Policy, 1966–1976: Selected Speeches and Documents* (Ottawa: Carleton Library Series #118, 1997), 18.

41 Canada, House of Commons, *Debates*, 19 December 1969, 4149.
42 'Nuclear Non-Proliferation Treaty: The Canadian Position,' 19.
43 Canada, Lieutenant-General E.L.M. Burns, 'Canadian Statement on Non-Proliferation,' *Statements and Speeches* (27 February, 1967), 1.
44 Quoted in Barrie Morrison and Donald M. Page, 'India's Nuclear Option: The Nuclear Route to Achieve Goal as World Power,' *International Perspectives* (July/August 1974), 24.
45 Canada, House of Commons, *Debates*, 22 December 1976, 2255.
46 Berhanykun Andemicael, Merle Opelz, and Jan Priest, 'Measure for Measure: The NPT and the Road Ahead,' *IAEA Bulletin* 37, no. 3 (1995), 30–8. Available online from www.iaea.org/worldatom/Periodicals/Bulletin/Bull373/priest.html
47 Office of the Prime Minister, 'Notes for an Address by Prime Minister Brian Mulroney, Johns Hopkins University, Baltimore, Maryland' (21 May 1992), 5.
48 Canada, *Canada in the World: Government Statement* (Ottawa: Canada Communications Group, 1995), 32.
49 William Epstein, 'Indefinite Extension – with Increased Accountability,' *Bulletin of the Atomic Scientists* (July/August 1995), 27–30. Also see Susan B. Welsh, 'Delegate Perspectives on the 1995 NPT Review and Extension Conference,' *Nonproliferation Review* (Spring/Summer 1995), 1–24.
50 See SCFAIT, *Canada and the Nuclear Challenge*; Department of Foreign Affairs and International Trade, *Government Response to the Recommendations of the Standing Committee on Foreign Affairs and International Trade on Canada's Nuclear Disarmament and Non-Proliferation Policy* (Ottawa: DFAIT, 1999); and DFAIT, *Nuclear Disarmament and Non-Proliferation: Advancing Canadian Objectives* (Ottawa: DFAIT, 1999).
51 Part of this section was published previously as Duane Bratt, 'Canada's Nuclear Schizophrenia,' *Bulletin of the Atomic Scientists* 58, no. 2 (March/April 2002), 44–50.
52 See Bothwell, *Eldorado*, and Eggleston, *Canada's Nuclear Story*.
53 Fawcett, *Nuclear Pursuits*, 60.
54 Finch, *Exporting Danger*, 105.
55 House of Commons, *Debates*, 3 June 1965, 1948–9. Interestingly, the change in uranium policy was directed more at the French than the Americans or British. The Pearson government did not want to assist the French with their nuclear weapons program, but, politically, how could it refrain from selling uranium to Paris when it was still selling uranium, for the very same purpose, to Washington and London? The answer was to demand assurances from all purchasers of Canadian uranium that it would only be

used for peaceful purposes. See John English, *The Worldly Years: The Life of Lester Pearson, 1949–1972* (Toronto: Knopf, 1992), 321–3.

56 Canada, House of Commons, *Debates*, 17 February 1953, 2010.

57 Ibid., 2 June 1954, 5397.

58 Quoted in Buckley, *Canada's Early Nuclear Policy*, 8.

59 John Clearwater, *Canadian Nuclear Weapons: The Untold Story of Canada's Cold War Arsenal* (Toronto: Dundurn, 1998), 23.

60 John Clearwater, *U.S. Nuclear Weapons in Canada* (Toronto: Dundurn, 1999), 12.

61 For a recent study that explores Canada's decision to acquire, and then purge, the bomb, see Erika Simpson, *NATO and the Bomb: Canadian Defenders Confront Critics* (Montreal: McGill-Queen's University Press, 2001).

62 Tom Keating, *Canada and World Order: The Multilateralist Tradition in Canadian Foreign Policy* (Toronto: Oxford University Press, 2002), 91.

63 Robert S. Norris, William M. Arkin, and William Burr, 'Where They Were,' *Bulletin of the Atomic Scientists* 55, no. 6 (November/December 1999), 26–35.

64 Quoted in Buckley, *Canada's Early Nuclear Policy*, 113.

65 Clearwater, *Canadian Nuclear Weapons*, 23.

66 Pierre Elliott Trudeau, 'Disarmament: The Problem of Organizing the World Community,' speech to the UN Special Session on Disarmament, New York (May 26, 1978), in Arthur Arthur E. Blanchette, ed., *Canadian Foreign Policy, 1977–1992: Selected Speeches and Documents* (Ottawa: Carleton Library Series #183, 1994), 45.

67 MacGuigan, *An Inside Look at External Affairs*, 183n55.

68 EMR, *Nuclear Policy Review*, 275.

69 The best single source on the role of human rights and Canadian foreign policy remains Robert O. Matthews and Cranford Pratt, eds., *Human Rights in Canadian Foreign Policy* (Montreal: McGill-Queen's University Press, 1988).

70 Kim Richard Nossal, *The Politics of Canadian Foreign Policy*, 3d ed. (Toronto: Prentice-Hall, 1997), 114.

71 Robert O. Matthews and Cranford Pratt, 'Conclusion: Questions and Prospects,' in Matthews and Pratt, *Human Rights in Canadian Foreign Policy*, 294.

72 External Affairs Minister Don Jamieson, 'Human Rights: One of the Most Complex Foreign Policy Issues,' *Statements and Speeches* (16 March 1977), 7.

73 DFAIT, *Human Rights and Canadian Foreign Policy*, retrieved, 5 September 2005 from www.dfait-maeci.gc.ca/foreign_policy/human-rights/forpol-en.asp

74 DFAIT, *Canada in the World: Canadian Foreign Policy Review* (Ottawa: DFAIT, 1995). Available online at www.dfait-maeci.gc.ca/foreign_policy/cnd-world/menu-en.asp

75 See T.A. Keenleyside and Patricia Taylor, 'The Impact of Human Rights Violations on the Conduct of Canadian Bilateral Relations: A Contemporary Dilemma,' *Behind the Headlines* 42 (November 1984), and Margaret Doxey, 'Human Rights and Canadian Foreign Policy,' *Behind the Headlines* 37 (June 1979).

76 For a more recent account of how Canada's trade interests have impeded its efforts at human rights protection see Heather Smith, 'Niche Diplomacy in Canadian Human Rights Policy: Ethics or Economics?' in Rosalind Irwin, ed., *Ethics and Security in Canadian Foreign Policy* (Vancouver: UBC Press, 2002), 77–94.

77 This point is developed in Duane Bratt, 'The Ethics of CANDU Exports,' in Irwin, ed., *Ethics and Security in Canadian Foreign Policy*, 229–48.

78 T.A. Keenleyside, 'Development Assistance,' in Matthews and Pratt, eds., *Human Rights in Canadian Foreign Policy*, 191.

79 Marcia Valiante, 'Legal Foundations of Canadian Environmental Policy: Underlying Our Values in a Shifting Landscape,' in Debora L. VanNijnatten and Robert Boardman, eds., *Canadian Environmental Policy: Context and Cases*, 2d ed. (Toronto: Oxford University Press, 2002), 3.

80 David Jackson and John de la Mothe, 'Nuclear Regulation in Transition: The Atomic Energy Control Board,' in Bruce Doern, Arslan Dorman, and Robert W. Morrison, eds., *Canadian Nuclear Energy Policy: Changing Ideas, Institutions, and Interests* (Toronto: University of Toronto Press, 2001), 100. For a good history of the origins and development of the AECB, see Sims, *A History of the Atomic Energy Control Board*.

81 Atomic Energy Control Board, *Annual Report, 1997–1998* (Ottawa: AECL, 1998), 1.

82 The CNSC behaves very much like the AECB but has greater legal powers for nuclear regulation. The name change was done because 'antinuclear critics sometimes attacked the AECB because of the similarity of its acronym to that of AECL, which suggested that the two organizations were in collusion.' Jackson and de la Mothe, 'Nuclear Regulation in Transition,' 104.

83 Representative of Canada's position during these early years is discussed in 'The Threat of Atomic Radiation,' in Blanchette ed., *Canadian Foreign Policy, 1955–1965*, 85–8.

84 Prime Minister Pierre Trudeau, 'Canada's Obligations as a Nuclear Power,' *Statements and Speeches* 75/22 (17 June 1975), 6.

85 Quoted in L. Ray Silver, *Fallout from Chernobyl* (Toronto: Deneau, 1987), 7.
86 UNSCEAR, 'Appendix J: Exposure and Effects of the Chernobyl Accident' (2000), 504. Available online from www.iaea.org/worldatom/Press/Focus/Chernobyl-15/unscear_report.pdf
87 AECB, *The Accident at Chernobyl and Its Implications for the Safety of CANDU Reactors* (Ottawa: AECB, 1987).
88 Ontario Nuclear Safety Review, F. Kenneth Hare, Commissioner, *The Safety of Ontario's Nuclear Power Reactors: A Scientific and Technical Review* (Toronto: Queen's Printer, 1988), i–ii.
89 IAEA, 'The International Nuclear Event Scale (INES),' IAEA Doc. GC(40)/INF/5, Part C, Annex C-5, Appendix C-5-8, retrieved 5 September 2005 from www.iaea.org/About/Policy/GC/GC40/Documents/gc40inf5ac-5-8.html
90 IAEA, 'The International Nuclear Event Scale,' *Fact Sheet*, retrieved 5 September 2005 from www.iaea.or.at/Publications/Factsheets/English/ines-e.pdf
91 SCFAIT, *Canada and the Nuclear Challenge.*
92 The Standing Senate Committee on Energy, the Environment, and Natural Resources, *Canada's Nuclear Reactors: How Much Safety Is Enough? Interim Report* (February 2000), 7, retrieved 5 September 2005 from www.parl.gc.ca/37/1parlbus/commbus/ senate/com-E/ENRG-E/REP-E/repintjun01-e.htm
93 OECD, *Nuclear Power in the OECD*, 170–1.
94 Richard Rhodes and Denis Beller, 'The Need for Nuclear Power,' *Foreign Affairs* 79, no. 1 (January/February 2000), 32.
95 Hans Tammemagi and David Jackson, *Unlocking the Atom: The Canadian Book on Nuclear Technology* (Hamilton: McMaster University Press, 2002), 140.
96 Ibid., 139.
97 Canadian Environmental Assessment Agency, *Report of the Nuclear Fuel Waste Management and Disposal Concept Environmental Assessment Panel* (Ottawa: Minister of Public Works and Government Services Canada, 1998). Available online from www.ceaa-acee.gc.ca/010/0001/0001/0012/0001/report_e.htm
98 Tammemagi and Jackson, *Unlocking the Atom*, 140.
99 Peter A. Brown and Carmel Létourneau, 'Nuclear Fuel Waste Policy in Canada,' in Doern, Dorman, and Morrison, *Canadian Nuclear Energy Policy*, 114–15.
100 For a good comparative study of how countries are responding to the problem of nuclear waste, see Michael E. Kraft, 'Policy Design and the

Acceptability of Environmental Risks: Nuclear Waste Disposal in Canada and the United States,' *Policy Studies Journal* 28, no. 1 (2000), 206–18.

101 Campaign for Nuclear Phaseout, *High-Level Nuclear Waste: No End in Sight*, retrieved 5 September 2005 from www.cnp.ca/issues/high-level-waste.html

102 Canadian Environmental Assessment Agency, *Report of the Nuclear Fuel Waste Management and Disposal Concept Environmental Assessment Panel.*

103 Natural Resources Canada, 'Nuclear Fuel Waste Legislation Announced,' *Press Release* 2001/27 (25 April 2001).

104 P. Stothart, 'Nuclear Electricity: The Best Option Given the Alternatives,' *Policy Options* 17, no. 3 (March 1996), 15.

105 World Nuclear Association, *Global Warming* (2003), retrieved 5 September 2005 from www.world-nuclear.org/info/inf59.htm

106 Quoted in Mycle Schneider, *Climate Change and Nuclear Power* (Gland, SWITZ: World Wide Fund for Nature, 2000), 8.

107 World Nuclear Association, *Global Warming.*

108 Hans-Holger Rogner, *Nuclear Power and Climate Change* (Vienna: International Atomic Energy Agency, 2003).

109 Juhani Santaholma, *Nuclear Energy: A Long-Term Energy Option to Address Climate Change – Finish Energy Industries Federation* (2003), retrieved 5 September 2005 from www.world-nuclear.org/wgs/cop9/js_finland.ppt; Richard Myers, *The Role of Nuclear Energy in U.S. Climate Policy* (2003), retrieved 5 September 2005 from www.world-nuclear.org/wgs/cop9/myers.ppt

110 Robert Van Adel, *Smog Season Calls for Fresh Look at Nuclear Energy* (August 2002), retrieved 5 September 2005 from www.aecl.ca/images/up-RVA_0208.pdf

111 Ralph Goodale, 'Notes for a Speech to the Canadian Nuclear Society Climate Change and Energy Options Symposium,' *Natural Resources Canada* 99/95 (18 November 1999).

112 Herb Dhaliwal, 'Notes for a Speech to the Canadian Nuclear Association Annual Winter Seminar Reception,' *Natural Resources Canada* 2003/14 (18 March 2003).

113 'Nuclear Power to Receive Tax Breaks as Clean, Green Power,' *Nuclear Canada* (9 July 2003). Available online from www.cna.ca/english/newsletter.asp

114 NRCan, *Statements and Speeches* 2001, 29 (26 March 2001).

115 Robert Morrison, *Nuclear Energy and Sustainable Development* (Toronto: Canadian Nuclear Association, 2000).

116 International Nuclear Forum, *Policy Statement* (June 1999), retrieved

5 September 2005 from www.cna.ca/english/files/Climate%20Change/
intlnuclearforum.pdf

117 Canadian Nuclear Association, *Climate Change: Qinshan Nuclear Project*
(2000), retrieved 5 September 2005 from www.cna.ca/cl5.html

118 Andrew Duffy, 'Europeans Won't Buy CANDU Green Credit,' *Calgary
Herald*, 10 October 1999, A6, and 'Germany Vetoes Emissions-Credit Plan,'
Globe and Mail, 2 November 1999, A8.

119 Campaign for Nuclear Phaseout, 'Canada's Federal Government is
Wrong: Nuclear Power Is Not a "Solution" to Climate Change' (January
2001), retrieved 5 September 2005 from www.cnp.ca/issues/nuclear-not-
solution.pdf. Also see Sierra Club, 'The Canadian Nuclear Lesson: Why
the Kyoto Protocol Should Not Subsidize the Dying International Nuclear
Industry' (June 2001), retrieved 5 September 2005 from www.sierraclub
.ca/national/nuclear/reactors/nuclear-and-clim-chg-6-01.html

120 S. Andseta, M.J. Thompson, J.P. Jarrell, and D.R. Pendergast, *CANDU
Reactors and Greenhouse Gas Emissions* (Toronto: Canadian Nuclear Association, 2000).

121 Tammemagi and Jackson, *Unlocking the Atom*, 69.

122 Ralph D. Torrie and Richard Parfett, *Phasing Out Nuclear Power in Canada:
Toward Sustainable Electricity Futures* (Ottawa: Campaign for Nuclear
Phaseout, 2003).

123 Rhodes and Beller, 'The Need for Nuclear Power,' 32–5.

124 Bruce Doern, Arslan Dorman, and Robert Morrison, 'Conclusions,'
in Doern, Dorman, and Morrison, *Canadian Nuclear Energy Policy*,
207–9.

125 Tammemagi and Jackson, *Unlocking the Atom*, 121.

126 Ontario Clean Air Alliance, *Expanding Exports, Increasing Smog* (June
2002), 9, retrieved 5 September 2005 from http://www.cleanair.web.ca/
resource/submarine.pdf

127 Robert Morrison, 'Global Nuclear Markets in the Context of Climate
Change and Sustainable Development,' in Doern, Dorman, and
Morrison, *Canadian Nuclear Energy Policy*, 46.

128 Steven Mark Cohn, *Too Cheap to Meter: An Economic and Philosophical
Analysis of the Nuclear Dream* (Albany: State University of New York Press,
1997), 304.

129 Export Development Corporation, 'Who We Are,' retrieved 5 September
2005 from www.edc.ca/corpinfo/whoweare/index_e.htm.

130 Morrison, *Nuclear Energy Policy in Canada*: 1942 to 1997 (Ottawa: Carleton
Research Unit on Innovation, Science and Environment, 1998), 53.

131 Export Development Corporation, *Summary Report to Treasury Board on*

Canada Account Operations Fiscal Year 1998–99, retrieved 5 September 2005 from www.edc.ca/corpinfo/pubs/1998–1999_CanAcctRep_e.pdf

132 Quoted in 'Canada: Nuclear Exports Threatened,' *Petroleum Economist* (April 1999), 35.

133 Ibid., 7–8.

134 Morrison, 'Global Nuclear Markets,' 42.

135 Export Development Corporation, *Summary of the Report to the Treasury Board on EDC's Canada Account Operations for the Fiscal Year 1997–1998,* retrieved 5 September 2005 from www.edc.ca/corpinfo/pubs/1997-1998_CanAcctRep_e.pdf

136 DFAIT, 'Government of Canada Financial Support Finalized for Romanian Project,' *News Release* 2003/1 (3 January 2003).

137 Peter Berg, *Nuclear Power Production: The Financial Costs* (Ottawa: Library of Parliament, 1993), 10.

138 David H. Martin, *Financial Meltdown: Federal Nuclear Subsidies to AECL* (Ottawa: Campaign for Nuclear Phaseout, 2000), 7.

139 Berg, *Nuclear Power Production,* 10.

140 David H. Martin and David Argue, *Nuclear Sunset: The Economic Costs of the Canadian Nuclear Industry* (Ottawa: Campaign for Nuclear Phaseout, 1996), 20.

141 Quoted in AECL, *Annual Report, 1998–1999* (Ottawa: AECL, 1999), 34.

142 AECL, *Annual Report, 1999–2000* (Ottawa: AECL, 2000), 45.

143 Martin, *Financial Meltdown,* 21.

144 Quoted in ibid., 22.

145 David H. Martin, *Exporting Disaster: The Cost of Selling CANDU Reactors* (Ottawa: Campaign for Nuclear Phaseout, 1996), 9.

146 For information on India's nuclear reactors, see International Nuclear Safety Center, *Data for Nuclear Power Plants,* retrieved 5 September 2005 from www.insc.anl.gov/plants, and IAEA, *Nuclear Power Plants Information.*

147 I would like to thank an anonymous reviewer for making this point.

148 Martin and Argue, *Nuclear Sunset,* 10.

149 CCNR, 'What Does the Nuclear Industry Think of CCNR?' retrieved 5 September 2005 from www.ccnr.org/ccnr_by_aecl.htm

150 Campaign for Nuclear Phaseout, 'Background on CNP,' retrieved 5 September 2005 from www.cnp.ca/support-cnp/about-cnp.html

4. The Need to Establish Markets, 1945–1974

1 Quoted in Reiss, *Without the Bomb,* 217.

2 For a description of the institutional framework for India's nuclear policy,

see K.K. Pathak, *Nuclear Policy of India: A Third World Perspective* (New Delhi: Gitanjali Prakashan, 1980), 27–58.

3 Itty Abraham, *The Making of the Indian Atomic Bomb: Science, Secrecy and the Postcolonial State* (London: Zed Books, 1998), 66n45.

4 David Hart, *Nuclear Power in India: A Comparative Analysis* (London: George Allen and Unwin, 1983), 34.

5 Ibid., 36.

6 Quoted in Lonergan, *Negotiations between Canada and India*, 59.

7 Quoted in Bothwell, *Nucleus*, 352. Bothwell gives credit to Cavell for initiating the CIRUS project, but Iris Lonergan argues that it was Bennett or A.E. Ritchee of the economic division of external affairs who had the original idea. Regardless of whether the idea came from the Colombo Plan, AECL, or DEA, the fact remains that it was the Canadians who approached India. Lonergan, *Negotiations between Canada and India*, 53–4.

8 Quoted in Bothwell, *Nucleus*, 353.

9 Lonergan, *Negotiations between Canada and India*, 63.

10 Ibid., 63.

11 Ibid., 71

12 Lermer, *Atomic Energy of Canada Limited*, 39.

13 Quoted in Lonergan, *Negotiations between Canada and India*, 74.

14 Quoted in ibid., 56.

15 Sims, *History of the AECB*, 192.

16 Quoted in Lonergan, *Negotiations between Canada and India*, 76–7.

17 Ibid., 58.

18 Fawcett, *Nuclear Pursuits*, 111.

19 See M.S. Rajan, 'The Indo-Canadian Entente,' *International Journal* (Autumn 1962), 358–4, and Reid, *Envoy to Nehru*.

20 Holmes, *The Better Part of Valour*, 19.

21 Bothwell, *Eldorado*, 404.

22 Quoted in Geoffrey A.H. Pearson, *Seize the Day: Lester B. Pearson and Crisis Diplomacy* (Ottawa: Carleton University Press, 1993), 50.

23 Quoted in ibid., 52.

24 Ibid., 57.

25 Quoted in Finch, *Exporting Danger*, 33.

26 Lonergan, *Negotiations between Canada and India*, 132.

27 Quoted in ibid., 59.

28 Quoted in Bothwell, *Nucleus*, 353.

29 Ibid.

30 Department of External Affairs, Box 50219-AC-1-40, 145–75 (31 October 1956).

31 Statement by the Canadian Representative Burns in the First Committee of

the UN (November 2, 1965), in J.P. Jain, *Nuclear India*, vol. 2 (New Delhi: Radiant Publishers, 1974), 176.

32 Bothwell, *Nucleus*, 370.
33 Quoted in Morrison and Page, 'India's Option,' 25.
34 Lonergan, *Negotiations between Canada and India*, 171.
35 Constance D. Hunt, 'Canadian Policy and the Export of Nuclear Energy,' *University of Toronto Law Journal* 27 (1977), 77.
36 Bothwell, *Eldorado*, 405. In this respect, the Canadians were exactly right. After all, India did not detonate its nuclear test until 1974, eighteen years after CIRUS. I am indebted to James F. Keeley for reminding me of this point.
37 Agreement on the Canada–India Colombo Plan Atomic Reactor Project (New Delhi: April 28, 1956), Article III.
38 Ibid., Article XI.
39 Lonergan, *Negotiations between Canada and India*, 160.
40 Department of External Affairs, Box: 50219-AC-40, 90-50 (21 March 1956).
41 Department of External Affairs, Box: 50219-AC-40, 129-50 (24 February 1956).
42 Department of External Affairs, Box: 50219-AC-40, 90-50 (21 March 1956).
43 Ibid.
44 Department of External Affairs, Box: 50219-AC-40, 129-50 (3 February 1956).
45 Department of External Affairs, Box: 14001-3-1, 74-68 (19 July 1957).
46 Bothwell, *Nucleus*, 362.
47 Quoted in ibid.
48 Girilal Jain, 'India,' in Goldblat, ed., *Non-Proliferation*, 91.
49 Cited in Alex Roslin, 'Indo-Pakistani Nuclear War? CANDU!' *Saturday Night*, 1 May 2002, 43.
50 Jain, 'India,' 91.
51 Quoted in Morrison and Wonder, *Canada's Nuclear Export Policy*, 18.
52 Quoted in Peter Pringle and James Spigelman, *The Nuclear Barons* (New York: Holt, 1981), 377.
53 Bothwell, *Nucleus*, 360–1.
54 Quoted in Pathak, *Nuclear Policy of India*, 20.
55 Department of External Affairs, Box: 14001-2-6 (23 July 1960).
56 Ibid.
57 Department of External Affairs, Doc: RG25 Box 380 14001-2-6-pt8 (24 May 1961).
58 Department of External Affairs, Doc: RG25 Box 380 14001-2-6-pt7 (29 November 1960).

59 Department of External Affairs, Doc: RG25 Box 380 14001-2-6-pt8 (24 May 1961).
60 Canada Treaty Series, *Rajasthan Atomic Power Station Agreement between Canada and India* (New Delhi: Dec 16, 1963), Preamble and Articles IX–XIII.
61 The IAEA's safeguards system was approved in 1965, but provisionally extended and revised in 1966 and 1968. The current system is contained in IAEA, *Information Circular* INFCIRC/66/Rev.2.
62 Quoted in Zia Mian and A.H. Nayyar, *Pakistan's Chashma Nuclear Power Plant: A Preliminary Study of Some Safety Issues and Estimates of the Consequences of a Severe Accident*, Report No. 321 (Princeton, NJ: Princeton University, Center for Energy and Environmental Studies, 1999), 23.
63 Canada Treaty Series, Agreement between the Government of Canada and the Government of Pakistan for Co-operation in the Peaceful Uses of Atomic Energy 1960 No. 14 (Ottawa: 14 May 1959), Preamble and Articles II–IV.
64 Canada Treaty Series, Agreement between the Government of Canada and the Government of Pakistan relating to the Construction of the Karachi Nuclear Power Station 1965 No. 26 (Karachi: 26 Dec. 1965).
65 Canada Treaty Series, Agreement between Canada, Pakistan, and the International Atomic Energy Agency 1969 No. 15 (Vienna, 17 October 1969).
66 KANUPP was still under construction when the 1965 war broke out. 'We had to stop work for a while,' recalled William Brown, who was in charge of engineering at KANUPP. 'Construction was interrupted for nine to 12 months (out of concern for) the security of Canadian personnel. We were getting a little nervous having our staff there.' Quoted in Roslin, 'Indo-Pakistani Nuclear War? CANDU!' 44.
67 Ashok Kapur, *Pakistan's Nuclear Development* (London: Croom Helm, 1987), 19.
68 Ibid., 19, 59.
69 Bothwell, *Nucleus*, 385.
70 After being awarded the contract to build Pakistan's nuclear reactor, a Nuclear Reactor Export Promotion Committee was created with members from ITC, DEA, the Export Credits Insurance Corporation, and AECL. Its mission, and $2 million worth of funding, was to support CGE's export promotion campaign. Nevertheless, the operation was unsuccessful and CGE died as a designer of nuclear reactors. AECL was left alone to head the Canadian nuclear industry. Bothwell, *Nucleus*, 386–391.
71 Quoted in Finch, *Exporting Danger*, 41.
72 Bothwell, *Nucleus*, 383–4.

73 EMR, *Nuclear Policy Review*, 314. It is interesting to note that CGE actually made a profit on KANUPP. See Bothwell, *Nucleus*, 391.
74 EMR, *Nuclear Policy Review*, 312.
75 Quoted in Bothwell, *Nucleus*, 365.
76 Ibid.
77 Ibid., 367.
78 Ibid., 366.
79 Pathak, *Nuclear Policy of India*, 125.
80 Quoted in Reiss, *Without the Bomb*, 213–14.
81 Ibid., 216.
82 Hadwen, 'A Foreign Service Officer,' 161.
83 Quoted in Roslin, 'Indo-Pakistani Nuclear War? CANDU!' 44.
84 Ashok Kapur, *India's Nuclear Option: Atomic Diplomacy and Decision Making* (New York: Praeger, 1976), 194.
85 Canada Treaty Series, Agreement between the Government of Canada, the Government of India and the International Atomic Energy Agency 1971 No. 36 (Vienna, 9 June 1971), Articles VI–XI and XVIII.
86 Quoted in Edwards, 'Myth of the Peaceful Atom,' 136.
87 Bothwell, *Nucleus*, 425.
88 Finch, *Exporting Danger*, 48.
89 John W. Holmes, *Canada: A Middle-Aged Power* (Ottawa: Carleton Library Series #98, 1976), 164.
90 Finch, *Exporting Danger*, 48.
91 Ann Auman, 'Lack of Ties with Taiwan blocks Candu Sale,' *Toronto Star*, 18 January 1983, B1.
92 Edwards, 'Myths of the Peaceful Atom,' 136.
93 Martin, *Exporting Disaster*, 56.
94 Quoted in Morrison and Wonder, *Canada's Nuclear Export Policy*, 20.
95 House of Commons, *Debates* (23 March 1970), 5374.
96 Quoted in Morrison and Wonder, *Canada's Nuclear Export Policy*, 20.
97 Quoted in ibid., 21.
98 Ibid.
99 Export Development Corporation, *Annual Reports, 1974–9* (Ottawa: EDC, 1974–9).
100 For more information on the nuclear motivations and capabilities of Argentina and Brazil, see Reiss, *Bridled Ambition*, 45–88.
101 Stephen Handleman, 'Is Canada Expanding Argentina's Killing Ground,' *Maclean's*, 4 October 1976, 62.
102 Quoted in Finch, *Exporting Danger*, 60.
103 'Payments to Agents by AECL,' *International Canada* 7 (November 1976), 268.

104 Export Development Corporation, *Annual Reports, 1974–9.*
105 See Keenleyside and Taylor, 'The Impact of Human Rights Violations.'
106 Quoted in Finch, *Exporting Danger,* 91n19, 170.

5. Strengthening Safeguards, 1974–1976

1 Quoted in Abraham, *The Making of the Indian Atomic Bomb,* 1.
2 Quoted in Pathak, *Nuclear Policy of India,* 141.
3 Editorial, *Globe and Mail,* 20 May 1974, 6.
4 Letter to the editor, *Globe and Mail,* 23 May 1974, 6.
5 George Quester, 'Can Proliferation Now Be Stopped?' *Foreign Affairs* (1974), 273–4.
6 Morrison and Wonder, *Canada's Nuclear Export Policy,* 62.
7 At the 1975 NPT conference, Ivan Head, Prime Minister Trudeau's special foreign policy adviser, reminded Kissinger 'that CIRUS stood for "Canada India Reactor United States," because the United States had earlier supplied the heavy water employed as a moderator and coolant in the small reactor and had asked that its name be added to the device as a means of public recognition.' Head added that 'had the Americans been as vigilant then as they now claimed to be in hindsight ... they could have insisted on much more vigorous safeguards.' Ivan Head and Pierre Trudeau, *The Canadian Way: Shaping Canada's Foreign Policy, 1968–1984* (Toronto: McClelland and Stewart, 1995), 122.
8 Kapur, *India's Nuclear Option,* 219.
9 Privy Council Office, 'Notes on Nuclear Questions,' *Memorandum to Cabinet* (29 July 1975) Cabinet Doc. 39695.
10 EMR, *Nuclear Policy Review,* 342–3.
11 Allan J. MacEachen, 'The Nuclear Non-Proliferation Treaty – An Essential Shield,' *Statements and Speeches* 75/13 (7 May 1975), 3.
12 Canada, House of Commons, *Debates,* 22 December 1976, 2255.
13 Ibid., 2256.
14 Privy Council Office, 'Notes on Nuclear Questions,' *Memorandum to Cabinet* (29 July 1975) Cabinet Doc. 39695.
15 Finch, *Exporting Danger,* 99.
16 Christopher Kukucha, 'Canada and India: An Analysis of the Political and Economic Relationship, 1947–88' (Master's thesis, University of Windsor, 1989), 194.
17 Quoted in SIPRI, *Yearbook 1975* (Stockholm: SIPRI, 1975), 16.
18 Robert W. Reford, 'Problems of Nuclear Proliferation,' *Behind the Headlines* (May 1975), 15. When Prime Minister Morarji Desai succeeded Indira

Gandhi as Indian leader in 1977, one of his first policy statements was to denounce Gandhi's policy on PNEs. T.T. Poulose, 'India's Nuclear Policy,' in T.T. Poulose, ed., *Perspective of India's Nuclear Policy* (New Delhi: Young Asia Publications, 1978), 100–101.

19 Reford, 'Problems of Nuclear Proliferation,' 12–13.

20 Quoted in Morrison and Page, 'India's Option,' 24.

21 See Stephen Gorove, 'Distinguishing "Peaceful" from "Military" Uses of Atomic Energy: Some Facts and Considerations,' *Ohio State Law Journal* 30 (1969), 495–501.

22 For a comprehensive discussion of India's thinking on peaceful nuclear explosions, see R. Ramanna, 'Peaceful Nuclear Explosions,' in Poulose, *Perspectives of India's Nuclear Policy*, 16–51.

23 Ashok Kapur, 'The Canada–India Nuclear Negotiations: Some Hypotheses and Lessons,' *World Today* (August 1978), 313n2.

24 Pathak, *Nuclear Policy of India*, 139.

25 James R. Walczak, 'Legal Implications of Indian Nuclear Development,' *Denver Journal of International Law and Policy* 4 (1974), 239.

26 Quoted in Pathak, *Nuclear Policy of India*, 129–30.

27 Hart, *Nuclear Power in India*, 56.

28 Quoted in Pathak, *Nuclear Policy of India*, 120.

29 Walczak, 'Legal Implications,' 243–4.

30 A list of countries which accepted the peaceful nature of the Indian test included France, the Soviet Union, Nepal, Bangladesh, Sri Lanka, Bhutan, Maldives, Iran, Argentina, Senegal, Lebanon, and Kenya. Meanwhile, a list of countries that viewed the explosion in military terms included Canada, Britain, the United States, Japan, and Pakistan. See Pathak, *Nuclear Policy of India*, 134–6.

31 Pathak, *Nuclear Policy of India*, 134.

32 Charles K. Ebinger, 'International Politics of Nuclear Energy,' *Washington Papers* 57, no. 6 (1978), 44.

33 'Nuclear Non-Proliferation Treaty: The Canadian Position,' 19.

34 Ashok Kapur, 'Canadian Images of Indian Nuclear Policy,' paper presented at the annual meeting of the Canadian Political Science Association, Laval University, Quebec City, 30 May 1976, Appendix II.

35 Ibid.

36 Quoted in Morrison and Page, 'India's Nuclear Option,' 24.

37 Morrison and Wonder, *Canada's Nuclear Export Policy*, 62.

38 EMR, *Nuclear Policy Review*, 269.

39 Privy Council Office, 'Canadian Nuclear Reactor for the Republic of Korea,' *Memorandum to Cabinet* (10 December 1974) Cabinet Doc. 676-74.

40 Jungmin Kang and H.A. Feiveson, 'South Korea's Shifting and Controversial Interest in Spent Fuel Reprocessing,' *Nonproliferation Review* (Spring/Summer 2001), 72.
41 Reiss, *Without the Bomb*, 91.
42 Quoted in Gary Clyde Hufbauer and Jeffrey J. Schott, *Economic Sanctions Reconsidered: History and Current Policy* (Washington, DC: Institute for International Economics, 1985), 505–6.
43 Quoted in *International Canada* (June 1975), 170.
44 Reiss, *Without the Bomb*, 92–3.
45 Ibid., 95–103.
46 Canada Treaty Series, *Agreement between Canada and the Republic of Korea* 1976 No. 11 (Seoul, 26 January 1976), Article I, Article III, Article V, Note I.
47 Morrison and Wonder, *Canada's Nuclear Export Policy*, 72.
48 Ibid.
49 Canada, Privy Council Office, 'Sale of CANDU Reactor to Argentina,' *Memorandum to Cabinet* (30 December 1975).
50 Ibid.
51 Canada, Privy Council Office, 'Sale of CANDU to Argentina: Negotiation of Safeguards,' *Memorandum to the Cabinet* (27 October 1975) Cabinet Doc. 602–75.
52 Canada Treaty Series, *Agreement between Canada and Argentina* 1976 No. 12 (Buenos Aires: January 30, 1976), Article I, Article III, and Article V.
53 Canada, Privy Council Office, 'Summary of the Relevant Parts of the Discussion on the Argentina Sale' (3 November 1975).
54 Canada, Privy Council Office, 'Sale of CANDU to Argentina: Negotiation of Safeguards,' *Memorandum to the Cabinet* (27 October 1975).
55 EMR, *Nuclear Policy Review*, 313.
56 Finch, *Exporting Danger*, 53.
57 'Payments to Agents by AECL,' *International Canada* 7 (November 1976), 268.
58 '$4 Million Bribe Given on CANDU Argentina Says,' *Toronto Star*, 13 June 1985, A1; Joel Ruimy, 'RCMP Should Probe Bribery Scandal in CANDU Sale to Argentina,' *Toronto Star*, 14 June 1985, A1.
59 James Fleming, 'The Deal that Never Was,' *Maclean's*, 15 October 1979, 45.
60 Quoted in Morrison and Wonder, *Canada's Nuclear Export Policy*, 19–20. Emphasis added.
61 Canada, House of Commons, *Debates*, 18 May 1976, 13615.
62 Morrison and Wonder, *Canada's Nuclear Export Policy*, 78.
63 Kapur, 'The Canada-India Nuclear Negotiations,' 311–20.
64 Canada, House of Commons, *Debates*, 18 May 1976, 13615.

65 Ibid., 23 March 1976, 12057.
66 Ibid.
67 It is interesting to note that Trudeau and Head were 'chagrin[ed]' and 'dismay[ed]' by the attitude of those cabinet members which prevented the Head agreement from being implemented. Head and Trudeau, *The Canadian Way*, 127.
68 Ashok Kapur, 'Nuclear Energy, Nuclear Proliferation and National Security: Views from the South,' in Robert Boardman and James Keeley, eds., *Nuclear Exports and World Politics: Policy and Regime* (New York: St. Martin's, 1983), 173.
69 Quoted in Robert Bothwell, 'The Further Shore: Canada and Vietnam,' *International Journal* 56, no. 1 (Winter 2000–1), 112–13.
70 Head and Trudeau, *The Canadian Way*, 127.
71 Quoted in Morrison and Page, 'India's Nuclear Option,' 24.
72 William Epstein, 'Canada and the Problem of Nuclear Proliferation' (paper presented at the Canadian Peace Research and Educational Association, Quebec City, May 1976), 20.
73 This is 'the approximate amount of plutonium of all isotopes discharged, if the plant is operating. This gross amount is not net of, if any, annual plutonium charge or loading. Seven kilograms of reactor-grade plutonium is assumed to be required for a crude nuclear bomb.' Brian G. Chow, *Civilian Nuclear Programs in India and Pakistan* (Santa Monica, CA: Rand, 1996), 3–4.
74 Canada, House of Commons, *Debates*, 23 March 1976, 12065–6.
75 Reiss, *Without the Bomb*, 232.
76 Morrison and Wonder, *Canada's Nuclear Export Policy*, 79.
77 Louis A. Delvoie, 'Taming the South Asian Nuclear Tiger: Causes, Consequences, and Canadian Responses,' in Fen Osler Hampson, Michael Hart, and Martin Rudner, eds., *Canada among Nations 1999: A Big League Player?* (Toronto: Oxford University Press, 1999), 245.
78 Richard P. Cronin, 'Prospects for Nuclear Proliferation in South Asia,' *Middle East Journal* (1983), 598.
79 Nuclear Engineering International, *World Nuclear Industry Handbook 1992* (Surrey, UK: Reed Business Publishing Group, 1991), 21.
80 International Atomic Energy Agency, Power Reactor Information System, 'Reactors Connected to the Grid' (31 December 1996). Available online from www.iaca.org/programmes/a2/
81 Rodney W. Jones, 'Nuclear Supply Policy and South Asia,' in Rodney Jones, Cesare Lerlini, Joseph Pilat, and William Potter, eds., *The Nuclear*

Suppliers and Nonproliferation: International Policy Choices (Lexington, MA: Lexington Books, 1985), 169.

82 Quoted in Girilal Jain 'India,' in Goldblat, ed., *Non-Proliferation*, 122.

83 IAEA, 'Reactors Connected to the Grid.'

84 IAEA, 'Nuclear Power Reactors in operation and under construction at the end of 1995.'

85 Gary Milhollin, 'Stopping the Indian Bomb,' *American Journal of International Law* 81 (1987), 595–8.

86 House of Commons, *Debates* (Dec. 22, 1976), 2258.

87 Quoted in Steve Weissman and Herbert Krosney, *The Islamic Bomb* (New York: Times Books, 1981), 40.

88 Ibid., 46. In a more scholarly treatment, Ashok Kapur concurs that one of Bhutto's first decisions as president of Pakistan was to authorize the development of nuclear weapons. See Kapur, *Pakistan's Nuclear Development*, 136–78.

89 Weissman and Krosney, *The Islamic Bomb*, 67.

90 Chow, *Civilian Nuclear Programs in India and Pakistan*, 3–4.

91 Hadwen, 'Canada's Nuclear Policies,' 164.

92 Quoted in Zalmay Khalilzad, 'Pakistan: The Making of a Nuclear Power,' *Asian Survey* (1976), 589.

93 Quoted in Pringle and Spigelman, *The Nuclear Barons*, 388.

94 Hufbauer and Schott, *Economic Sanctions Reconsidered*, 503.

95 M. Raxiullah Azmi, *Pakistan-Canada Relations: 1947–82* (Islamabad: Area Study Centre for Africa, North and South America, 1982), 102.

96 Ibid.

97 Ibid., 104.

98 Ibid., 106.

99 In 1979, France, under a great deal of international pressure, decided to suspend its reprocessing deal with Pakistan. However, 'the suspension occurred after 95% of the blueprints for the reprocessing plant had been transferred by France to Pakistan and before the reprocessing equipment was supplied by France.' Kapur, *Pakistan's Nuclear Development*, 6.

100 Azmi, *Pakistan–Canada Relations*, 111.

101 Morrison and Wonder, *Canada's Nuclear Export Policy*, 79.

102 Quoted in Azmi, *Pakistan–Canada Relations*, app. 8.

103 Quoted in ibid., 97–8.

104 House of Commons, *Debates*, 22 December 1976, 2258.

105 Canada Treaty Series, *Agreement between Canada and Pakistan* 1960 No. 14 (Ottawa, 14 May 1959), Article IV and VII.

106 Quoted in Mian and Nayyar, *Pakistan's Chashma Nuclear Power Plant*, 24.
107 Cronin, 'Prospects for Nuclear Proliferation in South Asia,' 600.
108 IAEA, 'Reactors Connected to the Grid.'
109 IAEA, 'Nuclear Power Reactors in Operation and Under Construction at
    The End of 1995,' retrieved 5 September 2005 from www.iaea.org/
    NewsCenter/Focus/Nuclear Power/table_of-reactors.pdf
110 Quoted in Mian and Nayyar, *Pakistan's Chashma Nuclear Power Plant*, 24–5.

6. Suffering the Consequences, 1977–1989

1 EMR, *Nuclear Industry Review*, 24.
 2 EMR, *Nuclear Policy Review*, 345.
 3 Morrison and Wonder, *Canada's Nuclear Export Policy*, 83.
 4 In 1988, a former Romanian spy, Ion Pacepa, asserted that Romania had
   stolen Canadian nuclear technology during the early and mid-1970s.
   'CANDU Heavy Water Technology Reportedly Stolen,' *Globe and Mail*,
   21 December 1987, A10.
 5 Edwards, 'Myths of the Peaceful Atom,' 143.
 6 Wally Keeler, 'Canada's CANDU Sale to Romania,' *Peace Magazine*, June/
   July 1989, 8–9.
 7 Stevie Cameron, 'Ceausescu Planned to Use CANDU Data for Bomb,
   Author Says,' *Globe and Mail*, 2 May 1990, A11.
 8 Canada Treaty Series, *Agreement between Canada and the Socialist Republic of
   Romania*. 1978 No. 10 (Ottawa: June 14, 1978), Articles III and IV.
 9 Quoted in Morrison and Wonder, *Canada's Nuclear Export Policy*, 83.
10 Thomas S. Axworthy, '"To Stand Not So High Perhaps but Always
   Alone": The Foreign Policy of Pierre Elliott Trudeau,' in Thomas S.
   Axworthy and Pierre Elliott Trudeau, eds., *Towards a Just Society: The
   Trudeau Years* (Markham, ON: Viking, 1990), 44.
11 Department of External Affairs official (name withheld by request),
   telephone conversation with author, Ottawa, ON, 6 June 1992.
12 Quoted in Jennifer Wells, 'Going Critical,' *Report on Business Magazine*,
   June 1995, 41.
13 Export Development Corporation, *Annual Report, 1978–1979* (Ottawa:
   EDC, 1979).
14 Wells, 'Going Critical,' 41.
15 Michael Ornstein, *Canadian Policy-Makers' Views on Nuclear Energy*
   (Toronto: York University Institute for Behavioral Research, 1976), 87.
16 Canada, House of Commons, *Debates*, 26 October 1976, 475.
17 P.R. Johannson, 'Canada and the Quest for International Nuclear Security,'

in Robert Boardman and James F. Keeley, eds., *Nuclear Exports and World Politics: Policy and Regime* (New York: St. Martin's, 1983), 81.

18 Richard Gwyn, 'CANDU Sense and Nonsense,' *Toronto Star*, 4 October 1979, A10.

19 Warner Troyer, *200 Days: Joe Clark in Power* (Toronto: Personal Library Publishers, 1980), 114–15.

20 Julio C. Carasales, a former Argentine ambassador, has recently written that Argentina never desired to acquire nuclear weapons. 'For 30 years, Argentina pursued a peaceful program whose objective was to achieve mastery of the complete nuclear fuel cycle, so as to make the country independent of foreign suppliers and influence. Argentina's nuclear program never had the goal of developing a nuclear weapon.' Julio C. Carasales, 'The So-Called Proliferator that Wasn't: The Story of Argentina's Nuclear Policy,' *Nonproliferation Review* 6, no. 4 (Fall 1999), 51. Even assuming that Carasales is correct, which is quite a stretch, the Canadians did not have the benefit of hindsight in assessing the nuclear ambitions of Argentina.

21 John Deverell, 'Big Labor Battles Reactor Deal,' *Toronto Star*, 11 July 1979, A10.

22 Ian Adams, 'The Real McGuffin: Selling the Bomb, Confessions of a Nuclear Salesman,' *This Magazine*, May 1982, 19.

23 Handleman, 'Is Canada Expanding Argentina's Killing Ground?' *Maclean's*, 4 October 1976, 61–2.

24 For additional information on human rights violations in Argentina during the 1970s, see Amnesty International, *Argentina: The Military Juntas and Human Rights* (London: Amnesty International Publications, 1987). For Canadian relations during this period, see Keenleyside and Taylor, 'The Impact of Human Rights Violations on the Conduct of Canadian Bilateral Relations.'

25 Bob Carty, 'No CANDU for Argentina,' *New Internationalist*, March 1978, 27.

26 Edwards, 'Myths of the Peaceful Atom,' 146.

27 Editorial, 'Must the CANDU Go the Way of the Arrow?' *Globe and Mail*, 30 October 1979, A6.

28 G. Bruce Doern, 'The Politics of Canadian Nuclear Industry,' in Doern and Morrison, *Canadian Nuclear Policies*, 47.

29 Jeff Caruthers, 'CANDU Held in Need of Ottawa Backing,' *Globe and Mail*, 30 August 1979, B1.

30 Ontario, Royal Commission on Electric Power Planning, *A Race Against Time: Interim Report on Nuclear Power in Ontario* (Toronto: Queen's Printer, 1978).

31 Cited in Ross Howard, 'Our Nuclear Industry's In Big Trouble,' *Toronto Star*, 16 December 1978, C5.

32 Jeff Carruthers, 'AECL Thinks Nuclear Deal with Argentina Impossible,' *Globe and Mail*, 4 October 1979, B19.

33 J.R. Redick, 'The Tlatelolco Regime and Nonproliferation in Latin America,' *International Organization* 35, no. 1 (1981), 119.

34 For a pair of good case studies of the embassy case, see Charles Flicker, 'Next year in Jerusalem: Joe Clark and the Jerusalem Embassy Affair,' *International Journal* 58, no. 1 (Winter 2002–2003), 115–38; and Norrin M. Ripsman and Jean-Marc F. Blanchard, 'Lightning Rods Rather Than Light Switches: Arab Economic Sanctions against Canada in 1979,' *Canadian Journal of Political Science* 35, no. 1 (March 2002), 151–74.

35 Jeffrey Simpson, *Discipline of Power: The Conservative Interlude and the Liberal Restoration* (Toronto: Personal Library Publishers, 1980), 132.

36 For a personal account of MacDonald's battles with her own department, and especially Alan Gotlieb, see Flora MacDonald, 'The Minister and the Mandarians,' in Mark Charleton and Paul Barker, eds., *Crosscurrents: Contemporary Political Issues*, 2d ed. (Scarborough, ON: Nelson 1994), 171–7.

37 J.L. Granatstein and Robert Bothwell, *Pirouette: Pierre Trudeau and Canadian Foreign Policy* (Toronto: University of Toronto Press, 1990), 209.

38 Margaret Munro, 'Argentine CANDU Haunts Govt,' *Ottawa Citizen*, 23 April 1982, 1.

39 Quoted in Michael Fox, 'Ottawa Hesitant over Second Reactor for Argentina,' *Financial Post*, 21 January 1978, 11.

40 Carruthers, 'AECL Thinks Nuclear Deal with Argentina Impossible,' A1.

41 Quoted in James Fleming, 'The Deal that Never Was,' *Maclean's*, 15 October 1979, 45.

42 Secretary of State for External Affairs Flora MacDonald, 'An Examination of Conscience at the United Nations,' *Statements and Speeches* (25 September 1979), 5

43 Stephen Handelman, 'Canada Takes a Tougher Line on Nuclear Export Safeguards,' *Toronto Star*, 25 September 1979, A2.

44 Flora MacDonald, interview with the author, Cornwallis, NS, June 18, 1998. An interesting question is why MacDonald did not resign or why Clark did not fire her for this blatant disregard of the principle of cabinet solidarity.

45 Quoted in Troyer, *200 Days*, 119–20.

46 'CANDU Bid Lost to W. Germany,' *Winnipeg Free Press*, 2 October 1979, 1.

47 William Courtney, 'Nuclear Choices for Friendly Rivals,' in Joseph A. Yager, ed., *Nonproliferation and U.S. Foreign Policy* (Washington, DC: Brookings Institution, 1980), 249.

48 IAEA, 'Nuclear Power Reactors in Operation and Under Construction at the End of 1995.'

49 For an elaboration on the political factors that have constrained Japan's exploration of nuclear weapons, see Reiss, *Without the Bomb*, 109–37.

50 Quoted in Michael W. Donnelly, 'Japan's Nuclear Power Strategy,' *Canada and the Pacific: Agenda for the Eighties*, No. 25 (Toronto: The Joint Centre on Modern East Asia, 1984), 11. For more information on the Canada–Japan CANDU negotiations, see Frank Langdon, *The Politics of Canadian-Japanese Economic Relations 1952–1983* (Vancouver: University of British Columbia Press, 1983), 110–15.

51 MacGuigan, *An Inside Look at External Affairs*, 69.

52 Michael W. Donnelly, 'Japan's Nuclear Power Strategy,' *Canada and the Pacific: Agenda for the Eighties*, No. 25 (Toronto: The Joint Centre on Modern East Asia, 1984), 21.

53 Ibid., 20–1.

54 Langdon, *Politics of Canadian-Japanese Economic Relations*, 110.

55 Israel also took a tentative step towards beginning negotiations for a CANDU export. In 1989, the Israeli energy minister, Moshe Shachal, expressed a 'very strong interest in CANDU.' However, Michel Hebert of AECL, quickly reiterating Canada's policy, replied that 'we have our rules and all of the changes (in policy) would have to be on the Israeli side if they are really interested in CANDU.' 'Israel Keen to Buy CANDU from AECL, Official Says,' *Globe and Mail*, 27 October 1989, A1.

56 Walker and Lönnroth, *Nuclear Power Struggles*, 151.

57 Canada Treaty Series, *Agreement between Canada and the Arab Republic of Egypt* 1982 No. 6 (Ottawa, 17 May 1982).

58 EMR, *Nuclear Industry Review*, 28.

59 Jennifer Lewington, 'CANDU Financing Plan Set for Mexican Bid,' *Globe and Mail*, 12 January 1982, B1.

60 IAEA doc. INFCIRC/209, Communication Received from Members Regarding the Export of Nuclear Material and of Certain Categories of Equipment and Other Material (September 3, 1974).

61 The membership of the NSG has grown steadily. From these original seven members to fifteen by 1978, to twenty-five today. For more information on the development of the NSG, see IAEA doc. INFCIRC/539/Rev.1, *The Nuclear Suppliers Group: Its Origins, Role and Activities* (29 November 2000).

62 See IAEA, 'Communication Received from Certain Member States Regarding Guidelines for the Export of Nuclear Material, Equipment and Technology,' *Information Circular* INFCIRC/254/Rev.1 (July 1992). Available online from www.iaea.org/Publications/Documents/Infcircs/2003/

infcirc254r6p1.pdf. The Nuclear Suppliers Group guidelines, which were originally agreed to in 1977, were substantially revised in 1992. The revised guidelines included restrictions on dual-use equipment, material and related technology whose transfer its members would restrict through national export legislation. They also agreed to export such items only to states that had either ratified the NPT or had accepted comprehensive IAEA safeguards. Thus, since 1992, all of the nuclear suppliers, including Canada, have similar export controls on nuclear materials, equipment, and technology.

63 Pringle and Spigelman, *The Nuclear Barons*, 380–5.
64 EMR, *Nuclear Industry Review*, 50.
65 AECL, *Annual Reports, 1983–1984* to *1990–1991* (Ottawa: AECL, 1984, 1991).
66 Department of Energy Mines and Resources, 'AECL and the Future of the Canadian Nuclear Industry: A Proposed Discussion Paper' (Ottawa: EMR, 1988), 4.
67 Ibid., 56–7.
68 Ibid., 97–8.
69 The federal government would provide $31.1 million, Ontario Hydro $30 million, Quebec $3 million, and New Brunswick $1 million. EMR, *News Release* (30 March 1990), 1.
70 Department of Energy, Mines and Resources official (name withheld by request), telephone conversation with author, Ottawa, ON, 14 June 1992.

7. Nuclear Renaissance, 1990–1996

1 Ray Silver, 'AECL Signs Agreement to Build Second 680–MW CANDU at Wolsong,' *Nucleonics Week*, 3 January 1991.
2 AECL, AECL Information: Media Questions and Answers (1992), Q&A #2.
3 Michael Bociurkiw, 'Wolsong 2 Lifts AECL's Spirits,' *Globe and Mail*, 8 October 1991, C6.
4 'AECL Eyes Indonesian Nuclear Job,' *Financial Post*, 11 October 1991, 5.
5 Interviews with AECL officials (May to June 1992). Despite the government's assistance with AECL's intense marketing effort – which included a number of one-on-one meetings between Chrétien and Indonesian president Suharto – no reactor contract was ever achieved. Carol Goar, 'Chrétien Makes Pitch to Sell CANDU to Indonesia,' *Toronto Star*, 15 November 1994, B2, and Bob Cox, 'Chrétien Boosts Trade with Indonesia,' *Halifax Chronicle Herald*, 18 January 1996.
6 In 1991, Canada's exports to South Korea were $1.8 billion, while its

imports were $2.1 billion. Statistics Canada, *Imports by Country*, Catalogue No. 65-006 (Ottawa: Statistics Canada, Jan.–Dec. 1991), 118–20, and Statistics Canada, *Exports by Country*, Catalogue No. 65-003) (Ottawa: Statistics Canada, January–December 1991), 148–52.

7 Bociukiw, 'Wolsong 2 Lifts AECL's Spirits,' C6.

8 Department of Energy, Mines, and Resources official (name withheld by request), telephone conversation with the author, Ottawa, ON, June 1992.

9 Department of External Affairs official (name withheld by request), telephone conversation with the author, Ottawa, ON, February 1992.

10 For more information on South Korea's decision to stop pursuing a nuclear weapons program, see Reiss, *Without the* Bomb, 78–108.

11 David Fischer, *Stopping the Spread of Nuclear Weapons: The Past and the Prospects* (London: Routledge, 1992), 225.

12 Alexandre Y. Mansourov, 'The Origins, Evolution, and Current Politics of the North Korean Nuclear Program,' *Nonproliferation Review* 3, no. 1 (Spring/Summer 1995), 25–38.

13 Yong-Sup Han, 'North Korean Behaviour in Nuclear Negotiations,' *Nonproliferation Review* 7, no. 1 (Spring 2000), 41–54.

14 Rick Doust, 'Canadian–Korean Partnership Works towards a Tandem Fuel Cycle,' *Nuclear Engineering International* (April 1992), 36.

15 EMR and DEA officials, interview with author, Ottawa, ON, June–July 1992.

16 James C. Wendt, *The North Korean Nuclear Program: What Is to Be Done?* (Monterey, CA: Rand, 1994), 1.

17 For an excellent account of this episode, see Leon V. Sigal, *Disarming Strangers: Nuclear Diplomacy with North Korea* (Princeton, NJ: Princeton University Press, 1998).

18 For more information on North Korea's missile program, see Daniel A. Pinkston, 'Domestic Politics and Stakeholders in the North Korean Missile Development Program,' *Nonproliferation Review* 10, no. 2 (Summer 2003), 1–15.

19 Jean du Preez and William Potter, 'North Korea's Withdrawal from the NPT: A Reality Check,' Research Story of the Week. Center for Nonproliferation Studies at the Monterey Institute of International Studies (10 April 2003), retrieved 5 September 2005 from http://cns.miis.edu/pubs/week/030409.htm

20 See the North Korea Special Collection put together by the Center for Nonproliferation Studies at the Monterey Institute of International Studies, available online from http://cns.miis.edu/research/korea/index.htm

21 James Clay Motz and C. Kenneth Quinones, 'Getting Serious about a Multilateral Approach to North Korea,' *Nonproliferation Review* 11, no. 1 (Spring 2004), 136–44.

22 Freedom House, *Freedom in the World, 2001–2002: The Democracy Gap*, retrieved 5 September 2005 from www.freedomhouse.org/research/survey2002.htm

23 Martin, *Exporting Disaster*, 35–6.

24 Wells, 'Going Critical,' 36.

25 Government of Canada, *News Release* No. 199 (17 September 1991).

26 These arguments were obtained from information provided in a telephone interview with an EMR official, Ottawa, ON, June 1992.

27 Telephone interview with DEA official, Ottawa, ON, June 1992.

28 Ibid.

29 Secretary of State for External Affairs Joe Clark, Ottawa, letter to the author, 15 January 1990.

30 See Dave Todd, 'Forced Labour Used in Romanian CANDU,' *Toronto Star*, 30 December 1989, A1, A20; Dave Todd, 'Conscripts Built CANDU Reactor: Government Never Protested to Romanians,' *Toronto Star*, 30 December 1989, A20; and Paul Watson, 'Life Harsh for 14,000 CANDU Workers,' *Toronto Star*, 3 January 1990, A1, A17.

31 Martin, *Exporting Disaster*, 27.

32 Marc Keillor, 'CANDU in Romania: Setting the Record Straight,' *Ascent* 9 (1990), 6; and William Walker, 'CANDU Overseer Dismisses Reports of Forced Labour,' *Toronto Star*, 3 January 1990, A17.

33 Quoted in Charlotte Montgomery, 'Knew Romanian Work Conditions Were Harsh, CANDU Official Says,' *Globe and Mail*, 25 May 1990, A1, A2.

34 Joe Clark, letter to the author.

35 Geoffrey York, 'Romanian Palace Cast in New Light,' *Globe and Mail*, 4 May 1996, A14.

36 Freedom House, *Freedom in the World, 2001–2002*.

37 Quoted in Wells, 'Going Critical,' 39.

38 Ibid., 46.

39 Cited in ibid., 46–7.

40 AECL, *Annual Report, 1990–1991* (Ottawa: AECL, 1991), 11.

41 David Stewart-Patterson, 'Candu Suppliers Face Hard Negotiations,' *Globe and Mail*, 11 August 1983, B3.

42 Ian Austen, 'CANDU Deal for Food, Goods, Hurt Romanians, Critics Charge,' *Ottawa Citizen*, 5 January 1990.

43 Edward Clifford, 'Romania Tangles Contracts on CANDU,' *Globe and Mail*, 4 January 1984, A1–A2.

44 Canada, House of Commons, *Debates*, 14 May 1990, 11370.
45 Wells, 'Going Critical,' 38.
46 Quoted in B. Michael Frolic, 'Re-engaging China: Striking a Balance between Trade and Human Rights,' in Fen Osler Hampson, Maureen Appel Molot, and Martin Rudner, eds., *Canada among Nations, 1997: Asia Pacific Face-Off* (Ottawa: Carleton University Press, 1997), 332.
47 Weixing Hu, 'China's Nuclear Export Controls: Policy and Regulations,' *Nonproliferation Review* 1, no. 2 (Winter 1994), 3.
48 Natural Resources Canada, *Speech* 96, 116 (26 November 1996).
49 Miro Cernetig, 'China Aspires to Nuclear Self-Reliance,' *Globe and Mail*, 15 April 2000, A6.
50 Department of Foreign and International Trade (DFAIT), *Statement* 94/25 (31 May 1994), 3.
51 Quoted in Rosemary Spiers, 'A Court Challenge to the Way the Chretien Cabinet Sells CANDUs,' *Toronto Star*, 27 November 1999, A1.
52 Office of the Prime Minister, 'Notes for an Address by Prime Minister Jean Chrétien. Canada China Business Council Luncheon. Shanghai, China' (26 November 1996).
53 DFAIT, *Speech 96/50* (26 November 1996).
54 There is currently a debate in the United States over whether China is trying to enhance its nuclear technology through civilian cooperation. Michael Beck, 'Reforming the Multilateral Export Control Regimes,' *The Nonproliferation Review* 7, no. 2 (Summer 2000), 91–103.
55 Hu, 'China's Nuclear Export Controls,' 6.
56 Mian and Nayyar, *Pakistan's Chasma Nuclear Power Plant*, 16.
57 Ibid.
58 DFAIT official, telephone interview with author, Ottawa, ON, May 1998.
59 Mark Nichols, 'China Syndrome: Critics Flail a $4-billion Canadian Nuclear Deal,' *Maclean's* 9 December 1996, 29.
60 Frolic, 'Re-engaging China,' 329.
61 Quoted in Paul Gecelovsky and T.A. Keenleyside, 'Canada's International Human Rights Policy in Practice: Tiananmen Square,' *International Journal* 50, no. 3 (1995), 566.
62 Ibid., 589.
63 Human Rights Watch, 'China and Tibet,' *World Report 2002*, retrieved 5 September 2005 from http://hrw.org/wr2k2/asia4.html
64 Amnesty International, 'China,' *2002 Report*, retrieved 5 September 2005 from www.amnesty.org
65 Freedom House, *Freedom to the World 2001–2002*.
66 Department of Foreign Affairs and International Trade, Notes for an

Address by the Honourable Raymond Chan, Canadian Secretary of State (Asia-Pacific), to the Society of Democratic Movement, Vancouver (28 May 1995).

67 Raymond Chan, 'Canada and Asia Pacific,' in Hampson, Appel, and Rudner, eds., *Canada among Nations 1997*, 112.

68 Frolic, 'Re-engaging China,' 333.

69 Quoted in Cox, 'Chrétien Boosts Trade with Indonesia.'

70 Department of Foreign Affairs and International Trade, Notes for an Address by the Honourable Raymond Chan.

71 Jeff Sallot, 'Ottawa Skips Reactor Advice: Liberals Ignore Recommendations in Studies before Selling Nuclear Plants to China,' *Globe and Mail*, 11 August 1997, A4.

72 This evidence was contained in an affidavit that Elizabeth May filed in conjunction with the Sierra Club's court challenge. A copy of the affidavit is at www.sierraclub.ca/national/nuclear/candu-case/affidavit.html

73 Sierra Club, 'Environment Group Plan Legal Challenge to CANDU Export Deal with China,' *Press Release* (November 26, 1996), retrieved 5 September 2005 from www.sierraclub.ca/national/media/candu2.html

74 For a copy of the Sierra Club's request for judicial review of the Qinshan project, see www.sierraclub.ca/national/nuclear/candu-case/jud-rev.html

75 Quoted in Speirs, 'A Court Challenge,' A1.

76 Sallot, 'Ottawa Skips Reactor Advice,' A4.

77 Ibid.

78 Canada, House of Commons, *Debates*, 8 November 1996, 6314.

79 Quoted in Spiers, 'A Court Challenge,' A1.

80 Sallot, 'Ottawa Skips Reactor Advice,' A4.

81 AECL official, telephone interview with author, Ottawa, ON, June 2001.

82 Canada, House of Commons, *Debates*, 29 November 1996.

83 Quoted in Andrew Duffy, 'Right to Secrecy Denied in Sale of Nuclear Reactors to China,' *Ottawa Citizen*, 21 December 1999, C15.

84 Sierra Club, 'AECL to Sierra Club: Include Us in Your Court Case: The Question Is Why?' *Press Release* (28 April 1998), retrieved 5 September 2005 from www.sierraclub.ca/national/media/candu-case-April-98.html

85 Duffy, 'Right to Secrecy,' C15.

86 *Sierra Club of Canada vs Canada (Minister of Finance)*, 2002 SCC 41, File No: 28020 (26 April 2002).

87 Elizabeth May, 'Why the CANDU Case Was Dropped' (August 2003), retrieved 5 September 2005 from www.sierraclub.ca/national/programs/atmosphere-energy/nuclear-free/candu-case/candu-case-2003.html

88 Quoted in Aaron Freeman, 'Financing Disaster: Canada's Export Development Corporation,' *Canadian Dimension*, May 2000, 19.

89 House of Commons, Standing Committee on Foreign Affairs and International Trade, *Exporting in the Canadian Interest: Reviewing the Export Development Act* (December 1999). Available online from http://192.197.82.11/committee/CommittePublication.asp

90 A copy of EDC's Environmental Review Directive is located at www.edc .ca/corpinfo/csr/environment/Environmental_Review_Directive_e.pdf

91 EDC, 'Comments on EDC's Environmental Review Directive and D3 of EDC's Disclosure Policy,' retrieved 5 September 2005 from www.edc.ca/corpinfo/csr/disclosure/comments_e.pdf

92 Robert Morrison, 'Global Nuclear Markets in the Context of Climate Change and Sustainable Development,' in Doern, Dorman, and Morrison, eds., *Canadian Nuclear Energy Policy*, 41.

93 Barrie McKenna, 'Canadian Firms See $2.7 Billion in Candu Deals,' *Globe and Mail*, 9 November 1995, B1, and Michael Urlocker, 'China's Deal for CANDUs Won't Cure AECL's Ills,' *Financial Post*, 11 November 1994, 6.

94 Ray Silver, 'Morden Upbeat about CANDU Sales Despite "onerous" Chinese terms,' *Nucleonics Week*, 15 February 1996, 8, and Ray Silver, 'Demand for Price Cuts May Kill AECL Bid to Sell CANDUs to China,' *Nucleonics Week*, 14 March 1996, 4.

95 Natural Resources Canada, *Speeches* 96/116 (26 November 1996).

96 Ray Silver, 'AECL, CNNC Ink Contracts for Two CAND-6s at Qinshan,' *Nucleonics Week*, 28 November 1996, 9–10.

97 Sierra Club, *Financing Disaster: How the G8 fund the Global Proliferation of Nuclear Technology* (Toronto: Sierra Club, 2001), 38.

98 Terence Corcoran, 'The CANDU Man,' *Globe and Mail*, 29 November 1996, B2.

8. New Challenges and New Opportunities, 1997–2005

1 Quotes from David Albright, 'The Shots Heard 'Round the World,' *Bulletin of the Atomic Scientists* 54, no. 4 (July/August 1998), 20–1.

2 Jaswant Singh, 'Against Nuclear Apartheid,' *Foreign Affairs* 77, no. 5 (September/October 1998), 50.

3 Quoted in John Stackhouse, 'Suspicion Helped Fuel Nuclear Blasts,' *Globe and Mail*, 15 May 1998, A10.

4 Quoted in John Stackhouse, 'Pakistan Angered by 2 More Blasts,' *Globe and Mail*, 14 May 1998, A8.
5 T.V. Paul, 'The Systemic Bases of India's Challenge to the Global Nuclear Order,' *Nonproliferation Review* 5, no. 4 (Fall 1998), 1–11.
6 Singh, 'Against Nuclear Apartheid,' 43.
7 Delvoie, 'Taming the South Asian Nuclear Tiger,' 237.
8 For a more comprehensive examination of India's decision-making that led to the 1998 test, with an emphasis on the role of the BJP, see Gaurav Kampani, 'From Existential to Minimum Deterrence: Explaining India's Decision to Test,' *Nonproliferation Review* 5, no. 4 (Fall 1998), 12–24.
9 'U.S. Hits India with Heavy Sanctions for Tests,' *Globe and Mail*, 14 May 1998, A8. In total, there were fifteen countries that placed sanctions on India and Pakistan. For an examination of the impact of these sanctions, see Daniel Morrow and Michael Carriere, 'The Economic Impacts of the 1998 sanctions on India and Pakistan,' *Nonproliferation Review* 6, no. 4 (Fall 1999), 1–16.
10 'Indian Bomb Raises Fears of Cold War,' *Globe and Mail*, 13 May 1998, A1.
11 Department of Foreign Affairs and International Trade, *Statements* 98/40 (26 May 1998).
12 Ibid.
13 Quoted in John Stackhouse, 'Pakistan Goes Nuclear,' *Globe and Mail*, 29 May 1998, A1.
14 Department of Foreign Affairs and International Trade, 'Axworthy Condemns Pakistan's Nuclear Weapons Tests and Announces Sanctions,' *Press Release* 136 (28 May 1998).
15 Quoted in John Saunders, 'Canada Steers Clear of India,' *Globe and Mail*, 14 May 1998, A8.
16 Cited in House of Commons Standing Committee on Foreign Affairs and International Trade (SCFAIT), *Canada and the Nuclear Challenge: Reducing the Political Value of Nuclear Weapons in the Twenty-First Century* (December 1998). Available online from www.parl.gc.ca/InfoComDoc/36/1/FAIT/Studies/Reports/faitrp07-e.htm
17 Quoted in Nomi Morris, 'Is Canada to Blame?' *Maclean's*, 8 June 1998, 41.
18 Roslin, 'Indo-Pakistani Nuclear War? CANDU!' 46.
19 Ibid.
20 Hadwen, 'Canada's Nuclear Policies,' 164.
21 'Rigid Garter Springs May Have Saved KANUPP From Tube Fracture,' *Nucleonics Week*, 13 January 1994, 6. Also see Ray Silver, 'Canadian Team Explores Safety Aid to India Under 1990 Policy Change,' *Nucleonics Week*, 13 April 1995, 13.

22 CANDU Owners Group, *1994–1995 Annual Report* (Ottawa: COG, 1995), 1.
23 'AECL, Indian Officials Meet Secretly, CTV Says,' *Globe and Mail*, 7 April 1995, A1.
24 John Stackhouse, 'How the Nuclear Ban Bent for India,' *Globe and Mail*, 15 June 1998, A1, A9.
25 Ibid.
26 John Stackhouse, 'Canadian Businesses Protest Tough Stand on India, Pakistan,' *Globe and Mail*, 23 November 1998, A10.
27 DFAIT, Notes for a statement by the Honourable Lloyd Axworthy Minister of Foreign Affairs to the Standing Committee on Foreign Affairs and International Trade 'India's Nuclear Testing: Implications for Nuclear Disarmament and the Nuclear Non-Proliferation Regime' (May 26, 1998).
28 Telephone interview with EMR official, Ottawa, ON, 14 June 1992.
29 Turkey, *Basic Facts Concerning the Proposed Nuclear Power Plant at Akkuyu*, retrieved 5 September 2005 from www.mfa.gov.tr/grupa/an/akkuyu.htm
30 Department of Foreign Affairs and International Trade, Commercial Division, Canadian Embassy, Ankara, Turkey, *Report on Turkish Energy Sector Resources, Policies & Opportunities* (January 1997), retrieved 5 September 2005 from http://www.dfait-maeci.gc.ca/english/trade/market/europe/84770.htm
31 Turkey, *Basic Facts Concerning the Proposed Nuclear Power Plant*.
32 Mustafa Kibaroglu, 'Turkey's Quest for Peaceful Nuclear Power,' *Nonproliferation Review* 4, no. 3 (Spring/Summer 1997), 36.
33 Cited in Martin, *Nuclear Threat in the Eastern Mediterranean*, 70.
34 Quoted in David H. Martin, *The CANDU Syndrome: Canada's Bid to Export Nuclear Reactors to Turkey* (Ottawa: Campaign for Nuclear Phaseout, 1997), 21.
35 Kibaroglu, 'Turkey's Quest for Peaceful Nuclear Power,' 35.
36 Martin, *Nuclear Threat in the Eastern Mediterranean*, 67.
37 Quoted in ibid., 68.
38 Allan Thompson, 'Reactor Sales Come Under Fire,' *Toronto Star*, 9 July 1998, A25.
39 For example, the Greek Cypriots have announced that they would be purchasing surface-to-air missiles from Russia to protect itself from the Turkish military. This has only increased tension on the island. 'Turkey Set to Strike Cyprus, Report Says,' *Globe and Mail*, 10 January 1997, A10.
40 Amnesty International, *The 1995 Report on Human Rights around the World* (London: Amnesty International Publications, 1995), 291.
41 Amnesty International, *News Release* (24 September 1996), retrieved 5 September 2005 from www.amnesty.org/news/1996old/44413796.htm

42 Heinz Kramer, 'Turkey and the European Union: A Multi-Dimensional Relationship With Hazy Perspective,' in Vojtech Mastny and R. Craig Nation ed., *Turkey between East and West: New Challenges for a Rising Regional Power* (Boulder, CO: Westview, 1996), 216–22.

43 'Turks Told Not to Expect Early EU Membership,' *Globe and Mail*, 27 March 1997, A14.

44 Stephen Kinzer, 'Secular Turks Wary of Government,' *Globe and Mail*, 14 February 1997, A14.

45 See Jonathan Lyons, 'Turkish Generals Continue to Flex Muscles,' *Globe and Mail*, 12 May 1997, A14; Stephen Kinzer, 'Turkish Army Rattling Sabres under Prime Minister's Nose,' *Globe and Mail*, 13 June 1997, A13; and 'Turkish PM Agrees to Hand Over Power,' *Globe and Mail*, 14 June 1997, A18.

46 Editorial, 'Turkey's "Soft" Coup,' *Globe and Mail*, 6 March 1997, A20.

47 Amnesty International, 'Turkey,' *Annual Report 1995* (London: AI, 1995), 294.

48 Amnesty International, 'Turkey,' *Annual Report 2000* (London: AI, 2000), 2.

49 Cited in Mian and Nayyar, *Pakistan's Chashma Nuclear Power Plant*, 25.

50 Mark Abley, 'Canada's Nuclear Industry Reeling: No Sales at Home,' *Montreal Gazette*, 4 July 1998, A1.

51 Cited in Mian and Nayyar, *Pakistan's Chashma Nuclear Power Plant*, 25.

52 Abley, 'Canada's Nuclear Industry Reeling,' A1.

53 CANDU Owners Group, *1990 Annual Report* (Ottawa: COG, 1990), 1.

54 SCFAIT, *Canada and the Nuclear Challenge*.

55 Quoted in Mian and Nayyar, *Pakistan's Chashma Nuclear Power Plant*, 26.

56 'Canada to Aid Some KANUPP Upgrades but only to Ensure Plant Safety,' *Nucleonics Week*, 25 February 1996, 17–18.

57 Mian and Nayyar, *Pakistan's Chashma Nuclear Power Plant*, 26.

58 Ontario Hydro, 'Report to Management IIPA/SSFI Evaluation Findings and Recommendations,' *News Release* (August 13, 1997).

59 Paul Waldie and Chad Skelton, 'Documents Itemize How Nuclear Plants Earned Low Rating,' *Globe and Mail*, 15 August 1997, A4.

60 Ontario Hydro, 'IIPA/SSFI Evaluation Findings and Recommendations.'

61 Bruce Doern, Arslan Dorman, and Robert Morrison, 'Conclusions,' in *Canadian Nuclear Energy Policy*, 205–6.

62 Quoted in Tom Spears, 'CANDU Believes Ontario's Woes Will Hurt Sales,' *Calgary Herald*, 21 August 1997, A7.

63 Quoted in Shawn McCarthy, 'Hydro Fallout May Hit CANDUS: Reactor Sales Could Suffer,' *Globe and Mail*, 14 August 1997, A4.

64 Natural Resources Canada, *Speech* 98/2 (9 February 1998).

65 Ibid.

66 Quoted in McCarthy, 'Hydro Fallout May Hit CANDUS,' A4.

67 Standing Senate Committee on Energy, the Environment, and Natural Resources, *Canada's Nuclear Reactors: How Much Safety is Enough? Interim Report* retrieved 5 September 2005 from www.parl.gc.ca/37/1parlbus/commbus/senate/com-E/ENRG-É/REP-E/repintjun01-e.htm

68 Natural Resources Canada, *Speech* 98/2.

69 Shawn McCarthy, 'Cabinet Approves Loan to Help AECL Win Turkish Deal,' *Globe and Mail*, 5 November 1997, A6.

70 Allan Thompson, 'Reactor Sales Come Under Fire,' *Toronto Star*, 9 July 1998, A25.

71 Quoted in Anne McIlroy, 'PM Defends Selling Reactors after Quakes,' *Globe and Mail*, 18 November 1999, A1.

72 Turkey, *Basic Facts Concerning the Proposed Nuclear Power Plant*.

73 Larry Shewchuk, 'Should Canada Try to Sell Nuclear Reactors to Turkey? Yes,' *Toronto Star*, 15 September 1998, A24.

74 Cited in Martin, *Nuclear Threat in the Eastern Mediterranean*, 59.

75 I would like to thank an anonymous reviewer for making this point.

76 Cited in Martin, *Nuclear Threat in the Eastern Mediterranean*, 61.

77 Quoted in ibid., 58.

78 Quoted in Jessica Aldred and Christina Frangou, 'Quake Prompts Call for Canada to Withdraw Nuclear Sale Bid,' *Calgary Herald*, 27 August 1999, A13.

79 Quoted in Thompson, 'Reactor Sales Come Under Fire,' A25.

80 AECL, *Cernavoda Unit 2 Nuclear Power Plant: Environmental Assessment Summary* (Ottawa: AECL, 2001), 9.

81 Romania, Nuclearelectrica, *Public Debates on Cernavoda NPP Unit 2 Completion Works*, retrieved 5 September 2005 from www.nuclearelectrica.ro/News.asp

82 Sierra Club, Comments by Non-Government Organizations on Atomic Energy of Canada Limited's (AECL) Cernavoda Reactor 2 Environmental Assessment Summary (Toronto: Sierra Club, 2002), 1–2.

83 Ibid., 4–6.

84 Ibid., 2.

85 *Financing of CANDU Bid to Turkey*, 'Memorandum to Cabinet from Minister of Natural Resources and Minister of International Trade' (December 1993), 29. This document was cited in Martin, *Nuclear Threat in the Eastern Mediterranean*, 78. Also see Shawn McCarthy, 'Ottawa Approves

$1.5 Billion Loan to Turkey Despite Earlier Refusal,' *Globe and Mail*, 29 October 1998, A1.

86 *Financing for Two CANDU Reactors to the Republic of Turkey*, Record of Cabinet Decision/The Cabinet Committee on Economic Development Policy, Meeting of 24 April 1997, Confirmed by Cabinet on April 27, 1997,' 29 August 1997. This document was leaked to the public. See McCarthy, 'Cabinet Approves Loan,' A6.

87 Reid Morden, 'CANDU Exports and Opportunities,' *Canadian Nuclear Society Bulletin* 18, no 1 (May 1997), 1.

88 Shawn McCarthy, 'ACEL Seeks More Public Funding to Extend Bid for Selling CANDU to Turkey,' *Globe and Mail*, 22 July 2000, B3.

89 Shawn McCarthy, 'Candu Loan Rejected as Risky Was for Less Than One Approved Later,' *Globe and Mail*, 10 December 1998, A5.

90 A brand new nuclear plant would be an attractive target for the PKK who have a history of attacking oil pipelines. For an elaboration on the security risk of the proposed Akkuyu reactor see Martin, *Nuclear Threat in the Eastern Mediterranean*, 53–4.

91 Jeff Sallot, 'Bribery Alleged in AECL Bid,' *Globe and Mail*, 10 May 2001, A7.

92 'Crown Corporations Told: No Bribes,' *Ottawa Citizen*, 10 December 1998, A2.

93 In 1998, about 63 per cent of the civilian engineering and 4 per cent of the electromechanical work had been completed for Cernavoda II. Anne MacLachlan, 'AECL offers Romania Financing to Begin Cernavoda-2 Completion,' *Nucleonics Week*, 5 March 1998, 3.

94 AECL, 'Romania Awards $200 Million Contract for Work on Cernavoda Unit 2,' *News Release* (April 27, 1998), retrieved 5 September 2005 from www.aecl.ca/news980505–e.htm

95 Energyonline, 'Nuclear Officials "Optimistic" on Reactor Financing,' *News Reports* (26 May 1998), retrieved 5 September 2005 from www.energyonline.com/Restructuring/news_reports/news/e26rom.htm

96 Jeff Sallot, 'Romanian Leader Rails against West,' *Globe and Mail*, 27 May 1998, A12.

97 Uranium Institute, 'Romania,' *News Briefing* NB00.38–8 (13–19 September 2000), retrieved 5 September 2005 from http://world-nuclear.org/nb/nb00/nb0038.htm

98 'Government Approves Export Financing for Romanian Reactor,' *Nuclear Canada*, 8 January 2003.

99 Quoted in Geoffrey York, 'AECL Wants Hard-up Romania to Buy Another CANDU,' *Globe and Mail*, 13 August 1998, A1.

100 Florian Glodeneanu et al., 'The Cernavoda Project – Past and Future,' *1995 Uranium Institute Symposium*, retrieved 21 October 2002 from www.uilondon.org/uiabs95/glod.html

101 It is not just Canada that is subsidizing the Romanian nuclear industry. AECL's partner in Romania is the Italian firm ANSALDO, and in 1998 Italy offered to buy electricity from Romania so that it could afford to finish construction on Cernavoda II. Uranium Institute, 'Romania,' *News Briefing* NB98.21-10 (20–26 May 1998), retrieved 5 September 2005 from http://world-nuclear.org/nb/nb98/nb9821.htm

102 York, 'AECL Wants Hard-up Romania to Buy Another CANDU,' A1.

103 Quoted in ibid.

104 AECL, *Annual Reports, 1990–1991* to *1998–1999* (Ottawa: AECL, 1991, 1999).

105 AECL, *Annual Report, 1996–1997* (Ottawa: AECL, 1997).

106 Peter O'Neil, '$100–Million a Year in Public Funding for CANDU Questioned,' *National Post*, 16 January 2002.

107 McCarthy, 'Cabinet Approves Loan,' A6.

108 Shewchuk, 'Should Canada Try to Sell Nuclear Reactors to Turkey? Yes,' A24.

109 Natural Resources Canada, *Speech* 96/116 (26 November 1996).

110 Nuclear Engineering International, *World Nuclear Industry Handbook 1992*, 18–20, and Nuclear Engineering International, *World Nuclear Industry Handbook 1997* (Surrey, UK: Reed, 1997), 17–22.

111 If the reactors that Ontario Hydro has shut down are included in this ranking – as anti-nuclear groups have argued - the CANDU's efficiency rating would drop even lower, to 49.25 per cent. See Martin, *Nuclear Threat in the Eastern Mediterranean*, 20.

112 AECL official, telephone interview with author, Ottawa, ON, June 2000.

113 Quoted in 'Lepreau Officials Take Hot Seat Over Nuclear Power Plant,' *Moncton Times/Transcript*, 2 November 1999, A1.

114 For its lifetime rating as of 1996 see IAEA, *Power Reactor Information System*, 'Reactors Connected to the Grid' (December 31, 1996). Available online at www.iaea.org/programmes/a2/. For its 1999 rating, see 'Nuclear Electricity Generation for December 1999,' *Nucleonics Week*, 10 February 2000.

115 Morrison Campbell, 'Lepreau Nuclear Plant Is Lagging,' *Fredericton Daily Gleaner*, 4 November 1999, A1.

116 Martin and Argue, *Nuclear Sunset*, 15–17.

117 Lermer, *Atomic Energy of Canada Limited*.

118 George Lermer, 'The Dismal Economics of CANDU,' *Policy Options* (April 1996), 16–20.

119 Bruce Doern, Arslan Dorman, and Robert Morrison, 'Precarious Opportunity: Canada's Changing Nuclear Energy Policies and Institutional Choices,' in Doern, Dorman, and Morrison, eds., *Canadian Nuclear Energy Policy*, 3.

120 David Torgerson, 'Letter to the Editor – Nuclear Energy is Integral to Solution,' *Winnipeg Free Press*, 18 April 2002.

121 Donald N. Dewees, 'The Future of Nuclear Power in a Restructured Electricity Market,' in Doern, Dorman, and Morrison, eds., *Canadian Nuclear Energy Policy*, 147–73.

122 Bruce Doern, Arslan Dorman, and Robert Morrison, 'Transforming AECL into an Export Company: Institutional Challenges and Change,' in Doern, Dorman, and Morrison, eds., *Canadian Nuclear Energy Policy*, 78.

123 Doern, Dorman, and Morrison, 'Conclusions,' 201.

124 Ibid., 203. Emphasis in original.

125 For a recent examination of the nuclear market in Britain, see Steve Thomas, 'Nuclear Power and Deregulation in the United Kingdom,' in Doern, Dorman, and Morrison, eds., *Canadian Nuclear Energy Policy*, 52–73.

126 'AECL, British Energy Studying CANDU Deal,' *Toronto Star*, 2 November 2001.

127 Wendy Stueck, 'CANDU Officials Hope for Sale to Britain,' *Globe and Mail*, 1 October 2001, A14.

128 Doern, Dormand, and Morrison, 'Transforming AECL into an Export Company,' 74–95.

9. Explaining CANDU Exports

1 Cranford Pratt is the foremost advocate of this perspective. See Cranford Pratt, 'Dominant Class Theory and Canadian Foreign Policy: The Case of the Counter-Consensus,' *International Journal* 39, no. 1 (Winter 1983–4), 99–135; Cranford Pratt, 'Canada: An Eroding and Limited Internationalism,' in Pratt, ed., *Internationalism under Strain: The North-South Policies of Canada, the Netherlands, Norway, and Sweden* (Toronto: University of Toronto Press, 1989), 24–69; and Cranford Pratt, 'Competing Perspectives on Canadian Development Assistance Policies,' *International Journal* 51, no. 2 (Spring 1996), 235–58.

2 Pratt, 'An Eroding and Limited Internationalism,' 54.

3 Cranford Pratt, 'Ethical Values and Canadian Foreign Policy: Two Case Studies,' *International Journal* 56, no. 1 (Winter 2000–2001), 50–1.

4 Pratt, 'An Eroding and Limited Internationalism,' 54.
5 Ibid., 55.
6 Pratt, 'Ethical Values and Canadian Foreign Policy,' 50–1.
7 Doern, Dorman, and Morrison, 'Precarious Opportunity,' 13.
8 'A Nuclear Cult Ran Reactors: Chairman Reacts to Scathing Report,'
   Toronto Star, 14 August 1997, A1.
9 Morrison and Wonder, *Canada's Nuclear Export Policy*, 8.

Appendix

1 For additional technical information on nuclear energy and the CANDU
   that is accessible to the layperson, see Tammemagi and Jackson, *Unlocking
   the Atom*; Atomic Energy of Canada Limited, *Canada Enters the Nuclear
   Age*; Fawcett, *Nuclear Pursuits*; Whitlock, 'The Canadian Nuclear FAQ,'
   www.nuclearfaq.ca; John McCarthy, 'Nuclear Energy FAQ,' www.
   formal.stanford.edu/ jmc/progress/nuclear-faq.html; the World Nuclear
   Association, www.world-nuclear.org; and Joseph Gonyeau, 'Virtual
   Nuclear Tourist,' www.cannon.net/ ~gonyeau/nuclear/index.htm
2 Proponents of nuclear fusion 'claim that with fusion there is an unlimited
   supply of cheap fuel, there is no danger of a divergent chain reaction, and
   the radioactive wastes are much more manageable, since there is no need
   to mine uranium and no fission products or plutonium are produced.
   Nevertheless, at the current rate of research and spending (about $2 billion
   a year worldwide), nuclear fusion as an energy source is not expected to
   become a reality until about 2050.' G.C. Hanna, 'Accelerators and Fusion,'
   in AECL, *Canada Enters the Nuclear Age: A Technical History of Atomic Energy
   of Canada Limited as Seen from Its Research Laboratories* (Montreal: McGill-
   Queen's University Press, 1997), 186.
3 For a more complete examination of different fuel systems, see the IAEA,
   Country Nuclear Fuel Cycle Profiles, Technical Reports Series No. 404
   (Vienna: IAEA, 2001).
4 This section draws heavily on H.K. Rae, 'The CANDU Reactor,' in AECL,
   Canada Enters the Nuclear Age, 207–14, and Gordon L. Brooks and John S.
   Foster, *CANDU Origins and Evolution*, www.cns-snc.ca/home_eng.html
5 EMR, *Nuclear Policy Review*, 273.
6 In the 1960s, a heavy-water plant was built at Glace Bay, Nova Scotia.
   However, it was a technical and financial disaster, eventually being shut
   down after producing no heavy water.

Bibliography

Primary Documents

Canada Nuclear Industry

Andseta, S., M.J. Thompson, J.P. Jarrell, and D.R. Pendergast. *CANDU Reactors and Greenhouse Gas Emissions*. Toronto: Canadian Nuclear Association, 2000.

Atomic Energy of Canada Limited. *Annual Reports, 1951–52 to 2002–2003*. Ottawa: AECL, 1951–2003.

– *Canada Enters the Nuclear Age: A Technical History of Atomic Energy of Canada Limited as Seen From its Research Laboratories*. Montreal: McGill-Queen's University Press, 1997.

– *Cernavoda Unit 2 Nuclear Power Plant: Environmental Assessment Summary*. Ottawa: AECL, December 2001.

Atomic Energy Control Board. *The Accident at Chernobyl and its Implications for the Safety of CANDU Reactors*. Ottawa: AECB, 1987.

Canadian Nuclear Association. *Climate Change: Qinshan Nuclear Project* (2000). Retrieved 21 October 2002 from www.cna.ca/cl5.html

– *Nuclear Canada Yearbook 2002: Annual Review and Buyers Guide*. Toronto: CNA 2002.

Ernst and Young. *The Economic Effects of the Canadian Nuclear Industry*. Toronto: Ernst and Young, 1993.

Leonard and Partners Ltd. *Economic Impact of the Nuclear Energy Industry in Canada*. Toronto: Leonard and Partners Ltd., 1978.

Van Adel, Robert G. 'Nuclear Power Generation in Canada: A View to the Future.' *Notes for Remarks: CNA Panel Discussion on Nuclear Energy and Innovation* (19 March 2003). Retrieved 5 September 2005 from www.aecl.ca/images/up-RVA-CNA-030319.pdf

Canadian Federal and Provincial Governments

Blanchette, Arthur E., ed. *Canadian Foreign Policy 1955–1965: Selected Speeches and Documents*. Ottawa: Carleton Library Series #103, 1977.
– *Canadian Foreign Policy 1966–1976: Selected Speeches and Documents*. Ottawa: Carleton Library Series #118, 1977.
– *Canadian Foreign Policy 1977–1992: Selected Speeches and Documents*. Ottawa: Carleton Library Series #183, 1994.
Canada. House of Commons. *Debates*, 1945–2004.
Canada. House of Commons Standing Committee on Foreign Affairs and International Trade. *Canada and the Nuclear Challenge: Reducing the Political Value of Nuclear Weapons in the Twenty-First Century* (December 1998). Available online from www.parl.gc.ca/InfoComDoc/36/1/FAIT/Studies/Reports/faitrp07-e.htm
– *Exporting in the Canadian Interest: Reviewing the Export Development Act* (December 1999). Available online from http://192.197.82.11/committee/CommitteePublication.asp
Canada. Senate Standing Committee on Energy, the Environment, and Natural Resources. *Canada's Nuclear Reactors: How Much Safety is Enough? Interim Report* (February 2000). Retrieved 5 September 2005 from www.parl.gc.ca/37/1/parlbus/commbus/senate/com-E/ENRG-E/REP-E/repintjun01-e.htm
– *Canada in the World: Government Statements*. Ottawa: Canada Communications Group, 1995.
Canadian Environmental Assessment Agency. *Report of the Nuclear Fuel Waste Management and Disposal Concept*. Ottawa: CEAA, 1998.
Department of Energy, Mines, and Resources. *Nuclear Policy Review: Background Papers*. Ottawa: EMR, 1981.
– *Nuclear Industry Review: Problems and Prospects, 1981–2000*. Ottawa: EMR, 1982.
– 'AECL and the Future of the Canadian Nuclear Industry: A Proposed Discussion Paper.' Ottawa: EMR, 1988.
Department of Foreign Affairs and International Trade. *Canada in the World: Canadian Foreign Policy Review*. Ottawa: DFAIT, 1995. Available online from www.dfait-maeci.gc.ca/foreign_policy/end-world/menu-en.asp
– Commercial Division, Canadian Embassy, Ankara, Turkey. *Report on Turkish Energy Sector Resources, Policies & Opportunities* (January 1997). Retrieved 5 September 2005 from www.dfait-maeci.gc.ca/English/trade/market/europe/84770.htm
– *Human Rights and Canadian Foreign Policy* (September 1998). Retrieved

5 September 2005 from www.dfait-maeci.gc.ca/foreign_policy/human-rights/forpol-en.asp

- *Government Response to the Recommendations of the Standing Committee on Foreign Affairs and International Trade on Canada's Nuclear Disarmament and Non-Proliferation Policy.* Ottawa: DFAIT, 1999.
- *Nuclear Disarmament and Non-Proliferation: Advancing Canadian Objectives.* Ottawa: DFAIT, 1999.

Export Development Corporation. *Annual Reports, 1974–2002* (Ottawa: EDC, 1974–2002).

- *Summary Report to Treasury Board on Canada Account Operations Fiscal Year 1998–99.* Retrieved 21 October 2002 from www.edc-see.ca/CorpInfo/Pubs/CanAcc9899_e.pdf

Natural Resources Canada. *Quarterly Report on Canadian Nuclear Power Programme.* Ottawa: NRC, 1999.

Ontario Nuclear Safety Review. F. Kenneth Hare Commissioner. *The Safety of Ontario's Nuclear Power Reactors: A Scientific and Technical Review.* Toronto: Queen's Printer, 1988.

Ontario. Royal Commission on Electric Power Planning. *A Race Against Time: Interim Report on Nuclear Power in Ontario.* Toronto: Queen's Printer, 1978.

Statistics Canada. *Exports by Country.* Catalogue No. 65-003. Ottawa: Statistics Canada, Jan.–Dec. 1991.

- *Imports by Country.* Catalogue No. 65-006. Ottawa: Statistics Canada, Jan.–Dec. 1991.

Other Countries and International Organizations

Andemicael, Berhanykun, Merle Opelz, and Jan Priest. 'Measure for Measure: The NPT and the Road Ahead.' *IAEA Bulletin* 37, no. 3 (1995): 30–8.

International Atomic Energy Agency. *Statute of the International Atomic Energy Agency.* Vienna: IAEA, 1956.

- *The Structure and Content of Agreements between the International Atomic Energy Agency and States Required in Connection with the Treaty on the Non-Proliferation of Nuclear Weapons (NPT Model Safeguards Agreement).* Vienna: IAEA, 1971.
- *IAEA Safeguards: An Introduction.* Vienna: IAEA, 1981.
- *Financing Arrangements for Nuclear Power Projects in Developing Countries.* Technical Reports Series No. 353. Vienna: IAEA, 1993.
- *Power the Reactor Information System.* 'Reactors Connected to the Grid' (31 December 1996). Available online from www.iaca.org/programmes/a2

- *Country Nuclear Fuel Cycle Profiles.* Technical Reports Series No. 404. Vienna: IAEA, 2001.
- *Nuclear Power Plants Information: Number of Reactors in Operation Worldwide.* Retrieved 5 September 2005 from www.iaea.org/programmes/a2/index.html
- 'The International Nuclear Event Scale.' *Fact Sheet.* Retrieved 5 September 2005 from www.iaea.org/Publications/Factsheets/English/ines-e.pdf
International Nuclear Forum. *Policy Statement* (June 1999). Retrieved 5 September 2005 from www.cna.ca/english/files/climate%20Change/intlnuclearforum.pdf
International Nuclear Safety Center. *Data for Nuclear Power Plants.* Retrieved 5 September 2005 from www.insc.anl.gov/plants/
Nuclear Engineering International. *World Nuclear Industry Handbook 1992.* Surrey, UK: Reed, 1992.
- *World Nuclear Industry Handbook 1997.* Surrey, UK: Reed, 1997.
Organization of Economic Cooperation and Development. *Business as Usual and Nuclear Power.* Paris: OECD, 2000.
- *Nuclear Power in the OECD.* Paris: OECD, 2001.
Romania. Nuclearelectrica, *Public Debates on Cernavoda NPP Unit 2 Completion Works.* Retrieved 5 September 2005 from www.nuclearectrica.ro/News.asp
Turkey. *Basic Facts Concerning the Proposed Nuclear Power Plant at Akkuyu.* Retrieved 5 September 2005 from www.mfa.gov.tr/grupa/an/akkuyu.htm
United States. Board of Consultants to the Secretary of State's Committee on Atomic Energy. *A Report on the International Control of Atomic Energy,* U.S. Department of State Publication 2498. Washington, DC: U.S. Government Printing Office, 1946.
World Nuclear Association. *Nuclear Power Plants in Commercial Operation.* London: WNA, 2000.
- *Nuclear Fuel Cycle.* Retrieved 5 September 2005 from www.world-nuclear.org/info/inf03.htm
- *Global Warming* (2003). Retrieved 5 September 2005 from www.world-nuclear.org/info/inf59.htm
- 'World Nuclear Reactors 2002–2003 and Uranium Requirements.' Retrieved 5 September 2005 from www.world-nuclear.org/info/reactors.htm

Secondary Sources

Abraham, Itty. *The Making of the Indian Atomic Bomb: Science, Secrecy and the Postcolonial State.* London: Zed Books, 1998.
Adams, Ian. 'The Real McGuffin: Selling the Bomb, Confessions of a Nuclear Salesman.' *This Magazine,* May 1982, 18–19.

Albright, David. 'The Shot Heard 'Round the World.' *Bulletin of the Atomic Scientists* 54, no. 4 (July/August 1998): 20–5.

Amnesty International. *Argentina: The Military Juntas and Human Rights.* London: Amnesty International Publications, 1987.

– *The 1995 Report on Human Rights around the World.* London: Amnesty International Publications, 1995.

– *Annual Reports, 1991–2002.* London: Amnesty International Publications, 1991–2002.

Arquilla, John, and Paul K. Davis. *Modeling Decisionmaking of Potential Proliferators as Part of Developing Counterproliferation Strategies.* Santa Monica, CA: Rand, 1994.

Axworthy, Thomas S. '"To Stand Not so High Perhaps but Always Alone": The Foreign Policy of Pierre Elliott Trudeau.' In Thomas S. Axworthy and Pierre Elliott Trudeau, eds., *Towards a Just Society: The Trudeau Years.* Markham, ON: Viking, 1990.

Axworthy, Thomas S., and Pierre Elliott Trudeau, eds. *Towards a Just Society: The Trudeau Years.* Markham, ON: Viking, 1990.

Azmi, M. Raxiullah. *Pakistan–Canada Relations: 1947–82.* Islamabad: Area Study Centre for Africa, North and South America, 1982.

Beck, Michael. 'Reforming the Multilateral Export Control Regimes.' *The Nonproliferation Review* 7, no. 2 (Summer 2000): 91–103.

Berg, Peter. *Nuclear Power Production: The Financial Costs.* Ottawa: Library of Parliament, 1993.

Bidwai, Praful, and Achin Vanaik. *New Nukes: India, Pakistan and Global Nuclear Disarmament.* Oxford: Signal Books, 2000.

Boardman, Robert, and James F. Keeley, eds. *Nuclear Exports and World Politics: Policy and Regime.* New York: St. Martin's, 1983.

Bothwell, Robert. *Eldorado: Canada's National Uranium Company.* Toronto: University of Toronto Press, Toronto 1984.

– *Nucleus: The History of Atomic Energy of Canada Limited.* Toronto: University of Toronto Press, 1988.

– 'The Further Shore: Canada and Vietnam.' *International Journal* 56, no. 1 (Winter 2000–2001): 89–114.

Bratt, Duane. 'Is Business Booming? Canada's Nuclear Reactor Export Policy.' *International Journal* 51, no. 3 (1996): 487–505.

– 'The Future of CANDU Exports.' Canadian Institute of Strategic Studies. *Strategic Datalink* #66 (October 1997).

– 'CANDU or CANDON'T: Competing Values Behind Canada's Sale of Nuclear Reactors.' *The Nonproliferation Review* 5, no. 3 (1998): 1–16.

– 'Canada's Nuclear Schizophrenia.' *The Bulletin of the Atomic Scientists* 58, no. 2 (March/April 2002): 44–50.

- 'The Ethics of CANDU Exports.' In Rosalind Irwin, ed., *Ethics and Security in Canadian Foreign Policy*. Vancouver: UBC Press, 2002.
Brown, Peter A., and Carmel Létourneau. 'Nuclear Fuel Waste Policy in Canada.' In Bruce Doern, Arslan Dorman, and Robert W. Morrison, eds., *Canadian Nuclear Energy Policy Changing Ideas, Institutions, and Interests*. Toronto: University of Toronto Press, 2001.
Buckley, Brian. *Canada's Early Nuclear Policy: Fate, Chance, and Character*. Montreal: McGill-Queen's University Press, 2000.
Campaign for Nuclear Phaseout. *High-Level Nuclear Waste: No End in Sight*. Retrieved 5 September 2005 from www.cnp.ca/issues/high-level-waste.html
- 'Canada's Federal Government is Wrong: Nuclear Power Is Not a "Solution" to Climate Change' (January 2001). Retrieved 5 September 2005 from www.cnp.ca/issues/nuclear-not-solution.pdf
Carasales, Julio C. 'The So-Called Proliferator that Wasn't': The Story of Argentina's Nuclear Policy.' *Nonproliferation Review* 6, no. 4 (Fall 1999): 51–64.
Carty, Bob. 'No CANDU for Argentina.' *New Internationalist*, March 1978, 27–8.
Chan, Raymond. 'Canada and Asia Pacific.' In Fen Osler Hampson, Michael Hart, and Martin Rudner, eds., *Canada among Nations 1997: A Big League Player?* Toronto: Oxford University Press, 1997.
Charleton, Mark, and Paul Barker, eds. *Crosscurrents: Contemporary Political Issues*. 2d ed. Toronto: Nelson, 1994.
Chow, Brian G. *Civilian Nuclear Programs in India and Pakistan*. Santa Monica, CA: Rand, 1996.
Clearwater, John. *Canadian Nuclear Weapons: The Untold Story of Canada's Cold War Arsenal*. Toronto: Dundurn, 1998.
- *U.S. Nuclear Weapons in Canada*. Toronto: Dundurn, 1999.
Cohn, Steven Mark. *Too Cheap to Meter: An Economic and Philosophical Analysis of the Nuclear Dream*. Albany: State University of New York Press, 1997.
Cole, Paul M. *Sweden without the Bomb: The Conduct of a Nuclear-Capable Nation without Nuclear Weapons*. Santa Monica, CA: Rand, 1994.
Cooper, Andrew F. *Canadian Foreign Policy: Old Habits and New Directions*. Toronto: Prentice-Hall, 1997.
Courtney, William. 'Nuclear Choices for Friendly Rivals.' In Joseph A. Yager, ed., *Nonproliferation and U.S. Foreign Policy*. Washington, DC: Brookings Institution, 1980.
Cronin, Richard P. 'Prospects for Nuclear Proliferation in South Asia.' *Middle East Journal* (1983): 594–616.

Daudelin, Jean. 'Trapped: Brazil, Canada and the Aircraft Dispute.' In
    Norman Hillmer and Maureen Appel Molot, eds., *Canada among Nations
    2002: A Fading Power.* Toronto: Oxford University Press, 2002.
Delvoie, Louis A. 'Taming the South Asian Nuclear Tiger: Causes, Conse-
    quences, and Canadian Responses.' In Fen Osler Hampson, Michael Hart,
    and Martin Rudner, eds., *Canada among Nations 1997: A Big League Player?*
    Toronto: Oxford University Press, 1997.
Doern, Bruce. *The Atomic Energy Control Board: An Evaluation of Regulatory and
    Administrative Processes and Procedures.* Ottawa: Law Reform Commission of
    Canada, 1976.
– 'The Politics of the Canadian Nuclear Industry.' In Bruce Doern and
    William Morrison, eds., *Canadian Nuclear Policies.* Montreal: Institute for
    Research on Public Policy, 1980.
Doern, Bruce, Arslan Dorman, and Robert Morrison, eds. *Canadian Nuclear
    Energy Policy: Changing Ideas, Institutions, and Interests.* Toronto: University
    of Toronto Press, 2001.
Doern, Bruce, and Robert Morrison, eds. *Canadian Nuclear Policies.* Montreal:
    Institute for Research on Public Policy, 1980.
Donnelly, Michael W. 'Japan's Nuclear Power Strategy.' *Canada and the Pacific:
    Agenda for the Eighties,* no. 25. Toronto: The Joint Centre on Modern East
    Asia, 1984.
Doxey, Margaret. 'Human Rights and Canadian Foreign Policy.' *Behind the
    Headlines* 37 (June 1979).
du Preez, Jean, and William Potter. 'North Korea's Withdrawal from the NPT:
    A Reality Check.' Research Story of the Week. Center for Nonproliferation
    Studies at the Monterey Institute of International Studies (10 April 2003).
    Retrieved 5 September 2005 from http://cns.miis.edu/pubs/week/
    030409.htm
Ebinger, Charles K. 'International Politics of Nuclear Energy.' *Washington
    Papers* 57, no. 6 (1978).
Edwards, Gordon. 'Canada's Nuclear Dilemma.' *Journal of Business Adminis-
    tration* 13, nos. 1–2 (1982): 217–63.
Edwards, Gordon. 'Myth of the Peaceful Atom.' In Ernie Regehr and Simon
    Rosenblum, eds., *Canada and the Nuclear Arms Race.* Toronto: Lorimer, 1983.
Eggleston, Wilfrid. *Canada's Nuclear Story.* Toronto: Clarke, Irwin, 1965.
English, John. *The Worldly Years: The Life of Lester Pearson, 1949–1972.* Toronto:
    Knopf, 1992.
Epstein, William. *The Last Chance: Nuclear Proliferation and Arms Control.* New
    York: The Free Press, 1976.
– 'Canada and the Problem of Nuclear Proliferation.' Paper presented at the

Canadian Peace Research and Educational Association, Laval University, Quebec City, May 1976.
- 'Canada.' In Jozef Goldblat, ed., *Non-Proliferation: The Why and the Wherefore.* Stockholm: SIPRI, 1985.
- 'Indefinite Extension – with Increased Accountability.' *Bulletin of the Atomic Scientists* (July/August 1995): 27–30.
Fawcett, Ruth. *Nuclear Pursuits: The Scientific Biography of Wilfrid Bennett Lewis.* Montreal: McGill-Queen's University Press, 1994.
Finch, Ron. *Exporting Danger: A History of the Canadian Nuclear Energy Export Programme.* Montreal: Black Rose Books, 1986.
Fischer, David. *Stopping the Spread of Nuclear Weapons: The Past and the Prospects.* London: Routledge, 1992.
Flicker, Charles. 'Next Year in Jerusalem: Joe Clark and the Jerusalem Embassy Affair.' *International Journal* 58, no. 1 (Winter 2002–3): 115–38.
Freeman, Aaron. 'Financing Disaster: Canada's Export Development Corporation.' *Canadian Dimension*, May 2000, 18–20.
Frolic, B. Michael. 'Re-enging China: Striking a Balance between Trade and Human Rights.' In Fen Osler Hampson, Michael Hart, and Martin Rudner, eds., *Canada among Nations 1997: A Big League Player?* Toronto: Oxford University Press, 1997.
Gecelovsky, Paul, and T.A. Keenleyside. 'Canada's International Human Rights Policy in Practice: Tiananmen Square.' *International Journal* 50, no. 3 (1995): 564–93.
Gendron, Robin S. 'Educational Aid for French Africa and the Canada-Quebec Dispute over Foreign Policy in the 1960s.' *International Journal* 56, no. 1 (Winter 2000–2001): 19–36.
Goldblat, Jozef, ed. *Non-Proliferation: The Why and the Wherefore.* Stockholm: SIPRI, 1985.
Gorove, Stephen. 'Distinguishing "Peaceful" from "Military" Uses of Atomic Energy: Some Facts and Considerations.' *Ohio State Law Journal* 30 (1969): 495–501.
Gowing, Margaret. *Independence and Deterrence: Britain and Atomic Energy, 1939–1945.* Vol. 1, *Policy Making.* London: Macmillan, 1974.
- *Independence and Deterrence: Britain and Atomic Energy, 1945–1952.* Vol. 2, *Policy Execution.* London: Macmillan, 1974.
Granatstein, J.L., and Robert Bothwell. *Pirouette: Pierre Trudeau and Canadian Foreign Policy.* Toronto: University of Toronto Press, 1990.
Hadwen, J.G. 'A Foreign Service Officer and Canada's Nuclear Policies.' In David Reece, ed., *Special Trust and Confidence: Envoy Essays in Canadian Diplomacy.* Ottawa: Carleton University Press, 1996.

Hampson, Fen Osler, Maureen Appel, and Martin Rudner, eds. *Canada among Nations 1997: Asia Pacific Face-Off*. Ottawa: Carleton University Press, 1997.

Hampson, Fen Osler, Michael Hart, and Martin Rudner, eds. *Canada among Nations 1999: A Big League Player?* Toronto: Oxford University Press, 1999.

Han, Yong-Sup. 'North Korean Behaviour in Nuclear Negotiations.' *Nonproliferation Review* 7, no. 1 (Spring 2000): 41–54.

Hanna, G.C. 'Accelerators and Fusion.' In AECL, *Canada Enters the Nuclear Age: A Technical History of Atomic Energy of Canada Limited as seen from its Research Laboratories*. Montreal: McGill-Queen's University Press, 1997.

Hart, David. *Nuclear Power in India: A Comparative Analysis*. London: George Allen and Unwin, 1983.

Head, Ivan, and Pierre Trudeau. *The Canadian Way: Shaping Canada's Foreign Policy, 1968–1984*. Toronto: McClelland and Stewart, 1995.

Hillmer, Norman, and Maureen Appel Molot, eds. *Canada among Nations 2002: A Fading Power*. Toronto: Oxford University Press, 2002.

Holmes, John W. *The Better Part of Valour: Essays of Canadian Diplomacy*. Ottawa: Carleton Library Series #49, 1970.

– *Canada: A Middle-Aged Power*. Ottawa: Carleton Library Series #98, 1976.

Hu, Weixing. 'China's Nuclear Export Controls: Policy and Regulations.' *Nonproliferation Review* 1, no. 2 (Winter 1994): 3–9.

Hufbauer, Gary Clyde, and Jeffrey J. Schott. *Economic Sanctions Reconsidered: History and Current Policy*. Washington, DC: Institute for International Economics, 1985.

Hunt, Constance D. 'Canadian Policy and the Export of Nuclear Energy.' *University of Toronto Law Journal* 27 (1977): 69–104.

Huntley, Wade. 'Nonproliferation Prospects After the South Asian Nuclear Tests.' *Nonproliferation Review* 5, no. 4 (Fall 1998): 85–96.

Irwin, Rosalind ed. *Ethics and Security in Canadian Foreign Policy*. Vancouver: UBC Press, 2001.

Jackson, David, and John de la Mothe. 'Nuclear Regulation in Transition: The Atomic Energy Control Board.' In Bruce Doern, Arslan Dorman, and Robert W. Morrison, eds., *Canadian Nuclear Energy Policy Changing Ideas, Institutions, and Interests*. Toronto: University of Toronto Press, 2001.

Jain, Girilal. 'India.' In Josef Goldblat, ed., *Non-Proliferation: The Why and the Wherefore*. Stockholm: SIPI, 1985.

Jain, J.P. *Nuclear India*. 2 vols. New Delhi: Radiant, 1974.

Johannson, P.R. 'Canada and the Quest for International Nuclear Security.' In Robert Boardman and James F. Keeley, eds., *Nuclear Exports and World Politics: Policy and Regime*. New York: St. Martin's, 1983.

Jones, Rodney W. 'Nuclear Supply Policy and South Asia.' In Rodney Jones,

Cesare Lerlini, Joseph Pilat, and William Potter, eds., *The Nuclear Suppliers and Nonproliferation: International Policy Choices*. Lexington, MA: Lexington Books, 1985.

Jones, Rodney W., Cesare Lerlini, Joseph F. Pilat, and William C. Potter, eds. *The Nuclear Suppliers and Nonproliferation: International Policy Choices*. Lexington, MA: Lexington Books, 1985.

Kampani, Gaurav. 'From Existential to Minimum Deterrence: Explaining India's Decision to Test.' *Nonproliferation Review* 5, no. 4 (Fall 1998): 12–24.

Kang, Jungmin, and H.A. Feiveson. 'South Korea's Shifting and Controversial Interest in Spent Fuel Reprocessing.' *Nonproliferation Review* 8, no. 3 (Spring/Summer 2001): 70–8.

Kapur, Ashok. *India's Nuclear Option: Atomic Diplomacy and Decision Making*. New York: Praeger, 1976.

– *Canadian Images of Indian Nuclear Policy*. Paper presented at the Annual Meeting of the Canadian Political Science Association, Laval University, Quebec City, 30 May 1976.

– 'The Canada-India Nuclear Negotiations: Some Hypotheses and Lessons.' *World Today* (August 1978): 311–20.

– 'Nuclear Energy, Nuclear Proliferation and National Security: Views from the South.' In Robert Boardman and James Keeley, eds., *Nuclear Exports and World Politics: Policy and Regime*. New York: St. Martin's, 1983.

– *Pakistan's Nuclear Development*. London: Croom Helm, 1987.

Keating, Tom. *Canada and World Order: The Multilateralist Tradition in Canadian Foreign Policy*. 2d ed. Toronto: Oxford University Press, 2002.

Keeler, Wally. 'Canada's CANDU Sale to Romania.' *Peace* Magazine, June/July 1989, 8–9.

Keeley, James F. 'Canadian Nuclear Export Policy and the Problems of Proliferation.' *Canadian Public Policy* 6 (1980): 614–27.

Keenleyside, T.A. 'Development Assistance.' In Robert O. Matthews and Cranford Pratt, eds., *Human Rights in Canadian Foreign Policy*. Montreal: McGill-Queen's University Press, 1988.

Keenleyside, T.A., and Patricia Taylor. 'The Impact of Human Rights Violations on the Conduct of Canadian Bilateral Relations: A Contemporary Dilemma.' *Behind the Headlines* 42 (November 1984).

Keillor, Marc. 'CANDU in Romania: Setting the Record Straight.' *Ascent* 9 (1990): 6.

Khalilzad, Zalmay. 'Pakistan: The Making of a Nuclear Power.' *Asian Survey* (1976): 580–92.

Kibaroglu, Mustafa. 'Turkey's Quest for Peaceful Nuclear Power.' *Nonproliferation Review* 4, no. 3 (Spring/Summer 1997): 33–44.

Kokoski, Richard. *Technology and the Proliferation of Nuclear Weapons*. Stockholm: SIPRI, 1995.

Kraft, Michael E. 'Policy Design and the Acceptability of Environmental Risks: Nuclear Waste Disposal in Canada and the United States.' *Policy Studies Journal* 28, no. 1 (2000): 206–18.

Kramer, Heinz. 'Turkey and the European Union: A Multi-Dimensional Relationship with Hazy Perspective.' In Vojtech Mastny and R. Craig Nations, ed., *Turkey between East and West: New Challenges for a Rising Regional Power*. Boulder, CO: Westview, 1996.

Kukucha, Christopher. 'Canada and India: An Analysis of the Political and Economic Relationship, 1947–88.' Master's thesis, University of Windsor, 1989.

Langdon, Frank. *The Politics of Canadian–Japanese Economic Relations 1952–1983*. Vancouver: University of British Columbia Press, 1983.

Lermer, George. *Atomic Energy of Canada Limited: The Crown Corporation as Strategist in an Entrepreneurial, Global-Scale Industry*. Ottawa: Economic Council of Canada, 1987.

– 'The Dismal Economics of CANDU.' *Policy Options* (April 1996): 16–20.

Leventhal, Paul L., Sharon Tanzer, and Steven Dolley, eds. *Nuclear Power and the Spread of Nuclear Weapons: Can We Have One without the Other?* Washington, DC: Brassey's, 2002.

Levitt, Joseph. *Pearson and Canada's Role in Nuclear Disarmament and Arms Control Negotiations, 1945–1957*. Montreal: McGill-Queen's University Press, 1993.

Lonergan, Iris Heidrun. 'The Negotiations between Canada and India for the Supply of the N.R.X. Nuclear Research Reactor 1955–56: A Case Study in Participatory Internationalism.' Master's thesis, Carleton University, 1989.

– 'Canada and India: The Negotiations for the Supply of the N.R.X. 1955–56.' *bout de papier* 8, no. 2 (1991): 12–15.

MacDonald, Flora. 'The Minister and the Mandarians.' In Mark Charleton and Paul Barker, eds., *Crosscurrents: Contemporary Political Issues*, 2d ed. Scarborough, ON: Nelson, 1994.

MacGuigan, Mark. P. *An Inside Look at External Affairs during the Trudeau Years: The Memoirs of Mark MacGuigan*. Edited by Whitney Lackenbauer. Calgary: University of Calgary Press, 2002.

Mansourov, Alexandre Y. 'The Origins, Evolution, and Current Politics of the North Korean Nuclear Program.' *Nonproliferation Review* 3, no. 1 (Spring/ Summer 1995): 25–38.

Martin, David H. *Exporting Disaster: The Cost of Selling CANDU Reactors*. Ottawa: Campaign for Nuclear Phaseout, 1996.

- *The CANDU Syndrome: Canada's Bid to Export Nuclear Reactors to Turkey.*
  Ottawa: Campaign for Nuclear Phaseout, 1997.
- *Nuclear Threat in the Eastern Mediterranean: The Case against Turkey's Akkuyu
  Nuclear Plant.* Uxbridge, ON: Nuclear Awareness Project, 2000.
- *Financial Meltdown: Federal Nuclear Subsidies to AECL.* Ottawa: Campaign for
  Nuclear Phaseout, 2000.
- *Canadian Nuclear Subsidies: Fifty Years of Futile Funding 1952–2002.* Ottawa:
  Campaign for Nuclear Phaseout, 2003.

Martin, David H., and David Argue. *Nuclear Sunset: The Economic Costs of the
  Canadian Nuclear Industry.* Ottawa: Campaign for Nuclear Phaseout, 1996.

Mastny, Vojtech, and R. Craig Nation, eds. *Turkey between East and West: New
  Challenges for a Rising Regional Power.* Boulder, CO: Westview, 1996.

Matthews, Robert O., and Cranford Pratt, eds. *Human Rights in Canadian
  Foreign Policy.* Montreal: McGill-Queen's University Press, 1988.

Mian, Zia, and A.H. Nayyar. *Pakistan's Chashma Nuclear Power Plant: A Prelimi-
  nary Study of Some Safety Issues and Estimates of the Consequences of a Severe
  Accident.* Report No. 321. Princeton, NJ: Princeton University, Center for
  Energy and Environmental Studies, 1999.

Milhollin, Gary. 'Stopping the Indian Bomb.' *American Journal of International
  Law* 81 (1987): 593–609.

Morden, Reid. 'CANDU Exports and Opportunities.' *Canadian Nuclear Society
  Bulletin* 18, no. 1 (May 1997).

Morrison, Barrie, and Donald M. Page. 'India's Option: The Nuclear Route to
  Achieve Goal as World Power.' *International Perspectives* (July/August 1974):
  23–8.

Morrison, Robert. *Nuclear Energy and Sustainable Development.* Toronto: Canadian Nuclear Association, 2000.

Morrison, Robert. 'Global Nuclear Markets in the Context of Climate Change
  and Sustainable Development.' In Bruce Doern, Arslan Dorman, and Robert
  W. Morrison, eds., *Canadian Nuclear Energy Policy Changing Ideas, Institutions, and Interests.* Toronto: University of Toronto Press, 2001.

- *Nuclear Energy Policy in Canada: 1942 to 1997.* Ottawa: Carleton Research
  Unit on Innovation, Science and Environment, 1998.

Morrison, Robert, and Edward F. Wonder. *Canada's Nuclear Export Policy.*
  Ottawa: Norman Paterson School of International Affairs, 1978.

Morrison, Robert W., and Edward F. Wonder. 'Canada's Nuclear Export
  Policy.' In Bruce Doern and Robert Morrison, eds., *Canadian Nuclear Politics.*
  Montreal: Institute for Research on Public Policy, 1980.

Morrow, Daniel, and Michael Carriere. 'The Economic Impacts of the 1998

Sanctions on India and Pakistan.' *Nonproliferation Review* 6, no. 4 (Fall 1999): 1–16.

Motz, James Clay, and C. Kenneth Quinones. 'Getting Serious about a Multi-lateral Approach to North Korea.' *Nonproliferation Review* 11, no. 1 (Spring 2004): 136–44.

Myers, Richard. *The Role of Nuclear Energy in U.S. Climate Policy* (2003). Retrieved 5 September 2005 from www.world-nuclear.org/wgs/cop9/ myers.ppt

Norris, Robert S., William M. Arkin, and William Burr. 'Where They Were.' *Bulletin of the Atomic Scientists* 55, no. 6 (November/December 1999): 26–35.

Nossal, Kim Richard. *The Politics of Canadian Foreign Policy*, 3d ed. Toronto: Prentice-Hall, 1997.

Ontario Clean Air Alliance. *Expanding Exports, Increasing Smog.* Toronto: OCAA, 2002.

Ornstein, Michael. *Canadian Policy-Makers' Views on Nuclear Energy.* Toronto: York University Institute for Behavioral Research, 1976.

Pathak, K.K. *Nuclear Policy of India: A Third World Perspective.* New Delhi: Gitanjali Prakashan, 1980.

Paul, T.V. 'The Systemic Bases of India's Challenge to the Global Nuclear Order.' *Nonproliferation Review* 5, no. 4 (Fall 1998): 1–11.

– *Power versus Prudence: Why Nations Forgo Nuclear Weapons.* Montreal: McGill-Queen's University Press, 2000.

Pearson, Geoffrey A.H. *Seize the Day: Lester B. Pearson and Crisis Diplomacy.* Ottawa: Carleton University Press, 1993.

Perkovich, George. 'Nuclear Power and Nuclear Weapons in India, Pakistan, and Iran.' In Paul L. Leventhal, Sharon Tanzer, and Steven Dolley, eds., *Nuclear Power and the Spread of Nuclear Weapons: Can We Have One without the Other?* Washington, DC: Brassey's, 2002.

Pilat, Joseph. 'The Major Suppliers: A Baseline for Comparison.' In William C. Potter, ed., *International Nuclear Trade and Nonproliferation: The Challenge of the Emerging Suppliers.* Lexington, MA: Lexington Books, 1990.

Pinkston, Daniel A. 'Domestic Politics and Stakeholders in the North Korean Missile Development Program.' *Nonproliferation Review* 10, no. 2 (Summer 2003): 1–15.

Poulose, T.T., ed. *Perspectives of India's Nuclear Policy.* New Delhi: Young Asia Publications, 1978.

Potter, William C., ed. *International Nuclear Trade and Nonproliferation: The Challenge of the Emerging Suppliers.* Lexington, MA: Lexington Books, 1990.

Pratt, Cranford. 'Dominant Class Theory and Canadian Foreign Policy: The

Case of the Counter-Consensus.' *International Journal* 39, no. 1 (Winter 1983–4): 99–135.

– ed. *Internationalism under Strain: The North–South Policies of Canada, the Netherlands, Norway, and Sweden.* Toronto: University of Toronto Press, 1989.

– 'Competing Perspectives on Canadian Development Assistance Policies.' *International Journal* 51, no. 2 (Spring 1996): 235–58.

– 'Competing Rationales for Canadian Development Assistance.' *International Journal* 54, no. 2 (Spring 1999): 306–23.

– 'Ethical Values and Canadian Foreign Policy: Two Case Studies.' *International Journal* 56, no. 1 (Winter 2000–2001): 37–53.

Pringle, Peter, and James Spigelman. *The Nuclear Barons.* New York: Holt, 1981.

Quester, George. *The Politics of Nuclear Proliferation.* Baltimore: Johns Hopkins University Press, 1973.

– 'Can Proliferation Now Be Stopped?' *Foreign Affairs* (1974): 77–97.

Rajan, M.S. 'The Indo-Canadian Entente.' *International Journal* (Autumn 1962): 358–84.

Ramanna, R. 'Peaceful Nuclear Explosions.' In T.T. Poulouse, ed., *Perspectives of India's Nuclear Policy.* New Delhi: Young Asia Publications, 1978.

Redick, J.R. 'The Tlatelolco Regime and Nonproliferation in Latin America.' *International Organization* 35, no. 1 (1981): 103–34.

Reece, David, ed. *Special Trust and Confidence: Envoy Essays in Canadian Diplomacy.* Ottawa: Carleton University Press, 1996.

Reford, Robert W. 'Problems of Nuclear Proliferation.' *Behind the Headlines* (May 1975).

Regehr, Ernie, and Simon Rosenblum, eds. *Canada and the Nuclear Arms Race.* Toronto: Lorimer, 1983.

Reid, Escott. 'Canada and the Struggle against World Poverty.' *International Journal* 25, no. 1 (Winter 1969–70): 142–57.

– *Envoy to Nehru.* Toronto: Oxford University Press, 1981.

Reiss, Mitchell. *Without the Bomb: The Politics of Nuclear Nonproliferation.* New York: Columbia University Press, 1988.

– *Bridled Ambition: Why Countries Constrain Their Nuclear Capabilities.* Washington, DC: Woodrow Wilson Center Press, 1995.

Rhodes, Richard, and Denis Beller. 'The Need for Nuclear Power.' *Foreign Affairs* 79, no. 1 (January/February 2000): 30–44.

Ripsman, Norrin M., and Jean-Marc F. Blanchard. 'Lightning Rods Rather Than Light Switches: Arab Economic Sanctions against Canada in 1979.' *Canadian Journal of Political Science* 35, no. 1 (March 2002): 151–74.

Roberts, Brad. 'Proliferation and Nonproliferation in the 1990s: Looking for the Right Lessons.' *Nonproliferation Review* 6, no. 4 (Fall 1999): 70–82.

Rogner, Hans-Holger. *Nuclear Power and Climate Change.* Vienna: International Atomic Energy Agency, Vienna 2003.

Roslin, Alex. 'Indo-Pakistani Nuclear War? CANDU!' *Saturday Night,* 1 May 2002, 42–7.

Santaholma, Juhani. *Nuclear Energy: A Long-Term Energy Option to Address Climate Change – Finish Energy Industries Federation* (2003). Retrieved 5 September 2005 from www.world-nuclear.org/wgs/cop9/js_finland.ppt

Scheinman, Lawrence. 'The Nonproliferation Regime and Fissile Materials.' In Paul L. Leventhal, Sharon Tanzer, and Steven Dolley, eds., *Nuclear Power and the Spread of Nuclear Weapons: Can We Have One without the Other?* Washington, DC: Brassey's, 2002.

Schmidt, Fritz. 'NPT Export Controls and the Zangger Committee.' *Nonproliferation Review* 7, no. 4 (Fall/Winter 2000): 136–45.

Schneider, Mycle. *Climate Change and Nuclear Power.* Gland, SWITZ: World Wide Fund for Nature, 2000.

Sierra Club. *Financing Disaster: How the G8 fund the Global Proliferation of Nuclear Technology.* Uxbridge, ON: Sierra Club, 2001.

– 'The Canadian Nuclear Lesson: Why the Kyoto Protocol Should Not Subsidize the Dying International Nuclear Industry' (June 2001). Retrieved 5 September 2005 from www.sierraclub.ca/national/nuclear/ reactors/nuclear-and-clim-chg-6–01.html

– *Comments by Non-Government Organizations on Atomic Energy of Canada Limited's (AECL) Cernavoda Reactor 2 Environmental Assessment Summary.* Uxbridge, ON: Sierra Club, 2002.

Sigal, Leon V. *Disarming Strangers: Nuclear Diplomacy with North Korea.* Princeton, NJ: Princeton University Press, 1998.

Silver, L. Ray. *Fallout from Chernobyl.* Toronto: Deneau, 1987.

Simpson, Erika. *NATO and the Bomb: Canadian Defenders Confront Critics.* Montreal: McGill-Queen's University Press, 2001.

Simpson, Jeffrey. *Discipline of Power: The Conservative Interlude and the Liberal Restoration.* Toronto: Personal Library Publisher, 1980.

Sims, Gordon H.E. *A History of the Atomic Energy Control Board.* Hull: Supply and Services, 1981.

Singh, Jaswant. 'Against Nuclear Apartheid.' *Foreign Affairs* 77, no. 5 (1998): 41–52.

Smith, Heather. 'Niche Diplomacy in Canadian Human Rights Policy: Ethics or Economics?' In Rosalind Irwin, ed., *Ethics and Security in Canadian Foreign Policy.* Vancouver: UBC Press, 2002.

Speier, Richard H., Brian G. Shaw, and S. Rae Starr. *Nonproliferation Sanctions.*

Santa Monica, CA: Rand, 2001.

Stockholm International Peace Research Institute. *Yearbook 1975*. Stockholm: SIPRI, 1975.

– *Internationalization to Prevent the Spread of Nuclear Weapons*. London: Taylor and Francis, 1980.

Stothart, P. 'Nuclear Electricity: The Best Option Given the Alternatives.' *Policy Options* 17, no. 3 (March 1996): 1–16.

Tammemagi, Hans, and David Jackson. *Unlocking the Atom: The Canadian Book on Nuclear Technology*. Hamilton: McMaster University Press, 2002.

Thomas, Steve. 'Nuclear Power and Deregulation in the United Kingdom.' In Bruce Doern, Arslan Dorman, and Robert W. Morrison, eds., *Canadian Nuclear Energy Policy Changing Ideas, Institutions, and Interests*. Toronto: University of Toronto Press, 2001.

Torrie, Ralph D., and Richard Parfett. *Phasing Out Nuclear Power in Canada: Toward Sustainable Electricity Futures*. Ottawa: Campaign for Nuclear Phase-out, 2003.

Troyer, Warner. *200 Days: Joe Clark in Power*. Toronto: Personal Library Publishers, 1980.

Valiante, Marcia. 'Legal Foundations of Canadian Environmental Policy: Underlying Our Values in a Shifting Landscape.' In Debora L. VanNijnatten and Robert Boardman, eds., *Canadian Environmental Policy: Context and Cases*, 2d ed. Toronto: Oxford University Press, 2002.

VanNijnatten, Debora L., and Robert Boardman, eds. *Canadian Environmental Policy: Context and Cases*, 2d ed. Toronto: Oxford University Press, 2002.

Walczak, James R. 'Legal Implications of Indian Nuclear Development.' *Denver Journal of International Law and Policy* 4 (1974): 237–56.

Walker, William, and Mans Lönnroth. *Nuclear Power Struggles: Industrial Competition and Proliferation Control*. London: George Allen, 1983.

Weissman, Steve, and Herbert Krosney. *The Islamic Bomb*. New York: Times Books, 1981.

Welsh, Susan B. 'Delegate Perspectives on the 1995 NPT Review and Extension Conference.' *The Nonproliferation Review* 2, no. 2 (Spring/Summer 1995): 1–24.

Wendt, James C. *The North Korean Nuclear Program: What Is to Be Done?* Monterey, CA: Rand, 1994.

Yager, Joseph A., ed. *Nonproliferation and U.S. Foreign Policy*. Washington, DC: Brookings Institution, 1980.

Index

The Institute of Public Administration of Canada Series
in Public Management and Governance